Judgment Ridge

ALSO BY MITCHELL ZUCKOFF:

Choosing Naia: A Family's Journey

ALSO BY DICK LEHR:

Black Mass: The Irish Mob, the FBI, and a Devil's Deal
(co-author)

The Underboss: The Rise and Fall of a Mafia Family
(co-author)

Mitchell Zuckoff *and* Dick Lehr

HARPERCOLLINS*PUBLISHERS*

Judgment

THE TRUE STORY BEHIND THE
DARTMOUTH MURDERS

Ridge

JUDGMENT RIDGE. Copyright © 2003 by Dick Lehr and Mitchell Zuckoff.
All rights reserved. Printed in the United States of America.
No part of this book may be used or reproduced in any manner whatsoever
without written permission except in the case of brief quotations embodied in critical
articles and reviews. For information, address HarperCollins Publishers Inc.,
10 East 53rd Street, New York, NY 10022.

HarperCollins books may be purchased for educational, business, or sales
promotional use. For information, please write: Special Markets Department,
HarperCollins Publishers, Inc., 10 East 53rd Street, New York, NY 10022.

FIRST EDITION

Designed by Jennifer Ann Daddio

Library of Congress Cataloging-in-Publication Data
Zuckoff, Mitchell.
Judgment Ridge : the true story behind the Dartmouth murders /
by Mitchell Zuckoff and Dick Lehr.—1st ed.
p. cm.
ISBN 0-06-000844-X
1. Juvenile homicide—New Hampshire—Hanover. 2. Juvenile homicide—Psychology.
3. Murder—Investigation—New Hampshire—Hanover. 4. Criminal investigation—New
Hampshire—Hanover. 5. Criminal investigation—Vermont—Chelsea. I. Lehr, Dick. II. Title.
HV9067.H6Z83   2003
364.15'23'0974363—dc21   2003044970

03 04 05 06 07 ❖/RRD 10 9 8 7 6 5 4 3 2 1

Contents

Part I

Part II

Part III

"So there they go, Jim running slower to stay with Will,

Will running faster to stay with Jim,

Jim breaking two windows in a haunted house because Will's along,

Will breaking one window instead of none, because Jim's watching.

God, how we get our fingers into each other's clay.

That's friendship, each playing the potter to see what shapes we can
   make of the other."

FROM *SOMETHING WICKED THIS
WAY COMES*, BY RAY BRADBURY

Part I

1

A Stranger
at the Door

At just past ten on a cool summer night, Andrew Patti nestled with his eleven-year-old son on a worn blue sofa in the living room of their Vermont vacation home. Burning logs hissed and popped in the red-brick fireplace as Patti read aloud to Andy Jr. from an adventure story about a hunter pursuing a wise and elusive buck.

Bam-bam-bam-bam-bam. A staccato burst of pounding on the front door interrupted him in mid-sentence.

Startled, Patti rose to his feet, silently motioning to Andy to stay put. It was too late for visitors, and the knocks were too sharp, too insistent to come from the hand of a friend. Someone must be in trouble or looking for trouble.

As Patti stood, he reached under the untucked hem of his work shirt for the nine-millimeter Glock pistol he always wore on his right hip. With a quick flip of his thumb, he unsnapped the safety latch and slid the matte black gun from its leather holster. Patti walked slowly to the door, holding the Glock out of sight, tucked close against the right rear pocket of his faded jeans.

With his empty left-hand he pushed aside the blind covering the nine small windows on the upper half of the door. On his front porch stood a young man Patti had never seen before. He was about six feet tall, lanky, dressed in a white T-shirt, black cargo pants, and black military boots. The young man—maybe in his late teens, Patti thought— leaned in close, his hot breath leaving vapor clouds on the glass. His hands were half-clenched like bear claws, his eyes wide and intense. The weak rays of a bug-yellow porch light cast a sickly glare on his pale skin.

"What's up?" Patti asked roughly.

"I have car trouble. Can you help me out?" the stranger answered just as roughly.

They stood for a moment face to face, inches apart, separated by only a pane of glass, each waiting to see what the other would do.

Andrew Patti was forty-seven, a trim, good-looking man of medium height, with thick, dark hair flecked with gray. He was a lifelong New Yorker with the accent and toothpick-chewing habit to prove it. Though raised in a cookie-cutter suburb of tract houses and strip malls, as a teenager Patti had grown enchanted by the mountains and forests of Vermont. As his only child and namesake approached manhood, Patti wanted Andy to know the embrace of untamed woods, the snap of a fish latching onto a hook, the smell of fresh-cut trees, the ping of a tin can pierced by a well-aimed bullet.

Patti and his wife, Diane, also forty-seven and a native New Yorker, lived and worked on Long Island, running an agency that provided services for infants and toddlers with special needs. It was successful enough to allow them to purchase their getaway home in the town of Vershire, on the eastern side of Vermont, halfway between Massachusetts and Canada. Vershire's name was an amalgam of Vermont and New Hampshire, owing to the abundance of hills offering views from the former to the latter, some fifteen miles away across the Connecticut River.

One of the hills was called Judgment Ridge, named for a defunct ski area once located there. Judgment Ridge was less than a mile from the Pattis' house, just off the main road that connected the neighboring town of Chelsea to Interstate 91. Once on the interstate, it was a short drive south to Hanover, New Hampshire, home of Dartmouth College, and from there to the world beyond.

Vershire was best known to outsiders as home to The Mountain School, a private school that doubled as a working farm, allowing high school students to combine traditional studies with lessons on sustainable rural living. Vershire also was a magnet for second-home owners like the Pattis, many of them New Yorkers searching for solitude, serenity, and bargain property. Locals called them "flatlanders" during civil, if occasionally dismissive, conversations. Some natives called the outsiders much worse in private.

The Pattis first saw the cedar-shingled house next to a postcard-perfect pond in September 1999, and then spent eight months struggling to get clear title and overcome a maddening series of obstacles to their purchase. It finally became theirs two months before the stranger came to the door. Locals knew the place as The Sugar House, and indeed, the home on Goose Green Road was a symbol of the changing community. It was built in 1993, replacing a landmark wooden shack where generations of Vershire residents had marked each spring by boiling maple sap into sugary syrup.

During their first weeks in the house, Andrew and Diane tried to make it homey without Long Island-izing it. Their signature decorative touch was a mounted head of a six-point buck Diane's father had shot years earlier, hung high on a living-room wall next to the fireplace. The deer's limpid eyes stared down at anyone who entered the front door, above which a plaque read: HOME IS WHERE THE HEART IS.

Soon after they moved in, the Pattis got a taste of life in a house built close to a country road: twice, just weeks apart, two strangers came to the door late at night seeking help with broken-down cars. The first was a young man who tentatively tapped on the door, then stepped briskly, submissively backward when Andrew Patti answered. The stranger's solicitous air convinced Patti there was no danger, and in a display of new-neighbor helpfulness he hitched the stalled car to Diane's SUV and towed it to the man's home. The second uninvited guest was a young woman who politely asked to use the phone to call Ward's Garage, a half-mile up the road. Again, Patti felt safe and obliged.

The Pattis didn't sense any hostility from their neighbors, but they wondered if some locals resented them. Andrew Patti thought his sparkling blue BMW with its New York plates gave some people the misimpression that he was a rich, liberal city boy who came north to smell flowers, hug trees, and call out "Look, it's Bambi!" at the sight of a deer. Several times during their first visits to their new home, the Pattis noticed a silver Audi whizzing down Goose Green Road, its occupants yelling something hostile but unintelligible out the windows as they sped past. It happened often enough that Andrew took steps to avoid seeing the silver Audi—when he and Andy fished in their pond they'd paddle their raft to its farthest reaches, an area hidden from the road by a stand of trees.

On Monday, July 17, 2000, Diane went to work while Andrew and Andy packed the BMW for the five-hour drive from Long Island to Vershire. They brought along their dog, a champagne-colored standard poodle puppy named Roxie. Their plan was simple: spend a week of Andy's summer vacation together, father, son, and pup, fishing for bass and pickerel, hiking deep into the woods, and eating whatever struck their fancy. At night they'd play cards and read books before the well-stoked fire.

Sometimes they'd take target practice in the woods, but Andrew Patti wasn't a hunter. Years earlier he'd come face-to-face with a deer in a stream and realized he couldn't imagine killing it. Still, he was a serious gun enthusiast who liked firearms the way he liked sharp cars. He respected their coiled power and enjoyed his ability to control and command them. The feel of a well-oiled gun at his side satisfied his own father's most frequent warning—"Be careful. Strange things happen." Andrew had passed his love of guns to Andy. One of the boy's prized possessions was a dime with a small bullet hole he had placed dead center.

Toward the end of their first full day in Vermont, Tuesday, July 18, Andrew, Andy, and Roxie lost their way during a hike in the unfamiliar woods. As they hunted for the path home, the elder Patti checked his pockets for matches and began silently calculating how they could stay warm and safe until daybreak. By the time they found their way home, a light rain was falling, fish were jumping in the pond, and brown bats were swooping and soaring, feasting on mosquitoes in the darkening sky. Around nine o'clock, tired but exhilarated, they called Diane to recount their adventure. Then they settled onto the couch for their nightly ritual of stories read aloud.

At one point, Roxie heard something outside the house and let loose a rumbling bark. Patti was in no mood to walk her again, so he shushed her and returned to reading. But something was bothering him, too. He had the uncomfortable sense that someone was watching him through a window where the shade didn't fit quite right. He tried to shake it, but the feeling of eyes boring in on the back of his neck continued to gnaw at him. Patti pulled out his gun and his son teased him—"You're going to shoot a hole through the window, Dad"—so he holstered it, sat back down, and continued reading.

Then came the pounding on the door.

P atti carefully considered the young man and his complaint of car problems. He decided this was no time to be neighborly.

"No," Patti answered the stranger's request for help.

"Do you have jumper cables?" the young man persisted.

"No," Patti repeated.

"Let me in. Can I use your phone?"

"No."

"C'mon, let me use your phone."

The stranger kept his face close to the window, his outsized nose almost pressed against the glass. Patti grew convinced that he and Andy were the targets of what New Yorkers call a "push-in" crime: a homeowner opens a door a crack and the criminal forces his way inside to rob, rape, or kill. Patti looked over to his son, who was still curled up on the sofa. Roxie was nowhere in sight; she had responded to the tension by finding a place to hide.

Though Patti sensed danger, it was even worse than he knew. Patti was unaware that the stranger had brought along two deadly weapons. One was an old but sharp hunting knife tucked in his military boot. The other was his best friend. While the stranger knocked on the door, the friend—also a teenager, a year younger than the young man at the door—crouched in a bush around the side of the house. He was dressed all in black, his face covered with a ski mask that revealed only his close-set eyes. The friend also had a hunting knife in his boot, and around his waist he wore a utility belt with pouches filled with duct tape, a jackknife, and plastic ties that could bind a person hand and foot.

Nor did Patti know that before coming to his house, the two young men had spent hours digging a grave, five feet long and three feet deep, in the rocky soil next to an abandoned house up a nearby road. If their plan held true, that grave would soon be filled with earth and the lifeless bodies of Andrew and Andy Patti, and maybe their dog, too.

"Andy, get over there," Patti said in a soft but firm voice, motioning his son toward a wall away from the front windows, out of harm's way. When Andy was in place, Patti brought his gun out from behind his back. Still holding the blind with his left hand, he gave the stranger an eyeful of the Glock.

"Whoa, whoa, whoa, whoa. I just want to use your phone," the stranger said. But he didn't seem scared by the sight of the gun. It only seemed to agitate him.

"I'll tell you what I'll do," Patti said. "I'll call Ward's Garage for you."

"OK. Please do that. But please do that now."

Patti let the blind drop and hustled over to a phone in the kitchen, not twenty feet from the door. Andy fell in step behind him, so close he was almost hugging his father from behind. Patti picked up the phone, the same phone he had used not two hours earlier to call Diane.

Silence.

"Oh shit. The phone's dead."

Alarmed, he and Andy ran upstairs to try the phone in the master bedroom. Again, nothing.

"What's going on, Dad?"

"They've cut the wires," Patti told his son.

He was on full alert, trying to keep Andy calm while assessing the situation. Patti surmised that when he refused to open the door, the stranger changed tactics and wanted him to discover that the phones were dead. Maybe then Patti would go outside to check the wires on the side of the house. Even with his gun, outside in the dark Patti might be vulnerable. "If I check the phone lines," he thought, "they'll bushwhack me." No matter what happened, he'd stay inside.

They ran back downstairs—Patti wanted to be there, Glock ready, if the stranger tried to bust through the door or the windows. Adrenaline pumping—half from fear and half from anger at the thought of someone hurting his son—Patti fought to keep a cool exterior to prevent Andy from panicking. They huddled on the living room floor, feeding the fire and waiting for a rock or a person to come crashing through the window. They had seen only one face at the door, but Patti remembered the queasy feeling of being watched. He was sure the young man at the door wasn't alone, and he wondered how many others might be out there. All he could do was hope they had been spooked by the gun, and wait.

As minutes passed and nothing happened, Andy's fear began giving way to exhaustion. Patti lay his son down on the sofa, covered him with a blanket, and told him everything was fine. Soon Andy was asleep. But Patti wouldn't let down his guard.

He spent the next few hours sitting on the hard floor, gun in hand, blinking to stay awake. He didn't dare sit on the couch or a chair because the cushiony comfort might lull him to sleep. As the silence stretched into hours, fatigue crept up on him. Patti lay down on his back, his head toward the fireplace and his feet toward the door, so he could watch for intruders just by lifting his head.

Patti spent the rest of the night that way—staring at the door, listening to night noises, hoping for daybreak— his gun on his chest, rising and falling with every breath.

2

Chelsea

In a sleepy hollow five miles or so from the Pattis' rural retreat is Chelsea, Vermont. A soccer field sits alongside Main Street. Bordering the field to the north is a farm, to the west a footbridge that crosses a stream and, beyond the stream, sloping hills smothered in trees. Three "bleachers" near the road are, in fact, three large benches. Then there's the south end of the field, where a large soccer "shooting board" is located. The board only recently became a permanent fixture.

The wall of wood is built from sheets of plywood, each four by six feet, nailed soundly together and then grounded firmly to withstand the hard shots of Chelsea kids. But there's something else about this new shooting board—one of the panels had a prior use that is of particular and peculiar interest. This single slab was originally a campaign sign in a 1999 student council election at the Chelsea Public School.

Neatly hand-painted on a side hidden from public view, the sign reads:

VOTE FOR
ROBERT & CASE
STUDENT COUNCIL '99

Robert was Robert Tulloch, candidate for student council president in the fall of his junior year. "Basically he wanted to run for school president to show everybody that he could be the school president," his best pal, Jim Parker, said later. Indeed, Jim helped Robert campaign and persuade other students to vote for a candidate originally considered a long shot.

To guarantee that voters would take notice, Robert and his running mate, fellow junior Casey "Case" Purcell, positioned the large plywood sign right outside the school's main entrance. To further grab voters' attention, Robert decorated the sign with four fictitious blurbs:

"THEY ROCK"—*Rolling Stone*

"THEY HAVE A STYLE AND FASHION
ALL TO THEIR OWN"—*Vogue*

"THEY'RE HELLUVA COOL"—*Time*

"THEY'RE LEADERSHIP SKILLS
ARE UN-PARELELED"—*Newsweek*

It was a sign, replete with mistakes in spelling and grammar, displaying teen creativity and friendship. And it worked: Robert and Casey won, and their buddy Jim Parker was elected sophomore-class representative.

More than anything, the dual life of a piece of plywood—high-spirited campaign sign and later, permanently, as soccer shooting board—captured the brio of youth and represented the very thing Chelseans proudly say their town is all about: kids and community.

Down a few hundred yards from the soccer field is the town center, a tree-lined village featuring two town greens that Chelseans use for picnics, a farmers' market in the summer, an annual flea market, and high school graduation. During and after school, kids often hang out around the greens, throwing Frisbees or skateboarding. Kids also gather in warm weather to shoot hoops at an asphalt court across the street.

Main Street is a mix of old homes and small businesses. Laundry flaps from clotheslines. Tractors pulling manure spreaders chug along during planting season. People actually wave to strangers. "Just yell north, and I'll hear you," said one villager, directing a visitor from the North Common to her home up the street. The business sector amounts mostly to one of each—a bank, a bar named The Pines, a food market, a funeral home, a restaurant named Dixie II's, an auto repair shop, a pizza shop, a coin laundry, a feed-and-grain store, and Will's Store, with its wildly varied offerings: video rentals, newspapers, ice cream, beer, milk, worms and crawlers for fishing bait, and ammunition for turkey and woodchuck shooting.

The Town Hall and library share a nineteenth-century, red-brick building located next to the North Common, and on the library's shelves are the few books that tell the story of this quintessential New England town, including *A History of Chelsea, Vermont,* compiled by W. Sydney Gilman and a committee from the Chelsea Historical Society.

Farming and family were the twin pillars upon which the community was founded in the eighteenth century. The original charter of 1781 explicitly says as much—both were conditions for moving to the area. The charter required that settlers, most of whom were of English descent and came from lower New Hampshire, Massachusetts, and Connecticut, "shall plant & cultivate Five acres of Land and build a house at least Eighteen feet square on the Floor, or have one Family Settled on each respective share or right of Land in said Township, with the Term of Four Years." For the next two centuries, farming defined life in Chelsea, a community where change has always come as slowly as a soft breeze. In 1840, the population peaked at 1,959 residents. By the year 2000 it was about 700 fewer. Many of the outdoor activities and social traditions established throughout the 1800s are the same ones practiced two centuries later—the fishing, hunting, snowshoeing, skiing, and ice skating, along with the minstrel shows and tree-plantings. It's the essence of country life found in just about any small New England town. One distinguishing characteristic of Chelsea is its long affinity for the dramatic arts. Sydney Gilman, the late local historian, noted, "A sense of drama has been inherent in Chelsea's history." Town Hall was itself once called The Opera House, and community drama clubs, with names like The Chelsea Dramatic Company or, later, The Chelsea Players, always seemed at work on one production or another.

Not far from Chelsea are greater concentrations of up-country wealth—to the west in Stowe, Vermont, for example, or to the south in Hanover, New Hampshire, home to Dartmouth College. For all its bucolic trappings, Chelsea is the seat of one of Vermont's more hardscrabble counties. Per capita income in Orange County in 1999 was $21,164, the tenth lowest of the state's fourteen counties. Real estate still sells relatively cheap—thirty acres of Chelsea woodland was on the market in 2002 for $33,900. A four-bedroom, 1926 Dutch Colonial on ten acres of land near the village was listed at the reduced price of $159,900. The town does not have its own police department and pays about $4,500 to the county sheriff's office for law enforcement—mostly to handle accidents, speeding, and drunken driving.

The core of the town has always been rock-ribbed conservative. In the 2000 presidential election, George W. Bush carried Chelsea with 350 votes to Al Gore's 272. Hanover, in contrast, went for Gore by a three-to-one margin—3,391 votes to Bush's 1,541. Another reminder of Chelsea's conservative mindset was the big sign in block letters hanging from a house overlooking the North Common: TAKE BACK VERMONT, the slogan used by those opposed to the state law recognizing the vows of same-sex couples.

While many other Vermont villages have turned into ultra-quaint destinations for skiers and tourists, Chelsea has not. Fewer than five miles of the town's seventy miles of roads are paved; instead, dirt and gravel roads zigzag through West Hill, where most Chelseans live, and some of those roads are impassable during the winter months and the mud season that follows. The town may cover thirty-seven square miles, but seventy percent is thickly forested. In a way, Chelsea has always lived in a cocoon, a by-product of geography and location. When the era of highway construction began in the 1950s, the region's two major routes—Interstates 91 and 89—came no closer than twenty-five miles to Chelsea. For the longest time the world was out there, and starting in the late 1970s, photographers and writers began showing up to document Chelsea's rustic, lived-in feel and seemingly unchanged ways. As part of a *New England Monthly* article in 1985, more than half the town turned out to pose for a photographer in front of the white Greek Revival courthouse. Thirteen years earlier, in *Vermont Life*, a similarly themed story featured a photo album of Chelsea's farms, meadows, the village, and local kids playing soccer and basketball. Nearly identical photographs could be taken today.

Both photo spreads featured the two town greens, North and South Common. In truth, the rectangular swatches of grass seem unremarkable to anyone familiar with the parks or large commons in cities like Boston or Montpelier, Vermont's capital. But context is everything, and what makes Chelsea's greens special is the fact that none of the neighboring communities have anything like them. Places like Vershire, Thetford, and West Fairleigh possess comparatively meager town centers, with town offices, libraries, post offices, and homes built practically on the curb of a main road. There's no bona fide common area at which to dally, just a state road cutting into and out of town. Chelsea's two greens are therefore a rarity, a twin treasure, its own Boston Common—and a draw over the years for townsfolk from other towns.

Years ago, the South Common was also the site of a whipping post and a set of stocks. The first county jail was built in 1796 on a site where today's brick jail sits, and the first courthouse atop South Common was built in the early 1800s. Crimes throughout the county are adjudicated in Chelsea. But then, as now, the criminal court docket has never been a crowded affair. Throughout the town's history, the crime log has featured the kind of petty offenses that occur anywhere—vandalism, thefts, and break-ins. Just as in any rural place suffering through long winters, Chelsea has also coped with crimes often hidden from public view, like domestic abuse. By the same token, just as in most of Vermont, there is nowhere near as much crime as cities see.

The most notorious incident took place in the early nineteenth century involving Rebecca Peake, who was not actually from Chelsea but lived in Randolph, the next town to the west. In the summer of 1835, Peake was charged with poisoning her husband with arsenic. The murder case was that era's headline-grabbing, high-profile story. The court record described Peake's conduct this way: "Not having the fear of God before her eyes, but being moved and instigated by the Devil, and of her malice aforethought," she killed her husband, Ephraim, on August 12, 1835. The December trial drew so many spectators that the proceedings were moved out of the courthouse and into the Congregational Church at North Common. Following Peake's conviction, gallows were built at South Common, and February 12, 1836, was set as the day Rebecca Peake "would be hanged by the neck until she is dead." Despite a major snowstorm that Friday morning, curiosity seekers filled the South Common to watch a civics lesson in capital punishment. But the hanging never happened. Peake had stockpiled opium a local doctor had provided to help her sleep, and she slipped the hangman's noose by committing suicide. "Woman Cheated Gallows," read one newspaper headline.

The gallows didn't stay there long. In Chelsea, it's simple—murder is not part of the town's experience. Until recently, most wouldn't know if anyone from town had ever been charged with homicide. Few can place the name Rebecca Peake—and her case doesn't really count because she was from Randolph. Only the true old guard can come up with a lone case from local history. In 1978, a thirty-four-year-old Chelsea man was charged with manslaughter after killing his brother with a shotgun blast to the chest at the house in West Hill the two men shared with their mother. Questions arose at trial about the shooter's mental health and his possible diminished capacity, and following deliberations a Vermont jury came back with a not-guilty verdict.

It was a case that unfolded in the local news as a new couple was just settling into Chelsea. John Parker and Joan Essery, both twenty-nine years old, had an outdoor wedding in Chelsea on September 30, 1979. Planning to raise a family, the Parkers soon went about building a home on nineteen acres on West Hill.

By the dawn of the twenty-first century, Chelsea was a place where, on a typical Friday night in the spring, quiet was the village's most ear-splitting trait. There was the burbling brook, running between the two greens, that eventually empties into the First Branch of the White River; the trilling of spring peepers breeding in vernal pools; the rattle of a pickup truck idling in front of a country store while the driver paid for a twelve-pack of Bud; the fading laughter of two boys on their bikes weaving into the dark past homes south of town; the low growl of logger Jack Johnson's twenty-two-wheeler, its shiny blue-gray hood sporting the names of his four sons painted in a proud and fancy script, lumbering through the village toward home after a long day of hauling logs and pulp wood. The world might be hopping elsewhere but not in Chelsea, and the tranquility could at once be comforting and disconcerting for outsiders. More than 75 percent of Americans live in or around urban centers; Chelsea's entire population of 1,250 could fit in a single waterfront apartment building in Boston. There are no traffic lights in Chelsea, cell phones rarely function, and the nearest highway is at least a thirty-minute drive—a town, all in all, where less is more.

It's a town embodying the extreme in the cultural concept that the world is a small place, a web where people link up to one another within a half-dozen or so connections. The playwright John Guare popularized the idea in his play, *Six Degrees of Separation*. In Chelsea, forget about six degrees. Try two. Chelseans know one another directly or are only one step removed, a familiarity that begins in the community's lone school. Each elementary grade at the Chelsea Public School has a single class. There are years when some grades have fewer than ten kids. Overall, the K-12 school has only about 270 students, and many of the high schoolers are not even from Chelsea but are tuition-paying students from nearby towns. By high school, many of the students have known and played with one another since they were toddlers struggling to stay on their feet. "In Chelsea we're all woven together, whether we like it or not," one resident said.

The pillars of the community are the old-time Chelseans whose ancestors go back for generations and who continue the farming and logging traditions. Logger and selectman Jack Johnson grew up in nearby Corinth, and his wife, Annette, grew up in Chelsea, where they met in high school. She now works in the school cafeteria. Jack's father was a logger, as are two of his sons. "My father always logged and ever since I was five years old I helped out in the woods," Jack Johnson said. Down the road from their house and the hundred acres they own on West Hill, the Johnsons have built the Johnson Family Sugar House for making maple syrup each March. Their youngest son, Brad, was a standout high school athlete, excelling in basketball, becoming the first player to score one thousand career points his junior year. The Johnson boys, like so many Chelsea boys, grew up logging, sugaring, camping, and hunting. "Brad was born with a basketball in one hand and a gun in the other," his mother, Annette, said.

Yet big, albeit slow, change has come to Chelsea—trends affecting both the town's farm-based economy and the culture. Older Chelseans talk about life on the farm. "There was always work to do," said Chelsea native Doug Lyford. Lyford grew up on his family's farm, became a teacher in town, and farms once again full-time at age fifty-four. When he was a boy in the 1950s, he woke to chores and after school picked up where he'd left off. Free time was an unfamiliar concept. Borrowing a term from today's baby boomers, the farm kids of Chelsea were "overbooked."

But that time has long passed. The number of dairy farms in Chelsea—nearly two hundred a century ago—dwindled to about eleven by 1995. "We've changed from more of an agricultural community into more of a bedroom community," said Lyford, "where both parents work out, and the kids are kind of latchkey kids." To Lyford, these changes aren't a good thing. "The way I look at kids," he said, "is when they're small they're almost like dogs and horses. All three of those categories—dogs and horses and kids—they need a little direction from adults. And if they don't get it, you know, dogs will run wild, the horses are no good, and the kids run a little wild, too."

The 1960s brought a cultural shock that rocked old Chelsea— what locals still refer to as the "hippie invasion." Town historian Gilman noted in 1984 that "many of the new arrivals brought a change of lifestyle with long hair, bare feet, a permissive use of drugs, and a change in sexual mores which clashed with traditional habits." Instead of the standard fare at the annual Town Meeting—school budgets and road maintenance—Chelseans were suddenly hotly debating Vietnam or the war in El Salvador. Drawn to Chelsea during this time were people like Cora Brooks, a poet, antiwar protester, and single mother. Brooks, petite and pretty in a no-frills way, bought a beat-up old house on Main Street in 1977 and later told a magazine writer she picked Chelsea "because I wanted to see the stars clearly. I wanted to see trees and hear birds and see wildflowers and learn about elements like fire and ice and mud and fresh air." She also wanted to end war. In 1981, Brooks and six others—the so-called Chelsea Seven—were arrested at a draft registration protest outside the post office. Trespassing charges were eventually dropped.

Drawn to Chelsea five years before Brooks was a young doctor from Chicago named Andrew Pomerantz. "I was the hippie doctor," Pomerantz said about his arrival in 1972, long hair and all, with his wife, Jill, and their baby son. They spent their first summer camping in a tent, then bought some land and dug in. Pomerantz aspired to be a country doctor. "We wanted a small town, and a small town away from the interstate." Chelsea fit the bill. "I figured twenty miles was a reasonable distance to cut down on some of the schlocky tourist stuff that was beginning to grow up around Vermont." Pomerantz became a family practitioner in the village.

"Flatlanders" like Brooks and Pomerantz brought diversity to Chelsea—cultural and socio-economic rather than ethnic. The old and new had some trouble mixing. Pomerantz found Chelsea to be "one of the last bastions of conservatism. When I first got here, the big national issue was Watergate, and a lot of people here thought Nixon was framed." But Pomerantz found in Chelsea a town that cared, with people who, in time, looked past the ponytail and protest politics. "I found early on people could get past that fairly quickly and begin to see people for who they were and what they had to contribute." The town's smallness and intimacy had produced conservatism with a heart. "Primal American values—family and community," said Pomerantz. By the late 1970s, many of the early hippies had moved on, but Cora Brooks stayed, becoming a frequent substitute teacher at the Chelsea school, a poetry teacher, and an advocate for battered women. Pomerantz and his wife stayed, too, raising three kids. Eventually he became a psychiatrist and took a job at a hospital thirty miles away in White River Junction.

Newcomers continued to trickle in, though, drawn just as Pomerantz and Brooks had been to the elbow room and slower pace of an out-of-the-way place. "Chelsea provides a life free from what I call kitsch—cheap commercial," said David Savidge, who moved to the area in the early 1970s. "You don't need a forty thousand-dollar SUV or an eight hundred thousand-dollar home to enjoy life here." Savidge, his wife, Mary, and two sons live four miles outside Chelsea village, just over the line in the town of Washington. His boys go to the Chelsea school. Savidge grew up in Princeton, New Jersey, and attended the private Hun School, but wanted none of that life for his sons. "Too much wealth and waste out there."

Locals sometimes call the new brand of arrivals "Ivy League carpenters" or "granola types," people who'd mostly come of age during the time of Flower Power and now wanted small-town life for their families. From the first, Chelsea has always been just that—a family-styled town. It said so in the founding charter. It's why John and Joan Parker built a house there two centuries later, in 1979. It's why thirteen years after that, in 1992, another young family, Mike and Diane Tulloch and their four kids, moved to town after a brief, difficult spell in Florida. Chelsea was a place to call home.

3

An
American Dream

On a cold, wet day in March 1976, the Zantop family trudged down the gangplank of a Polish freighter docked at the Port of Montreal. The sea-weary family—Half, Susanne, and their daughters, four-year-old Veronika and two-year-old Mariana—had boarded the ship ten days earlier in Hamburg, in the Zantops' native Germany. They arrived in Montreal bundled against the cold, en route to a new life in Hanover, New Hampshire, where Half had accepted a job teaching geology at Dartmouth College.

Half was thirty-seven, tall and handsome, with a close-cropped dark beard and a quiet bearing. Susanne was thirty, petite and pretty, with dark hair and a manner that was at once warm and intense. They had crossed the Atlantic in search of a safe, stable community in which to raise their daughters, who arrived looking like china dolls in sweet dresses, barely a word of English between them. The first sign that the Zantops had chosen their destination well materialized even before they crossed into the United States. Waiting for them at the bustling Montreal dock was a Dartmouth emissary, a legendary geology professor at the Ivy League school named Richard "Dick" Stoiber.

Knowing that the Zantops would be arriving with most of their worldly possessions, Stoiber had driven to Canada in convoy with a second car, a rented station wagon driven by a graduate student named Jim Reynolds and his wife, Haidee. After a long wait for the Zantops to clear Customs, the group got some bad news—a labor dispute had idled all porters, and no handcarts were available. Soaked by an icy rain, the three male academics—Half Zantop, Dick Stoiber, and Jim Reynolds—did mules' work, hauling twenty-two suitcases and duffel bags from the ship to the cars. The men made the wearying trek in hundred-foot increments, while Susanne, Haidee, and the bewildered little girls stood guard over the moving piles of luggage. To lighten the load, Stoiber joked that the luggage-moving team reminded him of penitents reenacting the Stations of the Cross. While the girls clung to her legs, Susanne fell into conversation with Haidee about politics, expressing her hope that Jimmy Carter would win the presidency in November.

They stuffed the bags into the Reynoldses' car, while the Zantops piled in with Stoiber for a four-hour drive to Hanover. Almost as soon as they got under way, Veronika and Mariana were asleep in the back seat. By the time they reached Hanover, the dockside drizzle had turned into a downpour. Stoiber and Reynolds drove directly to the home of another of Half's new colleagues, Richard Birnie, like Half, a promising young geologist who had just joined the Dartmouth earth sciences faculty. In time, Birnie would come to admire Half as the conscience of their department and a first-rate geologist, at home in a classroom but happiest in rock-strewn field. At their first meeting, Birnie greeted the Zantop family with the most down-home fare he could rustle up: grilled hamburgers and hot dogs. Veronika and Mariana were still rubbing sleep from their eyes when Stoiber brought them each a huge, juicy burger on a paper plate. He offered it with the benediction: "This, my dears, is the American dream."

Over the next twenty-five years, the Zantop family would achieve that dream to a remarkable extent.

Half—pronounced *hahlf*, from the German "to help"—was the fourth of six children of a printer and a homemaker. Before his birth and throughout his youth, Half and his family bounced back and forth between Spain and Germany, tossed on the tides of war and recession.

In 1925, the German economy was in ruins after World War I, and Half's father moved the family to Barcelona in search of work, eventually running a profitable printing and box-making factory. The Zantops remained in Spain until 1936, when upheaval caused by the Spanish Civil War sent them back to their homeland.

Half was born two years later, on April 24, 1938, in Eckernforde, in far northwestern Germany, a port city on the Baltic Sea that was home to the German U-boat school. Half spent his infancy in a country ruled by Adolph Hitler, a Germany where Jews had been stripped of their rights by the Nuremberg Race Laws. German troops occupied the Rhineland, and just a month before Half's birth, Germany announced the Anschluss, or union, with Austria. Germany would soon invade Poland.

With the Spanish Civil War ending and Germany leading the world toward war, the Zantops returned to Barcelona when Half was one. Three years later, in 1942, the family came home to Eckernforde, to live for the next six years on a relative's farm. In 1948, the family went yet again to Barcelona, where Half spent his teenage years attending a German school. His older brother, Wolf, remembered Half as a young man who wasn't blessed with special gifts in the classroom or on the playing field, but who excelled through effort and determination. "He was a normal young man, not the fastest, not the smartest, but he would work harder," Wolf Zantop said.

Half returned to Germany for college, receiving a geology degree from Karl Ludwigs-Universitate in Freiburg in 1960. Rootless, his life divided between Germany and Spain, he went even farther afield, earning another geology degree in 1961 from Washington State

University. He felt out of place at first in America, so he hung out at the Cosmopolitan Club, an organization for foreign students. There he met Alex Bertulis, a native of Lithuania and architecture student who would become a lifelong friend. They debated international affairs, and soon they realized they shared a passion for mountain climbing. As a boy, Half had climbed in the Pyrenees with his father, developing a love for the sport and taut, powerful muscles on his rangy frame. Together, Half and Alex spent several years in the early 1960s challenging themselves on some of the toughest mountain ranges in North America.

They climbed Canada's spectacular Bugaboos, North America's answer to the French Alps, and they mastered the toothy, glacier-marked Picket Range in Washington state. Whenever possible they chose the hardest routes, some never climbed before. On a ten-day, late-summer climb in 1963, they made what was believed to be the first complete traverse of the Pickets. Along the way they climbed the aptly named Mount Fury, Mount Challenger, and Mount Terror, making a harrowing, first-ever descent of Terror's forbidding north face. They were six thousand feet up when they had to rappel down two thousand feet of vertical rock—weaving their way through a fault that divides the mountain's twin summits. Exhausted from the effort, they slept that night hanging by ropes pinned to the rock.

On another trip, in the Cascades of Washington state, they climbed a sleeping volcano called Mount Adams and watched as loose rocks tumbled down the mountain perilously close to them. At the end of a day of arduous climbing, they bivouacked on a small ledge and enjoyed a magnificent mountain sunset. The next morning they woke early to reach the summit at nearly thirteen thousand feet. Several of their exploits were recorded in the bible of the sport, the *American Alpine Journal*.

Half's climbing days came to an abrupt end—nearly along with his life—on a trip to Yosemite National Park in 1965. By then, Half was enrolled at Stanford University in California, pursuing his Ph.D. and a young German woman he had met there named Susanne Korsukewitz.

Half was leading the way up majestic Echo Peak when he lost his grip on the granite wall. In the argot of climbers, Half "peeled off." Grabbing air instead of mountain, he fell backward, his head narrowly missing a ledge. Though he avoided a potentially fatal head injury, Half's leg hit the rock, shattering his ankle. Bertulis held fast to the rope that connected them and slowly lowered Half to safety. He fashioned crutches for Half from the branches of Ponderosa pines and carried Half's pack along with his own. Half hobbled back to their car, frightened, exhausted, and grimacing with pain. It was the end of his days as a serious climber. The friendship endured, but mountains were left to their memories.

In his later years, Half would stare out the windows of airplanes when he flew over mountain ranges and think wistfully of his youthful exploits. In 1994, almost three decades after their last climb, Half wrote Bertulis to express how deeply the fall had affected him. In a letter consoling Bertulis on the death of his wife, Half wrote: "Last night it struck me that some of my fondest memories and most challenging feats of my life have been fully your doing. The traverse of the Picket Range and the wild-goose chase to climbing areas in the Canadian Rockies, the Tetons, and Wind Rivers, and finally the Sierra Nevada, after we were snowed out of other possibilities. You saved my head when I fell on Echo Peak, and I suppose the broken ankle and meeting Susanne finally forced me to finish my long-overdue Ph.D. and embark on my professional career."

Susanne Liselotte Marianna Korsukewitz was born August 12, 1945, in Kissingen, in southern Germany. Hitler was dead by his own hand; Germany had surrendered three months earlier. Atomic bombs had been dropped over Hiroshima and Nagasaki just days before Susanne's birth.

Susanne—pronounced *soo-ZAHN-uh*—was the eldest of three children, two girls and a boy, in a comfortable, middle-class home run by a father who managed a brick factory, and a mother who was a homemaker. The family spent the postwar years outside Frankfurt, in a rural community dotted with medieval castles and small farms that grew wheat and potatoes and kept pigs, chickens, and cows.

Susanne's mother, Marianne Korsukewitz, was enchanted by the darling, gifted daughter who was a fixture at the top of her class. The word she used most often to describe her eldest child was "wonderful." When pressed for more details, she would add, "always happy, always good." Susanne skipped several grades in school "because she was too great in her classes," her mother said with deep pride and a thick German accent.

When she wasn't studying, Susanne mastered Mozart and Beethoven on piano, swam the breaststroke, played badminton, kept cats as pets, wrote fanciful stories, and devoured every book she could get her hands on, with a particular interest in history. She had a gift for languages even as a young girl, recalled her brother Thomas, a gastroenterologist.

In 1967, Susanne received the German equivalent of a bachelor's degree in political science from the Free University of Berlin, and then set her sights on America and a master's degree, also in political science. She was accepted at Stanford University on a scholarship.

Though Susanne and Half were both multilingual, expatriate German students, from the very first they were a study in contrasts. Half had grown to his full height of six feet and a lean 150 pounds. He was private and deliberate, a man who climbed a mountain, took a test, or faced a problem with the same patient approach, moving with confidence and care toward the summit. Sometimes progress was slow, and sometimes there were setbacks, but by refusing to quit he always made progress. Later in life, when a love for sailing replaced mountaineering, Half would reveal the same steadiness, maintaining an even keel through life's squalls.

If Half was rock solid, Susanne was quicksilver. A little more than five feet tall, she was a gregarious sprite, a crackling bundle of controlled energy. Passionate, engaging, engaged. She dressed simply, in pants or a straight skirt—"professor chic," her friends said. She wore her brown hair cropped short, with rarely even a drop of makeup on her animated face. She radiated warmth, from her eyes behind wire-rimmed reading glasses to a broad smile that accented her cheekbones. She had a memorable laugh. Yet she could be high-strung and impatient, especially with intellectual laziness or lapses that offended her moral and ethical codes. More often, her impatience was directed at herself. She rushed toward challenges, moving mountains if need be rather than picking her way through crags and crevasses.

Susanne received her master's degree from Stanford in 1968, and the next year Half earned his Ph.D. By then they were a steady couple, destined for marriage. Half took a job as a geologist for the mining industry, working for the Kennecott Corp. and Bethlehem Steel. They lived together in Argentina, and in 1970 they were married at the foot of the Andes Mountains, in Mendoza, Argentina. Susanne's family thought Half was a wonderful man and together they made a beautiful couple. Half's family was equally happy with the union of two such different yet kindred spirits.

After Argentina the Zantops spent a year in Colombia, where Susanne became pregnant. Then Half accepted a job in Spain, so the family returned to Europe. Susanne gave birth prematurely, while in Germany, and spent several months there with the daughter they named Veronika before joining Half in Spain, where they spent the next five years. Half continued his work as a mining geologist and Susanne gave birth to their second daughter, Mariana. Susanne taught German and literature at a college in Santiago de Compostela, a city in far northwest Spain where, legend has it, the remains of the apostle Saint James were found and where more Catholics make pilgrimages than anywhere except Rome. Their proximity to the shrine did nothing to incite religiosity; both Zantops considered themselves atheists.

As much as Half loved being a field geologist, the pull of the academic world was strong. As a teacher, he could spend more time with his wife and daughters. From 1975 through 1976, he was a research fellow in ore microscopy at the University of Heidelberg. Then Dick Stoiber recruited him to Dartmouth, and the Zantop family boarded the Polish freighter to begin their new lives in Hanover.

When they arrived at Dartmouth, Half poured himself into work as a junior faculty member in the school's earth sciences department. He specialized in work that melded the study of geology, economics, and political science, the interplay of which was critical to the pursuit of valuable ore deposits. During those first years in Hanover, Susanne's focus was on their daughters—Jim Reynolds's lasting memory at the Montreal dock was of Susanne protecting the girls from the cold and rain. But her ambition and energy soon drove her to seek a second master's degree, in comparative literature, from the University of Massachusetts in Amherst, a two-hour drive from their home.

Wherever she went, Susanne enlarged the couple's circle of friends. In the autumn of 1978, Alan Fair was an exchange student at UMass taking a class in German philosophy when he first came into contact with what he called the "inordinate intellect" of a young woman with a German accent. He saw her again soon after at a reading group and was impressed anew by her analytical skills. Much later, Fair would call Susanne "that rare creature, an intellectual with warmth and humanity. Not for her the aloofness of the Brahmin, but rather the friendliness of the comrade who seeks to make the world a better place through the virtues of friendliness and compassion."

Christmas came a few months after Fair met Susanne. Fair and his wife were hunkered down far from family in their small university apartment. On the morning of Christmas Eve, there was a knock at their door. Susanne made the hundred-mile drive to Amherst to insist that Fair and his wife come to Hanover. The Fairs spent Christmas Eve in the Zantops' home, talking art and politics and warmed by fine food, well-chosen wine, and the Zantop family's embrace. The Fairs ended up spending five memorable days with Half, Susanne, Veronika, and Mariana. "We all agreed that while we were Europeans, we felt a special affinity with Americans and America, and they had found a place that they could call home," Fair recalled. More than two decades later, Fair loved looking at the photos they had taken that Christmas morning, when they were young and happy together.

As the Zantop girls moved impressively through the Hanover public schools, Susanne continued her education, receiving a Ph.D. in comparative literature from Harvard University in 1984. Susanne's return to school meant Half had to take more responsibility at home, and he relished the opportunity to spend time nurturing their daughters. Friends were impressed by how the couple sought to be equal partners in all respects—in their family lives as well as their intellectual and professional pursuits.

Susanne had already been teaching at Dartmouth for two years when she received her doctorate. With Ph.D. in hand, she jumped on the fast track to becoming a professor of German and comparative literature. By 1988, she had published her first book, *Zeitbilder: Geschichtsschreibung und Literatur bei Heinrich Heine und Mariano Jose de Larra,* an academic examination of Heine, a romantic, humanistic German poet on whom Susanne had written her dissertation, and Larra, a melancholy, suicidal Spanish satirist.

The same year, Half coauthored the book *International Mineral Economics.* For much of his career, he focused on the economic and environmental impact of mining. He studied the geology of manganese and iron deposits, sulfide deposits, and precious metal deposits. He explored the silver mines of Fresnillo and Guanajuato in Mexico, the Aguilar base metal deposit in Argentina, and volcanic activity in El Salvador, Nicaragua, Guatemala, and elsewhere. Volcanoes were a particular interest, and by coincidence he and Susanne eventually found a home in Etna, a village of Hanover that by some accounts was named for the frequently erupting volcano in Sicily.

His coauthor, Werner Gocht, was repeatedly impressed by Half's devotion to the environment. "Mining is a dirty business. Half was always interested in finding ways to minimize the harm of mining," Gocht said. On a visit to a coal mining area in Germany, Gocht recalled, Half focused almost entirely on reforestation plans. "Geologists are interested in investigating rocks, but he was also a man who knew the plants and the animals, who saw nature as a whole." If someone was looking for a conversation about the environment, Half was always ready to take part.

Though he was a skilled researcher, Half's greatest gifts lay in teaching. It was a surprising discovery to him, as pleasantly unexpected as coming upon a vein of silver in a mine thought to have been stripped clean. Half once told a student that he loved being a field geologist, but gave it up for the classroom because it was a better fit with his family life; long stretches in the mountains and constant moves required of his earlier jobs made it impossible for him to be the father and husband he wanted to be.

"If I were not teaching, I don't know where I would be," Half said, his meaning both literal and figurative.

Still, at times he would wistfully tell stories of exotic cities and far-flung exploration, of shimmering deposits of gold and silver, of adventures with native guides, and of close calls with bandits. He could grip listeners with tales of mine disasters befitting an Indiana Jones movie. But if he regretted his decision to come in from the field, it never showed in his work.

Students and colleagues consistently ranked him among the top teachers in the department, and even one of the best at Dartmouth. Students praised his ability to make the most difficult subject matter understandable even to non-scientists. "Half is the best professor I've ever had at Dartmouth," was a comment that appeared regularly on his student evaluations. He would ask questions that teased the correct answers from confused students. He told stories about the provenance of a rock the way a historian would weave a fabulous tale from a trove of ancient writings. And often he did it with a wry sense of humor— just because they were studying rocks didn't mean Half's classes had to be dull. During slide presentations on rock formations, he might slip in a shot of a mallard or students sunbathing during a field trip. Beyond the humor, there was never a question that Half was an authority on the subject: Graduate students sometimes referred to him as The Rock God. "But he wasn't overly proud," said former student Kristina Kleutghen. "He knew what he didn't know and when he got things wrong."

Field trips were the highlight of students' time with Half because they got the best of him as both teacher and geologist. Dartmouth graduate Melanie Kay recalled a 1998 trip throughout Mexico in which Half, nearing sixty, outpaced students one-third his age. "Half was routinely the first one awake, the most eager to stay in the field until sunset, and the last one awake at night. And he never ate lunch. My fellow students and I could barely keep up. In the evenings, we would sometimes filter into Half's hotel room for cocktails and discussion, sometimes academically related but sometimes just for fun. Then, somehow, while we were all groaning at the 6:30 wakeup, Half was already downstairs completing his leisurely breakfast," Kay recalled. Half led the group of twenty students up a fifteen-thousand-foot volcano and down thousand-foot mine shafts, into the waves of a Mexican beach, and to a bar where he ordered a round of potent drinks called Coco Locos.

On the last night of the trip, Half took the group to a good restaurant to celebrate their journey. Kay sat next to Half, and they both smiled when the restaurant's photographer took their picture. Half bought an eight-by-ten print and a key chain with the photo, both of which he gave to Kay. She kept the key chain, but wrote "My Prize Student" on the larger photo and gave it back to Half with a note jokingly suggesting that he hang it on his office wall. And he did. Later, Kay wished she had written "My Prize Professor," which is what she really meant.

Some of his female students took note of his flattering beard—which over the years turned snowy white—and his "sexy German accent," recalled Julia Henneberry, a graduate student and former teaching assistant. But Half wasn't interested in extracurricular romance. In the quiet moments on those trips, Half would find somewhere to plug in his laptop computer and send Susanne e-mails saying how much he missed her.

What Half's students didn't know was that, for all his vigor, he was hiding a serious heart problem called atrial fibrillation—a fast, uncontrolled heart rhythm that can lead to stroke—that had been diagnosed more than a decade earlier. At first he ignored the diagnosis, continuing his jaunt through life. But in July 1998, the same year of the Mexico trip that Kay recalled so fondly, Half confided to his old friend Alex Bertulis: "About two years ago the doctors told me, 'You better watch out.' The heart was underperforming alarmingly, a little over 15 percent normal. . . . So now I am on a low-dosage beta-blocker and all seems well enough. Life as usual, after more than a year of the depressing feeling that it was all over. . . . The heart performance is back to lower limit of normal, and 'Las ganas de vivir' [the zest for life] has returned quite nicely."

From the moment she began teaching at Dartmouth, Susanne was a prolific scholar and an academic star. Starting with her book *Zeitbilder* in 1988, over the next dozen years Susanne authored or edited eight books and made regular contributions to several scholarly journals. She was coeditor of the *Women in German Yearbook,* an annual anthology of feminist articles in German studies. She became chairwoman of Dartmouth's German studies department in 1996 and won a five-year term, 1999–2004, as the Parents' Distinguished Research Professor in the Humanities. She was in great demand as a speaker.

A highlight of her career was her 1997 book, *Colonial Fantasies: Conquest, Family and Nation in Precolonial Germany, 1770–1870.* The book tied together two of her abiding interests: eighteenth and nineteenth century German history and, as she put it in the preface, "everything Latin American, from politics to literature to the many diverse cultures." Unexpectedly, she wrote, the work also gave her an opportunity to "exorcize some of the demons I had collected along the way: the trajectory from Berlin, Germany, to the United States, and from there to South America, then Spain, and finally back to the United States, first as a student, then as the wife of an employee of U.S. mining companies, then as an academic; and the trajectory from a self-satisfied, anti-imperialist sixties radical, to a guilt-ridden, reluctant participant in U.S. imperialism, to a critic of the culture of imperialism and my own involvement in it." It was pure Susanne: an outpouring of thoughts and feelings, intense, self-critical, and high-minded.

She was easier-going when it came to the book's final acknowledgments: "As I was working . . . I became keenly aware of how wonderfully supportive and nurturing even the much-maligned nuclear family can be. This book is therefore dedicated to them: to my mother, Marianne, whose unshaking faith in my ability to finish projects energized me throughout my life; to my father, Joachim, whose enthusiasm for cannibals and Amazons translated into many visits to libraries and much epistolary exchange on the subject matter; to my daughters, Veronika and Mariana, who bore with me through thick and thin, with leniency, love, and good humor; and to Half, in more than one sense my better half." She was known for making puns in three languages— English, German, and Spanish—so word play based on her husband's name was too tempting to resist.

And yet, because she wasn't a native English speaker, there were occasional linguistic miscues. Commenting on a colleague who ran herself ragged, Susanne observed, "She's a real busybody." Though more comfortable with English than Susanne, Half was susceptible to some of the same flubs. A pet peeve of his friend Dick Stoiber was the way Half would say "All by sudden," instead of the colloquial "All of a sudden."

In addition to her own scholarship, Susanne was a mentor, collaborator, and friend to a wide circle of other academics. But sometimes her willingness to help came at a price. "She really wanted to get the most out of life, so she was trying to pack the most things in," said Irene Kacandes, a close friend and member of the German studies department. "The downside is that you tend to feel a little stressed." Sometimes that stress showed itself on the roads around Hanover. "She drove like a bat out of hell!" recalled Bruce Duncan, another member of the German studies faculty. In fact, she became notorious—and picked up a few tickets—for speeding along the curved and hilly roads in her sporty red Volkswagen Jetta, usually leaving Half their practical but less nimble 1999 silver Subaru Legacy wagon.

Her frantic pace reflected Susanne's own perfectionism, friends said, as well as her tendency to take on huge loads of work. Some friends saw it as a sign of insecurity, others as evidence of her commitment to leading as full a life as possible. "She sometimes reminded me of a bouncing tennis ball, so energetic and always in motion," said her friend Margaret Robinson, academic assistant in the German department. "She could talk a mile a minute. When she got passionate, sometimes you had to ask her to slow down." Robinson also saw that side of Susanne's personality in her tennis game: aggressive and hard-hitting, though sometimes erratic.

Susanne was likely to be a professor students remembered long after leaving Dartmouth. They knew she was tough, and that she would push them, but always with compassion. One day several years after she had taken a class with Susanne, Dartmouth graduate Aarathi Sambasivan found herself thinking of Susanne when she visited The Jewish Museum on the Upper East Side of New York City. The memory was triggered by an exhibit on Morocco: "I found myself looking at the artifacts on display—the paintings, the clothes, the jewelry, the literature—and understanding the various connections between all these things and the reflections of a culture's beliefs in all of these things. These are all things I learned to do in her class. . . . Susanne had a way of inspiring her students. She made her class incredibly fun. She was a devoted teacher, one of the few that I would say 'taught' in what I consider the true sense of the word."

When Susanne was leading semester-long programs in Berlin, Half would fly over and spend several weeks with her. They would often stay in a two-bedroom apartment in the center of Berlin that Susanne's parents had given them. When they weren't using it themselves, they rented it out for six hundred fifty dollars a month.

Close friends saw the differences between Half and Susanne as dovetail complements. "Their mutual devotion was based on the respect they held for each other's ways of being—she for Half's methodical, exacting attention to detail, for his calm and thoughtfulness, his ingenuity and expertise; he for Susanne's tireless energy, critical and quick mind, her strong opinions, her intensity and passion for her work," friends Marianne Hirsch and Leo Spitzer once wrote.

"What they had in common was their endless generosity, the openness of their home, their commitment to social justice, and the high standards they set for themselves." Hirsch and Spitzer, married Dartmouth professors, were among the Zantops' closest friends. They called Susanne and Half "the nucleus at the center of the atom, holding us and so many friends, students, and colleagues within their orbit."

And yet, despite all they had achieved, Half and Susanne questioned whether they had done enough. "In the face of their remarkable accomplishments as scholars and teachers, there was always an anxious questioning—'Could I do better?'" said their friend and neighbor Audrey McCollum, a psychotherapist. "Susanne finished a book [*Colonial Fantasies*] and had a real dread that her colleagues would find it inadequate—a great deal of dread." In fact, *Colonial Fantasies* won an Outstanding Book Award from the German Studies Association. McCollum saw some of the same doubts in Half. "Half told me one day that before almost every lecture he gave, he would feel very, very nervous as to whether he'd be challenged or criticized."

Audrey McCollum and her husband, Bob, a retired dean at the Dartmouth Medical School, lived next door to the Zantops. Their homes were about four miles from the Dartmouth campus in Etna, on a street called Trescott Road.

4

Why Didn't You Jump Him?

Vermont State Police Sergeant Jocelyn Stohl was driving her cruiser toward a priority call when she came upon a car stuck in the snow next to the notoriously curving and narrow Bethel Mountain Road.

It was 2:55 on a Friday afternoon, which for January 19, 2001, meant it was practically twilight. Everything was gray—the sky, the road, and the woods. After snowing steadily, the sky seemed pressed down, the world closed in. The plows had come through, but the road was still a slushy, hazardous mess.

Even though Stohl was en route to a "possible despondent/suicidal subject" in the next town of Rochester, she knew to stop for the disabled vehicle. The trooper slowed her cruiser and pulled over just past the car to offer assistance.

Two teenage boys were standing outside the car, which Stohl noticed was a 1987 silver Audi with Vermont plates. Even before she spoke with them, the sixteen-year veteran trooper was reading the tire tracks in the snow to piece together what had happened. The driver had hit an ice patch and tried to straighten out with a quick back-and-forth of the wheel, she surmised, but then overcompensated, losing control and making matters worse. After a zig and a zag, the car traveled across the center line and onto the opposite shoulder, coming to a rest facing oncoming traffic.

The trooper climbed out of her cruiser, walked up to the two boys and asked them to tell her what happened. That's when the lies began. The boys acted as if there was nothing accidental about the fix they'd gotten themselves into. They'd pulled onto the shoulder on purpose, one of the boys tried explaining, so he could "take a leak."

The boys, the trooper noticed, were dressed mostly in black. The driver wore a light-colored top and black pants, the passenger a black sweatshirt, black jeans, and a black tuque.

Where are you heading? the trooper asked.

The driver hesitated before answering. "Skiing."

Whereabouts?

Hesitating again, the driver looked down at the ground. "Sugarbush."

The trooper put the boys through the paces, asking for licenses and registration. The driver scowled and acted as if she were wasting his time. But he complied, handing her a license that said he was from Chelsea, Vermont, DOB 5/24/84, 6 feet tall, 150 pounds, with brown eyes. His name was James Parker.

By contrast, the second boy, taller than the first, was accommodating, but in an exaggerated, overly solicitous way that struck the trooper as fake. To get his ID, the boy first asked her for permission to open the rear car door, and once in the back he rummaged around and found his license. It showed he was also from Chelsea, with a DOB of 5/8/83, making him a year older than his friend. Then Stohl matched the face in the picture to the boy standing before her and read the name: Robert Tulloch.

While Robert was retrieving his license, Stohl noticed two backpacks in the backseat, fully expanded and clearly full of something.

The trooper wasn't buying the skiing story. The car had been traveling east—the opposite direction from Sugarbush Mountain Ski Area. There were two backpacks, but she couldn't see ski apparel or ski equipment of any kind, either inside or on top of the car. What she did know was that she'd made a routine stop to assist a disabled vehicle and the driver was behaving angry in a nervous kind of way while the passenger was acting as cool as could be.

The trooper also knew the area had experienced some recent home burglaries.

Stohl's gut told her to pursue the matter further, and ideally that's what she would have done—put in a call for back-up and then ask the driver to consent to a car search. But at that particular moment there was little Stohl could do; she was in a hurry to a possible life-threatening situation while other troopers from the barracks were already tied up with other accidents and cars off the road. Stohl stayed long enough to run routine license and registration checks. But nothing came back when she punched in the names James Parker and Robert Tulloch.

In an incident report filed later, the trooper wrote, "Due to a priority call that I had to respond to and no other troopers available, I confirmed that a wrecker was responding to assist these subjects and went on my way."

Stohl told the two teens about the wrecker and left. She did so reluctantly. She hadn't liked the boys. They gave her a bad feeling and she felt they were up to no good. As soon as she heard their bogus skiing story, Stohl told herself not to turn her back on them at any time. "My suspicions of criminal activity were significant," Stohl wrote afterward.

That was the very last line of the report she filed about her encounter with Robert and Jim.

Sergeant Jocelyn Stohl was correct to feel creepy about the two boys dressed in black on the side of the road. The next morning, brassy as ever, Robert and Jim headed back over Bethel Mountain Road toward the town of Rochester. But not before making several adjustments.

They switched vehicles, for one, exchanging the Audi that Jim usually drove for his mom's green Subaru. More important, they gave up the black garb for the clothes of two ordinary high school students.

The dark attire had been part of one of their earliest ideas in the year since they had decided that the daring life was the only life for them. It was their after-hours option, in which they would jump some old man or woman as he or she arrived home at night. The student look was their new big thing, in which they'd pretend to be doing an environmental survey for school and, once inside a house, overtake the occupants. This option could happen in broad daylight, a ballsy move both liked. They valued "extreme thinking." Robert, who had the idea, especially liked the fake survey; it seemed so cynical. He liked cynical.

The one carryover from Friday was the backpacks. Of course they needed the backpacks.

The boys had a forty-mile ride ahead of them on mostly back roads. Jim was tempted to ignore any posted limits on speed. He was a charged-up kid, drawn to going fast in any direction someone pointed him. Robert certainly knew this about Jim because the two were best friends; in their minds, maybe the all-time two best friends ever. The boys sometimes talked about how lucky they were to have found one another in the first place. It was incredible that two boys who were so like-minded had come together in a country town they both agreed was a dead end.

On this morning, though, January 20, 2001, Jim knew he'd better not challenge the road. The last thing they wanted was to attract more trouble, like with the state trooper the day before. That was too close a call. Better to put that episode behind them, treat it as a bump in the road, a comma in their stream of higher consciousness, a tiny pause in their destiny.

Robert and Jim didn't want anything to get in their way. They headed south from Chelsea on Vermont 14, turning onto Vermont 107, then heading north on Route 12. They were back on Bethel Mountain Road, the winding, bumpy road that cut up and over a mountain ridge and led to their destination, North Hollow Road.

Robert and Jim knew about North Hollow Road from one of their reconnaissance drives in recent months, as they drove all around scouting out people and houses. They'd actually already broken into one of the houses on North Hollow, an older white Colonial-style home built close to the road. Jim had pried open a first-floor window, crawled inside, and unlocked the door for Robert. They'd stolen some mail and a map, but didn't come away with anything useful. Money was what they needed.

It was time to put up or shut up. They were a couple of hard-working students out doing a survey. They had the backpacks, the perfect props for two nerdy students. Inside the backpacks were two brand-new SOG SEAL 2000 knives. The boys had spent a lot of time researching the knives. They also had the ties and rope and other equipment they'd assembled, mostly from buying sprees at an Army-Navy store in Burlington.

They were going to get into one of the houses on North Hollow Road and be sitting around the table doing their fake survey and Robert would give the code that was a call to action. Forget about the scare with the trooper on Bethel Mountain Road. It was a glorious new day and the first day of the rest of their lives. They could taste it.

The boys made it over Bethel Mountain Road and, less than a mile from where they'd had the close encounter with Sergeant Stohl, they turned onto North Hollow Road. Fresh snow covered the meadows. Jim drove about a half-mile up the dirt road and buzzed by a house set hard against the road. They were thinking maybe this was one they should hit. But on quick inspection, they realized the house didn't hold a candle to the bigger one they'd passed, the biggest one they'd ever seen on North Hollow, a brand-new house.

Jim turned around the Subaru and headed back down the hill.

Their destination was 540 North Hollow Road, where Franklin and Jane Sanders were still in the process of breaking in the sprawling home they had recently moved into. Sanders was sixty-five, a retired utilities-and-insurance executive from New Jersey. He and his wife had only two months earlier completed construction of the modern, post-and-beam house on eighty-five acres of meadow and woods the couple had purchased in 1998. The home featured a large red barn, a big basement, and twelve rooms, with an assessed value of $650,700. The house was situated on a hillside, with a mountain range in back and a commanding view in front. In any affluent metropolitan suburb, the home would be labeled a trophy house, valued at many times the rural Vermont assessment. It was certainly a house that stood out among the mostly modest ranches, log homes, and double-wide house trailers that dotted surrounding roads.

Steering the Subaru onto the dirt driveway, the boys rode a couple hundred yards and pulled right up to the house. They noticed a dog pen alongside a garage, with access to an adjacent pen inside, so the dogs could go in or out on their own. Dogs were a potential concern, but not one to stop them at this point. Robert stepped out of the passenger side and strode toward the door. The two friends stood with their backpacks on the front steps when Franklin Sanders opened the door. They recognized at once he was an ideal target—an older man, meaning someone they could expect to subdue easily. Robert took the lead, telling Sanders they were students wanting to do an interview about the environment for school. They hoped he had some free time to help them with their project.

But Sanders was preoccupied. He was working on the new wave pool he'd begun installing over the Martin Luther King Jr. holiday weekend, when his son drove up from New Jersey to help him. The pool was an indoor aquatic-luxury item that was becoming popular with master swimmers and triathletes, or retirees with ailing hips and backs. The pools were designed to fit in sunrooms, garages, or basements, which is where Sanders was in the middle of putting his.

"No," he said, and he was curt about it.

The teenager doing all the talking wasn't even able to finish his presentation.

"I'm too busy. I'm tarring my pool." Sanders gave another reason, as well: After a lifetime in the utilities industry, where fights with environmentalists were as common as rate hikes, he had no interest in taking an environmental survey.

And then Franklin Sanders shut the door. It was that simple.

The boys stood there, stunned. That was it! Just like that—so totally dismissed!

The air went screaming out of their balloon.

Why didn't you jump him? Jim asked. It looked like the guy was home alone.

Didn't think of that, Robert admitted. It happened so fast. But Jim was right; he should have thought of that. Could have jumped the guy right at the door. Now it was too late.

They returned to the car and tossed the unopened backpacks into the back seat. They found themselves driving around, wondering what the heck had gone wrong. There was second-guessing, some sniping. They sounded like an old married couple, frustrated by the missed opportunities of life. Maybe they weren't prepared enough. The rebuff at North Hollow Road had been completely unanticipated.

The two left Rochester and were in Bethel, near Interstate 89, when they began to emerge from their funk. They weren't about to settle for this sort of setback, no way, not the two of them. They would just have to find new houses, and crank it up again. They reminded themselves of their calling as "Higher Beings." And they were nearing the route that would take them back home to Chelsea—which was ironic, because the whole point of their plan was to get away from Chelsea forever. Then one of them mentioned Hanover.

Hanover?

People in Hanover have a lot of money.

Hanover, New Hampshire—a great idea, and not only because Hanover did have a lot more money than most of the places they'd scouted. It was a great idea because no one would ever connect them to Hanover. They hated the college town and the conformist preppies who populated it. They almost never went there—the whole atmosphere was a turnoff, an insult to their self-images as brilliant adventurers and rugged individualists. None of their parents had business there, either, so there was no connection whatsoever. Best of all, Robert had some unfinished business from an angry brush with a debate team from Hanover High School.

So instead of heading back to Chelsea, they drove south on I-89.

Their mood picked up. Hanover was brilliant. Things might work out after all.

5

Trescott Road

It was easy to miss the house at 115 Trescott Road, situated in a small valley and hidden behind brush and trees and a low fieldstone wall. The house was barely visible from the heavily traveled street that connected Hanover to its bedroom suburb of Etna. But that's what the Zantops had been looking for: a respite from their busy lives, a place where they could feel swaddled by surrounding forests yet comfortable enough to entertain their many friends and colleagues.

Built in 1985 by Thomas Almy, a renowned Dartmouth Medical School professor, and his wife, Katharine, the two-story, 3,200-square-foot home had classic lines and a modern flair. Outside, the Almys sheathed it in vertical, blue-gray wood siding and topped it with a sloping roof covered by sheets of light-blue tin that made snow more likely to slide than stick. A fifty-yard gravel driveway curved in front of the house and led to an attached two-car garage. Circling the house was a swath of grass from which sprouted bushes, ferns, hostas, and an old-fashioned drying rack. Clothes hung there soaked in the fresh scents of the nearby woods. Inside were three bedrooms and a 600-square-foot living/dining room with an open kitchen, and just off the main room was an attached greenhouse.

When the Almys decided to sell in 1992, they wanted the buyers to love it as much as they did. People who'd appreciate the way beams of light shone through the large windows and reflected off the hardwood floors. The way the indoors and outdoors seemed to merge. The way the peaks of Killington Mountain loomed in the distance, over the border in Vermont. The way guests felt at home as soon as they walked in.

When the "For Sale" sign went up, the Almys' next-door neighbor, Audrey McCollum, leapt into action. She had known the Zantops for nearly a decade and had heard they were scouting around for a new home. Half and Susanne had been living close to the center of Hanover, but with their daughters off at college they were ready to indulge more rural desires. McCollum thought the Zantops would meet the Almys' requirements and also make ideal neighbors. She arranged an introduction and soon a deal was struck: In February 1992, the Zantops paid $322,600 for the home and just over three acres of surrounding land.

Shortly before the Zantops moved in, McCollum had brief second thoughts. Susanne mentioned how eager she and Half were to transplant their currant bushes to their new home. McCollum grew worried—currants harbor fungus that can endanger white pines, which flourished in their neck of the woods. If the Zantops insisted on moving the currant bushes, the two families might turn from Zantops and McCollums into Hatfields and McCoys. McCollum braced herself as she explained to Susanne the ecological conflict.

"We don't want to harm the environment," Susanne said, expressing a fundamental value she shared with Half. That was the end of that. Susanne and Half found a "foster home" for their currant bushes on property owned by friends, far from any white pines. The Zantops retained visiting rights to the shrubs, and Susanne continued to make her famous currant preserves.

To buy the Trescott Road home, the Zantops sold the house where they had raised Veronika and Mariana, on Hanover's Woodmere Drive. The buyer was Roxana Verona, a Dartmouth professor of French and Italian who met the Zantops at the real estate closing and quickly joined their inner circle of friends. Verona would call Half whenever minor repairs were needed at the Woodmere Drive house, and Half would grab his toolbox and head over. A native of Romania, Verona would joke that Bucharest and Berlin were never as close as when she and the Zantops were together. The Zantops' spirits came with the Woodmere Road house, Verona said, and "slowly we became one family with two houses."

Half and Susanne filled their new home with beautiful objects in a mix of tastes and styles, some of great monetary value and some whose worth was measured by emotional attachment. Upon entering the red-tiled foyer, guests followed an Oriental rug past a large pine-framed mirror, an antique cherry Chippendale desk, and an eighteenth-century banister-back armchair, on their way into the combination living/dining room, beyond which was the greenhouse.

Once in the house, they'd find a cast-iron wood stove, a Yamaha spinet piano, huge windows, book-lined walls, and a tan leather sofa—softened by the rumps of untold numbers of visitors—along with a black-and-tan striped love seat and a pair of low, tan chairs with the look and feel of corduroy pants. A brass floor lamp threw light that danced off a nineteenth-century silver tea set. Also on display were pieces of African tribal art—some brought back from Mariana's trips abroad—a pre-Columbian stone figure, and a pair of nineteenth-century carved wooden Foo dogs, fierce-looking creatures that are the sacred guards of Buddhist temples. The adjacent dining room held a modern, Danish-style oval table that usually was covered with Susanne's papers, but on special occasions would be set with silver flatware alongside blue-and-white plates with a frolicking pattern of onions and flowers, made by Meissen, the famed German porcelain company.

Bibliophiles and art lovers who had inherited important works from their parents, the Zantops had a nineteenth-century German Bible and a collection of leather-bound books from the late nineteenth and twentieth centuries. On a wall outside the couple's study hung the most valuable piece of property in the home: an elaborately framed, seventeenth-century still life of a claret jug and a fish plate on a table. Painted by the Dutch master Abraham van Beyeren, it was valued at $18,000. On a low bookshelf on the other side of the living room, the Zantops displayed a kneeling nude sculpture in bronze, called *Faunesse,* by Rodin, valued at $15,000.

Another favorite artist was the iconoclastic German painter Hans Thoma, whose 1911 self-portrait the Zantops treasured. Two other works by Thoma were nearby: an 1876 portrait of a lady with a bonnet and an 1882 portrait of an elderly woman dressed in black. The Zantops also owned a bronze nude by Tuaillon, worth $3,500. But not all the artwork was particularly valuable—their tastes were set by passion, not price. Half and Susanne owned a small, unsigned etching of a monkey painting a portrait of a donkey, titled *Ni mas, ni menos* (Neither more, nor less), worth perhaps $75.

Despite the value of their home and its objects, the Zantops focused little on money, preferring to concentrate on family, work, and friends. They gave dozens of dinner parties a year, large and small, where conversation flowed along with potent margaritas Half made from his secret recipe. Susanne filled the table with homemade cakes and German delicacies, like a soft cheese called quark, while Half might serve a salmon he had smoked himself. Discussions took place in multiple languages, about everything from world politics to academic intrigue to pop trivia. Half and Susanne had similar conversations in private, though alone with each other they spoke mainly in German.

With their next-door neighbors, the McCollums, they drank V&F Gonzalez pale dry sherry and ate goat cheese; a pâte of white beans, garlic, and lemon; and Smokehouse almonds. Susanne would decline the almonds at first, but with the slightest urging from Audrey McCollum she'd dive in with gusto. Other times they called each other to report backyard meadow sightings of wild turkeys, or a fox, or a doe with her fawns, or a black bear eyeing the bird feeders the Zantops had installed and the McCollums had followed suit. One time a bear brought down one of the feeders, and Half reacted with a string of German epithets. Audrey McCollum gave Susanne tarragon from her garden, and Susanne returned the favor with strangely shaped, home-grown tomatoes from the garden she tended as relaxation therapy. "That one's a grumpy old man," Susanne would say. "Or maybe a troll." Susanne and Half's green thumbs were more prominently on display in the lavishly filled greenhouse, where they grew exotic plants, with a special fondness for orchids.

As a salve for their hectic lives, the Zantops were always trying to squeeze in time for exercise. In winter, cross-country skis were usually resting by their front door; Susanne and Half loved to ski into the woods from their house, link up with a nearby stretch of the Appalachian Trail, and loop back home. Sometimes they'd drive five miles for a workout at the River Valley Club in nearby Lebanon. Careful of his heart, Half would work the Nautilus machines, pedal a stationary bicycle, or do strokes on a rowing machine. Susanne would swim a luxuriant breaststroke or join Half at the Nautilus stations. Sometimes she'd test herself by climbing the club's thirty-foot artificial rock wall, but Half never did. He had climbed real mountains, and it wasn't worth risking his heart on a fake one.

That wasn't a concern for two young wannabe climbers from Chelsea, Vermont, who decided one day in October 2000 to test them-selves on the River Valley Club's wall. They bought one-day passes, paying $15 each, and coached and coaxed each other up the same handholds where Susanne had climbed on other days. Robert Tulloch and Jim Parker took turns at the manmade challenge, one at a time on the fiberglass rock. They were tied together, literally. As Jim climbed, Robert held a belaying rope attached to Jim like an umbilical cord; if Jim slipped, Robert would pull the rope taut to prevent him from falling. Then they would switch positions and Jim would do the same for Robert. Each time they climbed together they drew closer, gaining confidence in themselves and in one another.

Proud of their German heritage, Susanne and Half waited more than twenty years after settling in Hanover to become naturalized United States citizens. Half amused friends by revealing that the one question that stumped him on the citizenship test was about the significance of July Fourth. The date had somehow never registered with him.

Even before they could vote in U.S. elections, both were committed to liberal politics—contributing to Democratic candidates, joining Amnesty International, and writing letters and e-mails to press their beliefs. Prejudice disgusted them, as did big egos, and both had a highly developed sense of fairness. Both were feminists, humanists, environmentalists.

Half rarely discussed his feelings about Germany and World War II, but Susannah Heschel, a professor of Jewish studies and a close friend, recalled how kind he was toward a student of his who had lost her grandparents in the Holocaust. The young woman was struggling with the thought of being taught by a German professor. "He felt in some way very responsible, and was extremely sensitive to her and her feelings," Heschel said. "I know some people who would respond with some defensiveness."

Susanne told several friends that learning about the Holocaust when she was thirteen had a profound impact on her life. "It was, I think, traumatizing that her country could have done such an appalling thing," Audrey McCollum said. "My own sense is that shaped her professional life. What I surmised, for both, was that it contributed to a conviction that they had to convince people to pay attention to their countries. . . . They engaged others to inform themselves, take a stand, and communicate their stand to government officials."

Still, it angered Susanne to be stereotyped because of her heritage, and friends recalled her saying in disgust: "Just because you're German, people think you're a Nazi!"

Susanne wept during the naming ceremony for Heschel's first child, who was named for relatives of Heschel's killed in the Holocaust. "I think it was a very sorrowful, sad part of their life," said

Fred Berthold, a friend who spent five decades teaching religion at Dartmouth. "But I don't think they allowed that to dampen their general optimistic and creative hopes for betterment." As an associate dean of the faculty, Berthold had been involved in hiring Susanne, a choice made easy by his first and lasting impression of her as "a tremendous person and scholar."

Yet all was not serious with the Zantops. Half sent friends wickedly funny e-mails and amused friends with his views of American life. Much as some men in New England track the Red Sox through newspaper box scores, Half gleefully followed a letter-writing battle in the local papers over whether a new bridge over the Connecticut River should be adorned with huge concrete spheres. Personally he thought them awful. Susanne loved self-deprecating humor and funny movies—Friday night was their steady "movie night." She poked gentle fun at the stereotypical attributes of Germans, even as she kept her home meticulously organized. And though she was devoted to her work, friends knew they could persuade her to sneak away from conferences by proposing to go shopping for pottery or gifts from local shops.

Though they loved their adopted hometown of Etna, the Zantops were happiest on a remote cove in Brooksville, Maine, where they vacationed for three weeks every summer for more than two decades. They and their daughters were fixtures at the rustic Hiram Blake Camp, a collection of fifteen wooden cottages where the Zantops spent days walking hand-in-hand, reading, or sailing their nineteen-foot Flying Scot, *Albatross*, across the waters of Penobscot Bay.

It was a place where time was dictated not by clocks but by whims and weather. They relished its remote location within a remote location: the cottages were at the end of an easy-to-miss, winding road to nowhere that looped back on itself. Susanne, Half, Veronika, and Mariana had a standing reservation from mid-July to early August in a cedar-shingled cabin named Maples with a wraparound porch overlooking the bay. Half spent days sailing, sometimes taking Susanne on trips to a nearby island to collect gooseberries. She spent hours "tipping and tailing" the tart berries—removing their tufts and stems—then turning them into preserves to spread over breakfast toast.

They'd collect mussels for lunch, or search the island woods for chanterelles—small, flat-headed yellow mushrooms with the fragrance of apricots that Susanne would sauté into rare delicacies. One summer before his death in 1984, Half's father joined them in Maine, and their friend Joan Blumberg was left with a vivid memory of the elder Zantop sitting quietly, painstakingly cleaning a huge basket of chanterelles. In her mind's eye, Blumberg could see a young Mariana hanging over the side of Half's boat, Half holding her by the ankles, as she tried to fix a problem for her captain father. She could see Veronika heading off to pick a few berries and returning with a shopping bag full. And Blumberg could see both girls happily diving into water so cold it reduced her own husband to shivering Jell-O.

Another Hiram Blake regular, Jim Zien, remembered the Zantops' departure at the end of their visit in August 2000. "They might have been running just a little late," Zien recalled. "Standing by the car, her summer canning complete, her perpetual knitting project one year and six inches further along, Susanne had perhaps begun to think about a conference or a paper or a course outline or a student or colleague in need of her attention. But Half had one last lesson in Maine coast geology to teach. A Swiss Army knife in his right hand, a rock in his left, and an inquisitive eight-year-old by his side, Half scratched the surface of beach treasures proffered, patiently distinguishing quartz from shale, copper from schist; quietly encouraging his young student to do the same."

Though busy with work, friends, and colleagues, the Zantops devoted themselves to their daughters. That remained true even after the girls left home as young women, Veronika to become a doctor doing a residency in family medicine at the University of Washington in

Seattle, and Mariana to attend the Columbia School of Public Health in New York and to receive training as a nurse midwife.

"They tended to know when the next exam was coming up, they tended to know when things were going well with the boyfriends and when things weren't," said their friend and colleague Irene Kacandes. "Sometimes the girls, like many young people, would not be very happy about what was going on in their life at that moment, and that would be a real sadness" to Half and Susanne.

In addition to Veronika and Mariana, the Zantops had unofficially adopted a "third daughter." Sujee Fonseca was a Dartmouth student from Sri Lanka who wanted desperately to go to medical school. In 1992, she found her way to Susanne's office. "Go ahead, Sujee," Susanne told her, "I'll stand beside you." That simple commitment created an enduring bond. Problems with immigration prevented Fonseca from attending an American medical school, so the Zantops, unknown to all but their closest friends, helped to arrange and pay for her to attend medical school in Canada. Fonseca spent Christmas 2000 with the Zantops, and she watched as Susanne came to Half with a broken ornament and a pouting face.

Half looked at Susanne with a gentle smile, and Susanne understood his message. She knew he was a fatalist—"What I have is what I have; if something's gonna happen, it's gonna happen," Half would say. Reading his mind, Susanne told Half: "Yes, I know. Nothing is permanent, my dear—except my love for you."

When Christmas was over, the approach of 2001 marked a return to their hectic lives. But they were considering a dramatic change. Susanne and Half had begun to mull retirement and had discussed whether Susanne, at fifty-five, seven years younger than her husband, should retire early. They were looking forward to more time for favored pursuits, like sailing in Maine and visits to their Berlin apartment. Mostly, friends said, they wanted more time together, knowing that Half's heart ailment might separate them too soon. "The love that

[Susanne] shared with her husband was so young and so beautiful and so free," said Saleeda Salahuddin, a Dartmouth student who, like Sujee Fonseca, considered the Zantops surrogate parents. "People would look at them and think that love like that didn't exist. But it did."

Susanne had taken a first step toward scaling back her work by stepping down as chairwoman of the German studies department, a job that required her to attend numerous meetings every week. Kacandes recalled how Susanne was once so busy and stressed out she developed stomach cramps so painful she couldn't straighten up. "The way she pushed herself all the time was very hard on a lot of us, including Half," Kacandes said. "She was tired, and she was aware she needed a better quality of life."

As for Half, there was only one dream he had yet to fulfill: becoming a pilot. But perhaps retirement—along with what he described as his renewed "zest for life"—would allow him to achieve that, too. Until then, the present was defined by their demanding careers and their circle of family and friends. All those threads came together in the first weeks of January 2001.

To celebrate the New Year, the Zantops hosted a party at their home that included their two closest friends, Dr. Eric Manheimer and his wife, Diana Taylor. The couple spent the night at the home on Trescott Road, and then pulled out of the driveway the next morning with Mariana Zantop in their car, to drive her back home to New York City.

In the weeks that followed, there were papers to write, speeches to prepare, classes to teach, and conferences to organize. All the while Susanne was talking regularly on the phone to her brother in Germany, planning a party to celebrate their father's eighty-fifth birthday in April. She even made a quick trip to Berlin, to speak at a conference. She also had been in Berlin a month earlier, to haunt film archives for a new project she was undertaking on German colonialism.

On Wednesday, January 24, Susanne received an e-mail from her friend Susannah Heschel, who was struggling with an article she was writing on American Jewish political thought. Heschel was nine months pregnant, which added to her discomfort. Though Jewish politics wasn't Susanne's area of expertise, she urged Heschel to drop by so they could talk about the paper over a pot of coffee. Heschel knew that Susanne wouldn't sugarcoat her thoughts—she always told Heschel when a lecture was good and when it wasn't, and Heschel loved that about her. They talked for more than an hour about the paper, and Susanne suggested a few books that might help. Then Susanne told Heschel about giving birth to Veronika and Mariana. In the midst of their conversation, Half phoned from his Dartmouth office, asking whether he should come home to share a cheese sandwich. Heschel was warmed by Half's desire to grab lunch with his wife of thirty years. Feeling better than she had in days, she went home and phoned her husband, James Aronson, a colleague of Half's in the earth sciences department. "I'm so happy," she told him. "I just can't believe how lucky I am to have her as a friend and colleague. I've known smart people, but never anyone who is so smart and so helpful." She went to the computer and dove into work, energized by her visit with Susanne. But the talk proved almost too invigorating: Heschel went into labor, giving birth to a girl the next day.

After Susanne's talk with Heschel, she, Half, and Roxana Verona went to Hanover's Nugget Theater to see the martial-arts love story, *Crouching Tiger, Hidden Dragon*. Afterward, Half and Susanne walked from the theater hand in hand.

On Friday, January 26, the Zantops went as usual to their Dartmouth offices. Susanne's was in stately Dartmouth Hall, built as a replacement for the oldest building on campus, which burned in 1904. Her office was filled with books, but its most striking feature was a giant umbrella plant, a species that can grow up to forty feet tall in the wild and seemed intent on doing the same under Susanne's care. A short walk up College Street, Half's office in the modern Sherman Fairchild Physical Sciences Center was, like him, more sedate, filled with rocks and microscopes.

Susanne spent the morning handling some administrative tasks and talking on the phone with Gerald Kleinfeld, executive director of the *German Studies Review* and a professor at Arizona State University.

She was chipper when she chatted with fellow German studies professor Bruce Duncan in the morning, but grumpy in the afternoon when she saw Margaret Robinson, the German department's academic assistant. Susanne groused to Robinson that she was en route to her second committee meeting of the day, and she knew she would have to spend much of the upcoming weekend catching up on work. Susanne also hoped to squeeze in a visit to the River Valley Club—she had scheduled her once-a-year facial.

That same day, Half taught his introductory metals course with his usual verve. A student's notes reveal a professor working hard to fill young minds with complex information about the formation of mineral deposits, malleable metals, and oxidation/reduction reactions. As always, Half stressed the need to be aware of the effect of mining on the environment.

After work, their friends Marianne Hirsch and Leo Spitzer dropped by the Zantops' home to borrow snowshoes. They were going to see Susannah Heschel's new baby, and Susanne decided to join them. On her way out the door, she went to her greenhouse and grabbed an impromptu present: a pot of spring daffodils. At Heschel's house, they took turns holding the baby. Then Heschel's three-year-old daughter Gittel came into the room to seek some of the limelight. "I wanna use a potty," she announced to the guests' delight. It was the first time she had made such a request, and it made Susanne reminisce about the long-ago days of toilet-training her own girls.

Hirsch and Spitzer drove Susanne home, and she urged them to stay for dinner. Soon the dining table was filled with sautéed shrimp and garlic, broiled trout, roasted potatoes, asparagus, and salad, served on colorful Mexican dishes Half and Susanne had brought back from one of their many trips. The foursome ate, laughed, and talked—no one faster than Susanne—about everything from Dartmouth to national politics to March vacations to a conference on German colonialism Susanne was planning for June. Half made some of his famously strong espresso, and afterward the group went to Dartmouth's Hopkins Center—"The Hop"—to see the movie *Best in Show*, a comedy about the strange world of canine competitions.

Before heading home, they made plans for a cross-country skiing and snowshoeing party on Sunday. The Zantops' other big plan for the weekend was to attend a ninetieth birthday celebration for Dick Stoiber, the now-retired geology professor who had met them at the Montreal dock and brought them to Hanover.

Half and Susanne woke early on Saturday, January 27, and threw themselves into their day. It wasn't uncommon for both to be up before dawn, though Half usually got out of bed first, around five o'clock, so he could bring Susanne tea in bed. Susanne often eased into her day by ironing clothes and listening to National Public Radio. By eight-thirty, they were sending the McCollums and other friends e-mail messages encouraging them to oppose conservative John Ashcroft's confirmation as attorney general. The McCollums wouldn't get the e-mail until much later; it was Bob McCollum's seventy-sixth birthday, and he and Audrey were getting ready to go skiing with their daughter and son-in-law. Around ten-thirty that morning, Susanne invited Roxana Verona to dinner.

It was a quiet day in town. The Hanover Police Department dealt with routine traffic stops, in most cases issuing warnings and sending the offending drivers on their way. Someone called in a report about a stray animal in the neighborhood, and a stranded motorist needed a hand. Police received two calls about found property and two others about permits to burn leaves. There was a report of a missing person— with no foul play suspected—and a report of a stolen car. The usual stuff in an Ivy League community where serious crime was a faraway problem.

Later that morning, there was a knock at the door of 115 Trescott Road. Susanne was chopping vegetables, so Half went to answer it. Before him stood two clean-cut young men, both tall and slim, not unlike Half in his youth. They said they were students from the Mountain School over the border in Vershire, Vermont, and they were doing an environmental survey for a class project.

"Hold on a second," Half said. "My wife is making lunch. I don't think I can do this."

He left them standing outside while he went to talk with Susanne.

How could he turn them away? He and Susanne were teachers and these boys were students. He and Susanne were environmentalists, and these boys wanted to talk about the environment.

"You know, I like what the Mountain School does," Half said, ushering them inside.

6

"Susanne? Susanne?"

Later that day, an hour past twilight, as a sliver of a crescent moon teetered in the sky, Roxana Verona turned the ignition on her blue-gray Saab. Alone in the car, she drove the familiar five-mile route from her home—the one she had bought nearly a decade earlier from Half and Susanne—to the Zantops' house on Trescott Road. Verona pulled down the gravel driveway, then did a three-point turn at the bottom so the car's nose would be pointed toward the street, to make it easier for her to navigate when she left in the dark.

Verona grabbed her purse and a bag with the salad she had prepared, got out of her car, and walked to the house. Her zippered black boots left small, perfectly formed impressions in an inch of freshly fallen snow. When she arrived at the front door, Verona rang the bell—she knew the Zantops always locked their home, whether they were inside or out, and even when they threw parties, Susanne or Half would unbolt and rebolt the door with each arrival. Sometimes their friends kidded the Zantops about that habit—around Hanover and Etna, many homeowners hadn't seen their house keys in years.

As she rang the bell, Verona placed her hand on the doorknob and was surprised to feel it turn. Susanne must have left it unlocked for me, Verona thought. Susanne usually showered before dinner, and she must have worried about leaving me stuck outside in the cold. How thoughtful of her, Verona thought. So like Susanne.

"I'm in," Verona called out. It was 6:35 P.M.

The dinner invitation had come that morning in a phone call from Susanne. They had missed each other the night before—Susanne had left a voice-mail urging Verona to meet them at The Hop to see *Best in Show,* but Verona hadn't heard the message in time. When they connected by phone, they chatted a few minutes about work and the movie—Susanne thought Verona would enjoy it—then Susanne suggested a quiet dinner for three.

"Why don't you come here?" Verona asked. No, Susanne said, I've already been to the food co-op and bought all we need. You come to our place. Verona agreed, promising to make a salad and arrive at their usual dinner hour, 6:30 P.M. Oh, Susanne added, I'll be alone when you get here. Half is going to a birthday party for Dick Stoiber. Susanne told Verona she was too busy to attend—her dining-room table was piled high with unfinished work. Susanne said Half would join them to eat—he didn't plan to stay at the party long.

Upon entering the house, Verona took off her coat and draped it with her purse on the ladder-back chair at the end of the entrance hall, then turned left to enter the main area of the first floor. Verona headed for the dining-room table, where she found room among Susanne's papers to drop her bag with the salad. She looked into the kitchen but saw no one.

"Susanne? Susanne?" she called out. No answer. The only sound was her own voice, calling her friend's name. Verona sensed something unusual about the silence. The shower wasn't running. No footsteps could be heard from the bathroom or master bedroom. The house seemed empty but for her.

Verona turned toward the study, where the light was on and the wooden door was wide open. Her mind expected the room to be as it always was, in perfect order, an efficiency expert's dream, with every paper in place and the hundreds of books on the floor-to-ceiling shelves lined up like soldiers at attention.

Instead, she saw bloody carnage. Verona's eyes burned with the sight of her dear friend Susanne, lying chest-down near the door, a halo of blood pooled on the hardwood floor around her head. Blood had also soaked through her brown-and-black pullover sweater and extended down to her tan corduroy pants. A card table was toppled over, resting on her calves. A few feet away, also on the floor of the study, was Half. He was lying on his right side, but it was an unnatural repose: His head was resting on the bottom shelf of a blood-spattered bookcase. The force of the impact pushed back a half-dozen books, including a thick volume on homeopathic medicine and a paperback called *How Your Heart Works*. Half's gray-and-white lambswool sweater was drenched in blood, and more blood outlined a ragged slit in the left leg of his blue jeans. Indeed, blood was pooled or sprayed everywhere—on papers and photographs strewn on the floor, on the bookcases, on an ergonomic computer stool, on a wicker trash basket pressed against Half's body, on a wooden folding chair, on an Oriental rug crumpled under Half's sock-clad feet.

There also were two items that Verona would never have seen before in the Zantop home: two black knife sheaths made from some kind of hard plastic. One was near Half's left foot, atop an overturned, bloodstained Birkenstock sandal that belonged to Susanne. The other sheath was four feet away, under an upright, metal-and-wood chair with a cane seat. The knives they had held were nowhere to be seen, but they must have been big. The sheaths were each more than a foot long and three inches wide.

Verona couldn't see Susanne's face—her head was turned from the open door—but she could see Half's. It was drained of blood, as white as the hair of his beard. Verona looked back to Susanne and saw her right hand, gripping her glasses, her skin the same lifeless shade as her husband's. In death, Half's arms stretched forward, reaching toward Susanne.

Verona was frantic; frightened, too. She thought of calling 911, but her friends were clearly beyond help, and whoever killed them might still be in the house. Verona ran to the foyer, grabbed her coat, and flew through the door. She ran to her car and turned the key, knowing almost without thinking where she was headed. She had dined several times with the Zantops' next-door neighbors, the McCollums, and she knew Bob McCollum was a doctor.

Inside the McCollums' tastefully furnished house, the cheese fondue was bubbling and the glasses were raised for a toast. Audrey and Bob were celebrating Bob's seventy-sixth birthday, joined by their daughter, Cindy, and her husband, John. They had spent part of the day in Woodstock, Vermont, at the Suicide Six ski area, then had come home to enjoy dinner and each other's company.

Their toast to Bob's health was interrupted by a pounding on the door and a woman's screams. They ushered Verona inside and listened as she choked out a garbled version of what she'd seen. Audrey McCollum called 911, while Bob and Cindy rushed out the door and drove next door. Verona returned as well, following in her own car.

"A guest went there for dinner and came to us in hysterics and said that the woman whose house it is was lying on the floor in a pool of blood," Audrey McCollum told the dispatcher. "My husband's a doctor and is going over now."

While she waited, wondering if her friends were dead and worrying that her husband and daughter might be in peril, Audrey McCollum called Steve Gordon, an editor of the local newspaper, *The Valley News*. She wrote occasional pieces for the paper, and she knew its reporters kept a close ear on the newsroom police scanner.

"Steve," she said, "something awful has happened next door. Have you heard anything on the scanner?"

"No," he said. "Oh, wait a minute. . . . They are saying, 'Two down at 115 Trescott.' "

Cindy McCollum called 911 a few minutes after her mother, from the Zantops' house, after seeing the horror Verona had found. Bob McCollum went to the doorway of the study and placed his hand on Susanne's right arm—it was cold to his touch—and felt for a pulse that wasn't there. He looked over to Half, but he didn't step toward him. A half-century of practicing medicine was more than enough for him to know his friends were gone.

While Bob McCollum viewed the bodies, his daughter ran outside to flag down a police officer. Meanwhile, Verona moved as far from the study as she could, holing up in the kitchen. In her mind she kept try-ing to lift Susanne and Half, to restore them to their normal, upright postures, to stop the horrible scene from replaying in her mind. Standing in the kitchen, Verona noticed a half-prepared meal. On the counter were cut vegetables, chopped herbs, sliced bread, two blocks of cheese, an unfinished soup, an open bottle of Merlot wine. Once the makings of a meal, now they were a way to estimate time of death.

Officer Brad Sargent of the Hanover Police Department was the first to respond to the McCollums' 911 calls. Within minutes he was joined at 115 Trescott Road by more than a half-dozen officers from Hanover, the New Hampshire State Police, and the Grafton County Sheriff's Department. They searched the home to make sure the killers were gone, then one by one walked to the study to witness what for some would be their first major crime scene. An ambulance was called as well, but Sergeant Patrick O'Neill looked inside the study and radioed the dispatcher: Cancel the ambulance and summon the medical examiner.

A few minutes later, Hanover Police Chief Nick Giaccone arrived. He and the other officers quickly noticed a trail of blood drops leading from the study out of the house. Giaccone saw a partial bloody boot-print in the foyer, and two more outside. Normally soft-spoken, with a

fondness for well-tailored suits, he looked around at the officers pouring into the house and issued a quick command: Everyone out!
Giaccone even ordered them to walk away from the house through virgin snow, to avoid smearing the footprints of the killer or killers.

A crime scene could be polluted in an infinite number of ways, and
Giaccone wanted to preserve as much evidence as he could for his
detectives and the New Hampshire State Police Major Crime Unit,
whose commander, Major Barry Hunter, would arrive the next morning. There had never been a double murder quite like this in Hanover,
and Giaccone was determined to get the investigation right.

When the Zantops' house was secured, officers told Roxana Verona
and Bob and Cindy McCollum to go home. Audrey McCollum went
outside when she saw her husband and daughter shuffling down their
driveway, heads bowed, escorted by a police officer with a flashlight.
Audrey ran toward them, yelling, "Don't tell me they're dead."

The policeman turned away. Cindy McCollum said, "Mom, come
in the house."

Around that time, a green Subaru drove down Trescott Road toward
the Zantop house. Inside the car were two young men, each of whom
had left a knife sheath at the house earlier in the day. As they drove
closer, they hoped they could drop by and collect their belongings
without anyone noticing. But as they neared 115 Trescott, they
noticed a New Hampshire State Police cruiser in the driveway.
Disappointed, they drove on past.

Word of what happened soon began to spread. It passed intimately
at first, investigator to investigator, then civilian to civilian. It raced
along the predetermined branches of a telephone tree that led from
one Dartmouth administrator to the next, from one faculty member to
another. Then it reached a Dartmouth College student named Omer
Ismail.

Earlier that evening, around the time Verona was finding the bodies, Ismail ate dinner with a friend at the Thayer Dining Hall a block from the Dartmouth Green. Then he walked next door to Robinson Hall, where he climbed the stairs to the offices of *The Dartmouth,* the college's five-day-a-week student newspaper. Ismail was twenty-one, a soft-spoken, studious-looking government major from Pakistan who had been elected the newspaper's president, a job that made him both publisher and editor-in-chief. When Ismail arrived, only one other person was hanging around the usually bustling office—there was no Sunday paper, so the next deadline was more than a day away, an eternity in the newspaper world. The other staffer soon left Ismail alone, which is just what he wanted. He had come to quietly exercise a perk of office: He planned to use the newspaper's phone to save himself the cost of a long-distance call to a friend at the University of Pennsylvania.

After his call, Ismail sat at a computer and began composing e-mails when the phone rang. A woman from a local television station was calling to ask if *The Dartmouth* had heard anything about a report that had crackled over the police scanner about two professors found dead at a home on East Wheelock Street.

"No, I haven't heard anything about that at all. I'll let you know," he answered.

Ismail hung up and immediately began trying to reach two friends and colleagues: managing editor Mark Bubriski, a twenty-one-year-old junior from West Stockbridge, Massachusetts, and features editor Julia Levy, also twenty-one, a junior from a Philadelphia suburb. Ismail left phone messages, and then, at 9:39 P.M., he sent both a hastily written e-mail: "come to the office now. its urgent." Ismail then sent another e-mail that would prove prescient, summoning Hank Leukart, a Dartmouth senior who managed the newspaper's Web site.

The messages connected. As soon as she walked into Robinson Hall, Levy began calling every college official and faculty member she could think of. Ismail and Bubriski hustled into a Jeep that Bubriski had borrowed from a friend and went searching for the crime scene. It was around 10 P.M.

The caller said the police scanner mentioned East Wheelock, a road that cuts through campus, so the two young journalists drove there looking for police cars. They found none, so they went to a nearby dormitory, the newly built McCulloch Hall, to ask if anyone had heard sirens or seen an ambulance. Again, nothing. Frustrated, Ismail and Bubriski returned to the newspaper office. Ismail called *The Valley News* to see if he could pry some information from his off-campus competitor. He got nowhere at first, but eventually a sympathetic *News* staffer relented, telling Ismail that something big seemed to be happening on Trescott Road in Etna.

In his three-plus years at Dartmouth, Ismail had never been over that way. It was only four miles away, a straight shot due east, but there was nothing in the sleepy village but nice homes and a few stores. For most students, life at Dartmouth revolved around the campus, the business district of Hanover, and the great outdoors. Ismail went to a computer and clicked on the *Yahoo.com* Web site to create an instant map of Trescott Road. In the meantime, Levy searched a campus directory for the names of professors who lived along the street. Ismail and Bubriski grabbed the list and left. Levy stayed behind and continued canvassing school officials for scraps of information.

Bubriski and Ismail drove along the winding, hilly blacktop, not quite knowing what they were looking for. But they knew immediately when they found it: a herd of police cars, lights flashing, parked outside a modern, ranch-style house largely hidden from the street. It was about a quarter to eleven at night.

Dartmouth reporters like Ismail and Bubriski don't get much practice working crime scenes, but they followed their instincts and began peppering officers with questions. Who lives here? What happened? Any arrests? They were repeatedly rebuffed. One cop after another told them they'd have to wait for a news conference scheduled for sometime after midnight.

But this was their turf. If two Dartmouth professors were dead, *The Dartmouth* wanted the story. They kept at it and eventually confirmed a small yet enormously important detail: the address. They checked the Trescott Road faculty list Levy had given them. Next to the number 115 they saw the name Zantop. Ismail and Bubriski looked at each other with the same thought: We're onto something.

The pair hurried back to the newspaper office and began working the phones with Levy. While they were gone, Levy's calls had been fruitless, but then she reached Edward Berger, dean of the faculty. Not long before, Berger had received a call from a campus safety and security official informing him of the Zantops' deaths. He provided Levy with the confirmation *The Dartmouth* needed.

With Levy calling out quotes and Ismail editing over his shoulder, Bubriski began typing as fast as he could. None of the three knew the Zantops, but they understood they had a major newsbreak on their hands. At 11:15 P.M., not five hours after the first 911 call, *The Dartmouth* posted a story on its Web site. It bore the bold headline: TWO PROFS DEAD; POLICE INVESTIGATING POSSIBLE DOUBLE MURDER.

"Two professors are confirmed dead," the story began, "and police are investigating the possible double murder late this afternoon at 115 Trescott Road in Etna, just miles from the campus, according to Dean of the Faculty Ed Berger. Professors Susanne and Half Zantop died sometime Saturday evening, but the police told *The Dartmouth* that they could not comment until after the state Attorney General Philip McLaughlin issued a press release." It was a sketchy story, with few details, but *The Dartmouth* had it. At roughly the same time, the local ABC affiliate, WMUR, reported the Zantops' deaths during its eleven-o'clock newscast.

The Dartmouth staffers knew that precious few students, faculty, or staff were reading the online newspaper or watching the TV news as midnight approached on a Saturday night. On the other hand, Dartmouth students were fanatical about checking their e-mail. Ismail turned to Hank Leukart, who had come to Robinson Hall as soon as he received Ismail's come-quick message. Ismail told Leukart to send an e-mail to the fifteen hundred people on *The Dartmouth*'s electronic subscriber list, repeating the headline and directing them to the story on the paper's Web site. The mass e-mail instantly connected, but it was too successful: Within ten minutes, the site was so overwhelmed it crashed. Their big story couldn't be read.

"Hank," Ismail implored, "what's going on?"

"Our Web site isn't capable of handling this," Leukart answered.

For fifteen anxious minutes, Leukart tried to reboot the system and restore the Web site, but nothing worked. Ismail made another decision. He knew that fifteen hundred people had received a disturbing e-mail that urged them to read *The Dartmouth* online, but *The Dartmouth* suddenly wasn't online. The newspaper was failing its readers—the staffers' friends and neighbors—by taunting them with an incendiary headline and directing them to a Web site that couldn't be reached. But there was another way: the BlitzMail system, Dartmouth's campus-wide e-mail service.

"Take the entire text of the story and send it to every student on campus," Ismail ordered.

Leukart looked at him skeptically. Under the limits of the school's computer system, he would have to send the story in a dozen or so separate batches, to three or four hundred students at a time, to reach the entire student body of forty-five hundred. *The Dartmouth* had done polls that way, and the circulation staff had sent friendly campus-wide messages urging people to subscribe to the paper. But as far as anyone knew, no news story, much less a murder story about two professors, had ever been BlitzMailed to every Dartmouth student at once.

Leukart was skeptical. "Are you sure?" he asked.

Ismail looked at Leukart from under the bill of his Dartmouth baseball cap.

"Yes, Hank. Do it."

Instantly word of the Zantops' death was all over campus. Among the first places it had an impact was at Tabard House, a co-ed fraternity named for Chaucer's inn. The Tabard's popular "Disco Inferno" party was in full swing when the newsflash came. Social chair Candice Adams stopped the music, grabbed a microphone, and announced that two professors had died. She asked everyone at the party to say a prayer.

While partygoers were absorbing the news—some left in tears, while others resumed dancing to the disco beat—Ismail, Bubriski, Levy, and Leukart remained at work. Soon they'd be covering the attorney general's news conference, and soon after they'd start around-the-clock updates of a story only beginning to unfold.

Ismail's decision to send an urgent bulletin reflected an undeniable fact: The Zantops' deaths would be major news, and the Dartmouth campus and the communities of Hanover and Etna would experience the onslaught of attention that comes with being the latest stop on the moveable media feast known as "The Big Story."

Much later, non-journalists would wonder why the Zantops' murders attracted so much scrutiny, especially when so many other murders were overlooked or even ignored. In response, reporters and editors turned that question on its head: "How could this story not be huge?"

In newsrooms large and small, near and far, journalists who heard about the Zantops' deaths instantly began doing the fuzzy calculus known as news judgment, feeding all the known elements and vaguely predictable possibilities into the information blenders that are their minds. At the *New York Times*, the three broadcast networks, CNN, *The Times of London,* the *Boston Globe, Time, Newsweek,* and *People* magazine, the *Sun Herald* of Biloxi, Mississippi, *The Scotsman* of Edinburgh, and hundreds of other print and broadcast outlets from New England to New Delhi, journalists came up with roughly the same answer. When two much-loved, middle-aged, married professors at an Ivy League school are brutally murdered in their home, with no immediate arrests or known motives, readers, viewers, and listeners want to know what happened, how it happened, and why. Especially why.

In the earliest stages of all such stories, a journalistic balancing act takes place, as no assigning editor wants to fall behind on what promises to be a competitive and potentially captivating story, yet at the same time feels reluctant to commit too many resources to a story that might quickly fizzle out. The lifespan of high interest, particularly for out-of-town media, depends on whether and how quickly an arrest is made, who the alleged murderer or murderers are, and what allegedly motivated them. The more easily those answers fall into the category of the tragically banal—say, it turns out the murderer was a disturbed neighbor who had feuded with the professors over a property line—the quicker the case falls off the media's Big Story radar screen.

As it happened, the stars were aligning to keep the Zantop murders front and center in the media's consciousness, a circumstance that would test patience and fray nerves in a community where love of isolation holds special status.

Unlike its peers in the Ivy League, Dartmouth wasn't founded to educate the elites. It traces its roots to the mid-1700s, when a Congregational minister named Eleazar Wheelock established Moor's Charity School in Lebanon, Connecticut, to train young Native American men for missionary work.

Wheelock wanted to grow the school into a college, but he wanted to build it far from what he considered the wicked influences of urban life. Wheelock thought a school in the wilderness would keep his students "free from a thousand snares, temptations, and divertissements which were and would have been unavoidable if this seminary had continued where it was, or been fixed in any populous town in the land." He also knew that Native Americans had been driven away from colonial centers along the Atlantic Coast, so more potential students could be found the farther inland he went.

In 1766, Wheelock dispatched to England his prized student, Samson Occom, a member of the Mohegan tribe, in search of financial support. Occom received the most lucrative reception from William Legge, the second earl of Dartmouth and secretary of state for colonies under King George III. The earl of Dartmouth's contributions earned him naming rights for the school. Occom would eventually loan his name to a campus pond, a road, and faculty housing. Wheelock's name would be used for a street bordering the campus Green.

In December 1769, Wheelock was granted a charter from the king establishing his college "for the education and instruction of Youth of the Indian Tribes in this Land . . . and also of English Youth and any others." It was the ninth college established in the colonies and the last under British rule. The land was provided by the royal governor of New Hampshire, John Wentworth, and it fulfilled Wheelock's every dream: a remote plateau blanketed with ancient, towering pines, flanked on the west by the Connecticut River and on the east by wooded hills that gathered like ruffles on the hem of the White Mountains. Its beauty was matched only by its inhospitality.

"Dartmouth men were compelled to be clannish when old Eleazar's ax-wielders slashed the room for their huts and cabins out of the virgin forests of a wilderness," wrote Wilder Quint in *The Story of Dartmouth*. "The feeling of loyalty and oneness got into the blood, and it has never gotten out." The harsh terrain and the lack of other diversions framed the character of the place and contributed to an almost fanatical loyalty, some might say insularity, even as those first huts were replaced over time by fine buildings of red and whitewashed brick, organized around the five-acre Green.

Even the nineteenth-century *Alma Mater*, later edited to reflect the admission of women starting in 1972, fixates on the school's physical qualities:

> *Dear old Dartmouth, give a rouse*
> *For the college on the hill!*
> *For the Lone Pine above her,*
> *And the loyal ones who love her,*
> *Give a rouse, give a rouse, with a will!*
> *For the sons of old Dartmouth,*
> *For the daughters of Dartmouth.*
> *Though 'round the girdled earth they roam,*
> *Her spell on them remains;*
> *They have the still North in their hearts,*
> *The hill-winds in their veins,*
> *And the granite of New Hampshire*
> *In their muscles and their brains.*

The location appealed not just to potential students, but also to parents hoping to keep their college-age children from harm's way. "The glories of 'Dartmouth out-o'-doors' are beginning to impress themselves far and wide, and fathers and mothers appreciate the situation of a college that has no easy access to the flash fascinations of metropolitan evil," Quint wrote. "This 'magnificent isolation' is the chief glory and hope of those who rule the college." The school's Latin motto translates as "The voice of one crying in the wilderness."

As years passed, Hanover became more connected to the world, helped by its location at the crossroads of interstate highways 89 and 91. A vibrant retail district emerged along Main Street, where the venerable Dartmouth Bookstore was kept company by such newcomers as the Gap and the Dirt Cowboy Café. The 2000 census counted nearly eleven thousand people in Hanover, almost 20 percent more than a decade earlier, with a college-skewed median age of twenty-two. Hanover also evolved into one of New Hampshire's wealthiest communities, with an average home price of $365,000. And yet, it clung to the self-image of a comfy little town in an out-of-the-way place, and with that came a feeling that Dartmouth and its surroundings were protected by a granite dome from big-city troubles.

The last time murder had touched Dartmouth was a decade earlier, in June 1991, when an Ethiopian man, Haileselassi Girmay, hacked to death two twenty-four-year-old Ethiopian graduate students, Selamawit Tsehaye and Trhas Berhe. Girmay, a geology teacher who had been working in Sweden, had been visiting the women and became enraged by Tsehaye's refusal to marry him. Girmay used an insanity defense at his 1993 trial, but jurors rejected it and found him guilty of murder. He was sentenced to life in prison without parole. Juror Richard Ryerson said the jury found Girmay sane "right off the bat." "Crazy?" scoffed Ryerson. "That could be a defense for anyone. You have to look at the evidence and ask yourself if he knew right from wrong." Girmay's insanity plea was fatally undermined by his purchase of an ax several days before the murders and his decision to hide it in the apartment beforehand.

Before the Girmay case, Hanover had gone four decades without a homicide. In 1950, a freshman football team member named Raymond J. Cirrotta was attacked by a group of upperclassmen for the offense of wearing a varsity sweater. He sustained head injuries and died several hours later. One senior, Thomas Doxsee, pleaded no contest in the beating. Amid reports that the investigation had been bungled, Doxsee was fined $500 and received a one-year suspended sentence.

Hanover's only other murder of the twentieth century also involved Dartmouth. In 1920, Theta Delta Chi fraternity brother Henry Maroney thought he had found a way around Prohibition—stealing a quart of whisky from a bootlegger named Robert Meads. Meads reacted according to the bootlegger handbook, pulling out a pistol and trying repeatedly to shoot Maroney. He succeeded on his fourth try, in Maroney's fraternity bedroom. The killing was ruled manslaughter and Meads received a twenty-year prison term.

Unrequited love could explain Girmay's actions. A lethal mix of alcohol and testosterone could explain Cirrotta's death. Maroney's murder could be attributed to rotgut revenge and Roaring Twenties gangsterism. There was no real mystery to any of them. On top of that, none of the victims was widely known on campus, and no one feared that urban ills had begun invading Dartmouth's snow- and pine-insulated world. After the Girmay ax murders, for instance, then-police chief Kurt F. Schimke said the shockwaves the crime sent around town were proof that "Hanover *is* the idyllic, Ivy League community that it is said to be."

As news spread of Half and Susanne's deaths, so did a veil of sorrow. The killers had chosen a couple who had spent a quarter-century cementing deep friendships around the campus and the world. "I could say Susanne was my best friend, but I know twelve other people would say the same thing," said Susannah Heschel, the Jewish studies professor whom Susanne had comforted three days before the murders. Phil Pochoda, associate director of the University Press of New England and a good friend of the Zantops, wondered: "How can they be the only two people that fate would obliterate? The thought that we would go on without them is now inconceivable."

A week after the murders, grief found an outlet and a salve at a memorial service inside the pink granite walls of Dartmouth's Rollins Chapel. Its Romanesque design, with a landmark peak-roofed tower, distinguished it from the stolid brick of most other historic Dartmouth buildings. It was built in 1885 with a $30,000 gift from a wealthy Dartmouth alum, Edward Ashton Rollins, a Philadelphia banker who had known his share of loss: He dedicated the chapel to the memory of his father, his mother, and his wife.

As more than seven hundred celebrants filed into the chapel to the soothing notes of a Bach organ chorale, each received a program with a blissful photo of the couple on its cover. In it, Half and Susanne stand together before a rock monolith, both of them wearing wide-brimmed sun hats and short-sleeved, loose-fitting shirts. Half's hat is set back on his head at a jaunty angle. They look lovingly at each other. Half's right hand reaches out, and Susanne holds it with both of hers. Her lips are pressed together, as if poised for a kiss.

"A teacher affects eternity," Dartmouth President James Wright told the crowd. "We learned much from their lives and we benefited. . . . Be free, good friends; be at peace." The Rev. Gwendolyn King spoke of the questions surrounding the deaths. "Shock, bewilderment, and disbelief are among the feelings we all had as news of Susanne and Half's deaths reached us. How could this be?" she asked. "Our hearts ache in the loss, and we have questions and seek answers that may never come." Through cascading tears, the Zantops' friend Herb Rowland said: "When we were with them we felt safe and taken care of. There was gentleness and grace, and both of them made time disappear on each occasion that we were with them. And I felt that I became a better person, more patient, more compassionate, more understanding, and more committed to social justice." Several of the fourteen speakers described Half and Susanne's professional achievements, but most focused on their hearts. Verona told the story of how her purchase of the Zantops' former home had led to a deep friendship, and how her life was shattered by her discovery of their bodies. "My house and I stopped breathing," she said. Yet like most of the speakers, Verona tried to find hope in the darkness. She told of new life on a plant Half and Susanne had given her. "A tiny bud from the hibiscus flower talks to me with my friends' voice," she said.

The celebrants stood and sang "Amazing Grace," recited the Lord's Prayer, and bowed their heads for the Jewish mourner's Kaddish, spoken by Heschel, her voice cracking with emotion. Most dressed in somber hues, but there was one dramatic exception: Audrey McCollum. Four weeks earlier, Half and Susanne had joined Audrey and Bob McCollum for an annual holiday dinner. Audrey wore a festive outfit that had become something of a tradition: black slacks, scarlet top, and a silver snowflake pin. "I knew what Audrey would wear," Susanne had said then, smiling. In tribute, McCollum wore the same celebratory outfit to the memorial service. "Susanne would have loved that," her husband told her.

At the close of the service, Veronika Zantop unexpectedly stood. She was twenty-nine, tall and attractive, articulate and composed. With an oval face and kind eyes, her looks favored her father. Next to her was Mariana Zantop, twenty-seven, an international relief worker based in New York City. She was shorter than her sister, with close-cropped dark hair and a resemblance to their mother.

In a sweet, clear voice, Veronika said: "I wanted to thank you for my sister and I from the depths of our hearts for all the love and support we've gotten from everyone here, as well as for the love and support you gave my parents during their lives. Thank you so much." Then the Zantop sisters became the first links in a "Circle of Light," with each participant holding a lit candle to symbolize how Half and Susanne illuminated the lives of those who knew and loved them. Veronika and Mariana were joined by Susanne's family, then Half's, then Half and Susanne's students, then Dartmouth staff members, then family friends, and on and on until it seemed nearly everyone in the chapel was included.

Unknown to the celebrants, a New Hampshire state trooper named Christopher Scott stood outside trying not to be noticed. He had been assigned to blend with the press and photograph people entering and leaving the chapel, as well as anyone loitering nearby, in the vague hope that the killer or killers might be among them.

Throughout the community, speculation swirled about the killers and their motives. "I think there may be a troubled student, and (Half) may have underestimated how troubled he was," Audrey McCollum said. Meanwhile, her husband quietly fulfilled one of the Zantops' last requests. Bob McCollum sent a letter to Vermont's U.S. senators, opposing appointment of John Ashcroft to the post of attorney general, speaking on behalf of the friends whose bloody bodies continued to flash before his eyes.

With minor variations, Audrey McCollum's sentiments about a targeted killing were echoed in conversations all over campus and throughout Hanover and Etna. "I would assume there was some connection between whoever did these crimes and the Zantops, and I don't think there's any reason to think there's some person who would be a threat to the community," said Marion Copenhaver of Etna, a former state representative whose husband was a retired Dartmouth professor. "Clearly there's a monster out there, but he has a specific target."

Still, just in case a murderer was among them, Dartmouth students began escorting each other around campus. "You wonder if this kind of violence has come to this little town," said Diana Allen, the mother of a prospective student from Los Angeles. "It's so charming here, but this is scary." Homeowners began searching for keys to deadbolts they rarely used. Others adopted an offensive posture. Eighty-four-year-old Robert Adams Sr. had lived peacefully in his Etna farmhouse for fifty-six years with his wife, Ruth; the Zantops' home was built on a portion of his old pastureland. Adams vowed he'd be ready if the killers were lurking in the woods. "I got a shotgun here," Adams said, "and it holds enough shells to keep 'em away."

Fueling the fear and speculation was the near-absence of information from authorities. The case was being investigated by more than thirty members of the Hanover Police Department and the New Hampshire State Police—some of whom strapped on snowshoes to search the grounds around the Zantop house. But the New Hampshire attorney general's office was the lead agency, and it kept an unusually tight rein on the release of information. (In most states, district attorneys prosecute murders, but because of New Hampshire's small size and relatively few murders—an average of twenty-one per year in the decade before the Zantops' deaths—homicide cases were the AG's domain.)

During the first few days after January 27, most of the circumspect public pronouncements came directly from Attorney General Philip McLaughlin, a graduate of Boston College Law School who had spent twenty-three years as a defense lawyer before being appointed attorney general in 1997. McLaughlin was fifty-six, the easygoing son of a police officer, a Democrat in a state run by Republicans. He was a father of five whose office overflowed with family photos, with one exception: he kept on his desk a photograph of a six-year-old girl who had been raped and killed. In daily meetings with the press, the normally articulate McLaughlin found himself in the impossible position of trying to reassure the public that all was well while subtly acknowledging that authorities had no idea who killed the Zantops. Compounding that conundrum, McLaughlin refused to reveal any details of the killings, including the cause of death, a position he recognized had the dual effect of protecting his investigation while intensifying the media's already unquenchable thirst.

As a result, McLaughlin's answers to reporters' questions tended toward the same shade of gray as the suits he favored. Asked if the community was at risk, the attorney general said: "We don't know the answer to that." On the other hand, he added: "If we have a specific, reliable reason to believe the community is at risk, we would express that because that would be our duty." A day later, he said, "I can assure the public there is progress that is being made," though under questioning he acknowledged he had "no idea" if the killers remained in the area or had fled. He refused to say whether a murder weapon had been found, whether one or more killers might have been involved, or whether he thought the crime was random. He said nothing of the knife sheaths.

Reporters groused about the official silence, and soon some of the Zantops' friends joined the chorus. "The lack of information just makes things that much harder to deal with," Richard Wright, chairman of the Dartmouth geography department, said three days after the killings. "If someone was caught or if someone was accused or charged, it would perhaps begin some kind of healing. But right now that's not happening."

The day after Wright's comments were published, McLaughlin disclosed that the Zantops were stabbed to death, possibly by someone they knew well enough to let into their home. Once again, though, he tempered that remark by saying it was only a "tentative assumption" that the couple knew their attackers. McLaughlin also addressed complaints about his approach with a subtle shot across his critics' bow: "This is a community that literally has thousands of people that are acculturated to asking detailed questions, and they feel frustrated when they don't get answers to them. We respect that, so we are trying to deal with this as accurately as we can." The attorney general also issued a public warning to the killer or killers: "The person who did this, who may well be watching this, should take no comfort in the fact that they have not yet been apprehended. Be patient; we'll be there."

A week after the killings, McLaughlin turned over the unenviable task of dealing with reporters to a telegenic thirty-two-year-old woman with large brown eyes, who at first glance seemed more likely to be a Noxema model than a murder prosecutor: Assistant Attorney General Kelly Ayotte. She received a less-than-warm welcome from the media when she announced that the public should be on the lookout for anyone who had recently exhibited suspicious behaviors such as absence from work, changed sleeping patterns, unnatural interest in the case, noted display of nervousness or irritability, or a change in usual consumption of drugs, alcohol, or cigarettes. When she finished the list, a wag in the press corps pointed out that she had just described the horde of reporters on the Zantop story. Ayotte wouldn't bite. "Just because one or more of those characteristics are observed doesn't mean that person was involved," she answered dryly. That same day,

Ayotte announced that daily press conferences would be suspended until further notice. Predictably, doubts arose about police and prosecutors solving the crime. "Two weeks after the murder of two Dartmouth professors, investigators appear as stumped as they were on the day of the crime," reported the *Boston Globe*.

But it was a mistake to underestimate Ayotte because of her youth, her looks, or her talent for keeping information from the press. Since joining the attorney general's office in 1998, Ayotte had prosecuted a man who had butchered a Manchester woman; a drifter who had raped and killed a girl in her bed; and a carpenter who had fatally shot a social worker on a Nashua street. When her pager first chirped with news of the Zantops' deaths, she was completing the prosecution of a woman who had killed her disabled boyfriend. Ayotte had been involved in perhaps thirty homicide cases and had brought a third of them to trial, winning convictions every time.

A native of Nashua, New Hampshire, Ayotte was athletic and outdoorsy, a ski racer in high school and a bicycle racer as an adult. She was a political-science major and a Delta Gamma sorority sister in Penn State's class of 1990, and while there, was elected president of the Pan Hellenic Council, which oversaw the activities of twenty-three sororities and more than two thousand women. After Penn State, Ayotte went to Villanova Law School with an eye toward environmental law. But that proved boring: "I like talking to people. There were fewer opportunities to meet people in environmental law." On her left hand she wore an impressive diamond, an engagement ring from a former Air Force pilot three years her senior who had also grown up in Nashua. He also gave her a foot-high silver bullet that stood like a trophy in her cluttered Concord office. The bullet came from an A-10 "Warthog" warplane her fiancé flew after leaving full-time military service and joining the Air National Guard. As the public face of a high-profile, seemingly stalled investigation, Ayotte needed all the silver bullets she could get.

Ayotte's right-hand man was another assistant attorney general, Michael Delaney. He was thirty-one, wiry as a greyhound, married to a defense lawyer, the father of two girls, a Massachusetts native whose father was a chief probation officer and whose mother was a guidance counselor in inner-city schools. Affable but wary, Delaney was another young but experienced prosecutor. He had recently won a first-degree murder conviction in a twenty-year-old case involving the strangulation, stabbing, and attempted rape of an eighty-one-year-old woman. DNA evidence was the deciding factor.

The lack of notable public comments from McLaughlin, Ayotte, or Delaney sent reporters looking for quotable criminologists, who obliged by clucking their tongues at the New Hampshire investigators. Several said the first seventy-two hours after a murder were critical and it appeared that this case had gone cold. A few cited statistics that seemed to equate the chances of solving the Zantop murders with the likelihood that Elvis would appear at Dartmouth's next commencement. One newspaper went through its files to find nine area murders that remained unsolved since 1982, while another quoted a criminal justice professor who suggested that solving the case might depend on "a wonderful stroke of luck." When the FBI joined the investigation two weeks after the crime, analysts were equally divided on whether it represented investigators' desperation or a sign that a fresh lead had been found.

The conflicting, unenlightening media reports had the combined effect of further rattling an already shaken public, leading some otherwise mature and highly civilized members of the Dartmouth community to consider vigilante justice. "For the first time, I'm having these fantasies: What if I ran into this person? I'd beat the hell out of him," Professor James Aronson, Half's colleague and friend, said a week after the murders. "Everyone's getting angry and worried. What if they don't catch this guy?"

Some people began to speculate that it was a random act, but most people who knew the Zantops doubted they would casually let a stranger into their house. "If an unknown came to the door, they would have to make a pretty good case to get in," Susanne's friend Margaret Robinson told police.

In the absence of hard information, reporters fought over scraps of news they could claim as scoops. In that atmosphere came the most explosive news story of all, published in the *Boston Globe* nearly three weeks after the murders.

Based on anonymous sources described as "authorities close to the case," the story began: "Investigators believe the killings of Dartmouth College professors Half and Susanne Zantop were crimes of passion, most likely resulting from an adulterous affair involving Half Zantop." The story touched off a firestorm, as Susanne and Half's friends rushed to defend their memories and reputations. Angry letters poured into the *Globe* as well as the *The Dartmouth*. "Was I reading the *Boston Globe* on Friday the 16th, or did the carrier mistakenly deposit a *National Enquirer* on the doorstep, with an anonymous story of sex and death in academe high above the fold?" Jim Zien wrote to the school paper. "My wife and I have shared a close friendship and close quarters in small sailboats with Susanne and Half Zantop for over fifteen years. Never in the intimate confines of our time and space together did any inkling surface of a relationship that might, in the *Globe*'s irresponsibly sensational speculation, motivate 'crimes of passion, most likely resulting from an adulterous love affair.'"

The strongest denials came from McLaughlin, the attorney general: "No responsible and knowledgeable law enforcement official would provide the *Globe* with the information it attributed to official anonymous sources," McLaughlin declared in a statement the day the story appeared. "In fact, investigators do not hold the belief attributed to them in the story." The *Globe* did have well-placed official sources, but they were misinformed, having based their comments on one of many unproven theories discussed among investigators during the frustrating weeks of heavy scrutiny and little apparent progress. Still, had the paper waited long enough to seek confirmation of its sources' claims, a painful episode might well have been avoided.

Five days after the story appeared, after new evidence emerged and the *Globe*'s sources admitted they had been in error, the newspaper published a page one retraction. It concluded: "It was certainly never our intent to increase the suffering of the Zantop family, their friends, or the Dartmouth College community, and we express regret for the pain our story undoubtedly caused them." Unknown to the *Globe*, the same day the story was being written, ground zero of the case had moved from Hanover across the Connecticut River, to an even sleepier and more isolated community.

7

Snow and Blood

When the Zantops were dead, Robert Tulloch and Jim Parker stepped over the bodies and bolted from the study. As they ran toward the front door, Jim handed his bloody combat knife to Robert, and both bounded through the snow to the green Subaru they had left waiting outside. As Jim turned the ignition on his mother's car, Robert stashed both knives under the passenger-side floor mat.

They had parked nose-in toward the Zantops' garage, so Jim had to back out to make their escape. But the vaporous heat that rose from their breath and bodies fogged the windows, making it impossible to see where they were going. Jim felt on the verge of panic, fearing that the car would get stuck in the snow outside a home with dead people inside, making any alibi they might come up with useless.

They rolled down the windows and stuck their heads out as Jim began inching backward up the driveway toward Trescott Road. "Am I hitting anything?" he screamed at Robert. "Am I hitting anything? Am I going off the road, or am I lined up?"

Robert assumed his usual role of providing guidance for Jim—not only was Robert a year older than Jim, by everyone's reckoning he was the smarter of the two. With his partner calling out directions, Jim pulled slowly onto the street—not like a day earlier, when they had briefly scoped out the Zantop house then pulled out too quickly from the driveway and nearly slammed into another car.

Jim looked at his right hand and saw smeared blood in the crook between his thumb and forefinger, blood that had dripped down the blade onto the handle then onto his skin. He knew it wasn't his; he was scared, but he was unmarked. Robert was worse off, physically at least. His khaki pants were drenched with blood from a deep cut above his right knee, and his pants and dark sweater were also sprayed with blood. His ruined clothes and painful wound aside, Robert was relatively placid.

"It was too easy," Robert marveled. "That was really weird."

His main focus for the moment was the wallet he had taken from Half Zantop. He rifled through its contents, counting out the money it held and trying to figure out if any of the numbers written on scraps of paper might be the code to the dead man's ATM card. But there were too many numbers, and it would be too dangerous to try one after another to see which one worked. That realization led to another: they had failed.

Not failure like six months earlier, when they had spooked the guy on Goose Green Road so badly he refused to open his door then flashed his gun. Not failure like the week before, when they slunk away once the guy on North Hollow Road told them he was too busy tarring his pool to talk with them. This time, they had succeeded by getting inside the house with their story of an environmental survey. They had failed because their efforts were only worth the $340 in cash Robert found in the wallet, barely making a dent in the $10,000 they calculated they would need to start new lives in Australia.

As those conclusions settled over him, Jim found himself "unsure about everything, surprised about how things went, pissed off because our plan didn't work."

"We screwed up," they agreed. "We didn't get, you know, any type of good money."

Jim didn't say so, fearing his partner would yell at him, but he had made a decision: "This is not the way I want to make money—killing people." He wasn't feeling particularly bad for their victims. He was feeling bad for himself, worrying about the potential fallout.

Robert was untroubled by such concerns. He announced: "We have to do something again." Jim let the remark pass.

Jim steered the car through Hanover then across the Connecticut River. As he drove across the waterway, Jim stared at the huge concrete spheres that adorned the bridge. They got onto Interstate 91, heading north toward home. But less than a mile later they noticed the Subaru's hood had partially unlatched, and they feared it might fly up altogether. Robert and Jim screamed at each other: "Oh shit, should we stop or should we not stop?" They decided one of them needed to get out and slam down the hood, so Jim pulled over and pushed open his door. Robert huddled in the passenger seat, worried that anyone who saw him might cast a suspicious eye and remark: "You've got some blood on your pants there, son."

Until that moment, being alone together in the car had always felt good. It was a private place to reveal themselves, to riff about using their superior brains and higher consciousness to become world-traveling adventurers, hired assassins, or both. They could fantasize about figuring out the codes that would let them cheat the computer program that they imagined ran the world, allowing them to do whatever they pleased with no fear of consequences. They could talk about what happens when someone dies, or how other people didn't understand them, or how Jim thought "people weren't having enough fun with their life." They could talk about what a waste of time college would be for them. They could argue about stupid things like the color of a rock-climbing shoe or how Robert always thought he was right, which Jim thought he wasn't.

Jim could talk about working for $10 an hour on construction sites for his "simpleminded" father, being fed health foods by his mother, and getting picked on by his older sister. Robert could complain about how his father was always angry, how his mother should leave—if she could "do her own thing she'd be much more happy"—and grouse that his parents "suck and don't have shit for money." Robert could fantasize about starting to run for president at twenty-five so by the time he was legally allowed to serve, at thirty-five, the nation would recognize his supreme greatness. From there, it was a quick hop to global conquest. Robert would talk about ruling the world, being a "higher power" who would bend the planet and its inhabitants to his will.

They could talk about becoming British Special Forces commandos, then decide it would be "a real pain in the ass to go through all the training." So instead they would train themselves to kill people and steal cars and whatever else they needed, and maybe hijack boats and sail them to different islands. After first learning to sail, that is. Once they got to the islands they could hunt with spears. That would be Robert's job because he thought killing animals would be good practice for killing people. Jim didn't like hunting and couldn't imagine why anyone would hurt an animal. Maybe they could figure out how to replace their bodies with robotic parts or make their way to Egypt to track down myths of immortality and "find some way to live forever."

None of that could happen, of course, as long as they were stuck at home.

Those thoughts were far away as they drove up Interstate 91 the afternoon of January 27, 2001. With blood literally on their hands, all they wanted was to get back home to Chelsea. They got off at Exit 14 in Thetford, Vermont, and drove on Route 113 past a Congregational church, a volunteer fire department, and the Hale Funeral Home. They drove deeper into Vermont on the winding, pitted, two-lane road, past weathered homes with satellite dishes, past country stores and silos. They could have driven Route 113 directly into Chelsea, but they weren't quite ready for that.

"What are we going to do next?" one asked. "We need to clean this stuff off."

Jim took a detour, turning onto Eagle Hollow Road, a hilly route with dense evergreen forests pressing in on both sides. They knew the area well—they had gone rock climbing at a boulder-strewn area just off Eagle Hollow Road in warmer weather. Jim pulled the car onto the shoulder and they walked into the woods. The two newly minted killers used handfuls of snow to scrub the blood from the knives and the floor mat, and Robert took off his pants and dropped his long johns to look at the cut on his leg. Then Jim realized something was missing.

"Oh shit, where's the knife sheaths?"

They searched the backpack they had used to carry their sheathed knives and fake survey papers into the Zantops' house, but the sheaths weren't there. They weren't in the car, either. As fear washed over them, they talked about turning around, but Jim said no. He didn't want to see the dead bodies. That didn't especially bother Robert, and he kept pressing the point.

For the moment, there was nothing to do but go home, change clothes, and consider their options. They got back into the Subaru, drove to the end of Eagle Hollow Road and turned onto Goose Green Road. That took them past Andrew and Diane Patti's vacation home and also past the road where they had dug graves for the Pattis six months earlier. Goose Green led back to Route 113, so they turned onto the road to Chelsea. Nearby was the defunct ski area known as Judgment Ridge, a place they had passed innumerable times. Now they had crossed over Judgment Ridge completely, literally and figuratively.

Route 113 dumped Jim and Robert into the heart of Chelsea, by the North Common and the county jail with the sheriff's office inside. They turned right onto Route 110, Main Street, and almost immediately pulled to a stop at Robert's house near the center of town. Jim waited in the car while Robert ran inside and changed pants, and then they went to Jim's house on the west side of town. Jim stopped outside his father's woodworking shack, a short distance from the house. They stuffed the knives, Robert's bloody pants, Half Zantop's wallet, duct tape, and plastic zip ties into a black gym bag and tossed it behind the front seat of a broken-down blue Volvo parked near the shack. Later they would return to fetch the knives and burn the pants and the wallet, minus the cash, in a furnace inside Jim's father's workshop.

After stashing the gym bag, they dropped briefly by Jim's house, where his parents were admiring a new entertainment center his father had just finished. Not knowing what to say, but knowing they couldn't just hang around and make small talk about furniture, Robert and Jim got back into the Subaru and headed north toward Burlington.

They drove to a Barnes & Noble bookstore where they hoped to find books about how to deal with killing people. They leafed through one, *On Killing: The Psychological Cost of Learning to Kill in War and Society,* an academic study by an Army colonel. But they didn't find it particularly useful, so they looked at magazines awhile, then left.

It was dark as they drove from Burlington. The initial fear had passed, and they knew their work wasn't finished for the day. As they approached Chelsea, they veered eastward, back toward New Hampshire. It was dangerous, they knew, but they had to return to Trescott Road to see if they could break into the house and retrieve the sheaths. If police found the sheaths first, Jim knew, "that could really screw us."

When they arrived they saw a New Hampshire State Police cruiser parked in the driveway. Frightened and downhearted, Jim kept driving, back to Chelsea.

They went to Robert's house and holed up in his room for the night. Outside they could hear the hum of cars and trucks passing by on Main Street, some heading where Robert and Jim dreamed of going—anywhere but here, out to the world beyond Chelsea. With each passing vehicle, the pitch of the motor and the tires grew higher as it approached and lower as it left town, like a train whistle across a prairie.

In the past, that had always been a comforting sound, a siren song luring them away from Chelsea forever. But now, tires on pavement made a frightful shriek. They lay awake much of the night, thinking each car they heard was a police cruiser, coming to get them.

Part II

8

The Crew

Cora Brooks walked into Jimmy Parker's fourth grade class in the fall of 1993 to begin a stretch as substitute teacher, and it was as if someone had declared that school would now be in perpetual recess. The dozen or so kids talked out of turn nonstop. Two boys huddling and whispering were in fact making a black-market trade—swapping a cheap cigarette lighter for a pocket knife. To top off the chaos, nine-year-old Jimmy Parker was standing on his desk, taking center stage. "He was clearly looking for attention, and he was getting it," Brooks said.

It was a class that already had a reputation, with some teachers thinking that certain parents, including Jimmy Parker's, went too far in encouraging "nonconformity." The arrival of a substitute simply stirred the pot further. Substitute teachers got the once-over all the time; it went with the turf. Furthermore, the students' rowdiness quotient was higher still because Cora Brooks was no stranger to the kids' kingdom. They knew Brooks well, mainly because each Halloween, trick-or-treaters counted on her to surprise them with unorthodox treats. Moving into her worn-out house on Main Street in the late 1970s, the single mother, poet, and pacifist had emerged as a Halloween heretic—eschewing candy and sweets for offerings with a deeper meaning or artistic purpose. Toothbrushes, blue ribbons, and pens were just some of the unordinary items she handed out in different years. But kids seemed to enjoy the eccentricity of Cora's basket and began flocking to her house. She might see two hundred young visitors some Halloweens, a stunning count for the tiny hamlet.

Over time, she became best known for *Sock Monster,* a self-published and self-illustrated children's story. The short tale, told in rhyme, was about a monster who lived by itself in a parking-lot Dumpster. The poet had sensed after moving to town that "Chelsea was a town where it may have been more honorable to cut down a tree than to read a book." *Sock Monster* became her way to encourage kids to read, and she made the short book one of her Halloween treats: "Socks were delicious, almost nutritious. Eating a sock made hardly anyone suspicious. Some socks were yellow, some socks were green. Some were red with spots of dried ice cream." Over the years she realized some Chelsea kids memorized some or all of the rhymes.

Jimmy Parker was one of those kids. His theatricality had caught her eye, and he became one of her favorites.

But what about classroom order, with unruly Jimmy up on his desk? Thinking quickly, the teacher decided the roomful of combustible kid energy presented a teaching opportunity rather than a disciplinary challenge. "I'm not going to ask him to come down off that desk," Brooks thought to herself, and she let the rowdiness run its course the rest of that day. The next morning she brought to class a children's book, *Five Chinese Brothers,* written by Claire Huchet Bishop and illustrated by Kurt Wiese. Cora informed her students that they would perform the book as a play. The story, a classic tale about five brothers, each possessing a unique trait—one brother could swallow the sea, another had a neck of iron, and so on—was one where

Jimmy could stand on the desk as part of the story. If Jimmy needed to stand on a desk to get some attention, well, then he could play the Third Chinese Brother, a character whose legs magically stretched and stretched and stretched. The funny, endearing story was infused with the simple message that everyone is special and gifted in some way. The class rehearsed and then invited the school's new principal, Pat Davenport, to watch. The classroom exercise was a success and Cora was pleased she'd found a way to channel Jimmy's antics artistically. The desktop routine that ordinarily might have turned out badly—"Young man, march yourself to the principal's office!"—had instead brought positive recognition.

That was brown-eyed Jimmy Parker—child actor and showman. Oddly enough, he reflected the community's long tradition in the arts and theater. Jimmy was a Chelsea Player, a kid with the quick smile that stretched across his round face. In yearbook after yearbook, Jimmy's grin measured the widest of all the elementary school kids.

Jimmy lived with his family in the house his parents had built up on West Hill. John and Joan Parker were a no-frills couple who slept in a shack while constructing a straightforward, wooden, red A-frame at the intersection of two dirt roads, Bradshaw Crossroad and Hook Road. Down a bit from the house, the shack was later put to use as a shop and office for John Parker's contracting business. With nineteen acres, the Parkers had plenty of elbow room. The property bordered an ancient cemetery, the Wills Cemetery, where about thirty-five of Chelsea's earliest settlers from the 1780s were buried.

Though outsiders, both Parkers established themselves in town. Especially John Parker. He became a community organizer, the boss of a house-building business, J. Parker Custom Construction, a JV basketball coach, and a rugged rebounder in the weekend games the men's basketball league played in the school gym. Joining the town's recreation committee, John Parker eventually became chairman and was the prime force in converting a few acres of farmland south of the village into new playing fields and a playground. His passion for bas-

ketball ran the gamut—from coaching to playing to collecting memorabilia. From a Web site he created, and by traveling to sport and card
shows, the elder Parker traded and dealt in basketball collectibles.
"This guy is a pillar of the community, a salt-of-the-earth type," friend
Kevin Ellis said about the trim but solidly-built six-footer whose worn,
toughened fingertips gave away his profession.

"He's a bit of an artist in the way he looks at things," Doug Brown,
a college roommate, said about his friend's success as a Vermont contractor. Brown said John Parker did meticulous work yet had a relaxed
manner about him. "He's not anal-retentive, not the kind of guy who
won't wear a shirt if it has a wrinkle."

John Parker grew up in upstate New York, attended a small liberal
arts college, Ohio-Wesleyan, and then headed west to San Diego,
where he met Joan Essery in the mid-1970s. "They fit together right
away," said Brown, who also settled in San Diego, where he became a
criminal defense attorney.

Joan Essery Parker was a vegetarian jock with that California feeling—a San Diego native and, for a time, a nationally ranked racquetball player who continued to compete regularly after motherhood and
worked as an instructor at courts in Barre, Vermont, and elsewhere.
Rarely seen wearing makeup, preferring a country-casual look, Joan
mostly wore her brown hair simply, straight down to her shoulders.

The Parkers—just like the Pomerantzes, David Savidge, Kevin Ellis,
or any number of other outsiders—set their sights on Chelsea as an
ideal canvas to paint their family's life, safely removed from the world's
woes, be it the nuclear reactor meltdown at Three Mile Island in 1979
or the bombing of New York's World Trade Center in 1993 or the violent crime rate that rose quickly throughout the 1980s and early
1990s.

"San Diego was too much of a big city for them," said Brown. "Both
had small-town interests." While visiting friends in Vermont, the couple was smitten by Chelsea's family orientation. "John and Joan were
effectively pacifists," said Brown. "Not in a dogmatic sense, but they
were not hunters, and there were no firearms in the house." They

hoped to raise children "to be interested in the world, to have strong family values, and to be kind and decent to other people."

The Parkers' first child was Diana, born in 1981. Popular in high school, Diana was serious about art, a passion reflected in the bold and colorful artwork decorating her upstairs room. Diana was salutatorian of the 1999 class at Chelsea Public School and headed off to an art college in Chicago after graduation. Growing up, brother and sister were never particularly close. "They pick on each other a lot," John Parker once said. Jimmy considered his older sister selfish and a general nuisance. But he also felt that enduring what he called her "unrelenting harassment" made him stronger mentally. Writing in the third person about himself in a school essay, Jimmy said he eventually "learned to ignore her, and went on with his life and left his ignorant 'sister' behind."

He lived a boy's life that was reflected in the look of the Parkers' property: the two tree forts that were built over time, the tire that swung from another tree, the basketball hoop that hung from a wooden pole, and the pedal bike that was later replaced with a dirt bike. Looking back, Jimmy portrayed himself in the school essay as "very brave and coordinated as a young boy, and [someone who] loved to eat." His toddler years were "full of energy and smiles." He learned "to walk, swim and bike at an early age" and he had parents who fed him "their simple—be kind and think for yourself—morals."

Jimmy said he "enjoyed praise," admitting he sought the spotlight. "He would never shut up," a teacher once laughed, talking about a boy who seemed to be here, there, and everywhere, bidding for an opportunity to make a splash—literally. Jimmy's early birthday parties were legendary among the other boys in town. The Parkers' large yard allowed for a long, running takeoff into the outdoor kiddie pool. "Jimmy was always the craziest one jumping in," said his longtime friend Zack Courts, a rangy, outgoing, upbeat boy with close-cropped dark hair and an easy smile. To the herd of preschool boys like Courts, who was a year older than Jimmy, the sprawling Parker homestead was "a cool setting," and "cocky" Jimmy Parker was an easy kid to like.

In elementary school, Jimmy hung around with Brad Johnson, a strong, outdoorsy boy the same age who lived about a mile away on West Hill. It was a friendship mixing new and old Chelsea—John and Joan Parker being from "away," while Jack and Annette Johnsons' bloodlines were pure Vermont. Brad's mom sometimes wondered what Jimmy's mom made of the fact that logger Jack Johnson cut down trees for a living. Joan Parker was what locals called a "tree-hugger." If privately Joan Parker disapproved, she never let on, and, besides, Jimmy and Brad got along fine.

Some people considered Jimmy a pain in the butt, like when he tagged along with his father on a work site and got in the way. Or John might take Jimmy to a sport-and-card show that the elder Parker was passionate about, and Jimmy would get restless and impatient. But Jimmy loved to fish and the Johnsons enjoyed having him around. The boys camped together and Jimmy even accompanied the Johnsons on a few family vacations.

Yet the two grew apart as they got older. Brad idolized Davy Crockett and was becoming an experienced hunter. Brad began with a BB gun and then his dad handed him a small rifle to practice target-shooting out back on their land. "It's kind of a parent, hereditary thing," Jack Johnson said. Brad eventually grew into felling deer with a .243-caliber rifle or a muzzle loader, a single-shot, long-barreled rifle. Jimmy, meanwhile, was a boy who, when they all went camping, was spooked by the dark—and would remain that way into his teens. He was against hunting, and began asking Brad, "How can you kill an animal?" Words right out of his mom's mouth.

Brad, filling out, was whole hog into team sports—soccer, basketball, and baseball—while Jimmy was a talented but indifferent participant. Jack Johnson and John Parker coached their sons in basketball in elementary and middle school, but Jimmy brought a different kind of game to the court. "He could have been a good ball player," said Brad's mom, "but he didn't care if he won or lost." John Parker would coach and play, year after year, but Jimmy would not. One by one, Jimmy bailed from organized sports, quitting basketball after freshman year and soccer the next year. John Parker's JV basketball team featured many of Jimmy's friends, but not his own son. Jimmy dabbled in other things. He briefly took karate with Jill Pomerantz. He began taking piano lessons at age seven. Trombone lessons followed. Turning thirteen, he started playing bass guitar and really got into it. By the time he was in high school, he had an electric keyboard set up in the living room and a full drum set in the cellar. Jimmy might not have been his father's son in terms of sports, but it didn't spark any tension at home. "They've always been really supportive with me and always there for me," he said later. His parents hung a framed collection of his school photos on one wall in their home, twelve oval spaces in all, arranged clockwise, with his first grade photo in the one-o'clock position, and so forth. By 2001, the circle was nearly complete, all but Jim's senior year photograph and a large space in the center for a graduation-day picture.

One consistent quality of his youth was a desire to stir things up. The sixth grade basketball team had won all but one game, so Jimmy challenged the coach: shouldn't we let the other team win now? "He was that kind of kid," said Annette Johnson. "Jimmy always wanted to stand out for being different."

It was why one day substitute teacher Cora Brooks found Jimmy standing on his desk in fourth grade. Some teachers considered Jimmy "needy." Jimmy later put it differently. "I'd say about the fourth grade I started getting really tired of school. Because it was slow for me," he said. He considered himself a "truly intelligent person." Looking around, Chelsea increasingly seemed like a yawner of a place to grow up in. "I just started thinking that I could be doing better things."

Clowning around helped to make life more interesting. The same with the dramatic arts. In middle school, Jimmy found himself teamed up with Cora Brooks for a movie tryout. Filmmaker Jay Craven was casting parts for a movie he was shooting in the area. The film was an adaptation of Howard Frank Mosher's *Stranger in the Kingdom,* a novel about a black minister who moves with his son to a tiny Vermont town in the late 1950s and eventually finds himself accused of murder. Among the casting needs were small parts for a mother and a son. Joan Parker telephoned Cora Brooks and asked if the poet would try out with Jimmy. Brooks threw herself into the tryout, tracking down a '50s-style, blue print dress with a white collar in a thrift store. She and Jimmy rehearsed together and then gave it their best shot. They didn't get called back, but Cora didn't mind. "For a few moments we were mother and son," she said. They had fun, and Cora told Jimmy he should pursue drama.

"I thought he was really good."

Jimmy seemed a natural—ever eager to assume a part and play out a fantasy that took him to places beyond Chelsea and turned him into characters other than himself.

Diane and Mike Tulloch and their four kids—two girls followed by two boys—began renting in Chelsea in 1992. People meeting the newcomers were quick to realize that Diane, quietly attractive, served as the family's point person. Mike was a background figure, a recluse who wore dark glasses as if to avoid eye contact and carried himself with an air of resignation. Mike once likened himself to the younger of his two daughters, who had a brain abnormality that resulted in developmental delays and impulse-control problems. Mike said he had a handicap of his own, "that is for me a serious one. I am painfully shy."

There was more to it than that. The road to Chelsea had not been an easy one for the Tullochs. Going back to the early years of their marriage in 1977, Mike had struggled with alcoholism and depression, and had at times been suicidal. The couple was from New Jersey originally—Mike from Jersey City and Diane from the more affluent Glen Ridge. They married in Frankford Township when Mike was twenty-three and Diane was twenty-two, with Mike listing his occupation on the marriage certificate as "paper carrier." Five or so years into the marriage, Mike had an affair, but he and Diane stayed the course and seemed to come out stronger for it. The couple had struggled personally and financially, and there were other struggles as well—such as trying to figure out where to make a go of it as the family grew.

During the 1980s, the couple had bounced around among several Vermont towns—North Pomfret, Bridgewater, and Sharon. Robert was born in North Pomfret, a home birth on a farm. Robert waxed romantic about his entry into the world. "No hospitals, no doctors, no medicine, a pure birth, just like the days of old," he once wrote. "I was born in the same manner as Jesus or Moses." The family's move to Sharon, wrote Robert, covering his toddler years in his auto-hagiography, marked "the humble beginnings of an intellectual giant."

"Sharon was great," he wrote. "I played every day, learned every day, and ate the best homemade food. We had a huge yard, and every neighbor would let us explore their land. We would pirate the seas of a giant green straw field, climb the castles of the forest, and rain down arrows on attackers.

"Our mother would go to the library and check out a billion different books. Dinosaurs, machines, animals, mysteries, biographies, everything a child would find interesting. She would read to us until we learned how to read ourselves. We did what we wanted, read what we wanted, and played at what we wanted. And then the food, the wondrous food of my childhood. Fresh jam, homemade pickles, fresh grown vegetables, four loaves of fresh bread every day, endless stacks of pancakes and waffles, excellent milk bought from a neighboring farmer, elaborate meals stacked to the ceiling, completely vanished by bedtime.

"I led a charmed life, a child could want for nothing more."

Robert and his family were acquiring a taste for the rhythms of life in the Green Mountain State. It seemed a natural fit, the Tullochs and rural Vermont. But they didn't decide on Vermont permanently until after taking a sharp detour into an entirely different world.

The Tullochs' two-year Florida experiment began the summer of 1990 when the family moved to Jensen Beach, a sun-drenched town about two hours north of Fort Lauderdale, where the big event was the annual Pineapple Festival. Diane's parents had moved to the neighboring town of Stuart a few years earlier, a major reason for making the Florida relocation in the first place. Years later, Robert would tell his girlfriend that his maternal grandparents were "really rich," but that was a gross exaggeration.

The Tulloch family found a home on one of the winding streets of Jensen Park Estates, a middle-class development whose name, in the Florida tradition, was far grander than reality. The modest, ranch-style homes were set close to each other and hard by the streets; few would command six figures. The Tullochs paid $90,000 for a three-bedroom house, tan with green trim, on Northeast Lima Calle. Robert shared a room with his brother Kienan, one year younger than Robert and the youngest of the four kids. The girls shared another room. There was Becky, five years older than Robert, and next came Julie, who had the brain disorder. The four kids were enrolled at the Jensen Beach Elementary School, a mile away, the "Home of the Vikings."

The Tullochs tried to fit in but never did. "Sort of a weird family," Bart Fletcher, another boy on the block, recalled. Bart was in first grade with Kienan, a year behind Robert, and he and his brother, Nick, would play with the Tulloch boys. They were joined by John Donovan, whose family also lived in Jensen Park Estates. The neighborhood kids at first thought Robert and Kienan were twins—both had mullet haircuts—bangs on top and long in the back—and both had dour expressions and frail-looking bodies. The Tulloch brothers shared clothes and had one dresser, but not much else for furnishings in their bedroom. They slept on two mattresses; their parents either never bothered or never could afford to buy them bed frames. There wasn't much in the way of toys either, so Robert and Kienan appeared regularly at Bart Fletcher's house to play with his stuff. Robert came off as kind of "strange" to older kids around the neighborhood. "He was picked on by other kids—an outsider, not really accepted," one neighborhood parent said. "You know, kids can be cruel," said Bart Fletcher. "They felt that."

Because Kienan was in their grade, Bart Fletcher and John Donovan initially played mostly with him. But they found Kienan cautious, Robert bolder, and gravitated to the older brother. "Robert was more outgoing, always, 'Let's go for it,'" said Bart Fletcher. "We connected more on that basis." In the neighborhood the boys played pickup games and built forts in a lot across the street from the Tullochs' house, on the edge of a small, manmade lake. They'd also experiment—like the time at the Tullochs' when they tried to poison lizards.

Robert and John Donovan mixed chemicals from Robert's chemistry set and used an eye dropper to shoot the potions in the lizards' mouths. "Nothing happened," said Donovan.

"Then we decided to try some ourselves—since we were macho guys. I ran home because I thought I was going to die and I told my parents."

Robert soon sold the chemistry set to Bart Fletcher for $20. He and John Donovan never heard if the lizard stunt got Robert in trouble, but they suspected it did. "The kids were afraid of the parents," Bart Fletcher said. Robert and Kienan told their friends about the severe discipline that came their way for infractions as slight as being late for dinner. Fletcher once went over to their house and found Robert sitting inside filling page after page with a one-line phrase beginning, "I will not . . ." Beyond that, Fletcher didn't know what form the punishments took.

Neighbors could tell the Tullochs didn't have much money. But it wasn't finances that set them apart. Most yards might be modest-sized but they were well-manicured. Not the Tullochs', which was ill-kept by neighborhood standards. Socially, Diane and Mike Tulloch were far from a dynamic couple on the cook-out circuit. "They were very withdrawn, quiet, rather asocial," said Bart Fletcher's mother, Ginny Luther.

"They kind of gave me the creeps," she said.

Part of the unease involved Julie Tulloch. There was the time Julie tried to teach the family's two green-and-blue parakeets to talk and lay eggs and ended up drowning them as part of the misguided "lesson." Julie also had a tendency to roam the neighborhood, collecting items that didn't belong to her.

"She'd take stuff from other houses," said Bart Fletcher. "That caused a lot of tension." Neighbors who couldn't find something would think: Julie Tulloch. "Julie would deny it, even if it was sitting right there, and it would be a big ordeal." Fletcher was once a victim, when Julie "borrowed" his scooter.

But Julie wasn't the only Tulloch with quick fingers. Not long after Robert left his house one day, Fletcher realized he was missing one of his most prized possessions, a Marvel trading card, encased in plastic, featuring a hologram image of the superhero Wolverine. Fletcher went to Robert's house and conducted a warrantless search of Robert's room. "I found it," Fletcher said. "He said, 'Yeah, I took it.' Like no big deal." Bigger and stronger than Robert, Fletcher decided it was time for an added dose of street justice. He informed Robert he was taking back the $20 he'd paid for Robert's chemistry set as further penalty. Robert stood by and surrendered the money, acting nonchalant about the whole affair.

Neighbors weren't surprised when they saw a "For Sale" sign go up on the Tulloch lawn. Diane Tulloch, for one, had been open about wanting out. "Diane once told me they just didn't like this area at all," Ginny Luther said. "They were kind of earthy people, I think. She said they didn't like the fast pace of life here."

"My mother hated it," Robert later wrote. Robert hated Florida, too. "The kids were mean. The environment was hellish and dangerous. The adults were greasy and sleazy, and the schools were horrible. As I look back at it, I compare it with hell." It was a time, noted Robert, when "my relationship with my parents faded." It was also a time when Robert self-consciously began to "carve my niche as the smart, witty kid."

Ginny Luther's husband, Jack, wasn't unhappy to see the Tullochs move away. "They weren't what you'd call an asset to the neighborhood," he said. Nearly two years would pass after their move to Vermont before they found a buyer for the house. It wasn't until August 1994 that they returned to close out the Florida chapter of their lives. They sold the place for $88,000, which meant after four years of owning the house they suffered a $2,000 loss.

"Beautiful Chelsea," Robert once wrote. "My last American home."

Florida had been a mistake. It was everything Vermont was not: palm trees, not maples; beaches, not ski slopes; flatland, not mountains; transient, not grounded. The Tullochs rented when they first came to Chelsea, but once they found buyers for their Jensen Beach home they were ready to commit to the town. Robert was in sixth grade and it was just days before Thanksgiving 1994 when they bought a house on Main Street from a weaver named Maggie Neale. It was a two-story yellow Colonial—the kind of old Vermont house breezes find their way into—located next door to Chelsea Mills, built in the 1820s and once the busiest grist mill in town. Her kids grown, Maggie Neale no longer needed a house that had provided more than enough room for a family and her weaving business, which she operated out of a first-floor front room. In the ten years she'd lived in the house, her ex-husband, a carpenter, the same profession Mike Tulloch had pursued, made major improvements to the kitchen. He'd installed new and bigger windows along one wall to brighten the room with natural southern light, pulled up the linoleum and put in a new wood floor, and covered the counters with two-inch-thick slabs of maple. Maggie put in a wood-burning stove. Large enough for a round table, a rocking chair, and a nook with a sitting cushion, the kitchen was the home's main gathering place. Set in back of the house, the kitchen was also the room providing the most privacy. Maggie's family, and the Tullochs later, mainly came and went through the kitchen by way of a back porch that was crowded with stacked wood, a gas grill, and usually a bike or two. The unpaved driveway ended there, between the porch and a small garage Maggie's ex had converted into a carpenter's workshop.

Diane Tulloch worried about the $93,500 price, but was taken by the rambling old house—so many rooms for the kids and even a workshop out back for her husband. In the small front yard something was always coming up—daffodils, Jacob's ladder, Solomon's seal, and, of course, the sweet-smelling lilacs that graced the entire village. "She loved what had been done to it and also what had not been done, because Michael was a carpenter," Maggie said. Looking finally to sink roots, the Tullochs took out a loan for $79,475 from a West Brattleboro mortgage company. Handling the closing was a lawyer from a small firm headed up by Dan Sedon, a young attorney originally from New Jersey who mostly practiced criminal law. Sedon, like so many newcomers to the Chelsea area, had migrated to Vermont during the 1990s for more breathing room.

The Tullochs' new home was across the street and a few doors down from Cora Brooks's place. Halloween was a month gone, but next year's treats were now only a few steps away. The foliage season was long gone, too. In southern New England, hillsides featured a salad bowl of greens as late as Halloween, but not so in Chelsea. Trees were already mostly barren; any leaves hanging on were rust-colored and brittle. The November daylight was noticeably slanted by mid-afternoon, casting long shadows on the Tullochs' backyard. The mountain-valley weather could change quickly—a hard, morning hail storm, for example, followed by a blustery wind, some sun, or clouds and maybe a late-day sprinkle. The Tullochs moved into their home during this season of meteorological surprise and fired up the wood-burning stove in the kitchen. Right away, Diane painted the kitchen a plum color. "Quite vibrant. It looked great," said Maggie Neale. "It was a bright and happy kitchen, a lot of good, natural light." The family dog, Ruby, and later two cats, Ocho and Mismatch, staked out territory around the warm kitchen stove.

The family didn't come close to having enough furniture to fill all the rooms. The television and VCR went in the front living room that had a second and prettier wood-burning stove, an oval-shaped, red-enamel parlor model. In the other front room, where Maggie Neale had weaved, the Tullochs put an upright piano, and later Mike had a workbench near the piano he used to assemble finely made wooden chairs. In a first-floor room between the kitchen and the room with the piano the Tullochs set up a Ping-Pong table. Overall, the interior of the house was a work in progress; some rooms, like the kitchen and living room, were pretty much finished, but other rooms looked as if they were in a permanent state of renovation, with exposed insulation or wooden wall sheathing. The front staircase, for example, featured hand-painted scenes on the risers of each step, one of a barn in a meadow, another of a cat seated contentedly. The unique artwork was already there when the Tullochs moved in. The front hall, meanwhile, was unpainted blue board, with sheetrock screws showing.

Upstairs, Robert took one of the front bedrooms. It was a corner room on the south end of the house that was reached by walking from the center staircase past one front bedroom, through a hallway door and then past a bathroom. The hallway door had the effect of dividing the upstairs, so that Robert's corner bedroom seemed to exist separately from the rest of the house. "When you entered this space it felt like a different area," said Maggie Neale. She'd actually rented out the bedroom and for a while had even considered building a private stairway and entrance from the outside. Robert had a mattress on the floor, just as in Florida, and eventually he kept a second mattress rolled up for when his friends slept over. In a portable closet hung some pants and shirts, a few ties, and a belt, and he used a metal rack to hang socks and underwear to dry. In one cardboard box on the floor, he kept his underwear, T-shirts, sweaters, and shorts. In another, a cardboard box that used to contain oranges, he kept a stack of comics. A bookcase held randomly arranged notebooks, folders for his writings, video games, and books.

It was his domain, sparsely decorated with a floor plant, a couple of homemade posters, and a United States flag he draped as a shade over one of the windows. Clothes were always scattered—socks and underwear on the floor, shirts, sweaters, and blue jeans piled on a chair. The unpainted walls were scarred and gouged when he got there, and the family never repaired them. In fact, Robert did his part to make it worse. "His door was a target for anything that would stick into it," Jimmy once said. The walls were "ugly . . . they're all falling apart."

But overall the room suited Robert fine. He could block out the rest of the family, and the family him.

The K-12 Chelsea Public School sat at the top corner of South Common, a two-story white-clapboard building that faced north and was next door to the county courthouse. The building was a hodgepodge of appendages and tacked-on additions that blended new with old. The original school structure, built in 1912, was right out of old Vermont, with its snow-white exterior, clapboard face, and rooftop cupola. Behind it, a new wing was added in the late 1970s to hold the high school. It was the most modern-looking part of the school complex, with a single ground-floor hallway leading to the library, offices for school administrators, eight high school classrooms, and science labs.

Joining teacher DeRoss Kellogg's sixth grade class the first day of school in 1994, Robert hustled up a narrow staircase that zigged, then zagged, and creaked with the rush of little kids, and was better suited for one-way traffic. Kellogg's class, located in back on the second floor, overlooked the playing fields and, beyond the fields, a cemetery on a hill. To the west, the room had a view across Main Street, past roof tops to the steep, rolling West Hill, covered with trees—some birch, fir, and pine, but mostly maple.

Robert still wore the mullet haircut he'd had in Florida—it was a style he kept through most of elementary school. His nose had not yet overtaken his face, and between his delicate features and the haircut he looked girlish in school photos. Becky was a high school junior, and Julie was in seventh grade, attending school despite her learning difficulties. Julie wore bangs, too, and in some photographs she and Robert looked a lot alike. Their younger brother, Kienan, was a year behind Robert, starting fifth grade, just like Jimmy Parker. Though Robert had been around Chelsea earlier, this was the first year the two boys would take notice of one another and begin forging their friendship.

Entering the classroom, Robert found the desks and chairs lined up in rows, and the walls decorated with standard fare—posters of current events and education-boosting rhymes and sayings. He also saw his new teacher's devotion to the Boston Red Sox. Displayed prominently on an inside wall was a poster of slugger Jim Rice, a picture Kellogg had hung early in both his and the left fielder's careers in the late 1970s. Low-slung bookcases lined one side of the room, full of well-worn and well-read paperback books, including such novels as Ray Bradbury's *Something Wicked This Way Comes,* an allegorical tale of good and evil, truth and deception. The book tells the story of two teenage boys, James Nightshade and William Halloway, forced to confront dark forces and themselves when a mysterious carnival rolls into their Midwestern town.

Robert also found a teacher who couldn't wait to have him in his class. Every year Kellogg and the fifth grade teacher swapped teaching math and science, so Kellogg had met Robert the year before when he taught math to fifth graders. Kellogg, a soft-spoken, slightly built man with a sparse handlebar mustache, felt an immediate connection: "I somehow knew we were kindred spirits almost the first day." He liked Robert's sense of humor. Teasing one another came easily. From the very first, Kellogg discovered Robert was a student "who grasps concepts quickly and easily."

"I looked forward all year to having him in sixth grade," Kellogg said.

Robert enjoyed Kellogg as well. "Sixth grade, the year of my awakening," he would write in a high school essay. "DeRoss Kellogg, one of the best teachers I will ever know, taught me to be independent in school. In his class I learned to distinguish myself and became a separate and confident individual. He encouraged each student to exercise their creativity and individuality with creative projects such as skits, short stories, presentations, and the like. We could do whatever we wanted, it felt free, and this was back when I was still interested in school."

It turned out that Robert and a handful of sixth grade classmates were an unusually bright group, the kind that comes along every once in a while for no apparent reason, a seemingly chance constellation. "It's almost like a UFO went over . . . and there was this small group that was way better, way more interested in academics than the average class," said Paul Callens, a high school math and physics teacher.

Robert's pal, Kip Battey, red-haired and freckle-faced, was one of the sixth grade go-getters, as were Anna Mulligan, Billy Funk, Emily Dumont, and Torry Hook. The class became one of Kellogg's favorites, with Robert one of the teacher's all-time prized students. The kids had a snap to them, an electricity that made teaching satisfying. It led Kellogg to ponder new ways to challenge Robert and his peers. He ran his ideas past school administrators and, with their support, began accelerating their course work, particularly in mathematics. They did so well that the next year Robert and the others skipped pre-algebra, the usual track for seventh graders. "The idea was let's see how they do," said Kip. "So we went in with the eighth graders and took regular algebra." The course was a year long, and when Robert and Kip finished seventh grade, they had earned the first of three math credits necessary for high school graduation. Pushing the students seemed a good idea in the short term. Possible long-term consequences could wait for another day.

For the Tullochs, Chelsea proved to be a better fit all around. Mike had his workshop out back. He printed up business cards—"Michael W. Tulloch, Finish Carpenter, Cabinets," it read in green print with a green border—and began picking up work. A loner, he strongly preferred working by himself. Over the years he did a few jobs for a carpenter-contractor in town with a much bigger and more lucrative business, John Parker, although the two men never became more than acquaintances. Mike Tulloch once said he "almost had no contact" with John Parker, "even though we're in a similar business. We very rarely have crossed paths." Mike didn't know Joan Parker at all. His wife knew Joan Parker a little from the food co-op both families belonged to.

Diane, mostly a stay-at-home mom, branched out and began taking nursing courses. Chelseans had a hard time getting to know the reclusive man of the house, but found Diane a kind person who seemed a natural for nursing. Licensed by the state of Vermont in July 1995, Diane began practicing her caretaking skills—and also providing the family with a much-needed steady income—as a visiting nurse with an office in Randolph, just west of Chelsea. The family also was comforted by the community's response to Julie, who was prone to outbursts and sudden mood shifts. Not only was Julie included in regular classes during elementary and middle school, the whole Chelsea feel was supportive. Julie was someone people looked after, not looked at cross-eyed, as in Jensen Beach. Sure, she tended to roam, but if she took something from Will's Store, it was handled with a quiet call to Diane and not the sheriff's office. Chelsea was a safety net.

Robert was busy doing what other elementary school–aged kids did—playing and fooling around. For a while he had a paper route, and he played on a Little League baseball team coached by Jack Johnson. The coach and teammates could tell he wasn't really interested in the sport even though he was clearly a coordinated kid. In school Robert had become fast friends with Kip Battey, whose mind was as quick as Robert's. Kip's family was one of those Chelsea families that went way back, and his father, Ned, an insurance salesman, was active on the school committee and coached sports. By middle school Robert had a new best pal—Zack Courts, an upbeat kid who loved the thrill of racing and got his first dirt bike when he was eight years old. Zack's parents were divorced and Zack spent a lot of time at his father's house on Main Street a few doors down from the Tullochs'. The two played on the same Little League team—"We laughed at each other's jokes," Zack said later—but didn't really connect until middle school. Zack had attended the alternative Wellspring School until seventh grade. Wellspring, located behind a white picket fence in a white clapboard house on South Common, was a Waldorf School, where exams were downplayed and course work was designed to blend mental, physical, and spiritual growth.

Meeting in the single seventh grade class at Chelsea Public School, Robert and Zack hit it off. They were joined by two other boys who'd been with Zack at Wellspring—Coltere Savidge and Casey Purcell. The new buddy system became Robert, Kip, Zack, Coltere, and Casey. The boys found Robert smart, quick-witted, and fun to be around. In his own words, Robert saw himself as developing "into an incredibly smart, witty, and scheming individual." Robert's mullet was history. The boys slept over at each other's houses, played sports, and romped in the woods. Sometimes a pretty, dark-haired girl in their class, Christiana Usenza, who'd also attended Wellspring, tagged along. Eventually Jimmy Parker entered the circle. On nice days, they might climb out Robert's bedroom window onto the flat roof above the front porch and lounge around, looking over Main Street. Zack eventually came up with a name for the six Chelsea boys: The Crew. "Robert laughed when he heard me using the name," said Zack, "but then he'd sometimes use it too."

The boys in Jensen Beach had thought Robert's parents were strict, while the Chelsea boys saw them as laissez-faire. Mike was distant and didn't have much to say. Diane was often busy coming and going with work. In fact, the parents were often not around. Robert's oldest sister, Becky, was like a third parent, especially in keeping track of Julie. They seemed like a functioning family that, as some in town came to learn, had managed a number of private crises—Julie's disability, Mike's drinking and depression, and chronic money concerns. Sometimes Chelseans spotted Diane and Mike walking down Main Street hand in hand. The couple might stop at Will's Store or S&L Video to pick up a movie and continue their walk around one of the commons before heading home. Renting movies was a Chelsea ritual—the nearest cinema was a thirty-minute drive.

But inside, all was not picture-perfect. The older Robert got, the edgier he seemed. The trouble could be his father or the household in general. "His relationship with his dad wasn't as good as mine is with my dad," Zack said later. By the time Robert was in high school, he was expected to pick up the slack now that Becky had graduated from high school and left the house to attend nursing school. In theory, Julie was next in line in the family pecking order to assume the role as "third parent," but her disability prevented that. She could not be counted on.

"Robert washed a lot of dishes," said Zack. "He mopped. He vacuumed. He carried a lot of wood. Robert carried a lot of chores on his shoulders."

Sometimes Robert couldn't take it anymore. "Goddamit, why do I have to do all these dishes!" he shouted one afternoon. Robert stood at the kitchen sink. He was washing, Zack was drying. The sooner they cleaned up the sooner they could run off. Julie prowled around the kitchen, and Robert began to badger her. He was fed up with her uselessness when it came to housework. If Julie were ever told to wash the dishes she'd probably forget to. Or, if she did remember, she'd do such a lousy job someone would have to wash them again.

"I do everything," Robert snarled at her.

Julie didn't cry, but she left abruptly. She went out the back door and toward the workshop. Minutes later, Mike Tulloch strode into the kitchen. Zack was taken aback, unaccustomed to seeing Mike Tulloch animated. Locking eyes with his son, Mike said firmly, "You cannot do that. She is not someone you can get mad at like that." The father turned on his heels and left. Robert didn't say a word.

Confrontations were an exception, not the rule, but Robert's chafing intensified regarding home life in general and his father in particular. "I think it was kind of rough for him," said Jimmy Parker. "His father was a very—he was grumpy a lot and probably had some kind of depression or something. He would get angry a lot at just different stuff, sometimes be unreasonable. . . . I mean Robert cared for everybody in his family, his father, too. He just seemed like he wanted better for everybody because they seemed to have a very . . . his father was always struggling with work. I don't know, I think I had a much better home life than he did."

Jimmy Parker came into The Crew during middle school by an altogether different route. Jimmy was neither in the same grade nor taking any of the same courses as Robert, Kip, Zack, Coltere, or Casey. He was Kienan's elementary school classmate. The leapfrog over Kienan to Robert had the echo of Jensen Beach, where the neighborhood boys first got to know Kienan and then gravitated to Robert. Initially, Jimmy hung out with "both Robert and Kienan, and then, ah, I just became better friends with Robert."

For Jimmy, choosing between the Tulloch brothers was no contest. Jimmy saw himself as a cool guy in the making. "I was maturing a lot and they weren't," Jimmy said about Kienan and other classmates. "They were still making fart and poop jokes." Jimmy concluded that Kienan was "silly, unintelligent, and very uncoordinated." Besides,

Kienan was shy and introverted, like his father, while Robert's energy and bounce matched Jimmy's. "Jimmy and Robert are kind of loud and very verbal, and Kienan isn't," Diane Tulloch once said.

It was Florida all over again—and Kienan let Robert know about it. "Kienan got upset," said Jimmy, "because Robert was taking his friend away, like he always does. I guess it might have happened before." Robert blew off Kienan and his complaints, making use of his verbal and physical edge. "He just kind of had all the advantages over him, so he could pick on him," Jimmy said. "You know, really make him feel bad."

For Jimmy, just as the Florida boys before him, Robert had an allure that Kienan lacked. "He's just ready, you know, to do something exciting," said Jimmy. "He's very intelligent. Maybe not enough common sense to go with it. That's kind of the same for both of us." The two complemented one another—Jimmy the actor, inspired by Robert's theories and direction; Robert the idea man, emboldened by a partner overflowing with creative energy. They were one another's best audience.

"We talked a lot about life in general, what's going on, you know, what we're supposed to be doing here—if this is it, maybe we should make the best of it.

"We didn't think people were making enough out of life."

Robert and Jim brought an attitude to The Crew. "Ninth grade and up, it was mostly, like, Casey, me, Zack, and Robert," said Jimmy. "Kip and Coltere, because Coltere was Zack's really good friend, so that was basically the group of friends we had."

By high school, Robert's house had become mission control. No one had a driver's license yet, so if Jimmy didn't go right to Robert's house from school, any plans to get together became complicated. "We would have to arrange things with our parents to drive me to his house, so that was a big pain in the ass." It worked out better for The Crew to just head directly there after school. Jim was there almost every day.

Robert was also the first one to get Nintendo 64. The console was hooked up to the television in the living room. The boys played *James Bond, Beetle Racing,* and first-person shooting games like *Doom.* "Robert would steer the guy and I would shoot," Zack said. Robert's parents weren't around much, and the boys often had the run of the place. The house became known as the best venue in Chelsea for ball tag. The rules were FFA—"free for all." One boy took the ball—maybe a Nerf ball, but usually a fake-leather mini-soccer ball—and chased the others, trying to nail one so he would be "it." The game was some-times played at Jimmy's or Casey's houses, but Robert's house was the best by far. It had front and back staircases and lots of rooms with two entrances, making it easier for players to avoid getting trapped. The popular contests were often expanded beyond the core crew to include Kienan and other boys. The house, said one boy, was "just awesome," and Robert "had the greatest moves."

There was plenty of outdoor action too. "Mostly within the area, because we couldn't drive anywhere yet," said Jimmy. "We'd go swim-ming a lot. We tried building a couple of forts. Taking boats down the river, canoes during the floods. Taking sticks into the woods and kick-ing down trees and stuff like that."

The boys always seemed to have one fort or another going all through high school. Robert and Zack were juniors in the spring of 2000, when Zack told Robert and Jimmy about a new spot he'd found. It was across the footbridge behind Zack's house on Main Street, in the woods and up a hill, a hidden spot with a commanding view across the village and the valley. The boys went to work: they found four trees that formed a square and cleared out the brush between them. They chopped down four other trees and nailed them to the standing trees to form a support for a platform. Kip joined the construction crew, and the four boys took time to carve the initials of their first names into one of the four supports. The site wasn't on the Courtses' land, and the boys probably should have asked for permission before starting the fort, "but do before ask is one of those things fifteen- and sixteen-year-olds are real good at," said Zack.

It wasn't an easy spot to reach, up a hill that got steeper and steeper and included a final stretch that was a rock face. Robert and Jimmy seemed to like the last part best, said Zack, so much so that rock climbing would become Robert and Jimmy's passion. "Rock climbing is hard, a challenge," said Zack, "and if there's anyone who likes to take up a challenge it was Robert."

The boys had other big plans, like installing a zip line to a nearby tree that would run down a back hill. It would be a thrill ride. But they never got that far; indeed, like so many projects, they never finished the fort. Instead one hot day someone had a new idea—why don't we dam the small waterfall down a bit from the fort and make a sitting pool to cool off in? Soon enough the boys were dragging the logs used in the viewing platform down to the waterfall. It was hardly an uncommon outcome, the boys racing through one idea to another. "This is fun, but I have a better idea," said Zack about the pattern. "Like Legos, the pleasure was in the building, not playing with what you've built."

It was Huck and Tom in Chelsea—and a good thing, too, because one fact of life for Chelsea boys all through the ages was the need to find ways to cope with the peace and quiet of a rural place. Older Chelseans all knew this. Like Will Gilman, owner of Will's Store and son of the town's late historian, who "learned early, if you wanted to do things you had to learn to make them up yourself. You entertained yourself." This was the yin and yang of Chelsea—there was everything and nothing to do. The everything was mostly outdoors: the camping and hunting, the hiking, biking, and skiing, the high school sports and traditional town events, like winter carnival, born decades earlier to combat the isolation. But there was little of what teenagers everywhere consider to be "something." To see a movie, go to a mall or superstore, eat Chinese food, go bowling—all that required a road trip to places like Barre, Vermont, twenty miles north on back roads. Said Gilman, Chelsea "is a great place to live if you like to hike or camp or hunt or bike. For kids who crave more excitement, it's a tougher place."

Growing up in Chelsea required imagination—never more so than when Robert and Jimmy and their friends hit their teen years in the late 1990s. They had more free time on their hands than teens in Chelsea had ever known. "There's really not a whole lot to do," said Kip Battey. Robert and Jimmy decided they were lucky to at least have each other.

"We were both very adventurous," Jimmy said. "A great pair."

9

The Sheaths

For three days after the Zantops' bodies were found, investigators scoured the house for clues. They seized 105 items they thought might offer evidence, from door knobs to a key ring, a wine glass to Post-it notes. They took a calendar, a Rolodex, a cell phone, a business card to Valley Acupuncture Health Clinic, two torn ticket stubs to *Best in Show*, a regional telephone book, twelve volumes of a bloodsplattered German encyclopedia, an Apple laptop computer, an Apple desktop computer, and anything else that might lead them to the killers.

Under the supervision of state police Sergeant James White and Timothy Pifer, director of the New Hampshire State Police Forensic Laboratory, a team of five state troopers and four lab technicians combed the rugs for hair. They took swabbings of five drops of what appeared to be blood. They documented five partial or near-complete bloody bootprints. They identified nineteen partial or complete finger- and palm-prints.

The next day, medical examiner Dr. Thomas Gilson collected fingernail clippings from Half and Susanne's bodies to see if either had scratched the killer or killers. He and his assistants took the couple's finger- and palm-prints, plucked hairs from their heads, and drew samples of their blood, to distinguish between evidence left by the killers and the victims. Upon completing the autopsy, Gilson concluded Half died from "multiple stab wounds with injuries of airway, heart, and lung." Susanne's death resulted from "multiple stab wounds with injuries of skull, brain, major vessel, thyroid cartilage/airway, intestine, and spleen." On both death certificates, Gilson wrote that death occurred within "seconds, minutes." Under manner of death, Gilson wrote "04," the code for homicide.

Throughout their work, investigators and medical examiners kept detailed logs of who did what, who went in or out, who handled what evidence, and who stood guard. They photographed everything in triplicate and videotaped the scene. When they were finished, they called a locksmith to change the locks and an alarm company to re-code the security system, then hung "No Trespassing" signs and yellow crime-scene tape along the property line bordering Trescott Road.

For all the painstaking work, all the evidence labeled, diagrammed, and shipped out for testing, every one of the investigators knew that two items stood out from the rest: the knife sheaths. They weren't smoking guns in the hands of a killer, but they were close. They had held the murder weapons. They had been touched by whoever murdered the Zantops. The fact that there were two of them strongly suggested there was more than one killer. They also were unusual, not the run-of-the-mill sheaths that could be found in the hands of everyone from Boy Scouts to longshoremen. They were the glass slippers of the Zantop murders: search the countryside to find their rightful owners and the mystery would be solved.

Given the sheaths' importance, Major Barry Hunter of the New Hampshire State Police knew he needed to entrust them to a particularly dogged investigator, a cop who wouldn't give up no matter how frustrating the work became, no matter how many days, weeks, or months passed. A cop who would grind calmly ahead, inch by inch, without fanfare, ego, or complaint. The word "tenacious" kept coming to Hunter's mind. So did the name Chuck West.

Trooper West had become something of a legend almost four years earlier, in August 1997. He was working a routine narcotics case when his radio barked out two dreaded words: "Officer down." West pointed his car north, racing seventy miles to the scene. On the way, he picked up details of the danger he was rushing toward.

The crisis had begun earlier that afternoon, a mile outside Colebrook, New Hampshire, a town of 2,500 souls in the state's remote North Country. A trooper from West's barracks named Scott Phillips was on his way to get a haircut at a little place called Joanne's Added Attraction when he saw a rattletrap 1974 Dodge pickup driven by a local misanthrope, Carl Drega. Most people around Colebrook knew the sixty-two-year-old Drega, and most knew it was best to stay clear of him. A carpenter and mechanic, Drega stood more than six feet tall, weighed more than two hundred pounds, and went everywhere armed, even to the end of his driveway to get his mail. He had feuded with almost everyone who crossed his path, particularly with town officials over zoning and property issues. Drega's belief system boiled down to my land, my rules.

Phillips had tangled with Drega a few times, and the trooper had discussed Drega's broken-down pickup with fellow trooper Les Lord. Both thought it wasn't roadworthy, and they resolved to take action the next time either saw him driving around town. When Drega pulled into the lot at the IGA market, Phillips flipped on his flashing blue lights and followed him. Phillips was thirty-two, the father of two, a friendly family man who lived in Colebrook and had been assigned to protect the area since joining the state police seven years earlier. Knowing that Drega was trouble, Phillips radioed Lord for backup.

Drega braked to a stop and Phillips pulled up behind him. As Phillips began walking toward Drega's pickup, Drega got out holding a

Colt AR-15 assault rifle. Before Phillips could react, Drega began shooting. Phillips returned fire, emptying his gun without hitting Drega; one of Drega's shots had struck him in the hand, making it difficult to aim and impossible to reload. Wounded, Phillips stumbled toward tall grass at the edge of the parking lot, hoping to hide and, perhaps, draw Drega away from shoppers in nearby stores. Just then, Lord pulled into the lot and Drega turned toward the approaching cruiser. Lord, known as "Lucky," was forty-five, the father of two, a man with more than two decades of law enforcement behind him. Drega leveled his gun and began firing. A bullet passed through the passenger-side window, hitting Lord in the head and killing him instantly. Drega returned his attention to Phillips. He strode purposely to the field and executed the bleeding trooper.

With two dead troopers sprawled behind him, Drega knew he had nothing to lose. He went back to his pickup, but it wouldn't start, so he climbed into Phillips's cruiser and drove a short distance to a brick building that housed the local newspaper, the *News and Sentinel,* and the office of Vickie Bunnell, a local lawyer and part-time judge who had taken out a restraining order against Drega. The two had faced off repeatedly over the years, starting in 1991 when Bunnell was a selectwoman in nearby Columbia and she ordered Drega removed from a meeting in handcuffs when he threatened her during a zoning dispute. When Bunnell saw Drega drive up in the bullet-pocked cruiser, she ran through the halls screaming, "It's Drega! He's got a gun!"

Drega stalked the forty-four-year-old lawyer through the building and out to the parking lot, where he fatally shot her in the back. Newspaper editor Dennis Joos tried to wrest the gun away. "Mind your own fucking business," Drega was heard to say as he executed the fifty-one-year-old Joos with eight shots.

Drega drove the cruiser home, shaved off his beard, changed clothing, and grabbed more ammunition. On his way out, he poured gasoline on his front door and set it ablaze. He apparently wanted to kill more police and firefighters—he had rigged an explosive device to his front door—but no one took the bait. Elsewhere on his property, he had stored eighty-six sophisticated pipe bombs and four hundred pounds of high-grade ammonium nitrate—a fertilizer that when mixed with fuel oil creates the same explosive used in the bombing of the Oklahoma City federal building.

Drega then headed west, toward Vermont, with New Hampshire troopers and game wardens in pursuit. Drega kept firing during the chase, hitting warden Warren Saunders through the windshield of his truck. Saunders's shield, pinned over his heart, stopped a second bullet that might have been fatal. Drega drove to a deserted logging road, parked the cruiser, and turned the police radio to high volume so it would be found. He slid into Phillips's bulletproof vest and donned the slain trooper's Stetson hat. Drega then hid on a nearby hill, giving himself a clear line of fire to the cruiser.

A team of Vermont and New Hampshire state and local police officers, along with a group of U.S. Border Patrol agents and a police dog named Major, converged on the scene. By then Chuck West was among them. The dog spotted movement on the hill, and Drega sprung his ambush, critically wounding New Hampshire Trooper Jeff Caulder and Agent John Pfeifer of the Border Patrol, and shooting a third officer in the foot. West stepped into the line of fire and dragged Caulder to safety. Then West and two other officers tried to rescue Pfeifer. Drega opened fire again. A gun battle raged for forty-five minutes while Pfeifer bled. Saving him meant stopping Drega.

"I really don't want to do this," West said, knowing he would do it anyway.

"This is really going to sting," responded Border Patrol Agent Stephen Brooks, who joined West in the mission.

With Drega hiding behind a tree, West led Brooks up the hill. When Drega came into the open, ready to kill again, the lawmen fired. West delivered the deadly blow, hitting Drega with a shotgun blast that crushed his chest despite the bulletproof vest. West and Brooks then carried Pfeifer to a Jeep for transport to the hospital. Four people were dead and four more were wounded, but Drega's siege was over.

For his heroism, West was named the nation's 1998 Police Officer of the Year by the International Association of Chiefs of Police. When he accepted the award to a thunderous standing ovation from ten thousand police officials gathered in Salt Lake City, West deflected the credit, praising Brooks and honoring the fallen troopers.

West was relaxing at home when he got the call about the Zantops' deaths, and he immediately drove his unmarked blue Chevy Lumina to the scene. He was forty-three but looked years younger, a Pennsylvania native with a wife and two teenage sons. West had a wrestler's build yet carried himself lightly, with a thoughtful, bemused look that could be mistaken for docility. He joined the state police in 1984, after stints in the Air Force and as a member of the Hampton, New Hampshire, police force. Though he had risen to plainclothes detective, West was more from the school of Columbo than Kojak.

Most days, working alongside West on sheath detail was Detective Frank Moran, a thirty-five-year-old lieutenant from the Hanover Police Department. Moran was a thirteen-year veteran of the department, with jet-black hair and a wary demeanor. As they dug into the task, West and Moran learned that they faced good and bad news in roughly equal proportions.

The best news was that the sheaths were indeed unique and hadn't been around very long. They were designed to fit a knife called a SOG SEAL 2000, a commando weapon with a seven-inch, powder-gray blade and a five-inch, contoured black handle. The SEAL 2000 had been sold for five years by a Washington State company called SOG Specialty Knives. The company's name came from an elite and once-secret American military unit, the innocuously named Studies and Observation Group. During the Vietnam War, highly mobile SOG teams operated behind North Vietnamese lines to sabotage military installations, pinpoint targets for U.S. bombing missions, launch psychological warfare missions, and rescue U.S. pilots downed in enemy jungles. The company's line of SEAL knives—in addition to the 2000, there were the shorter Pup and the longer Tigershark models—were named for the Navy SEALS, whose own name derived from their ability to fight on "sea, air, or land." The SOG SEAL 2000 had been honored as the "official knife" of the Navy SEALS. It could only be considered a hunting knife if the intended prey were human.

Although the SEAL 2000 had been on the market for five years, the sheaths were more recent additions to the product line. Made of a composite hard plastic called Kydex, each sheath found at the Zantops' home bore a one-inch-square SOG logo stamped on the back, which company officials told West and Moran had only been added in March 2000. That narrowed the search considerably, to sheaths and knives sold during the previous ten months. Investigators thought they also might find clues in a dagger-shaped design carved onto one of the sheaths.

The bad news was that the SOG SEAL 2000 was an extremely popular knife, the company's best-selling blade, with buyers from all over the world. When Moran first made contact with the company two days after the killings, assistant marketing director Vicky Karshna estimated roughly five thousand were made each year. They could be purchased directly from the company, in retail stores, through catalogs, and over the Internet. Some were sold by SOG to wholesalers, who in turn resold them to dealers who were lower in the weapons food chain. West likened it to a spider's web with a potentially infinite number of branches. Worse still, neither the knives nor the sheaths had serial numbers, and, unlike firearms, no laws required sales to be recorded or reported. Some sales were in cash, some sales came at small-time weapons shows, and some sales led to seemingly impossible to trace resales on a vague and shadowy secondary market. None of that especially troubled West.

The sheaths, for all the hurdles, were a known quantity. "We take what we can get," he shrugged. He'd stay focused on a process of elimination, keeping his spirits up and his energy from flagging by reminding himself how important the sheaths were to solving the case.

Unbeknownst to West, he was following a trail that had been blazed seventy-seven years earlier, in a similarly high-profile case: the investigation of the mysterious death of a wealthy Chicago boy named Bobby Franks. A pair of round, horn-rimmed reading glasses was found with the body, and the police concluded they had been left behind by the killer. The frames and the prescription were common, but some deft sleuthing determined that an unusual, patented hinge connected the earpiece to the nosepiece. Only three had been sold in Chicago, and detectives tracked down each. One belonged to a woman considered a particularly unlikely suspect. A second pair was owned by a lawyer who was traveling in Europe at the time. The third was sold to a brilliant but odd young man named Nathan Leopold. He read widely in philosophy, and was a devotee of Friedrich Nietzsche. Leopold subscribed to Nietzsche's notion that laws didn't apply to "the supermen." In Leopold's eyes, that title squarely fit him and his best friend, Richard Loeb. The lost glasses were eventually Exhibit A in the 1924 murder trial that ended with the convictions of Leopold and Loeb.

For the first few days of their search, West and Moran cast around with little to guide them. They called some sport shops and together went to the Dartmouth Outing Club, the largest organization on campus, to learn if the club kept knives among its equipment. It didn't. Two days after the killings, SOG produced the names of several mail-order catalogs that carried the SEAL 2000, companies with names like Ranger Joe's and Smokey Mountain Knifeworks. A day later, the company provided a list of merchants in New Hampshire, Vermont, Maine, Connecticut, and New York. West and Moran immediately began the painstaking process of contacting the sellers one by one, to ask if they had sold any SOG SEAL 2000s with Kydex sheaths since March, if they kept records of buyers, and most of all, if anyone had purchased more than one.

A day later, at West's request, SOG added a list of Arizona retailers. It was far afield, but West knew what he was doing. While he and Moran were chasing sheaths, several dozen other investigators were conducting scores of interviews, fielding dozens of phone tips, collecting and comparing thousands of pieces of information, to see if any reached the point of critical mass. Some of the first clues pointed them toward Arizona.

During the first days after the murders, investigators swept through the halls of Dartmouth, serially interviewing faculty members in Half and Susanne's departments. Two state police detectives went to Fairchild Hall to meet with Half's teaching assistant, Tom Douglas. Douglas had already been interviewed once, two days earlier, by West and Moran. During that interview, Douglas offered nothing much other than his belief that Half was "anal" about planning the academic field trips he led students on in Mexico. Douglas talked about two students he considered "cutters," but he meant they cut classes, not people.

During his second interview, though, Douglas said he had been puzzling over what might have happened and had come up with a name of someone he thought might have had reason to kill the Zantops: a geology professor from Arizona State University named Stanley Williams.

In the small world of geologists, Stanley Williams was a big name with an ego to match. He was forty-eight and something of a celebrity because of an event that nearly killed him. In 1993, Williams was leading a group of fifteen scientists, engineers, and tourists to the crater at the summit of an active volcano called Galeras in southwestern Colombia. As they got ready to leave, the walls of the crater began to shake. The earth opened with a roar, yielding to the pressure of gases that had collected under the volcano's dome. White-hot rocks spewed out in a fusillade, along with a cannonade of red-hot boulders the size of dishwashers. Nine members of the party died. Two of them were vaporized. A fist-sized rock plowed into Williams's head, driving pieces of his skull deep into his brain. His jaw was broken, his right leg was nearly severed, and the bone of his left leg jutted through his pants. Two vertebrae were cracked and his back and arms were badly burned. Williams was carried down the volcano a changed man. Beyond his broken body, he was permanently brain-damaged—he lost a piece of his brain the size of a peach pit. He retained his lopsided grin but tended to erupt in anger. He was prone to depression.

Williams had received his master's degree and his Ph.D. at Dartmouth under his friend and earth sciences mentor, Dick Stoiber. The same Dick Stoiber who had brought the Zantops to Hanover and had become Half's close friend. On the day of the Zantop murders, Williams was in Hanover, having flown in from Arizona to attend Stoiber's ninetieth birthday party. The same party Half had planned to attend. Douglas told the detectives that Williams seemed agitated at the party, sniping at him for failing to arrive early to park cars. Five minutes later, Williams's mood shifted abruptly. He put his arm around Douglas and offered him a drink from a bottle of champagne. Douglas also told the detectives that Williams had made it known that he wanted to return to Dartmouth, and as Douglas saw it, the only job Williams was qualified to fill was already occupied—by Half Zantop. It also emerged that Half had been the thesis advisor to Williams's wife, Lynda, when she received a master's degree in 1984, and that Susanne Zantop had been in Arizona a few months earlier for a conference.

Douglas's report sent investigators into high gear. Within hours, they had tracked down the white Daewoo sedan Williams had rented during his stay in Hanover. A search of the car revealed a large cardboard box in the trunk, stained reddish-brown by an unknown "organic material." Investigators seized Williams's rental contracts and his $188.34 bill, a pair of sunglasses he had accidentally left behind, and the remnants of a McDonald's meal. They took statements from Thrifty Car Rental workers, who said Williams was rude. They twice searched the guest bedroom and bathroom in the home where Williams stayed with friends on his long weekend in Hanover. They scoured records of his purchases at the Dartmouth Co-op. They re-interviewed members of the earth sciences faculty and asked pointed questions about Williams.

The height of investigators' interest in Williams came a week after the murders, when Moran took a break from sheath duty to join Assistant Attorney General Mike Delaney and New Hampshire State Police Sergeant Russell Conte on a trip to Arizona. They took blood samples and fingerprints from Williams, and interviewed him and his wife. In a two-hour interview at the Phoenix Police Department, Williams walked the investigators through his career, how he bumped into Half at Dartmouth the day before the murders, and his movements the day Half and Susanne were killed.

Well into the interview, Conte asked Williams flat out: "Did you kill the Zantops? Did you kill Half? Did you kill Susanne?"

"No," Williams answered. "I can't even see how you could kill anybody."

Conte persisted: "Did you hire anybody to kill the Zantops?"

"No," Williams said.

"Were you part of a conspiracy . . . ?"

"No," Williams said again.

Williams remained in investigators' sights for almost two more weeks, but in the end, authorities found no evidence against him. One of the most potentially damning findings, the stained cardboard box in the trunk, turned out to be much ado about moose stew. While taking the North Country delicacy to a friend's house for a dinner two days after the Zantops' death, Williams had placed the stew pot in the box to avoid soiling the car.

In the meantime, however, Williams's name had leaked to the media. His wife—not knowing that Half Zantop's teaching assistant had pointed investigators toward Williams—blamed reporters for the fallout. "Because of a moose stew stain," Lynda Williams wrote in a caustic letter to the media, "you have slandered my husband's work, insinuated he was a suspect in murder, and accused me of having an affair with my advisor. Your stories have sickened us and caused heartache for our teenaged children. There is no excuse." Investigators never corrected her misimpression about how Williams became their focus.

Meanwhile, Stoiber died February 9, two weeks after the Zantops, of natural causes. He was never told of their deaths, and never knew that his protégé Williams had been a potential suspect.

10

Smarter Than Everybody

Robert had the idea first: Let's get my CD from Casey's house.

But they're away, one of the other boys pointed out.

So what? said Jim—to most, he was no longer Jimmy. He'd stick with Robert.

We go in, Robert riffed, we get the game, we leave.

The others went along. Rash? Maybe.

"We were looking for something to do," Jim said later.

Along with Robert and Jim were Zack Courts and Gaelen McKee, another Chelsea boy who sometimes hung out with The Crew. Even though Gaelen was only a freshman, while Jim was a sophomore and Robert and Zack were juniors, the boys thought Gaelen was cool. Zack and Gaelen had baseball practice and needed to get back for that. Even so, if they hurried they might have enough time to squeeze in some fun at Casey's house—a game of ball tag.

Robert, acting on impulse, had found a way to kill yet another weekday afternoon on a cold day in April 2000. It was the conclusion of another long winter—a time known as "mud season"—when the thaw and vanishing snow wreaked havoc on the miles of unpaved roads, rendering many impassable until the dirt hardened and the ravines created by streams of water were filled in. To entertain themselves this time of year, some Chelsea boys went "mudding," a back-road sport where they piled into a pickup truck and raced up and down the roads, bouncing around the craters and mounds, rocking and rolling inside the cab.

To entertain themselves, Robert and Jim came up with their own version of rocking and rolling, by deciding to head over to the Purcells' house.

Robert wanted his CD game back. By now, all the boys had computers. They had CD games, they surfed the Internet, and they "instant-messaged" one another. But it wasn't as if they could spend endless hours online. Most hookups were through a family's one telephone line, which meant tying up the phone to go online. No problem when parents weren't around, but a single line hampered unlimited use. Jim was the exception; his parents put in a second telephone line for Internet use in one of the two computers the family had set up in a second-floor hallway. John Parker used one for work and the other one was Jim's domain. But none of the boys had high-speed service; they all had the maddeningly slow dial-up connection. In short order, Jim chose the screen name jimibruce—a compound moniker based on one of his favorite musicians, Jimi Hendrix, and the name of a family pet. "The Parkers got a kitten, a really neat, totally black kitten, when Jim was in high school," explained Zack Courts. "Jim named it Bruce, even though it was a girl." Zack was calzone07, because he'd eaten his first calzone right around the time he needed to pick a name. Robert was light08. Zack wasn't sure how Robert came up with that, except that Robert had always liked the word and often used it as a name when he played games on the computer or on Nintendo 64.

At the Tulloch house, the computer had started out in Robert's bedroom. This gave Robert mastery, but it also caused friction. Kienan liked playing computer games, even more so than Robert. Robert would come home and find Kienan on his turf. "You've been on the computer for a long time," Robert would say. "Get out of my room." Another friction point was that Kienan liked to stay up late playing on the computer, while Robert liked to hit the sack early. The solution to the fraternal standoff came when they eventually agreed to move the computer into Kienan's bedroom.

To head over to the Purcells', the boys left Robert's house and piled into a champagne-colored Porsche owned by Zack's father. Zack was the wheel man, Robert rode shotgun, and Jim and Gaelen folded themselves into the tiny backseat. The boys followed their standard policy of "My car, my music." Zack favored the hard, raucous sound of two punk-pop groups from California—blink-182 and Green Day. Robert's taste was more diverse: disco, the Beatles, the Bee Gees, heavy metal. He liked Bela Fleck and The Flecktones. Jim, the musician, liked jazz and dismissed anything remotely considered pop. That meant pretty much everything Zack liked.

From Chelsea, the boys headed east on Route 113, driving the mile or so to a turnoff past Ward's Garage. The Purcells were renting a section of a larger house occupied by another family. The boys didn't want the other family to notice them, so Zack pulled over before they got there and parked out of sight. The four boys hiked to the house and tried the door. It was locked. They tried the other doors—all locked. "What should we do?" Jim said.

Not to be denied, they checked windows and found one was unlocked. Soon they were inside. Robert looked around and found his CD game. He also came across a movie on videocassette belonging to Casey, one he hadn't seen, so Robert picked that up, too. Now they had something to do later. The boys munched on chips and someone grabbed a bottle of sparkling cider. "Stupid stuff," said Zack. The world was their oyster. There was even time for a brief game of ball tag. Zack said, "We're done here," and Gaelen scribbled a note for the Purcells: "Ate Food. Thank You."

It would have ended there—and likely stayed a secret—except the family from the other side of the house returned and realized some boys were rambling around in the Purcells' house. Knowing the Purcells were away, they called the sheriff's office. Thinking they had gotten away unnoticed, Zack drove the Porsche back toward town on Route 113, right past the sheriff's office and the North Common. The boys were inside the car talking, listening to music. Zack actually drove right past the sheriff, who was idling in an unmarked pickup truck. The sheriff did a U-turn and began to follow Zack, who was oblivious.

In town the sheriff pulled the boys over. The three passengers were dismissed, while Zack, as the driver, was questioned at the sheriff's office. "I got the third-degree," he said later. He missed baseball practice, but no criminal charges resulted. "It seemed innocent to me," Casey's mother, Fran Purcell, said after being told about the boys' escapade in her house. Casey wasn't bothered about it at all. Eventually, Zack performed three hours of community service, shoveling snow off the basketball court across from the South Common and working in the school library. Robert, Jim, and Gaelen got off scot-free. Just another afternoon filling free time in their hometown.

Teen life in Chelsea could indeed be dull, and part of the problem was school. Robert, Kip Battey, and the other high-octane students from DeRoss Kellogg's sixth grade class had gotten such a jump acquiring the twenty-three credits needed for a diploma that a free-time crisis had developed. It was an unintended consequence, but real nonetheless. It was also totally out of sync with much of the rest of the country. In towns and suburbs throughout the United States the operative term for teenagers was "overbooked." Baby boomer parents worried their kids were frantic and stressed out: too much homework, too many sports, too many clubs and extracurricular activities, too many social demands. Parents had become chauffeurs in the 24-7 ride around town to get kids to the next appointment on time. The grown-ups might fret, but, like an addiction, they couldn't seem to kick the habit of what had become the rat race of growing up in America. It became the stuff of newspaper lifestyle articles, cultural studies, and books with names like *The*

Overscheduled Child, with experts proclaiming the overbooking of kids a national curse. By 2000, one community even tried to counter the trend by organizing a townwide time-out to focus on family and family quality time. The people of Wayzata, Minnesota, created Family Life 1st and set up a Web site, *www.familylife1st.org.* The next year, the affluent New Jersey suburb of Ridgewood picked up on the idea, dubbing the slow-down "Family Night."

Chelsea wasn't part of that world. The concern wasn't about finding ways to lighten the teen load or soften teen stress. Educators and parents instead found themselves coping with high schoolers who had too much free time. Elsewhere, an empty appointment book might be a red flag for a teenager who was adrift and maybe heading for trouble. But in Chelsea it generally signaled the opposite—success. The Chelsea student with free time was the student who'd accelerated and piled up graduation credits way in advance of senior year, a trend that began in earnest with Robert and his sixth grade classmates.

Having finished algebra in seventh grade, Robert, Kip, and the others took algebra II at the start of eighth grade. It was a class mostly filled with freshmen and sophomores, and taking the course meant juggling the youngsters' schedules. The high school had adopted block scheduling, an increasingly popular format for carving up the school day. Instead of taking five courses a semester, with each daily class lasting about forty-five minutes, students took three courses a semester, with each period lasting ninety minutes. Instead of taking an entire year to complete a course, it took just one semester.

This meant Robert and the others earned their second math credit halfway through eighth grade. "We got done with algebra II and we all did pretty well and so we took geometry," said Kip. Before entering high school, the group of fourteen-year-olds had three credits—fully satisfying the Chelsea school system's graduation requirement in mathematics. Robert also studied French in eighth grade, earning a fourth credit.

Freshman year Robert went into academic overdrive. Before regular classes met, he'd arrive early to take an advanced-placement course. Then he took three regular courses as well as a half-credit course during "S block," a shorter, forty-five-minute period that was also part of the day's infrastructure. He was on a pace to earn four or more credits a semester, or about nine for the year. "Robert kind of got ahead of being ahead," said Kip. By the end of his freshman year, Robert had stacked up about thirteen of the required twenty-three high school credits; this meant he had three years to obtain just ten more credits. He then continued a full course load his sophomore year. By junior year he could take just one course a semester and still end up with more than enough credits to graduate.

It was an early release program of sorts that was not at all what educators had intended. Explaining to parents the difference between the old, conventional, seven-period school day and the more progressive block schedule, school officials stressed that ninety-minute-long classes enabled students to probe more deeply into a particular subject. The new three-period school day would "allow teachers to do more projects, group work," and the "work is often more in-depth."

In theory, educators had hoped students motivated to get ahead on credits would develop new and broader academic interests to pursue during their last two years. The idea was to treat juniors and seniors as "adult learners," said principal Pat Davenport. Like college freshmen, they would have freedom and flexibility in choosing what to study. Educators believed this would help "bridge" high school and college life.

Reality, however, was different. The combination of the block schedule and the acceleration of a special group of students in DeRoss Kellogg's sixth grade class became the engine of a new student culture. Students began piling up credits early on in high school so they would only have to take a few, if any, courses later on. The new dynamic might have begun with Robert's group, but it did not stop there. Jim Parker and his classmates, and succeeding classes, got on a roll of entering high school with a healthy head start in the race to acquire credits.

"Freshman and sophomore year we just like loaded up with classes," Brad Johnson, Jim's classmate, said about the strategy he and his friends adopted. "You're going into senior year and, it's like, it seems like I should be done with school."

"I am done," Matt Butryman said about his status at the end of his junior year. "Like all my requirements are finished up this semester. Next year I could do nothing if I wanted to. Which I won't. My parents wouldn't let me." The credit count was on the minds of most Chelsea teenagers. "I'm going to have all my credits done by second semester," projected Sada Dumont, a sophomore, about her upcoming junior year.

"Don't tell the principal this!" joked Tyler Vermette, who also had accumulated almost enough credits to graduate by the end of junior year.

Starting with advanced students like Robert and Kip, upperclassmen began taking fewer courses. Many Chelsea teens spent less and less time in school. The culprit, inadvertently, had been the block schedule format—aiding and abetting the increasing amount of free time kids had in a school day. For just as block scheduling created ninety-minute chunks of class time, it also created ninety-minute chunks of down time for students with a free block. The Chelsea school day, beginning at 8:30 A.M., went like this:

A Block: 90 minutes
B Block: 90 minutes
LUNCH: 11:50 A.M. to 12:30 P.M.
S Block: 45 minutes
C Block: 90 minutes

The accelerated students like Robert, who began cutting back his coursework in junior year, would make cameo appearances. They might arrive late in the morning for a half-day of school, or they might come in the morning and leave for good around lunch time—depending on whether the course they needed was held during A Block or C Block. Even though the Chelsea school officially was a closed campus, meaning students were to be in the building during school hours and not roaming about, the advanced students, with parental permission, were allowed to sign out. In practice, the school seemed far more open than closed. Robert generally came and went as he pleased. It was particularly easy for Robert, because he lived within a short walk of the school.

Easy come, easy go was a privilege the go-getters had earned—a sign not of dropping out but rather of achievement. High school mostly became a patchwork of classes and hang-time at one or the other's house. The problem, Kip Battey said, was that the school seemed front-loaded. "They had everything all lined up for us for the first two years of high school," he said. "By the time you get to junior and senior year, it's almost like they're pushing you away. Because they're not giving you a whole lot of options."

It wasn't as if educators and parents were blind to the new kid culture that had taken root with little fanfare. Fine-tuning was attempted along the way. The total number of credits necessary to graduate was increased, from twenty-one in 1996 to twenty-three by 1999. Some new upper-level courses were added, depending on the availability of funds. But given the budget constraints in a town as tiny as Chelsea, this was a rare luxury. In fact, the high school's program of studies directly addressed this limitation: "Because it is difficult for a small school to offer a large variety of courses or sometimes for a student to fit a regularly scheduled course into his/her schedule, an independent study option is available. It is the student's responsibility to initiate independent study through the teacher involved." Finally, sensing younger students were rushing to pile up credits at the front end of high school, some of the courses Robert and his classmates had taken as freshmen were put off limits, with enrollment open only to juniors and seniors.

Parents also began to wonder, where was the accountability? "What should happen to a senior who has completed all of his or her requirements?" asked one. "Should he or she be cut loose and told to come back at graduation time?" Even some students in Robert and Jim's classes were uneasy about how kids worked the system.

"It gives you just way too much free time," said Matt Butryman.

The 1980s and early 1990s had seen a steady stream of newcomers to Chelsea, folks like the Parkers, the Savidges, the Courtses, the

Purcells, the Tullochs, and others. New parents and young couples who were looking for a country upbringing for their newborns or soon-to-be born, and the pastoral town indeed seemed like toddler heaven.

But as their kids grew up, the teen years became another challenge altogether. The hard part of being a teenager in Chelsea? Teen after teen answers the question with an eye-roll. "It's *so* quiet," said Sada Dumont. Not only were many kids finding out they had more free time during the school day; the age-old, small-town quiet embraced by parents was suffocating to teenagers eager to flex. Cora Brooks, with the eye of a poet, sometimes detected faraway looks shadowing the faces of teenagers she'd known from Halloweens past. To her, the teenage impulse to want to get out into the world was always stronger in towns as isolated and small as Chelsea—an appetite only whetted by the Internet surfing that allowed the kids to "be all over the world" online. Emerging from their virtual world, they'd confront Chelsea reality—a community where people tended not to have much money, where you needed a car to get anywhere.

"Coming into Chelsea is like going back in time," Brooks would say. "It's a town that doesn't easily satisfy the wanderlust to want to discover the world."

The crew of boys coming into puberty around 1997 did have each other, the heyday of their togetherness occurring the first half of high school, their freshman and sophomore years. They'd invented games like ball tag, for example, or threw themselves into volleyball, golf or, best of all, Ultimate Frisbee. The Crew began playing in ninth grade, in the spring when the snow melted, and became addicted. They played all through the summer and then into the fall, usually taking over center field on the baseball diamond next to the school. They'd play during the school day, starting a contest during a free period and going until school was over when some boys had to split for soccer or baseball practice. Picking teams became an art, because each boy developed different strengths. Coltere Savidge had the reputation for being a good catcher, but, said Zack, his throw was "kinda funky." Casey also had great hands, "whereas Jimmy had a really nice throw." Zack and Robert were known for their all-around game. "Robert could throw a real good Frisbee too," said Zack. Their interest grew beyond Chelsea, in large part because they tired of the same old lineup. "It always sucked just playing each other," said Zack. The boys talked at one point about forming a team and joining a regional league, but the idea, like others, didn't pan out, and their playing days waned by the time Robert and the others became juniors.

Robert, Jim, and The Crew also participated in the annual town and school events, which in a small community practically required maximum kid participation if the events were going to come off. During Winter Carnival 2000, Jim performed in skits that drew hearty applause, applying blackface and a big round nose to portray the Big Bad Wolf. When a photographer moved about the carnival taking pictures, Jim mugged for the camera, flashing his trademark grin and pointing his finger at the lens, Gotcha! "He captured you on stage," one Chelsea school administrator said about Jim's theatrics.

During the Spring Festival 2000, Robert and Jim teamed up for the raft race down the snowmelt-swollen First Branch of the White River. The event was more hokey than competitive; this was Chelsea, after all. "The raft race is not really a race," said Kip. "Kids build these abominable rafts you'd never think would even float." Kip's younger brother and some friends tried putting an inflatable couch on some planks. "Half the time they were in the water," said Kip. "That's the competition." Robert and Jim were more serious about the race than most. "They actually made something that could go fast," Kip said.

Bystanders could clearly see how the two teens had sprouted. Robert had always been physically ahead of most of his classmates, taller and lanky, and he now towered at six-foot-three. His arms pulling the paddle through the water displayed a strength more man than boy, though his long legs were more bone than muscle. His nose had come to dominate his face, making his eyes seem recessed and his expression dour, almost sullen. Long gone was his pre-teen girlish look; now his light-brown hair was cut short, with bangs plastered on his forehead from the river spray. Jim had grown with him, particularly during a big spurt his sophomore year. Instead of the rounded, cheeky look of elementary school, his face was strong and lean, and he was over six feet himself—an inch shorter than Robert. His dark-brown hair—which at times he dyed blond—was even shorter than Robert's.

The two young men raced down the river, in shorts, shirtless, their chests covered only by flotation vests. Robert was in front, a study in focus, eyes ahead, leading them faster and faster downstream. Jim was, as always, right behind him, his shoulder and bicep muscles bulging as he stroked under Robert's command. Together, they paddled their inflated-tire raft from a starting point behind Will's Store to the finish line behind the Shire Inn on Main Street. Their teamwork was unmatched—though others might scoff at the absence of real competitors, Robert and Jim met their goal: they finished first. Then, just for kicks, Robert being Robert and Jim being Jim, they capsized their winning raft and tumbled into the river.

In some ways, The Crew was a bunch of straight-arrows: the boys were uninterested in the partying commonplace to teenhood. Generations of Chelsea teens drank beer and smoked pot at parties in the woods. "I've never been to one," Coltere Savidge once said about the gatherings. "A lot of people do." Zack Courts was the same as Coltere—just not into drinking or smoking. He'd rather race a motorcycle. Kip Battey, Casey Purcell, Robert, and Jim—the party circuit never became central to The Crew's lifestyle. The common ground they did share with boys in America was girls. Dating was more an individual pursuit than a group exercise. Jim dated different girls for brief periods, while during high school Robert mainly went out with Christiana Usenza. The two, said Jim, "were always trying to get together." It was one area Robert wasn't chatty about with Jim. "I'm going to be stereotypical here for a second, but I don't think guys really talk about that as much as girls do," Jim said.

The Crew could also play the role of merry pranksters. Like the time around Winter Carnival 2000 when Zack, Robert, and Jim drove to Montpelier and, under the cover of darkness, scaled the Vermont State Capitol. It was as if they'd come up with a carnival event of their own. To get to the top, the boys scurried behind the building and

boosted one another atop a rear entrance. They shimmied across a narrow, steep-sloping roof, climbed to a second, flat level, and then
climbed up a final flat roof. They scampered around the gold dome to
the front and took in the commanding view of the large green, the surrounding state office buildings and businesses, and the dark snow-
covered mountains beyond. Lights flickered like stars. Robert and Jim
returned months later on their own with a couple of golf clubs.
"There's kind of a rubber divider in one of the roofs," Jim explained, "so
we tried sticking tees in there and hitting golf balls. But that didn't
work." The golf outing was a bust, but they didn't mind.

"The fun part is climbing up there," said Zack.

Country boys being country boys. Cheap thrills, testing limits, and
straddling boundary lines, sometimes crossing them. Robert, Jim,
Zack, and Gaelen McKee once stole some golf balls from a driving
range in the nearby town of Washington, and Gaelen was stopped for
speeding afterward. A month after getting in trouble for going into
Casey's house when no one was home, the boys were back doing
another home entry. To Robert, Jim, Zack, and Gaelen, going into the
empty house of twin sisters they knew from school felt different than
the Purcells' house. The boys had permission this time and figured it
was OK.

It was late in May, just after Jim turned sixteen on May 24, 2000.
Gaelen knew Tess and Ivy Mix best. He'd often been to their house
in Tunbridge, just south of Chelsea. The girls lived there with their
mother, Susan Dollenmaier, a successful businesswoman who sold
high-quality fabrics and home furnishings through her company,
Anichini. Her husband, Robin Mix, was a ponytailed glassblower
whose studio inside an early-nineteenth-century brick-and-clapboard
Federal-style home had been renovated by Jim's dad, John Parker. The
couple was separated.

The twins' house was spacious—and ideal for ball tag. "Just a sweet
house," said Zack. The girls were on vacation with their mother in
Jamaica and had told Gaelen he and the others could hang out in the

house. It was a no-brainer to the boys, even if using the empty house constituted an exception to a rural community's customs. "You don't walk into a house when nobody's home, but you can just walk in if they are home and talk and do whatever you want," a Chelsea teenager explained. But with the twins' permission, the boys piled into Zack's Porsche and headed to Tunbridge.

The house was unlocked, and the first thing the boys did was make the interior contest-ready. They rounded up fancy vases, some artwork, and breakable glass objects, and deposited them inside a first-floor bathroom. Then, let the games begin—and in the annals of ball tag this was something else, having such a roomy house all to themselves. For an hour or more they played hard and fast. They played to exhaustion, only to realize they'd worked up a raging appetite. Game over, why not cook up a meal, maybe even take in a movie? They started cooking noodles, and Zack got worried. "Dudes, I don't know," he said. But the others insisted all was cool: the eating, movies—the twins had okayed everything.

Robin Mix walked into the house to the smell of boiling macaroni and sauce. He and Susan had agreed he would check on the house while she and the twins were away. No one had told him about the boys and ball tag. The boys were in a downstairs room in the dark watching a movie. Gaelen went upstairs to talk to him. Gaelen was the group's best representative; he was the only one who knew Robin, and he was the one to whom the twins gave permission. Besides, said Zack, Gaelen was "as cool as the other side of a pillow." From downstairs, Robert, Jim, and Zack listened as Gaelen pleaded their case. They couldn't make out the back and forth, but they did hear Robin's final take:

"This is *not* cool."

It was time for the boys to leave. Robin asked if they were going to eat the food they had cooked.

"We better go," they said in unison.

Robin Mix considered notifying their parents, but then checked with Susan and learned the twins had okayed the visit. No need, then, to make an issue of it. Certainly no reason to notify police. Some of the boys later joked about the episode, referring to it as a "B&E," standing not for "breaking and entering" but for "breaking and eating." It was seen as the stuff of boys, harmless errors all around. Yet for someone like Zack Courts the B&E seemed more—a learning moment. "That was a pretty stupid thing to do," he said. For him it was a cautionary yellow light. His friends Robert and Jim brushed it off. To them, the B&E was practice for bigger and better things to come. It was more like green light: Go.

"These kids could be wild, but they were good," said one Chelsea father. To most, Robert at first seemed a fairly engaged high school student. At the start of his junior year in the fall of 1999, folks saw Robert trying to stir interest in turning an empty storefront into a teen center. The property was owned by Kip Battey's dad, and Christiana Usenza's mom had rented it to run Café Ole, a Tex-Mex concept that eventually failed. The storefront was along North Common, providing easy access for kids. Robert and Casey Purcell talked up the idea with the Friends of Chelsea School, a parent-teacher group. No one disliked the idea in theory, but no one ever worked out a deal. The center proposal fizzled. Then Robert and Casey surprised classmates and their teachers by prevailing in the school council election. The boys waged a colorful, spirited campaign featuring the giant plywood sign they'd painted and installed right at the school's entrance. Jim was swept along on their coattails, winning election as a sophomore class representative. Later that fall, Robert added to his lineup of new activities: he joined the school's debate team, run by local filmmaker John O'Brien, himself a former Chelsea debater when he was at the high school in the early 1980s, before he went off to Harvard. "Robert just came up to me and was all hot to debate," O'Brien said about his first meeting with Robert that fall.

Most of Robert's days were free, however, and in his few classes he and Jim were more saboteurs than scholars. "Making jokes and comments and disagreeing with the teacher," said Jim about their general classroom approach. The two boys liked taking courses together.

"Sometimes we would make fun of other students," Jim said. "Sometimes we would have pen-marking fights when the teacher was teaching, you know, we'd sit next to each other and try to get each other marked on our clothes." Or Jim would showcase his flair for theater with a dramatic reading. "One of the things that I would do, is, you know, they'd pass around something that you could read and I'd read it in a funny accent, or I would read it really fast or I'd read it really slow. I'd change the words or something." Friends said Jim reminded them of a rubber-faced comic actor with the same first name—Jim Carrey.

Aping Robert, Jim came to have a fairly high opinion of himself. Writing in the third person in a school paper, he said if he had to have a letter sewn or burnt on his chest it would be the letter I: "I for INCREDIBLE," he wrote, "because, really, honestly, he was just one Incredible Guy. An 'F' also might do, for FABULOUS. But walking around with a big branded 'F' on his chest might get some funny looks, because it could also stand for demeaning words. Such as Failure, Fraud, Froth, and worst of all, people might think his name was Frank or something, and that would just flat out suck! Any-who, 'I' for INCREDIBLE worked."

Teachers considered both boys bright, especially Robert, whose voracious reading habits always impressed. For example, during middle school he read his way through novelist Russell Banks's complete body of work. In high school, his appetite for the written word took him to reading Friedrich Nietzsche on his own. Of particular interest was the German philosopher's exploration of nihilism—the existential notions that God is dead, that no absolute moral values exist, and that life itself has no intrinsic meaning. "Every belief, every considering something true is necessarily false, because there is simply no true world," Nietzsche wrote in the 1880s in his notebooks. Nietsche also wrote: "He who fights with monsters might take care lest he thereby become a monster. And if you gaze for long into an abyss, the abyss gazes also into you." Robert was gazing into the abyss.

Robert was clearly the more academic of the two. He acknowledged in school being impressed with a number of historical figures, but only in terms of inflating his own self-image. He told one teacher he admired Thomas Jefferson as a genius, but then could not resist including the comment that Jefferson's intelligence paled in comparison to what he called his own "divine intellect." His teacher thought his hubris was amusing.

Papers Robert wrote were usually heavy on opinion, short on evidence, with a racy style. Robert was not afraid to say pretty much anything. In an outline for an essay about the United States' entry into World War II, he wrote, "War sucks. We should have stopped Germany earlier, but late is better than never. We should learn from our mistakes. America has a responsibility to the rest of the world. Isolationism is neglect."

He wrote with similar verve about Thomas Jefferson, Adolf Hitler, Dalton Trumbo's *Johnny Got His Gun,* Mark Twain's *Adventures of Huckleberry Finn,* and F. Scott Fitzgerald's *Great Gatsby.* Robert despised *Gatsby,* calling the novel "one of the worst books ever." He told his teacher, "The trauma I suffered due to that book will never be repaired." His commentary was slick and way over the top. Only after reading about the Jazz Age did Robert begin "to forget the burn marks I had subjected myself to, trying to take my mind off the pain of that terrible, terrible Gatsby book. It was terrible! I can not express how absolutely horrible that book was. I have never seen such an impossibly boring, and drudgingly narrated, piece of crap!"

Henry David Thoreau was another matter. "Thoreau rocks!" Robert wrote in a paper. "He was an intellectual god, his ideas I completely identify with (here is where I get to brag)." But admiration was filtered through his own prism. "We're two peas in a pod, him and I." Robert saw Thoreau as caring only about his own interests. "Society means nothing to him," he wrote, "only that it brainwashes others before they truly learn anything. Of course he is probably a bit smarter than me, just a bit (hehe)." In yet another paper, Robert weighed in on the value of studying the mind. "Psychology is the way to higher learning (you can quote me when I am famous)."

It was a philosophy Jim came to embrace. The two friends decided they were beyond the reach of society. They thought of themselves as

"Higher Beings." They found they practically thought the same thoughts—or at least that was how it seemed to Jim after he absorbed Robert's nihilistic view of life. Both, for example, decided school was useless and boring and that most teachers were idiots. Robert once wrote school was mostly about "human stupidity." Their peers were "little pinheads" who wasted time in classes with "idiotic readings and making worthless points." It was up to them, the two boys decided, to find their own purpose when faced with this "whole heap load of ignorance in the world." They had to find a way out of the life they'd known so far.

For all his literacy, however, Robert's grades were unremarkable, with a high school average of between B-minus and B. Even so, Jim bragged that he and Robert would sometimes pull off academic magic. "When we wanted to, we would make really good reports," he said. Jim was particularly impressed with his pal's approach. "He would write a lot of his school papers that morning or before class and then hand it in and get a pretty good grade."

Robert was the first to admit he was intentionally disruptive, writing as much in self-evaluations required by some of his teachers. "During lectures I tried to think of intelligent questions, and I tried very hard to make snappy comments at inappropriate times," he wrote about one class. The teacher wrote back, "Robert, I really do appreciate your humorous wit." But then she added, "P.S.: as a teacher, your snappy comments can sometimes be difficult." Generally speaking, Robert was quite pleased with himself. He was opinionated, self-assured, never tongue-tied, always a charmer. Evaluating his "responsibility" in one course, he wrote: "Well hey, I finished all my stuff, except one set of little notes, and that doesn't matter!" Evaluating his effort, he wrote: "I had tons of that!" Yet another teacher told Robert she knew it was hard for him "not to rant, but give it a try!" She further urged, "Don't forget that goal!!! (Try modesty, attempting to be humble, patience with others, open mindedness.)"

Midway through junior year it was no surprise Robert had little connection to school. In Chelsea's small world Robert and Jim had become part-time students. "Usually I didn't need to come to school," said Jim. "I think I only had one main class a day, which was chemistry, so I didn't have to go to school very long. . . . I could leave and me and Robert would like go to his house and eat or just talk or go rock climbing or something." Things were changing for them in Chelsea.

More and more it was just Robert and Jim. Once part of a crew made up of at least four other Chelsea boys—and often more—by June 2000 it was pretty much Robert and Jim on their own. The change was subtle, not the sort that registered much on the social Richter scale in Chelsea's teen world. The boys of The Crew were, after all, still good friends. There hadn't been any big falling out of long-lasting proportion. They still did stuff together—ball tag at the twins' house, for instance—if less so. It was more a natural selection: Zack, Coltere, Kip, and Casey were branching out.

Coltere and Kip had gone off and spent a semester boarding at the rigorous and prestigious Mountain School in Vershire. For four months the two Chelsea boys had roomed, studied, and worked on the school's organic farm with students from all over the world.

Zack had his passion for motorcycles. By the time he was fifteen, he and his dad had begun racing vintage sidecars together. By the time he was sixteen, his dad had bought him his first motorcycle. Father and son traveled to compete in races in Ontario, Nova Scotia, and Georgia. Mostly they'd head over to the New Hampshire International Speedway in Laconia. Zack brought Robert along a couple of times. Robert not only got to watch the races, but also saw that Zack and Tim Courts had a special father-son relationship. His own father, meanwhile, was more distant than ever. Mike Tulloch had discovered the fine art of making Windsor chairs; during the prior year he'd begun attending weeklong programs at the Windsor Institute in New Hampshire. The new activity that drew father and son further apart did bring father and daughter closer. Julie Tulloch had always liked hanging around Mike's shop, and once he mastered the chair-making skills, Mike overcame his shyness to conduct a presentation for his daughter's special education class. It proved to be a success for all involved. Enchanted by the experience, Mike even wrote an article for a chair-making periodical in which he described a Zenlike joy that came from connecting parts of his life into a single experience. He wrote, "It is funny how things that can deeply affect and even change your life come to you. Sometimes they are right in front of you, and you do not see them until the time is right. My association with Windsor chairs contained a level of enrichment for me, for my daughter, and her classmates that I had not imagined."

Casey, meanwhile, had for some time tasted the world beyond Chelsea in travels with his parents prior to their divorce. Not long after the student council election, he began a new romance, and was swept away with that. The Crew was not alone in enjoying these broader experiences. Anna Mulligan, Robert's intellectual peer since grade school, also attended the Mountain School during junior year, and was making plans to spend part of her senior year in Ghana. Then there were the twins, Tess and Ivy Mix, who seemed always to go on trips to exotic places, like Jamaica.

Though most of the other boys who made up The Crew were also ahead on school credits, they spent more time on school grounds than off. "I always went to school," said Zack. "It's just the way I am." In school the other boys were playing varsity sports—soccer, basketball, and baseball—while Robert and Jim were not. The demise of their group sport, Ultimate Frisbee, occurred in part because Robert and Jim weren't regularly in school, which is where games had begun.

The Crew was getting older. Needing spending money, some got jobs. Coltere and Zack worked that summer at the Vershire Riding School. They hauled garbage, fixed fences, and painted a house while listening to a radio station that played Vitamin C's song "Graduation" so often they heard it in their sleep. The two didn't much like the grunt work, but steady work was steady work. Robert and Jim only occasionally worked for John Parker. "Anything that didn't require skill," said Jim. But the work, admitted Jim, was never "a full-time job type of thing."

The other boys were finding ways to stay busy, Chelsea-style: sports, new schools, travel, and summer jobs. If Kip Battey hadn't spent winter semester at the Mountain School, he wasn't sure what he would have done with himself. "Probably what Robert did," Kip said, "which wasn't a whole lot." The Crew was peeling off in different directions, so much so that by the fall, the start of Robert's senior and Jim's junior year, Zack said, "This is a period when I can't vouch for their whereabouts."

Indeed, Robert wasn't even enrolled in school. Jim, meanwhile, encouraged by his parents, felt he'd maxed out Chelsea's musical offerings. "They don't have much of a music program," he explained. "There's kind of like an advanced music class and we just kind of go fart around and play what kind of music you can . . . but it's mostly younger kids, and lower level of playing too." Jim began commuting to Spaulding High School in Barre, which was known for its music programs. Always flip, Jim admitted the school switch wasn't solely about studying music: "There were more girls there."

Most of The Crew—Zack, Kip, Casey, and Coltere—had their sights set on college. Robert and Jim did not. Robert glibly offered up his who-needs-college spin and enjoyed pointing out famous college dropouts. "Bill Gates never graduated from college," he liked to say. Jim earlier had thought he might try a college-level outdoor guide program, but that idea had faded. College was stifling, not for a free spirit like him.

"I thought it was confining and held you back," he said, adopting Robert's view.

John and Joan Parker noticed the two boys were spending all their time together, and were comfortable with the ironclad friendship. "I actually liked Robert," said John Parker, finding his son's best friend to be a "conscientious" kid with "a sense of humor."

Diane and Mike Tulloch were not as sanguine. "Jimmy always would eat us out of house and home and I got tired of having him for dinner every night," said Diane. She eventually ended up complaining to Joan Parker. "I don't really like to confront people, so it took a while, a real long time before I told Joan, you know, 'Could you pick up your son before dinner?'" Robert argued with his mother about Jim, wanting to know what the big problem was if he hung out while the Tullochs ate supper. But Diane said, "I hate to have somebody in the house if we're going to eat and they're not going to eat." Moreover, there were times Robert and Jim wrestled nonstop, a quasi WWF smackdown, as they slammed one another around the house. Diane Tulloch would have to yell at them to either cut it out or Jim would have to leave. "They'd be rough sometimes and break things," she said. "It was a stressor always having Jimmy there." Mike Tulloch was even less generous about Jim. "I just never took a liking to Jimmy, on a personal level," he said. "I think it was a personality clash." He found Jim's behavior "over the top. Loud—he was usually, if he was in the house, you knew it." Robert knew full well his father's feelings about his best friend—a rare area of communication between father and son. "Whatever my feelings were about Jim were totally known to Robert," Mike Tulloch said. "Communication with teenagers can be a hard thing for anybody, but . . . that was one thing that Robert knew about." His parents' position had no impact on Robert; if anything, he was in their face with Jim as his best friend, as if the friendship itself was in part an act of rebellion. Mike made it clear to Robert that one characteristic of the deepening bond he disliked most was that Robert and Jim operated as such an "exclusive team."

But that's exactly what Robert and Jim had become. "At that point, me and Robert had gotten really close," said Jim. If anything, this was an understatement. The two mostly hung out alone together in Robert's room. Or they went rock climbing together. Or they used their new paintball guns in the woods—having, as Casey Purcell once said, "gotten wicked into paintball" that spring and summer. Or they drove around for hours on end. Jim, once he'd turned sixteen in May, had use of the silver Audi his sister Diana drove before she went to college in Chicago. The car was unreliable at best, often in the shop for repairs, but it was Jim's to use and use it he did. Tooling around in Vershire that spring he and Robert had come across an abandoned house. It was off Goose Green Road, on a road leading to the Vershire Riding School, not far from the closed Judgment Ridge ski area. The white-clapboard house with black shutters was low-slung, surrounded by acres of uncut high weeds. Above the front door hung a gold-painted wooden eagle. Inside the boys found broken windows and a wide-plank wood floor that tilted and rocked underfoot. Doors hung at odd angles off their hinges. Dust coated a beat-up couch, an armchair, and the old rugs lying about. Brown wallpaper peeled off the first-floor walls. Empty beer bottles littered the attic, along with a Mitch Miller album and a few paperback books, including *Crime Without Punishment* by John McClellan, published in 1962. The house was a complete dump, but the boys staked their claim. Forget the failed teen center in Ned Battey's storefront on North Common; this was better, their own clubhouse and theirs alone.

"We tried to make it look nice," said Jim.

They were inseparable. Drive and talk, climb and talk, and talk some more. The two increasingly parroted one another's ideas. "We were always thinking all the time," Jim said. "Like too much thinking." Whether the subject matter was college or Chelsea, it didn't matter. The conclusion was always the same: it wasn't good enough for intellectual giants like them. Sometimes their shared ideas got weird. For instance, after much discussion, they concluded Hitler was "very cunning" and for that alone, they decided simplistically, Hitler should be admired.

"Sounds like he was not a very good guy," Jim said, "but I mean we agreed that he was a pretty smart guy and was really good at manipulating people, and we had a certain amount of respect of him for that. But there was nothing against the Jews."

Together they were developing a knack for turnings things inside out. The other boys, they decided, weren't leaving them behind with college, motorcycle racing, girlfriends, or jobs. In the world according to Robert and Jim, *they* were leaving The Crew. "We started excluding people a lot more," Jim said. The Crew, it turned out, was no longer up to snuff. "Because they just weren't much to talk to. We considered them really immature or below our level." Robert and Jim were sounding like the worker about to be fired who tells the boss, You can't fire me, I quit.

It wasn't just The Crew, either. The rest of Chelsea was suddenly beneath them. "We were smarter than everybody else," Jim said. "People didn't see things the way that we did. We thought, you know, what everybody was doing was silly. Like going to school and like wasting half your life with education that you're not going to even use." Even though he'd always liked his parents and felt their support, Jim was growing impatient with his mother's "incessant worrying," once writing that he was hoping he could "endure it for just a little longer."

The partners were determined to devise their own itinerary. "We basically just wanted to get out of Chelsea and start something else on our own." They had gotten into their discontented heads the inflated notion they were something special and, working together, they would come up with an escape plan.

Kip Battey and Coltere Savidge could go off to the Mountain School, Zack Courts on his racing trips with his dad. Robert and Jim, creative geniuses that they were, would find a different way out.

Different destinations altogether. First, though, they needed some money.

11

Dead Ends and College Dumpsters

Day after day, Detective Chuck West plugged away at the list of knife dealers. To speed his search, he obtained a subpoena requiring SOG Specialty Knives to produce a list of all sales accounts, worldwide. While waiting for that list, West focused on nearby knife shops, going down his list of dealers one by one—Peregrine Outfitters, the Edge Company, Burton Snowboard, The Fly Rod Shop, Trapper John's Knives and Swords. There were some tantalizing possibilities that would require follow-up, but nothing approaching a clean hit.

West also focused on Internet knife dealers. First, though, he had to familiarize himself with the World Wide Web. More comfortable outdoors than in front of a computer, West had only tried going online a month earlier. West's boss, Major Hunter, said dryly: "His assignment wasn't necessarily based on his computer expertise." West turned himself into a Web surfer, breezing through sites including Absolute

Knives, Knife Outlet, Knives Express, Knife Center of the Internet, Chesapeake Knife and Tool, and Merlo's Cutlery. Again there were some possibilities. Knives Express had sold two SEAL 2000s to a person in Madison, Connecticut, a week apart in July 2000. West added it to his growing list. Another Web knife dealer, Shoptimax, had sold two SEAL 2000s to someone in Canada less than four weeks before the murders. "Investigation continues," West wrote at the bottom of the Shoptimax report. The Wholesale Hunter sold two to a Missouri business, and two more to someone in Arkansas. The list grew longer. Some of the companies West contacted refused to cooperate without a subpoena, so West obliged by getting one.

On February 12, SOG produced a somewhat narrowed-down list of the individuals, companies, distributors, military accounts, and foreign accounts where it shipped SEAL 2000s. It was a sixty-nine-page report, with 297 separate listings, accounting for 4,929 knives. West had been working on the case for seventeen days, and the task seemed to keep growing larger rather than smaller.

To stay focused and relieve the tedium, West leafed through the SOG accounts like a salesman looking for hot prospects.

As days passed without a solution to the case, police found themselves plowing through a blizzard of suggestions and potential suspects that arrived via letters, phone calls, e-mails, and face-to-face interviews. The tips ranged from tantalizing to bizarre, with every category in between. And yet, given the lack of leads, a surprising number were deemed worthy of follow-up.

There were foreign-intrigue tipsters: "It is possible that the Zantops (especially Susanne, given her anti-colonialist, anti-imperialist, and feminist attitudes) got involved in some way with the 'Shining Path' PERU guerilla/terrorist organization," one e-mailer wrote to Hanover Police. "It is my considered opinion that this link deserves to be looked into by your investigation team, especially your FBI backup unit, Interpol, and possibly even the CIA."

Holocaust tipsters: "I found it interesting that Professor Zantop was killed on the European anniversary of Holocaust Remembrance Day, and that her work was given as a reading assignment on the Holocaust."

Simplistic tipsters: "Have you investigated the students that could have ties to the teacher, maybe an angry student?"

Racist tipsters: "There is a bigger problem here in the Upper Valley than a few people can handle. . . . We have Chinese around, too many. This has come to my attention recently."

Geographic tipsters: "The Appalachian Trail crosses Trescott Street within roughly a quarter mile of the Zantops' house. It is my belief that this intersection is not a coincidence, and that the murderer was traveling on the Appalachian Trail."

Conspiracy tipsters: "The recent campus murder was plotted and committed by none other than our government, the FBI, for George W. Bush, the payback kid, and his father, George P. Bush [sic]. The murderers of Professors Half Zantop and Susanne Zantop are the same group who murdered John Kennedy Jr., his wife and sister-in-law, Missouri governor Mel Carnahan, Congressman Julian Dixon, and many other people too numerous to name at this time."

Then there were the self-proclaimed psychics. One promised that the date of the Zantops' deaths could be realigned to reveal the killers' dates of birth. Or, if that didn't work, answers could be found in events in Germany in 1944. Another said the killer had used an insanity defense when charged with a previous crime. Some psychics saw a knife, one saw a dog, and—with police withholding news of the two sheaths—nearly all thought the killer acted alone. One said the Zantops had contacted her from beyond, and that they wanted their daughters to know they were in a good place and ready to "go into the light."

Mark Mudgett, a New Hampshire State Police sergeant who supervised the investigation, pored over each of the tips, deciding which to follow and which to file.

Police also collected Half and Susanne sightings. One woman told police she saw Half driving quickly out of the Mascoma Bank in Norwich, Vermont, a day before his death. Later that day, a different tipster said, Half inquired about romaine lettuce in the produce department of the Market Basket supermarket in Claremont. Another thought he saw the Zantops at the Ramada Inn in Lewiston, Maine, at 10 that night. A different tipster placed the Zantops at a restaurant called Molly's Balloon, eating lunch with a younger couple on the day of the murders. Most sightings proved wrong.

Some of the tips were little more than poignant memories. A student of Half's named Jennifer Flight told a state police sergeant that a month before the killings, three days before Christmas, Half had come to the jewelry store where she worked to have a diamond set in a pendant for Susanne. While there, he bought Susanne a pair of diamond earrings. Time and again, police heard about the Zantops' quiet acts of generosity, about how much the two loved each other, and how much they were loved by others.

One tip, though, struck investigators as especially intriguing. Paul Newcity, a contractor from Canaan, New Hampshire, swore that he saw a green Volvo station wagon speed out of the Zantops' driveway the afternoon before the murders. The car pulled out so fast it nearly hit the car Newcity was riding in, driven by his friend Jason Gilmore.

"You rich asshole!" Newcity had screamed as Gilmore swerved to avoid a crash. The forty-year-old Newcity told police the car's driver was white, male, thin, twenty to twenty-five, clean shaven, with dark hair. He had a look that made Newcity think "punk." Newcity only saw the car for an instant, but he thought it was a Volvo because of its rounded front end. That was a style the formerly boxy cars had adopted in recent years, which, it so happened, gave them a certain resemblance to some Subaru models. But Newcity said Volvo, and his account sent Hanover Detective Eric Bates on a lengthy search for every green Volvo around town.

Beyond the tips, investigators fattened the Zantop homicide file with hundreds of interviews, tracking down everyone from the Zantops' large circle of friends and colleagues to their mail carrier, cleaning woman, driveway snowplow driver, UPS delivery man, and the students who received the lowest grades in their classes. They canvassed the neighborhood, dove through Dartmouth Dumpsters and came up smelling like Ivy League garbage, tracked down Mariana Zantop's high school boyfriend, set up roadblocks to interview drivers on Trescott Road, and chased down reports of abandoned suitcases at the Manchester, New Hampshire, airport. They collected boxes of potential evidence, filled out reams of forms. They ordered scores of forensics tests on items including a blood- and grime-stained shirt found in the trash behind the Doug's Sunoco station and a bloody five-dollar bill passed at the Colonial Deli Mart.

The work yielded thousands of potential clues—and thousands of dead ends—as well as a handful of potential suspects. There was a Dartmouth junior from the Bronx, Pedro de los Santos, who had the bad luck of having what witnesses described as a "tense" conversation with Half in Spanish the day before the murders. A second strike against de los Santos was a scrape on the side of his face, accompanied by a bruise on his forehead. Investigators tried for a week, but couldn't find a third strike against him. Another potential suspect who quickly fell by the wayside was a Dartmouth basketball player named Jay Jenckes, a former student of Half's whose sometime girlfriend was disturbed by flippant comments Jenckes made about the Zantops' deaths. Two factors in Jenckes's favor were his enormous feet: He wore a size 20, far too large to have left the bloody footprints at the Zantop home.

Indeed, while cataloging tips and culling the list of suspects, police were poring over early reports from forensics testing. One of the most useful discoveries was that two of the bloody footprints at the scene matched a boot made by a company called Vasque Footwear. Specifically, it came from a boot with what Vasque called its Alpha outsole, and it appeared to have been from the left boot of a men's size 11 or 11½.

On February 14, eighteen days after the murders, Chuck West was fifty-six pages into the SOG sales report when something caught his eye. A Massachusetts company called Fox Firearms had bought 124

SEAL 2000 knives, a number that dwarfed the orders placed by nearly all other dealers.

West called the Massachusetts State Police for an assist, and received a callback at 4 P.M. from Detective Scott Berna. West asked Berna to interview James Fox, who ran Fox Firearms out of his home in the shoreline town of Scituate, Massachusetts, a half-hour south of Boston. Berna set immediately to work, calling Fox to set up a five o'clock meeting that night.

Fox was happy to cooperate, telling Berna that he had received his SEAL 2000s in June 2000, and had already sold eighty-four, all via the Internet. Fox printed out a computerized list of his customers, which Berna faxed to West along with a report on the interview.

The next morning, February 15, West looked over Berna's reports. Fox had sold the eighty-four knives to eighty-three customers; one person had bought two SEAL 2000s. The details of that purchase intrigued West almost enough to get him excited: there was proximity to the Zantop murders in terms of both timing and location. The buyer had ordered the knives less than four weeks before the killings, and he lived just thirty miles from Hanover, in Chelsea, Vermont. His name was Jim Parker, and he went by the computer screen name jimibruce.

West called Fox to see what else he could learn. Fox didn't know much, but he was pretty sure he still had the e-mails from Parker arranging the sale. While Fox searched for the e-mails, West began making calls, spreading news of the find and ordering a criminal background check on Parker. Two other troopers, Sergeant Robert Bruno and Trooper Russell Hubbard, drove to Chelsea to check out Parker's house. They found no one home, so they waited there. Late that afternoon, Fox faxed West printouts of the e-mails.

"I would like to purchase 2 of your seal 2000 knives," read the first, dated January 1. Jim, using the e-mail address *jimibruce@hotmail.com,* offered $180 for the pair, plus shipping and handling. He signed off, "thank you, Jim." By the next day, the deal was set, and Jim sent another e-mail requesting two-day shipping to his address: 10 Bradshaw Crossroads, Chelsea, Vermont 05038.

Five days later, on January 7, he sent Fox a third e-mail: "could you notify me when you receive the money order and when you send out the knives? thank you. Jim." Four days later, January 11, came a fourth and final e-mail, with impatience seeping into the tone: "i would like to know if you have received the money order yet, and if you have sent the knives. i sent the money order last week thursday. thanks. Jim."

West looked over the e-mails and began worrying about his fellow troopers, Bruno and Hubbard. This was a brutal double homicide, apparently committed by two people. Who knows what they might find, what trouble they might face. West grabbed his coat. He was going to Chelsea.

12

You're Just
a German

While their friends were thinking about college, Robert and Jim turned inward and toward each other. They devoted Y2K to reinventing themselves, each serving as the other's Dr. Frankenstein, working the other's clay. The plots they concocted and refined to escape Chelsea may have, at first, seemed like the fantastic, bizarre brainstorms of a couple of frustrated teens trapped by their stations in life. For someone like Jim the crazy ideas about cross-country flight and discovering immortality probably felt like good theater. He was, after all, the erstwhile Third Chinese Brother whose legs stretched magically in a fourth grade skit that won him the attention he always craved. For him, the role-playing would take him out of himself and Chelsea, and the changing storylines became rehearsals in a made-up drama that passed the time with a snap, crackle, and pop. Jim was the willing actor, and Robert was the director pushing to turn fiction into reality.

Family and friends, even in tiny Chelsea, mostly missed the pitch-black shadow making its way across the boys' souls. One reason was that Robert and Jim were so good at hiding what they did, for the most part keeping their internal journey a secret. Then there was the inti-macy of a small place like Chelsea; its zoom lens may have actually worked against detecting the boys' descent. Just as it often takes a vis-iting aunt to recognize what a parent has overlooked—a sudden growth spurt in one of the kids—the town's familiarity with Robert and Jim may have hindered notice that the boys were vanishing before their eyes.

Even so, the boys had their public moments. Taken alone, none may have been cause for a five-alarm fire response. But in hindsight, the public outbursts clearly indicated trouble. Particularly for Robert: In March 2000, two back-to-back public humiliations fueled his smol-dering anger and propelled his spiraling disaffection.

Robert was apoplectic that day in March when he plunked himself down in one of the chairs around the conference table in Pat Davenport's office. The school principal's quarters were windowless and claustrophobic. Besides Robert, seated at the table were Davenport, guidance counselor Steve Kamen, and students Ellen Knudsen, Lucy Johnson, and Casey Purcell, a member of The Crew and Robert's old pal.

Old pal? Hardly, figured Robert. He was pissed at all three stu-dents, but especially Casey. VOTE FOR ROBERT & CASE read the cam-paign sign he and Casey had used in pulling off their upset in the fall to become student council president and vice president.

Now Casey had joined the two girls in a bid to oust him from his presidency. There already was bad blood between Robert and Ellen; in winning office, Robert had defeated Ellen, the odds-on favorite. She was a serious student, bound for Middlebury College, who'd been on the council since seventh grade. Losing hadn't come easy for her, and Robert wasn't surprised by her role in a coup d'état. But Casey?

Fed up with his leadership style—actually, a lack of leadership—the other three students on the council's Executive Committee had decided to impeach Robert. Later on, some teachers speculated that the students' choice of such an unusual remedy was influenced by national affairs: the impeachment of President Bill Clinton. Whatever the move's origin, nothing like this had ever happened at Chelsea Public School. Once the idea got around, a few teachers chose to view it as democracy in action. But Robert was not one to appreciate its educational value, not when he was the target.

To him, this was mutiny at school.

Davenport summoned the key parties to her office to air it out. The tiny room was filled with contained rage. How dare they challenge him, was Robert's attitude. He was the victim of a gross injustice. Casey and the girls—they were the enemy. It was him against the world.

But the truth was, Robert shouldn't have been surprised by their disenchantment. Sure, he'd taken the election in the fall seriously and worked tirelessly. "He went for it," said Davenport. No half measures, she said, but total commitment. "He even began to dress the part." He might as well have been Chelsea's version of Robert Redford starring in *The Candidate*. Robert climbed into the one sports jacket he owned, added a stringy tie, and then hit the campaign trail. He worked the school hallways, schmoozing and charming student voters.

"He really got into it," said Zack Courts. "He'd go up to someone, and like a pol be real flattering to the person and say just the right thing, as if it were scripted by some Hollywood comedy writer. Something like, 'Hey, you look great!' Stuff like that. And he'd blab and flatter them and then say, 'Vote for me and Casey!'"

It worked. Robert conned his way into office. But his closest friends—The Crew—knew Robert's involvement was more style than substance. Jim, who that same fall was elected as the sophomore class representative, knew Robert just wanted to prove a point: that he was great. The whole campaign, Jim said later, was at best tongue-in-cheek. "Kind of a mockery of the system, I guess." Robert was not so much interested in governance as he was in looking for a stage to strut his stuff, show off, and win what he felt he was entitled to. Robert and his running mate may have run a hard, competitive campaign, and they really wanted to win, but, said Zack, it was basically "a joke to him and Casey."

When the time came for the council's real and often mundane work, Robert was mostly missing in action. "The win went to his head, I guess you could say," Zack said. Robert was at best an indifferent and half-hearted leader. He'd be bored one moment, imperious the next, and often played to his principal audience, Jim. "They were rude," said Matt Butryman, another council member. The moment something didn't go Robert's way, he recalled, Robert would "blow it off completely." During plenary meetings for Winter Carnival, for example, Robert lobbied to include Hacky Sack as an event. "He wanted that in, but no one else did," said Matt. "So he said things like, OK, let's stop, the meeting is over, we're done."

The council sputtered. "Things never got started," one teacher said later. "There were starts and stops and it was not a productive year." Said Zack, "To be honest it would've been better if Ellen was student council president. She was more responsible." By March the council was barely meeting, and then one day Robert, who'd missed a few days with the flu, returned to school and walked into an impeachment ambush.

In front of Davenport, both sides went at it. Robert, seething, told Casey that as vice president he could have conducted meetings in his absence. He spoke in a cutting, low tone. He took apart Ellen at one point, a performance that surprised some present because dressing down the poised and intelligent Ellen Knudsen was no easy undertaking. The other three came back with their own list of grievances—how Robert had let them down, had let the school down, by his indifference. He'd dropped the ball, they said, was unprepared and uninspired. He didn't seem to care. Time to go.

Even Robert's best friend knew the others were right. Robert didn't care what happened with the council. The thrill of winning soon wore off. Jim knew Robert's private attitude was, "This kind of sucks. I don't want to do this anymore." But facing impeachment, Robert went ballistic—mainly because the surprise action was not on his terms. It was OK if Robert chose to mock the council as idiotic and pointless, but the council had no right to hold him accountable; after all, he considered himself above reproach.

In Davenport's office, surrounded by his accusers, Robert refused to take any responsibility for the floundering council. Instead he counterattacked: the others had waged a cowardly coup. Robert staked out a position as the victim of a horrible injustice. The face-off concluded after an hour with bruised feelings all around, and afterward principal Davenport ruled against an impeachment as being unnecessarily punitive and excessive.

Word of the meeting got around school, but no one seemed to know exactly what had happened. Robert, saving face and twisting facts to his advantage, gave Jim the false impression that he had quit the council. Davenport later said that wasn't the case. Either way, the council never got back on track that year.

Further detaching himself from school, Robert put up a front, acting as if he didn't care. But friends like Jim and Zack knew otherwise. Robert was incensed at the school and the council. "Sure he was hurt by this," said Zack. "He got the most votes and then they want to impeach him? That sucks." For Robert, another cord was cut.

This was Robert's arc: strong start, lousy finish, and afterward no one better point the finger of blame at him. His council presidency certainly fit this pattern, and unfolding on a parallel track at exactly the same time was an even fuller display of Robert's modus operandi. It centered on his brief, unhappy life as a high school debater.

October in Chelsea was the time of year when the debate team was assembled. It was one of fewer than a dozen high schools in Vermont that had any sort of debate program. Vermont, or New England for that matter, is not a debate hotbed. That label belongs to the Midwest and the South, where large and intensely competitive leagues devote themselves to making annual pilgrimages to state, regional, and national tournaments. In Vermont the tradition was different—committed, to be sure, but low-key.

Given the small size of Chelsea, every October was a recruiting challenge, a small-scale hustle to coax enough students to sign up for the team. Tryouts? Not a chance in Chelsea. Organizers scooped up any kid who showed an inkling of interest.

The fall of 1999, Robert's junior year, was no different for the two grown-ups in charge of debate—Marilyn Childs, the school's veteran forensics coach, and John O'Brien. If anything, rounding up debaters had gotten tougher since O'Brien's high school days—thanks to the changing school culture of accelerated course work and block scheduling. Many juniors and seniors, having piled up their academic credits, weren't around the school much. Unable to depend on them, O'Brien had learned to focus his energy on persuading freshmen and sophomores to take a run at joining the novice debate squad.

O'Brien was naturally quite pleased, then, when Childs brought up the name of a junior during a preliminary meeting one October afternoon. "This boy Robert is interested in debate," Childs told the young debate coach. O'Brien had no idea whom she meant, but a few days later the coach met Robert Tulloch. "He seemed bright and enthusiastic, and anyone like that I was looking forward to working with," said O'Brien. The nature of Chelsea debate, however, would play right into Robert's hands. The cajoling and permissiveness required to field a squad and then maintain its viability throughout a season worked, in effect, to shift the balance of power from coach to student debater. The casual atmosphere became an ideal stage for Robert's oversized sense of himself; for him, debate became a license to kill, verbally. Soon enough, Coach O'Brien learned that Robert didn't come alone but as a package deal. With Jim.

O'Brien's personality seemed a good fit for the circumstances. In his late thirties, with curly hair, a boyish face, and easy smile that made him seem closer in age to Robert than to the veteran teachers in the school system, O'Brien was what in sports would be called a player's coach. Professionally he was also enjoying the afterglow of critical acclaim for a film he'd made about a seventy-seven-year-old Vermont farmer who ran for Congress. The film, *A Man with a Plan,* was a mix of fact and fiction, the story of Fred Tuttle as political neophyte taking on entrenched political power and money. The little guy wins. O'Brien, Tuttle, and the film ended up featured on the front page of the *New York Times,* an article that compared Fred's sudden stardom to Vermont's two established celebrities, "ice cream kings" Ben and Jerry. The film and feel-good story were also written about in *Life* magazine and received a full-page write-up in *Time* magazine. Fred became the focus of an adoring *New Yorker* cartoon.

Preparing for the 2000 season, O'Brien wasn't sure exactly why Robert Tulloch had surfaced. It might have been because one of Robert's friends, Kip Battey, had already joined the team. Whatever the reason, O'Brien was happy to have the junior turn up, especially because the coach was quickly impressed by Robert's confidence and bravado. Debate, said O'Brien, was not for shrinking violets. "Debate's a bit intimidating, but Robert didn't seem intimidated at all by it." Robert clearly seemed eager to take the center stage. "It helps if you are sort of cocky," the coach said.

O'Brien began meeting weekly with his young debaters after school, usually in the school library. In high school debate, a topic is chosen each year by the National Forensics League. The so-called resolution becomes the centerpiece of every high school tournament in the United States. During a debate, one team argued the affirmative and the other side the negative. The affirmative side outlined a specific plan that would fulfill the resolution's goal. The negative side then attacked the plan as unworkable, drawing on any evidence it could muster that the affirmative's plan was ill-conceived. Despite what non-debaters might think, a debate wasn't a contest in which one team sought to win over the other team or the judges to its side; rather, it was about the logic and reasoned attack one side launched to expose weaknesses and flaws in the other's position. In this way, the contest was less about the content of a particular plan than about the logic and evidence used in supporting or attacking it.

The topic chosen for the 2000 season was about federal efforts to improve academic performance in high schools: "Resolved: That the federal government should establish an education policy to significantly increase academic achievement in secondary schools in the United States."

For most teams, preparation meant devoting weeks to researching the issue, using the Internet, libraries, or both. Student debaters would have two goals in mind. First, they wanted to come up with an "affirmative plan" about how to upgrade high school education. Second, they wanted to figure out how to rebut the plans opposing teams devised. Teams often created evidentiary files, filling out index cards with data, and they'd arrive at a tournament lugging the material in boxes called "tubs" or "oxes."

Not so the Chelsea squad, which had more the feel of a club than a hard-driving team. But that was OK; the laid-back coach's expectations were modest. He was glad to have another team going, however ragtag. The weekly meetings became more like bull sessions than research grinds. The debaters would discuss generally the ideas opposing teams might concoct to improve secondary education, and O'Brien would outline tactics to attack those plans during a competition. In Chelsea there was no deep research.

In fact, best illustrating the softness of the Chelsea program was the fact that the coach—not the debaters—came up with the idea Chelsea would use as its affirmative argument. It was a fanciful claim that students' academic performance would improve with better classroom lighting. And not only did O'Brien come up with the novel idea, he even wrote the text for the students to read during a debate.

This suited Robert fine; he made it clear to O'Brien and the others on the team that he wasn't interested in real work. "Robert never really would do any research," the coach said. "He wasn't a hard worker." But Robert was supremely self-assured. "To him it was more fun if you were just a big B.S.-er talking off the top of your head."

Just as the season got under way, O'Brien also noticed that tagging along behind Robert to the weekly meetings was Jim Parker. The sessions became even less productive and more rambunctious. "Jimmy was both very funny and a clown and disruptive," said O'Brien. "We were in the library having a practice, and Jimmy and some other people would come in and just hang out there. I'd say like after five minutes of joking around, I'd be like, 'OK, we have to get back to debating,' and Jim wouldn't leave, and he and Robert would sort of spar and egg each other on." Maybe another coach on another team in another town would have come down hard on Robert and Jim. O'Brien would later concede, "Robert could be distracting and a smartass during practice." But no one in Chelsea ever really pushed back when it came to Robert and Jim, and the boys became accustomed to doing things their way. Moreover, playing hardball not only didn't fit O'Brien's warm style; having even one kid quit might sink the team.

The loose dynamic favored Robert, giving him a sense of being in charge.

High school debaters describe how during competition they get "high from talking." The contest can become a verbal high-wire act involving embarrassing spills and soaring thrills. Debaters talk about becoming engrossed in the moment, the debate equivalent of what athletes call playing in the zone—a perfect state of focus.

Robert experienced that high. He and Kip won all three rounds in the team's first tournament, held in Chelsea on January 8, 2000, against a half-dozen other schools. Robert even led all debaters on total "speaker points." O'Brien noticed how much Robert enjoyed the verbal jousting.

It's said that high school kids are drawn to debate because they get off on arguing—a brand of mental warfare where wit and quick tongue are the weapons of choice. Debaters might go into the contest acting mannerly and shake hands. They might dress in jackets and ties and blouses and skirts. But behind the decorum is an intense competition. Rivals end up talking trash, dissing one another, and becoming single-minded in wanting the verbal kill. It's teen combat featuring sharp tongues, tongue lashings, and an opportunity for adolescents—already in a life phase marked by testing limits—to explore wild ideas in the confines of an organized activity. Teen debaters, noted sociologist Gary Alan Fine, are often "determining how far they can trespass intellectually." In his study of the culture of high school debate, Fine quoted one coach describing the strategy she wanted her high school debaters to adopt during their turn at cross-examination. "You want to nail somebody to the cross in a nice, pleasant manner," the coach said, sounding like a Mafia boss explaining how to set up a hit by sweet-talking the target. Crudeness only provided the opposition a chance for a comeback. "If you stick in the knife, you don't want to leave it in because they can pull it out and survive," the coach said. "You want to turn it, but in a nice, polite fashion."

This was a world fit for Robert. Coming off the win in their first outing, Robert, Kip, and their coach were excited about the fast start. Robert was good, albeit rough around the edges. He picked up on issues quickly and seemed more aware of current events than most kids. "He was very smart and good at bantering, just the sort of guy you see at Harvard," O'Brien said. The coach also saw Robert relish the spotlight, as if he told himself, "Hey, I get eight minutes to really sound off here." He especially liked going second on the team, a slot usually taken by a team's strongest debater to cross-examine the opponent. It was an opportunity, said O'Brien, to "set the other person up and make them look foolish." Robert embraced this chance "to ding the other guy." Jim knew this to be true: "When he wants to be verbally abusive he is very verbally abusive."

But O'Brien grew quickly discouraged with his star. Robert might get psyched for the actual "performance" of the debate, but practices were still a joke to him. He fooled around with Jim and paid little to no attention. He was lazy. In fact, instead of building on his early interest and refining his technique, Robert grew more restless and cavalier. Instead of an upward growth curve, the arc of Robert's participation had that familiar backslide to it.

"He wasn't prepared," O'Brien said about the Robert who showed up at the later tournaments. The judges felt the same way. Time and again they noted Robert's intelligence, but also criticized him for being "really rude." Said another coach, who saw Robert at four debates, "He was always pushing the envelope with his remarks. Debate is argument and evidence, and Robert usually didn't have any evidence."

Robert won some, he lost some, and with every merit came a demerit. "The reason he did not become the best debater clearly that year is he didn't do the work," said O'Brien. "People who weren't nearly as good as he was, with their work, and using evidence, were always going to beat Robert." No one imposed any limits on him. He suffered no real consequences for being, as O'Brien said, "way too sarcastic."

There did come one moment when O'Brien had enough of the Robert and Jim Show. Even though they both were taking fewer classes and had an inordinate amount of time on their hands, they were invariably late. Jim, not on the team, simply assumed his perch as a pest in the peanut gallery. "He was just disrupting everything," said O'Brien. But instead of coming down hard on them, instead of insisting they quit their antics, instead of making pronouncements about accountability—"Hey guys, you're way out of line here, you're embarrassing our program, and if you get down off your high horses you'll see you're embarrassing yourselves, too"—the coach cut them slack. He challenged Jim to join the team, to partner with Robert at the final tournament on February 19 at Mount Saint Joseph Academy in Rutland. To up the ante, O'Brien bet Jim a dollar he'd lose.

Jim and Robert loved the idea—bring it on, they said. The debate was soon upon them and Robert and Jim took on all comers, to a fault. The team from Otter Valley High School argued that allowing Ebonics—the vernacular of some black youths—would help academics. Robert and Jim, assigned to argue that Ebonics was a lousy idea, seized the performance opportunity. Robert stood up and talked in Ebonics in his rebuttal. Jim rooted him on and tried the same when his turn came. The two used Ebonics the rest of the debate. Their coach was partly amused but mostly horrified. "They are both good mimics," he said, "and stayed in character way longer than I could. It was sort of like a *Saturday Night Live* skit." But at the same time, the coach said, "You know, they were both skirting racism, too."

No one was surprised when the Chelsea team lost hands down. But the drive back to Chelsea in O'Brien's Honda Civic was hardly a bummer. Robert and Jim were jazzed up, delighted with themselves for having sabotaged the debate. Jim at one point opened the car door, stuck out his leg, and howled at the top of his lungs.

O'Brien wasn't impressed, but the coach didn't know what to do. The one thing he did realize was that his big idea had backfired badly—Robert and Jim had turned the debate into a travesty. But the foolish Ebonics riff wasn't the end of it.

The state tournament was the climax of Vermont's high school debate season, held inside the gold-domed Capitol building in Montpelier every year in early March. O'Brien wasn't planning to send anyone in 2000. The reason had nothing to do with the Ebonics disaster—the Chelsea squad was down to one member: Robert.

Other kids had come and gone. Robert had started the season paired with Kip Battey, but by the winter Kip was no longer at school. Far ahead on credits to graduate, Kip and Coltere Savidge were tasting academic life beyond Chelsea, boarding at the Mountain School. O'Brien then matched up Robert with classmate Anna Mulligan, who had returned to school after spending the fall semester away, also at the Mountain School. O'Brien actually liked what he had in Anna and Robert, even if it was clear to the coach the classmates weren't the best of friends. Anna, attractive and graceful, had an "elegant style," while Robert was more "in your face and brash." The coach thought the good cop–bad cop tandem could work. But Anna's interest in debate waned quickly. Like Kip, Robert, Coltere, and other junior classmates who had gotten way ahead on their credits, Anna was pursuing interests beyond school. She wasn't interested in the state tournament on March 11.

Most other schools in the Vermont league were sending several two-person teams to compete at the all-day event. They'd be squaring off before a lineup of prominent judges, including state officials, attorney David Kelley, who'd waged an unsuccessful campaign for governor in 1994, and some "celebrity" judges, most notably the star of O'Brien's documentary, farmer Fred Tuttle. But Robert, without a partner, was left out in the cold.

This changed a few days before the tournament. O'Brien got a telephone call from the debate coach at Rutland Senior High School. Compared to Chelsea, Rutland was overflowing with talent; it was sending three teams. The Rutland coach also had a seventh debater without a partner, a freshman named Luke White. The Rutland coach wanted to find a partner so the fifteen-year-old boy might enjoy the experience of debating at the state tournament, even though a mixed pairing wouldn't be in contention to win a trophy. The coach had initially suggested to Luke a debater from Otter Valley High School, but Luke vetoed the match. Luke White had another teenager in mind: What about Robert Tulloch from Chelsea? The two boys had met at a tournament earlier in the season and become friendly, exchanging e-mails. Luke, an intense, ambitious student, had found something charming about the easygoing Robert. Between rounds during the often cutthroat competition, when other kids warily sized one another up, Luke liked that Robert seemed "laid back, very cool." Robert jumped at the offer. The two boys might not be able to win a school trophy, but Robert knew he'd still have the opportunity to show the league he was the best on his feet; he was still eligible to win Best Individual Speaker.

The state tournament captured Robert's season in a nutshell—fast, flashy start followed by rapid, nasty decline.

Robert and Luke faced one of toughest teams in the league in the opening round—and won, thrilling themselves and O'Brien. But once they lost their second-round match to another strong team, Robert's mood darkened. Luke, shrugging off the loss, sought to boost his partner's spirits. During the midday lunch break, he spotted a news photographer in the hallway of the Capitol, and he badgered the photographer to take a picture of him and his teammate. Robert, liking the attention, went along with the goof and the two boys played to the camera. They stood outside the governor's office, a few feet from an oil portrait of Richard A. Snelling, Vermont's governor from 1977 to 1985, and struck statesmen-like poses. The photograph in the next day's *Rutland Herald* showed Robert looking earnestly at a debate notebook he held open in his hands, while Luke, standing at his side, pointed to something in the book. "It was so staged," said Luke. "Robert was trying to look so attentive. We laughed about it afterwards. It was kind of cool we were in the paper."

But there was nothing cool about their third and final round.

Luke went first against the team from Mount Saint Joseph Academy. He was unfamiliar with the affirmative argument he and Robert were using—the plan O'Brien had devised about classroom lighting—so it made sense that Luke open by reading the plan. "In Genesis, when God said, 'Let there be light,' was he creating the universe, or proposing a plan to significantly increase academic achievement?" he began.

The two novice teams were crowded into a small upstairs room in the Capitol. Posters and paintings of cows and livestock revealed that this was the legislature's Agriculture Committee room. It had plush, ruby-red carpet and barely enough space for the long wooden table in the middle surrounded by upholstered chairs. The debaters sat tightly in a row on one side of the table piled with lawmakers' papers.

"We, the affirmative, say, 'Let there be light,'" Luke said.

Luke was on his feet, dressed in a dark blazer, a blue shirt, and a tie, his brown hair neatly combed to one side. Robert sat next to him. He wasn't wearing a sports jacket or a tie, but he looked tidy, having buttoned his plaid shirt all the way to his neck. Down the table sat the team from Mount Saint Joseph—Matt Gregg and Johannes Gamba. Johannes, lanky and as tall as Robert, was from a small village in Bavaria, about an hour from Munich, Germany. He was a foreign exchange student staying with a family in Rutland.

A few feet away, across the table, sat the judge, the former gubernatorial candidate David Kelley. O'Brien sat behind the judge with two friends, both journalists, who'd never seen a debate and had come along out of curiosity.

Luke worked his way through the Chelsea argument that better classroom lighting would boost academic achievement. He said, "Does anybody here feel more 'alive' in a fluorescent-lit room with no windows than in a bright, sunny room? Remember what Emerson said in *Nature*: 'Light is the first of painters. There is no object so foul that intense light will not make it beautiful.'" He finished with a flourish: "We must now watch the negative prove that gloominess is good for grades. But while you're listening to our esteemed opposition make the case for dimness, remember what Goethe requested on his deathbed: 'Light, more light!'"

Johannes Gamba sat listening to Luke with mounting dread. How could he answer the "weird speech" about installing skylights and windows to bring natural light into classrooms? The plan was out of left field and caught Johannes off guard. He and his partner had come armed with evidence and facts to attack more standard plans. Had their opponents tried to argue, for example, that school uniforms improved student performance, Johannes and Matt were ready to beat that plan into the ground. But this "Let there be light" plan was unusual.

For Johannes, the tournament was his final competition—and he'd had a blast being on the team. Indeed, his exchange year in the United States had been terrific. "I like America more than Germany, actually," he told his new friends in Rutland. His high school back home in the tiny village of Penzing didn't have any extracurricular activities, and Johannes had found the offerings at Mount Saint Joseph a dazzling smorgasbord. A non-athlete, a self-proclaimed computer geek, Johannes decided to join the debate team at his adopted high school. "I've always liked to debate about things in real life and I figured it would be even cooler to do it in a foreign language," Johannes said.

When his turn came, Johannes stumbled, only able to offer some bland, generic counterarguments against the lighting plan—like flatly asserting it was just a bad idea that would fail. The others in the room, Chelsea's O'Brien and his two journalist friends, could see that Luke and Robert had the upper hand.

Robert smelled blood. He stood to cross-examine Johannes. So far during the debate the other boys had been stiff and formal as they'd spoken. They'd all faced forward and looked at the judge rather than make eye contact with one another up and down the row. But right away Robert was different. He leaned toward Johannes and locked eyes with him. Robert rocked, his body language cocky.

John O'Brien shifted in his seat; something was up. O'Brien knew Robert had become increasingly soured by the day's events. Pushed in the first round, Robert rose to the occasion and pulled out a surprise win against the team that would end up winning the tournament. That round's judge even told O'Brien afterward that the debate had been "as good as any varsity debate." After round one, Robert briefly led all debaters in speaker points. But then came the second-round loss, and with that Robert's fantasy about winning the best speaker trophy was crushed. During the lunch break, O'Brien saw that Robert remained upset. Facing a team unable to offer much competition in round three, Robert was now spoiling for a fight.

He began by peppering Johannes with questions. His manner was heavy-handed and rough—the very opposite of the approach O'Brien would have coached when a team was clearly ahead. Robert and Luke could have tap-danced their way to a win. But Robert was no longer interested in the here and now, his manner turbulent and provocative as he opened his cross-examination with his trademark sarcasm.

Johannes couldn't keep pace with the grilling—"I didn't know the answer"—in large part because he wasn't able to follow Robert's rapid-fire English. When Johannes hesitated, Robert pounced.

"You're just a *German*. How can you know?"

Robert's voice ricocheted around the room.

"You're just a *German* . . . "

Instantly everyone knew the comment was out of bounds—everyone except, of course, Robert. Luke looked up, maybe even gasped. He preferred to think Robert hadn't intended any malice, but that didn't matter. Luke understood how the remark sounded. He leaned toward Robert and whispered to his teammate, "You've got to apologize." Even if Luke didn't think Robert's comment was a slur, Luke knew it would be viewed as abuse. "It's like saying another person is stupid. You can't do that."

In his seat, O'Brien hung his head. He knew immediately that Robert had gone too far, "in the same vein as the Ebonics thing." Robert had ignored the foul line once again and had put his team's fortunes in jeopardy. Seated beside O'Brien was his friend, Marialisa Calta, a free-lance writer, and she was thinking the same as the others: Robert's in trouble now. "Pointing out your opponent is not from the U.S. is not going to help you win," she said later. "It seemed really dumb."

Johannes smiled nervously. He didn't feel particularly stung by the insensitive remark. He was used to a certain amount of kidding about his accent from friends at school. He'd just turn around and joke about their upcountry Vermont accents. But Johannes understood that the context was different: Robert's comment had come during a debate. Robert, he thought, had gone and acted "pretty uppity."

Robert ignored Luke's entreaty and did not apologize. He just kept going until his time ran out, seemingly oblivious to the eye-rolling and gasps. He simply didn't get it. Johannes and his teammate, meanwhile, quickly realized that Robert had handed them something to work with. When his turn came, Matt Gregg tried repeatedly to draw the judge's attention to the remark and emphasize how rude Robert had been.

Luke tried to undo the damage, spending most of his rebuttal apologizing. Luke then tried to steer the debate back to the topic. He felt he'd succeeded, delivering a rebuttal he considered his best ever. After the debate, shaking Johannes's hand, Luke apologized again. Luke figured he and Robert had pulled it out. "I thought the fire was settled," he said.

O'Brien, too, was hopeful. Luke and Robert, in terms of the policy issue, had dominated; the other boys had been unable to make a dent in the lighting plan. He predicted the judge would award a "low-point win," meaning a narrow margin to reflect Robert's crude faux pas. Awaiting the outcome, even Johannes thought he and his teammate had lost. "Although we did think that the judge probably wouldn't like Robert's remark, we still expected the other side to win because of their better argumentation."

They were wrong. Judge David Kelley, who debated in high school and at the University of Vermont, was a purist. "I was tempted to end the debate right there and forfeit Chelsea and announce, 'Sorry, this is not the reason why we are here,'" Kelley said. "Simple civility is a building block of the competition." Robert, the judge said, "first struck me as particularly bright," but as the round unfolded Robert displayed "sheer arrogance." Kelley found the nationality remark "chilling."

"I was surprised and disappointed in this particular team, more so than in any debate I've ever judged." The judge ruled that Johannes and Matt had won. Robert's commentary, said Kelly, was "tantamount to watching a boxing match and having one of the boxers bring a fist into his opponent's groin."

Luke and Robert were crestfallen. But Luke got over it; he shrugged and accepted the fact that once Robert made the German comment the debate was no longer about their lighting plan. "Like when Holyfield fought Tyson and got his ear bit off," Luke said, echoing the judge's boxing metaphor. "Who's going to care who's winning the fight? Tyson obviously got disqualified, and the boxing didn't matter."

Robert was unable to accept the outcome. He was incensed. Outside in the hallway, in front of his coach and the coach's two friends, Marialisa Calta and Paula Routly, two women he'd never met before that day, Robert flipped out. "We're smarter than those guys. How could he do that to us?" Robert demanded to no one in particular.

Calta wondered how Robert could even think this way. "It was clear they weren't going to win" after Robert's ugly remark, she said. Routly, the publisher of an alternative weekly newspaper in Burlington, considered Robert's harangue a "verbal version of kicking the wall." She tried to calm Robert and move him off the subject, nodding in agreement that indeed life was unfair sometimes. She tried humor. But nothing worked. Robert was absorbed in his own angry world. "He certainly didn't need much interaction to keep going," said

Routly. "He wasn't asking questions, like what we thought about this. He wasn't really listening to us. It was like he needed an audience, but not much more. He just wouldn't let it go."

Weeks passed before O'Brien saw Robert again, a break that O'Brien didn't mind. But then one day O'Brien bumped into Robert near the school. It was all chitchat, with O'Brien asking Robert what he was up to and Robert casually replying he had big plans in the works. "I'm not going to be around here," he told his coach. "I'm going to be in Europe."

Europe? Where in Europe?

Robert shrugged. Europe, was all he'd say.

In the wake of his back-to-back humiliations in student council and debate, Robert was stepping up his talk with Jim about their breakout from Chelsea. Robert told some of his friends he was thinking of going to Germany's Bavaria region. "I'm not sure why he came up with that," Zack Courts said. "Maybe because it's a green and mountainous region, kind of like Vermont." Or maybe Robert wanted a rematch with debate opponent Johannes Gamba. Then Robert and Jim began talking about a destination even farther around the planet—Australia. Zack remembered them saying, "It would be sweet to go to Australia." Zack was quick to grasp the appeal of life down under, saying Australia "seems cool. It's foreign. It's weird, and they do speak English there."

Around this same time, Chelsea school officials and board members held a series of special sessions with parents, some of whom had grown alarmed by stories of drug use, bullying on school buses, and a general lack of discipline. The sessions began contentiously—one selectman called them "bitch-and-complain meetings"—but they proved productive. The school handbook was overhauled, spelling out beefed-up regulations and policies on everything from hazing to weapons. Principal Pat Davenport later said proudly the new handbook addressed "some post-Columbine issues."

But the new bright lines for student conduct had little impact on Robert and Jim—not with the growing free time they had on their hands, time they spent mostly with one another. Friends continued to hear accounts of their ambitious travel plans, although specifics were rarely forthcoming. The boys' means to their end remained a very private work in progress—disconnected from The Crew and a closely held secret. In a number of ways, though, Robert and Jim had commenced in earnest their training days.

After Robert had honed his sharp tongue and felt the intellectual high of debate, he and Jim were soon getting in shape and experiencing the physical kick of rock climbing. Climbing became an obsession during the spring of 2000, their new big thing to do. They spent hours on end at indoor rock-climbing facilities, mostly riding in Jim's car to Petra Cliffs in Burlington, an 8,500-square-foot training complex about an hour away. They bought and borrowed equipment and threw themselves into a sport that devotees say provides a supernatural and gravity-defying rush, an escape from life's ordinariness.

It was also a sport of bonding, where rope-mates had to learn to work as one, as one climber belayed, or managed the safety rope, for the other. Perfect for Robert and Jim. Climbing became a way to test themselves, to see if they had the nerve to push themselves to the next level, where the thrill was greater but so was the risk. Climbing meant relying on each other, hanging there together, driving toward a summit and prodding each other past fears and doubts. The goal could only be reached in tandem, each step along the way requiring careful and deliberate planning but also an ever-ready nimbleness to shift left or right if suddenly they faced a rough route. Only by talking it through and working closely together could they succeed.

Devoting themselves, they improved quickly. "I would say they were maybe not experts but upper-end intermediate climbers," said Petra Cliffs' owner, Chip Schlegel. In short order, he said, the two boys had become "strong climbers." Christiana Usenza tagged along on occasion and even tried climbing, but neither she nor any of The Crew took to climbing with the intensity of Robert and Jim. It was their thing, theirs alone. Kienan was once asked to identify his brother's rock-climbing friends. He replied: "He didn't have any rock-climbing friends—just him and Jim."

Just Robert and Jim.

13

Vasque Boots

In the first days after the murders, Robert and Jim tried to live as normally as possible—in denial, Jim called it—while plotting their long-planned, now-urgent departure from Chelsea. They knew the knife sheaths might lead police to Jim, and that would inevitably lead to Robert. Unless they escaped, that would destroy their dream of living lives of great adventure.

Robert returned to school the Monday after the killings, strolling into Joan Feierabend's advanced art class at 10:20 A.M. He announced that he was joining the class even though he had missed the first week of the semester. That didn't thrill Feierabend, who had last taught him in the sixth grade. DeRoss Kellogg might have thought Robert was wonderfully spirited, but she considered him grumpy and sarcastic. She let him know that attitude wouldn't work in a class filled with students serious about art. Robert said he understood, and to her surprise he seemed more subdued than usual.

The only other class Robert needed to take to graduate was environmental science, and before that class settled down to work his friend Kip Battey brought up the Zantop murders. "You hear about this?" Kip called to the teacher, Richard Steckler. As they talked about the mysterious killings, Robert sat impassively. He wasn't his usual quick-with-a-quip self, but he was as composed as ever.

After school that day Robert called his sometime girlfriend, Christiana Usenza.

"What'd you do this weekend?" she asked.

"Nothing," he lied. "I called you. I was really bored. I wanted to see what you were doing." As it happened, Christiana had spent Saturday taking the SAT.

On Tuesday, the day after their phone call, Robert visited Christiana at work at the Hunger Mountain Co-op in Montpelier. When he walked in, she noticed him carrying his careworn brown teddy bear. She ran over and gave him a hug. "Yay, you did it! You're ready to go," she said. For months she'd been hearing about his plans to leave Chelsea and see the world with Jim—she understood instinctively that bringing her his teddy bear was a sign that he was casting off his childhood and readying himself for the road.

One other person Jim and Robert told they were leaving was their friend Gaelen McKee, but they only told him they were going rock climbing in Colorado, saying nothing of their plans never to return. McKee wasn't especially alarmed by the news, knowing that both were ahead on credits in school and could probably afford some time off. Other friends noticed nothing strange about Robert and Jim.

While Robert was saying good-bye to Christiana, Jim was raising money for what they called their trip fund. For starters, they had $340 that had belonged to Half Zantop, the cash they had found in his wallet. To add to the pot, Jim sold his saxophone, bass guitar, and amplifier to a music store in Burlington, and his snowboard to Tim Courts, the father of his friend Zack Courts. He tried to sell his paintball gun and tennis racket, but couldn't find any takers, so he gave them to Gaelen in a cardboard box along with an old Frisbee. Together, Robert and Jim had about $800, but then they bought some fancy climbing shirts for more than $100 each, and then Robert wanted new rock-climbing shoes to match the ones Jim had been given for Christmas.

Those purchases reduced their stake by more than $300, which ate up the money they had taken from Half's wallet. In the rough math of robbery-murder, the lives of Half and Susanne Zantop were only worth two shirts and a pair of shoes to Robert and Jim.

They already owned the rest of the clothing, sleeping bags, and other gear they'd be bringing, including their matching SOG SEAL 2000 knives, minus their Kydex sheaths. Instead, they wrapped the blades in homemade sheaths, one made from a sock and the other from a mitten, both crudely cocooned in duct tape.

Jim and Robert had talked about throwing the knives in the river, or burying them, to rid themselves of damning evidence. But, as Jim put it, "If, you know, it became a problem to have the knives, then we were screwed anyway. We weren't thinking about trial or how we could maybe defend our case or anything like that. . . . Plus, we wanted to keep them, you know? Wherever we went we needed survival knives."

They also kept busy monitoring news of the Zantop murder investigation, looking at papers at Will's Store and once or twice in the school library. Later they did the same at home, surfing the Internet. Several times Jim typed in a simple search—"hanover and homicide"—and got back hundreds of responses. None of the news accounts suggested that police were working on hot leads, and none mentioned Chuck West and Frank Moran's painstaking search for SEAL 2000 sales. For the moment at least, Robert and Jim thought they were safe.

They planned to leave the same day Robert visited Christiana at the health-food co-op, but the weather was bad and Jim's mother wouldn't let him leave the house. They needed to keep their plans secret from their parents, and they didn't want to arouse suspicion by having Jim demand to go out that night. Their flight on hold, Robert invited Christiana to his house.

"Do you want to see my cut?" he asked her. Robert had visited school nurse Charlotte Faccio on the day he returned to school to have her tend to it. It was fresh, still bleeding and hurting badly, though his mother had looked at it a day earlier and told him it didn't need stitches. Faccio noticed it was two inches long, a horizontal cut across his right thigh, several inches above the knee. Robert told Faccio he had cut himself on a fence, but Faccio thought it looked like a surgical cut—made by a sharp knife—because it was too straight and clean to have come from a fence. She cleaned it, affixed a new bandage, and sent him on his way.

Neither Robert nor Jim knew exactly how Robert had gotten the cut, but they were certain where it had happened. "I think he had it during the murders," Jim said later, "because he didn't have it before and he had it afterward."

Robert first mentioned the cut to Christiana on the phone a day earlier, telling her only, "I ran into a metal thing." When they were alone in Robert's room, Christiana asked again how it happened.

"Well, it's embarrassing, so I just, I just told people I ran into a sap bucket in the woods," Robert said. The real story, he told Christiana, was he dropped a knife on his leg. Christiana didn't ask more about it, figuring it was one of those dumb things boys do.

They talked past midnight and made a list of fake names Robert might use on his journey, which he said he'd need to prevent his parents from tracking him down and making him come home. As they talked, Robert became unusually emotional. He got teary at the thought of not being able to say good-bye to his mother. Even the sight of his family's cat made him cry.

"You don't have to go right now," she told him. "You could wait until you have more money, 'til you graduate."

"Well, I have to go. I, I kind of have to go," he said. "I've done something bad."

"Really bad?"

"Yeah."

Christiana didn't press further, figuring Robert would have told her if he wanted her to know, and anyway it was probably nothing worse than him stealing something to raise money for his trip. She remembered how the previous spring he had told her about stealing an all-terrain vehicle then trying unsuccessfully to sell it to raise travel money.

Robert and Christiana fell asleep in his room at 1 A.M. They woke at eight the next morning and began saying their good-byes. After breakfast Jim showed up at Robert's door, his silver Audi waiting outside to take them away.

They drove an hour from Chelsea to the Vermont Transit Authority bus station in White River Junction. It was only a few miles from Hanover, just over the state border. They went to the counter and told ticket agent Brenda Johnson they wanted to go "somewhere warm." Their real goal was Colorado, but they didn't tell her that. The first place they mentioned was "Syracuse, California," but that destination had the disadvantage of not existing. Johnson suggested San Diego—not knowing it was Jim's mother's hometown. But one-way tickets there cost $159 each, and Robert and Jim balked—too heavy a strain on their wallets.

They borrowed an atlas from Johnson and leafed through the pages. They returned to the ticket window and told her they'd take two tickets to Amarillo, Texas, one way, at $139 each. Jim also paid for two weeks of parking, saying someone from his family would come by the station's lot to collect the Audi.

They hung around for nearly two hours, calmly waiting for the 1:50 P.M. bus. They didn't strike Johnson as nervous or upset, just a little confused. "They didn't seem to know just where they wanted to go," Johnson said later. "That's what stood out in my mind. Two young boys who didn't know where they were going."

They climbed aboard the bus and settled into their seats. By the following night, they had traveled through New York City, changed buses, and made it as far as St. Louis. But the reality of cross-country bus travel quickly took its toll. They were short on money, tired, and uncomfortable on the crowded, smelly bus. Neither could stomach fast food, and the bus only made pit stops at places like McDonald's. Making matters worse, Robert's leg was becoming infected and growing ever more painful.

The first night, Jim called his parents to say he and Robert were on a road trip but he wouldn't tell them where. "We needed to take a break," he told his father. "We're just taking off for a few days to go rock climbing." Despite Jim's assurances, the call sent Joan and John Parker searching for clues to where he was and fearing he was gone for good.

"Dad is really sad because he thinks Jim has left home to be out in the world," Joan wrote in an e-mail to her daughter, Diana. "He thinks he's too young, and he wants him to graduate and not be a dropout, and he will miss him. He is worried that this is it, and Jim is gone. I tend to think he's on a joyride, and will be back when he runs out of money. Mom."

"Geez," Diana responded. "I can't believe Jim sometimes, but maybe after he realizes that he can't make it out on his own, then he will come to his senses. I just hate that he thinks that he is Mr. Do-What-Ever-He-Wants cuz he is cool. And that he thinks he's so grown up and beyond everyone else."

When Diane Tulloch learned that Jim had called his parents, she was upset that Robert hadn't called her and Mike. She considered the disappearance Robert's first "strange behavior"—overlooking numerous earlier signs—while her husband considered it a huge surprise. Mike thought Robert hadn't shown any signs of trouble.

By the second day of their trip, Robert and Jim had had enough.

"What do you think, Jim?" Robert asked.

"Let's just go home," Jim answered. He explained later: "I kind of convinced myself that everything was OK. I really just wanted to go back home because I was tired, I was hungry, and ah, the bus ride sucked."

Around 9 P.M., on February 1, when the bus made a brief stopover, Jim called his parents a second time. They could hear in his voice that the adventure had gone out of him.

John and Joan Parker ordered Jim to come home immediately and he agreed, having already reached that same conclusion. He and Robert would fly from St. Louis to Manchester, New Hampshire. Robert called Christiana. "We're coming home," he told her. "America is gross. The food is gross. My cut's getting worse." He asked her to pick them up at the airport the next day at noon.

After meeting the weary travelers at the airport, Christiana drove them to the bus station to get Jim's car. Before leaving, they went into the station to seek $20 refunds on the unused portions of their tickets. When Brenda Johnson handed them the money, she said she was surprised to see them back so soon. They ran into bad weather, they told her, so they had turned around.

They returned to Chelsea, most of their money gone, their tails between their legs.

Home again, Robert and Jim ran into a storm of criticism and a barrage of questions. John and Joan Parker liked Robert, but now they weren't so sure this intense friendship was the best thing for their son. They denied Jim use of the car and the computer, and forbade him from seeing Robert for a month. The Parkers also warned him that, if it happened again, they'd call the police and file a missing persons report. Or, worse, they'd tell the police he had stolen their car. No one in Chelsea heard whether Robert was punished, but nothing in his behavior suggested there were consequences for his actions.

Kip Battey badgered Robert after his return, asking him why they went and doubting the answers. "I was thinking about, like, calling up the airlines to see if they really did fly back from St. Louis. I didn't really buy it," Kip said. He said he figured his friends "just screwed up really big and ended up doing something really, really stupid."

"First you think, 'Oh, you know, did they get caught drinking, or something like that, or drugs, or they got in trouble with their parents,'" Kip said. But drugs and drinking seemed unlikely pursuits for Jim and Robert, so Kip kept searching for an explanation.

No matter how many imagined offenses he ran through, Battey

never dreamed of a serious crime. If he had ticked off all the possible explanations for his friends' sudden disappearance and mopey reappearance, murder would have been "like, number 395" on the list. Also, though the Zantop murders had taken place only a few days earlier and a short drive away, Kip explained, "Hanover is in another universe, really."

He brought up Robert and Jim's trip at a debate team practice, tossing around theories with the other debaters about what kind of mischief their friends must have gotten into to make them take off. That was the first time debate coach John O'Brien heard about the trip. Later, O'Brien needled Robert, trying to get some answers.

He joked about Robert's wound and scoffed at his story. "What is this? A spout tap in the woods?" O'Brien said. He told Robert flat out that he didn't believe that story. But rather than react with his usual arrogance, Robert backed down, letting O'Brien's comments pass. It surprised the coach. He had expected Robert to go into hard-charging debate mode, snapping back at him, using knife-sharp rhetorical flourishes and fast-forming arguments to deflect O'Brien's challenge and strike back with a counteroffensive. O'Brien felt pleased when Robert didn't do any of that. He found himself liking this mellower, well-mannered, post-runaway version of Robert Tulloch. O'Brien thought it was a sign his young friend was maturing.

During the two weeks that followed, O'Brien wasn't the only one who noticed a more subdued Robert. Kip, among others, thought the antibiotics he was taking for the infected cut were making him lethargic.

Robert started attending school with greater frequency, but revealed little, even when discussions turned to the ubiquitous news stories about the murdered Dartmouth professors. At one point Christiana asked him, "Did you hear about the murders in Hanover?" "Yeah," Robert answered. "It's too bad." The conversation moved on.

His self-assessment of his work in Joan Feierabend's art class the week he and Jim returned to Chelsea had only a small hint of his usual smarter-and-better-than-everyone bravado: "Joan, It was a bad week. My leg, a botched trip, and a general negative attitude made my week a real downer. But I like art. I don't like doing stuff I don't like when

I'm angry. And it calmed me. It was relaxing and simplistically satisfying. I really like my sculpture. Thank you, Robert."

Privately, after returning to Chelsea, Robert and Jim willed themselves into denial and talked about what to do next. "We could make money other ways, and, you know, everything's going to be OK," Jim said. "We'll work for my dad and different stuff like that." Robert went along with that for a few days, but soon he reverted to form, telling Jim, "Let's do some illegal stuff again."

Jim wasn't interested. He told himself: "I want to graduate and just work." He was thinking about doing a national outdoor leadership program. Jim didn't share those thoughts with Robert because he knew that would have led to one of the brief but explosive arguments they had over anything from the best climbing shoes to the state of the world. Jim knew that Robert hated when people disagreed with him, and he hated it worse when anyone proved him wrong.

One thing they agreed on was a story they would tell if anyone asked about the knives. Jim couldn't deny buying them—jimibruce was his Internet handle, and the knives had been sent to Jim Parker of Chelsea, Vermont—so he'd claim to have sold them to a stranger at an Army-Navy store in Burlington, the same store where they'd bought their black commando sweaters. If anyone asked, Robert would corroborate that account.

As days passed, old routines reemerged. Jim retrieved his tennis racket, paintball gun, and Frisbee from Gaelen McKee. Movies were always a favorite pastime, but with Jim grounded, Robert needed a new film buddy. On Valentine's Day, February 14, he visited Christiana and then he and Kip Battey drove to Hanover, not far from the Zantops' house, to see the war-on-drugs film *Traffic*.

Kip and Robert talked the whole way there and back. Robert wasn't his usual witty and cynical self, Kip thought, but he wasn't much different from usual, and he never mentioned if something was bothering him. "He's normally very verbose," Kip said. "He still talked, but he seemed a little bit withdrawn. I just thought he was a little quieter."

The next day, at school, Sada Dumont saw both Robert and Jim, whom she had dated once a couple years earlier and always considered nicer than Robert. She noticed that Jim didn't seem as funny or happy lately, but that day Jim seemed his usual easygoing self. Robert joked around with her at lunch and played with the crutches she needed for an injured leg.

That night, just when it seemed they were in the clear, the police came knocking.

As Chuck West began his drive along the winding roads into Vermont, his two fellow New Hampshire State Police detectives were already making the rounds in Chelsea.

On the afternoon of February 15, Sergeant Robert Bruno and Trooper Russ Hubbard dropped by the local sheriff's office to get directions and find out what they could about the SEAL 2000 buyer, jimibruce, a.k.a. Jim Parker. A captain in the sheriff's office, Arnold Covey, surprised them with the news that they were looking for a sixteen-year-old boy. Covey couldn't add much beyond a record of a couple of traffic citations and a comment that, as far as he knew, Jim Parker wasn't one of the local teenage troublemakers. One more thing the New Hampshire detectives picked up at the sheriff's office was an escort. Bruno remembered that his friend Tim Page, a Vermont State Police sergeant, lived upstairs from the sheriff's office. It was good police practice to bring along a local officer when outside one's jurisdiction, so Bruno invited Page to join them.

It was shortly before 7 P.M. when Bruno, Hubbard, and Page arrived at 10 Bradshaw Crossroad. In the winter darkness, the red A-frame house radiated warmth, evoking in the troopers' eyes a comfortable place where they could imagine making a social visit. The New Hampshire detectives emerged from their heated cars into the deep snow and pitch-black night, wearing their usual plainclothes attire of parkas over jackets and ties, accessorized with holstered guns hidden under their coats. They looked as benign as Fuller Brush salesmen, but the effect was spoiled by Page, resplendent in his full uniform complete with Smokey the Bear hat.

Bruno knocked on the door and John Parker answered. We're

detectives, Bruno said, investigating the homicide of the Dartmouth professors over in Hanover. We'd like to talk with your son, James, about his purchase of two SOG SEAL 2000 knives. Just so you know, Bruno told the elder Parker, you're not obligated to talk with us, and you don't have to invite us in. It's completely up to you.

"Come on in and have a seat over at the kitchen table," John Parker said. He didn't know anything about his son buying commando knives, but the Parker family had nothing to hide from the police. As they walked in, the officers noticed one other person in the house: a wiry young man sitting on a kitchen stool.

"Will you need to talk with me?" the young man asked. As he asked the question, Jim thought: "Bummer . . . I'm screwed." Through his fear he formed a quick plan—he would answer the troopers' questions without providing enough information for them to place him in custody. If he could avoid jail for this one night, maybe he could avoid it forever. It was a passive alternative to a plan Robert had outlined several times since the murders, in the event police came to their homes. Robert's plan, as Jim understood it, involved "knocking one of them out . . . and maybe even killing them." The killing part didn't appeal to Jim, and Robert didn't make a big issue of it. Either way, once the cop was disarmed, Robert would use the gun to hijack a car, pick up Jim, and they'd escape. If police came first to Jim's house, Robert expected him to do the same in reverse. Now, though, with two detectives standing in his house, Jim modified the plan to exclude violence, focusing instead on avoiding arrest and getting away clean.

Bruno wasn't sure who the young man was, but he suspected it was Jim Parker. Answering the question of whether they'd need to speak with him, Bruno said, "We might." So Jim joined them at the table.

Before they got started, Bruno told John Parker that he didn't have to allow them to interview his son, but the elder Parker said that would be fine. Jim voiced no objections, either. As Bruno started asking questions—why did you buy the knives, how did you use them, where are they now—a change came over the young man who had been sitting so languidly on the stool.

The veins in his neck began to throb. His Adam's apple bobbed like

a cork in rough seas. The side of his neck pulsed so violently it reminded Bruno of the movie *Alien*—a creature seemed ready to burst
through Jim Parker's neck.

Soon, though, Jim settled his nerves and his pounding neck well
enough to tell Bruno, Hubbard, and Page the story of buying the
knives over the Internet from Fox Firearms to use with his friend
Robert. It was the first time investigators heard the name Robert
Tulloch.

In his fright, Jim couldn't remember if his best friend's last name
was spelled Tulloch or Tolluch, so Hubbard wrote it down both ways.
In response to one of Bruno's questions, Jim said he used the e-mail
name jimibruce for no special reason—it was just that Bruce was a
name he liked. He explained that he and Robert bought the knives for
camping and to cut branches and build forts, but they proved too cum-
bersome, so they sold them.

Jim described how they drove to Burlington one day in January—
he couldn't remember exactly when—to unload the knives at the
Army-Navy store. Jim said the guy behind the counter wasn't interested, but a scruffy-looking customer in the store overheard Jim's proposal and made an offer: $60 each. Jim said he haggled a bit on the
price—he had wanted at least $130 for the pair—but took the cash
because he and Robert were glad they'd recoup at least part of their
money.

Bruno circled back again and again, prying out new details. Soon
Jim was wavering on his description of the mystery buyer—first his
hair was black and then it was brown; first he was in his early twenties
and then he might have been in his thirties. Bruno thought Jim was
lying, mostly about not knowing the identity of the knife buyer. Bruno
also doubted Jim's claim that he hadn't heard about the Zantops' murders until the detective mentioned them.

Despite Bruno's skepticism, he considered it too far-fetched to
imagine that this teenage boy had killed the Zantops. What could his
motive possibly have been? How would a kid from a nice home like
this, with a supportive father sitting by his side, get mixed up in murder? Bruno's questions reflected investigators' initial belief that Jim's

involvement was limited, at most, to supplying the knives. Bruno figured Jim was scared to death of the real killer.

"Do you know who you gave the knives to?" Bruno asked again. "Is
that why you're so nervous?"

"No, it's just that I'm talking with police," Jim said.

Before a stalemate bogged them down, Bruno asked if Jim would
drive into town to be fingerprinted at the Orange County sheriff's
office, to compare his prints with evidence found at the murder scene.
John Parker said he had no objection. Neither did Jim.

By that time, Chuck West had arrived at the Parker house. He
quickly learned from Bruno what had been said and that Jim had
agreed to fingerprinting. West and the other detectives drove their cars
to the sheriff's office while John and Jim Parker drove over separately.

"You didn't do anything, did you?" John Parker asked his son as they
sat in his truck.

"No, I haven't done anything," Jim answered. "Come on, Dad, I'm,
I'm really scared about this whole thing. . . . This is, you know, weird."

"Just tell them the truth," his father said. "Just tell them what you
know."

When they arrived at the sheriff's office, West had Jim write out
his account of the purchase and sale of the knives. The scrawled
statement, complete with misspellings and curious punctuation,
never names Robert, describing him only as a "friend." It adds more
suspiciously vague details of the buyer, describing his height as five-
nine to six feet, and with "shortish hair, but not real short 4-6 inches
maybe." It was a description that fit nearly the entire adult male population of Vermont. The statement concluded: "The reasons we
chose these knifes is because they are really tough and we like to use
the best."

After reading Jim's account, West went to work. He sat with John
and Jim Parker in a kitchenette at the sheriff's office. With his usual
painstaking approach, West began searching for flaws, chipping away
little by little. Still, after going over Jim's story several times in several
ways, West didn't think he saw a murderer sitting in front of him. Like
Bruno, West thought Jim was simply a liar, a boy scared of someone he

knew, someone he sold the knives to, someone who used them to kill Half and Susanne Zantop.

"As a detective who's been around awhile, I can tell when I'm not being told a hundred percent truth," West told Jim and John Parker.

"Right," Jim said.

"And you," West added, "you agree, Jim? You agree?"

"I, I know, it's a . . . I don't, I don't like this story either," Jim answered. "I wish I had a different one, but . . . "

"Mmm-hmm."

"That's it," Jim said.

"Well, that's all right, Jim," West said. "I don't want to put any pressure on you. But what I'm telling you is I don't think you're being truthful, a hundred percent, because I think you're scared and I think you're afraid what's . . . going to unfold. So Jim, before you get too deep in a hole here . . . "

"OK."

"Tell us the truth," West demanded. "What happened?"

"It's all I've got," Jim said.

West kept at him, but the detective focused his efforts almost entirely on Jim's story of the mystery knife buyer. West never asked Jim if he had ever met the Zantops. And he never asked if Jim was directly responsible for their deaths. Indeed, West never mentioned the Zantops by name. The only name he was seeking was the person he imagined to be the real killer, the person to whom Jim gave or sold the knives.

The closest West came to the question of murder was to ask John Parker where he was on January 27.

"Uh, I don't remember," the elder Parker said. "I was, I think, I was finishing a job up in Stratford and I was there on Sunday that weekend, but the twenty-seventh, I was either at home or, um, at this job in Stratford."

Then West turned to Jim: "All right, so where were you on the twenty-seventh?"

Before Jim could answer, West interrupted: "I know what you're supposed to say, 'cause you're in . . . "

"I know," Jim said, "but um, we go to the movies sometimes."

"Mmm-hmm," West said, urging him on.

"Uh, we just sit around."

West let it drop.

With his father by his side, and the questions focused on the person to whom Jim supposedly provided the knives, Jim was able to hold onto the alibi he and Robert had hatched. At the end of the interview, John Parker even adopted West's own phrasing to support his son: "I believe Jim a hundred percent."

While West was dealing with the Parkers, Bruno, Hubbard, and Page drove a few hundred yards from the sheriff's office to the Tullochs' yellow house at 313 Main Street.

They arrived just after 8 P.M. and explained to Mike and Diane Tulloch that they had just spoken with Jim Parker about the purchase of two SOG SEAL 2000 knives. Now they'd like to speak with Robert. The Tullochs, who'd been watching a movie on their VCR in the living room, invited the detectives to take a seat at the kitchen table while Diane went upstairs to rouse Robert, who was fighting the flu.

Robert came downstairs with the pillow-haired look of someone fresh from sleep. While Diane made Robert a cup of tea, Bruno started firing questions at him. Bruno and Hubbard were struck by how different he seemed from Jim Parker. At seventeen, Robert was only a year older, but he struck Bruno as far more articulate, better educated, thoughtful even. Robert was cool, calm, and collected. No alien creatures were trying to escape from his neck. Bruno found it much easier to talk with Robert, mostly because he wasn't as tightly wound as Jim. When Bruno began the interview by saying Robert didn't have to speak with them, Robert answered confidently: "I'll talk to you."

Robert repeated Jim's story of buying the knives from Fox Firearms, deciding after they arrived that they were too big, and then selling them a week or so later at the Army-Navy store. He couldn't place the dates exactly, he said. Robert also couldn't describe the buyer because Jim had handled the sale. He echoed Jim's line about keeping the knife purchases secret from his parents because they wouldn't have approved.

It was the first Diane and Mike heard about SOG SEAL 2000s. When Diane learned they had ordered the knives over the Internet, her thoughts rushed back a few months to a similar incident, what she called "another one of their stupid things." Robert had said he needed climbing shoes, so she let him use her credit card to order a pair—if he agreed to pay half. Instead of shoes, Robert ordered two Stun Master stun guns, handheld, high-voltage devices whose primary use was to temporarily immobilize people. The box came addressed to Diane, and when she ripped it open she was shocked to find the weapons. When Robert came home, Diane confronted him for lying to her about the shoes and for buying such strange and troubling items. Robert answered her accusations with yet another lie, calculated on the spot to minimize the damage. He admitted ordering the Stun Masters, but told his mother they were for innocent mischief. He said he and Jim heard they could use stun guns to pop street signs off their posts—a harmless teen prank. In fact, Robert already had a stop sign affixed to his bedroom door. Diane thought it was a lame excuse, but she allowed herself to believe him. She didn't probe further. Her anger at his lie about the climbing shoes and her doubts about his street sign story carried next to no consequences. She sent the stun guns back to the seller, and when no refund came she made Robert and Jim reimburse her.

Diane didn't mention the stun guns to the troopers sitting in her house asking her son about his Internet purchase of two commando knives.

Robert volunteered to Bruno that he and Jim were rock climbers, and when Bruno asked if they had done much climbing lately, Robert told the detective about the deep cut on his leg. Bruno asked how it happened, and Robert said he climbed over a snow bank "to take a leak" and cut it on a maple-tree spigot. It was the lie he had told most often during the past three weeks.

Despite the link from Robert and Jim to the knives, and despite Robert's cut, Bruno—like West—still couldn't see these boys as the Zantops' murderers.

Just as he had done with Jim, Bruno asked Robert if he would voluntarily allow the detectives to fingerprint him. Robert agreed. Then

Bruno asked something else: "We'd like to look at your footwear." It was a question they hadn't asked Jim—it was suggested by Sergeant Russ Conte, another New Hampshire State Police detective, when Bruno called him from the sheriff's office to discuss what Jim had told them.

Mike Tulloch, who had been sitting quietly, piped up: "Do you want to look at them or do you want to take them?"

"At this point in time I just want to look at them," Bruno answered.

Robert went upstairs and returned with two pairs of shoes. He plopped them on the kitchen table—a pair of Nike sneakers and a pair of hiking boots.

"What make of shoes are those?" Hubbard asked.

"Vasque," Robert answered.

It was the same make of shoe that had left the bloody footprint in the Zantop house.

Bruno took Mike and Diane into the next room, to quietly tell them that a Vasque footprint had been found at the murder scene. He didn't say it, but Bruno knew that fact, plus the link between Robert and Jim and the knives, plus the cut on Robert's leg, might be adding up to something. Mike recognized as much on his own.

"This ups the level a bit," he said cautiously.

"You're absolutely correct. It does up the level," Bruno said.

"I don't know if I should talk to an attorney or not," Mike Tulloch said.

"That's a decision you and your wife have to make. I'm not going to advise you one way or the other," Bruno said. "If you tell me the boots stay here, they stay here."

"I don't think my son is involved in this case," Mike said. "You have my permission to take the boots as long as it's OK with Robert."

They went back into the kitchen.

"Robert," Bruno said, "I want your permission to take your boots. A print at the homicide scene was made by a Vasque boot. OK? I want to take your boots to compare them to that print that was found at the scene."

The question played to one of Robert's strengths—he had to

instantly calculate the risks and benefits of every possible answer. He understood intuitively that he faced a choice: Object to surrendering the boots and he'd cast doubt on his innocence, maybe ending up in custody as a result. Or play it cool and surrender the incriminating boots, buying himself enough time to run.

"Take the boots," he said, "as long as I get them back." Robert continued the nonchalant charade, saying they were his only pair of insulated winter boots and that he'd need them for the cold days ahead. Bruno said that wouldn't be a problem. That is, as long as they didn't match the footprint left at the scene. To be helpful, Diane got a brown paper bag and the boots were packed to go.

While Bruno stepped out of the room to speak with Mike and Diane, Hubbard asked Robert a question: By the way, what size are those boots?

Robert wasn't sure—they had been his father's and had been handed down to him. He thought they were size 12. No, maybe 11½.

Even with a Vasque boot the same size as the one that left the footprint, Bruno and Hubbard wouldn't allow themselves to get excited. It flickered in their minds that one or both of these teenage boys might be seriously involved, but they didn't allow the spark to burst into a flame. First off, the detectives were exhausted at the end of a long day that had followed a string of long days. Mostly, though, there had been too many dead ends in this case already. Until something was declared a perfect match—a fingerprint, a bootprint, anything—they needed to stay as calm as Robert seemed. Most of all, they still didn't have the murder weapons.

After taking the boots, Bruno, Hubbard, and Page escorted the Tullochs to the sheriff's office for fingerprints. While there, Robert caught brief sight of Jim.

No words passed between them, but none needed to. They were in the crosshairs of the police. If they were allowed to go home, both knew what they needed to do next—run. This time there would be no turning back.

14

Two SOG
SEAL 2000 Knives

Just as they had hoped, Robert and Jim were allowed to return home with their parents after being questioned and fingerprinted at the sheriff's office. Although Jim had purchased two SOG SEAL 2000 knives and Robert owned a pair of Vasque boots and sported a nasty cut on his leg, it still seemed too far-fetched to investigators to imagine these two bright boys from good homes were more than peripherally involved in the killings.

As midnight approached on Thursday, February 15, investigators were satisfied they were finally making real progress in solving the case. With the right questions and enough pressure to make these boys realize the trouble they were in, Robert and Jim would lead them to the killers. In the meantime, there didn't seem to be an urgent need to place them in custody.

The phone rang shortly after Robert and his parents returned home from the sheriff's office. It was his girlfriend, Christiana Usenza, checking to see if he was still suffering from the flu.

"Guess what happened to me?" he asked.

"What?"

"Um, the police came and questioned me about those murders in Hanover," Robert told her.

"WHAT?"

Robert explained that he and Jim had bought the same kind of knives used in the killings and that police had tracked their Internet purchase.

"Robert, this does look weird," Christiana said. "You have a cut on your leg. . . . Did you do it?"

"No, I didn't," Robert answered. He told her the story about selling the knives at the Army-Navy store before the murders.

"Well, then you should be OK because they'll find that guy and they'll figure out that [you] didn't have the knives at the time," Christiana said.

"Yeah," Robert answered, eager to get off the phone. "I gotta talk to Jimmy, 'cause I don't know if they've questioned him."

"Are you OK?"

"No," Robert said.

Christiana hung up, telling herself there was no way he was mixed up in murder. Yet something nagged at her enough to make her pray it was all a big mistake.

Meanwhile, in his house across town, Jim felt the same need to talk with Robert, so he dialed the Tullochs' phone number. Earlier, Jim had asked his parents if he could sleep at Robert's, or if Robert could come to their house, but they said no. Joan and John also told him not to speak with Robert, but he disobeyed that order by picking up the phone.

It was a brief conversation, summed up by a single phrase: "We're kind of fucked here." They agreed they'd be better off communicating via computer, using the AOL Instant Messenger system, in case their phones were tapped.

Jim went upstairs to the family computers and Robert went into his brother Kienan's room to use their shared computer. But soon Diane

Tulloch came in to see how he was doing. She believed her son's story about selling the knives, and now she wanted him to get some rest. When his mother asked how he was feeling, Robert answered, "I'm sick, I've missed school, and now I'm wanted for murder."

She told him to go to bed and stay in his room—a move that cut him off from the computer. Around the same time, John Parker realized his son was communicating with Robert over the Internet and ordered him to stop. After that, John and Jim sat together watching TV awhile, then John said what they all needed most was sleep.

When his parents went to bed, Jim called Robert again. "We'll meet at Red Ass," they agreed, using a nickname for Kip Battey as a code in case someone was listening in on their conversation. Each knew that "Red Ass" meant the Batteys' house near Chelsea's Beacon Hill, where the snowmobile trail crossed the road.

They hastily filled backpacks with whatever they thought might be useful: a compass, some fishing hooks and bobbers, the Boy Scouts' *Handbook for Boys,* a camping ax, cans of tomato soup and black beans, Chap Stick, pens and pencils, duct tape, matches, a flashlight, Band-Aids, climbing shoes, vise grips, and assorted clothing. Robert also grabbed a Vermont junior driver's license belonging to Kip Battey that had somehow found its way into his possession. Useful, perhaps, as false identification. They also grabbed whatever cash they had, a thin stack of bills including a fifty and a few twenties that together added up to far less than they had on their first flight two weeks earlier.

Before Jim left home, he tore a piece of paper from a notebook and scrawled a note to his parents:

I Just had
to talk
to Robert
alone, I will
be back
be th morning
don't call cops!!

It was after three in the morning on Friday, February 16, when Jim left the note on the kitchen counter and slipped out of the house. He climbed into his silver Audi and drove the winding back roads to the far side of Beacon Hill from the Batteys' house, parking the car on the side of the road and trudging through the snow along an unpaved route that was impassable to cars in winter. It was hard going, but he figured it was the safest way to meet up with Robert while avoiding any troopers who might be roaming through town.

As Robert prepared to meet Jim, he walked past his parents' bedroom.

"Robert, go back to bed," Diane called.

"I'm going down to get some tea," Robert lied on his way out the door.

They met as planned near the Batteys' house and from there hiked back to Jim's car for what would be their final departure from Chelsea. This was it: Chelsea was history; indeed, neither boy would step foot in town again.

Soon after they hit the road, Robert made a stunning announcement: In his rush to pack, he had forgotten the knives. It was an extraordinary admission, a loud echo of what had happened twenty days earlier when they left the sheaths at the Zantops' house. Now authorities would have two matched sets of knives and sheaths, shattering their alibi about selling the knives at the Army-Navy store.

Maybe it was simple forgetfulness by a teenage boy on the run from police. Or maybe Robert wasn't as prepared to leave home as he thought he was. Whatever the reason, Robert and Jim both recognized the risk. As they drove from town in the predawn darkness, they discussed going back for the SEAL 2000s. But almost as quickly they realized that returning to Robert's house might be just the opportunity his parents or the police would need to forever prevent them from leaving. They dropped that idea and pressed on, with Jim driving back roads from Chelsea then picking up Vermont Route 14 toward Interstate 89.

John Parker switched on the light in his bedroom when he heard Jim turn the ignition in the Audi. He and Joan ran to the window, threw it open, and yelled into the cold night for him to stop. But Jim was already pulling down the driveway.

The Parkers suspected Jim was headed to Robert's house, but it was anyone's guess where the boys would go from there. The Parkers called the Tullochs in a bid to intercept them. The phone rang awhile but no one answered, so John pulled on his clothes, grabbed his coat, and ran outside. He pointed his pickup truck toward Main Street.

Mike and Diane Tulloch were lying in bed when they heard the ringing phone that, unknown to them, was their last chance to prevent their son and his best friend from becoming fugitives. They never imagined the caller was John Parker desperately trying to reach them, and as they lay there hearing one ring after another they wondered why Robert wasn't answering it, as he had the earlier calls. After the ringing stopped, Mike rose from bed and checked Robert's room. Empty. He scoured the house, with no better luck. Before he and Diane could do anything more, they heard a knock on the door—John Parker. When he learned that Jim wasn't there and Robert had disappeared as well, John drove around town for more than an hour looking for them.

When John returned empty-handed, all four parents shared the hope that their sons had just gone off somewhere to talk, and that they'd be back by morning. The Parkers hadn't yet found Jim's note, but when they did a few hours later, it buoyed their spirits. Maybe he was just upset about the police visit and he'd come home, after all. But as more hours passed with no sign of them, a hard question formed in their minds. As Diane put it: "Why would these boys be running?"

The manhunt began around eleven that morning, about eight hours after Robert and Jim set off. It was triggered when John Parker realized that his son wouldn't be keeping the promise he made in his note. After talking with his wife and the Tullochs, John Parker called Detective Chuck West. "Jimmy's gone," he said.

Two months later, the Vermont sheriff whose territory included

Chelsea would blast New Hampshire authorities for not keeping a closer watch on the pair and for not asking him to do so. "If they even gave the slightest indication . . . that they would flee, we'd have watched them," fumed Orange County Sheriff Dennis McClure. New Hampshire authorities defended their approach, but there wasn't much they could say in response. The failure to post guards outside the boys' homes was the clearest evidence yet that, even after they questioned Robert and Jim, it remained too far a stretch for West, Bruno, Hubbard, and the other investigators to imagine them responsible for the crumpled, bloodied bodies in the Zantops' study.

Once they got out of Chelsea, Robert and Jim drove along Interstate 89 for more than an hour and then picked up Interstate 93, heading south toward Boston. They made their way to the Massachusetts Turnpike, the state's main east-west corridor, and headed west. It was a roundabout escape route, with only one apparent benefit: It kept Robert and Jim away from Interstate 91, which they considered the main highway through Hanover.

It occurred to them that the police would soon be on the lookout for Jim's Audi, so they decided to abandon it and try to hitch rides toward California with cross-country truckers—an idea they'd picked up from watching movies. Their first attempt was a dud. They stopped at a Massachusetts rest stop and asked about long-haul truckers only to learn that most of the truck traffic on the turnpike was involved in close-range work of a hundred miles or fewer. One trucker told them to head toward Sturbridge, Massachusetts, Exit 9 off the turnpike, where they might find truckers veering south toward New York and beyond.

From the exit they took a right onto Route 20 West, and from there they wandered onto Route 131 and into the parking lot of the Sturbridge Service Station. By this time Robert had taken the wheel to give Jim a break, and as he pulled into the station he noticed a tow truck idling in the lot. The driver was John Moran, a twenty-one-year-old, part-time police officer in Brimfield, Massachusetts, who was making ends meet by driving a wrecker while waiting for a full-time police job. Moran—no relation to Hanover detective Frank Moran—had just dropped off a car and was drinking coffee to stay warm and awake on the overnight shift when the Audi pulled in. Robert rolled down his window and asked Moran for directions to a gas station—Sturbridge Service had no gas pumps. Jim piped up from the passenger seat and asked how to get back to the turnpike. Moran gave them directions to both, then watched them drive off. Moran thought something about the two young travelers didn't seem right. They looked nervous, he thought. He considered checking their license plate to see if the car was reported stolen. To his regret, Moran let the idea pass and went back to work.

Six hours later, relaxing at home after his shift, Moran was watching the local news when he saw a report about two fugitive teenage boys. When he saw their pictures—the same faces he saw in the Audi—he ran to the phone and dialed the New Hampshire State Police. Moran was quickly transferred to the command center, and soon after he was talking to an FBI agent. Investigators had their first solid lead about where the duo was and which way they might be heading.

The town of Sturbridge would like to be best known for Old Sturbridge Village, a two-hundred-acre re-creation of what life was like in a small New England town in the years after the Revolution. But to most travelers, Sturbridge is most familiar for its location at the crossroads of New England. The town lies at the intersection of the Massachusetts Turnpike and Interstate 84, which makes Sturbridge the perfect place for a truck stop.

After following Moran's directions to an Xtra Mart for gas, Robert and Jim found their way to the Sturbridge Isles truck stop and eased the Audi into a parking spot in a rear lot. They walked into the Sturbridge Isles diner the morning of Friday, February 16, and began a daylong quest to find a trucker willing to give them a lift. One rejection followed another—insurance rules barred most truckers from taking riders. While they waited, Robert and Jim used the Audi as a base, returning several times to grab rest and their belongings.

Around four in the afternoon, short-order cook Joe Paquette parked his car nearby and saw the pair climb out of the Audi and slip on their backpacks. Left behind was the usual detritus found in a teenager's car—gloves, receipts, clothing, an atlas, a knapsack. There also were some other, less typical items. A brown wallet was tucked in the console between the front seats. In the trunk was a tool box containing two knives, one a hunting knife and the other a military knife. The blades were covered by worn sheaths held together with duct tape, but there was nothing special to distinguish them. Such knives and sheaths were as common in Vermont and New Hampshire as maple trees and rolling hills. Later, it would occur to investigators that if the Zantops' killers had used those knives and left behind those sheaths, they might never have been apprehended.

As darkness approached, Robert and Jim were sitting inside the truck-stop diner, where fifteen-year-old Zack Mathiew of Holland, Massachusetts, saw one smoking a cigarette and the other drinking coffee. Waitress Carrie Morris, a sixteen-year-old from Sturbridge, noticed how one sat in a booth while the other paced by a window, walking rapidly back and forth and looking nervous.

Paquette, the cook, saw the two again around 5:30 P.M., brushing their teeth in the men's bathroom. Jim had forgotten his toothbrush in his rush to pack—Robert wasn't the only forgetful one, but a toothbrush could hardly compare with the knives—so he bought a new one at the Sturbridge Isles. Diner hostess Sharon Palmer thought they were runaways, and she thought Jim might have been crying. Palmer watched as they walked through a lounge area, looking for friendly truckers heading toward California.

A few hours later, Palmer sent a male trucker into the men's room, to look for the pair and maybe eavesdrop on their conversation. Another waitress wondered aloud if they should call the police. But the trucker came out and said the bathroom was empty.

Robert and Jim had caught a ride.

That same afternoon, a Vermont State Police cruiser parked in front of the Tulloch house on Main Street. It was an unmistakably odd sight for Chelsea that got people talking. Something was clearly up, but no one knew what. Soon, word began to circulate that police were looking for the boys—a second cruiser was parked at the Parker house on West Hill. But why? It was fast becoming the talk of the town.

The weird quality of the day only grew stranger as the afternoon wore on. Pat Davenport, the school principal, took a call from a state police detective from the nearby barracks in Bethel. The two were familiar with one another because of their respective positions and, ordinarily, could talk easily. But Davenport found the normally affable Detective Sergeant Ray Keefe guarded.

Keefe asked her if Robert and Jim were in school.

Davenport checked the daily attendance list and told the detective the boys had not come in. But, she added, the two had been in school the day before, Thursday.

"Don't let them in," Keefe told her. The detective then advised her, "If you see them, lock them out." If anyone spotted the boys, notify him immediately.

The instructions unnerved the school principal. She asked what was going on.

The situation is dangerous, said Keefe.

How dangerous? Davenport asked.

Extremely dangerous, said Keefe.

The principal was looking for specifics, but got none. Finding herself in a verbal dance, unable to get a straight answer, she tried to come at it from another angle. Should I be concerned?

Very concerned, said Keefe.

The detective wasn't in a position to disclose any hard information, but the truth was that the police were worried the boys might show up at the school for a "Columbine-type thing." Rather than trigger panic by referring specifically to that bloodbath, Keefe stressed locking the boys out.

Davenport got the message. It wasn't just Keefe's manner, but also the fact that Keefe was a detective on the department's Bureau of Criminal Investigations. The BCI unit didn't bother with petty crimes; it focused on felonies like rape and murder. Davenport toured the school and checked to make sure doors that should be locked were, in fact, locked. Then she assigned a free faculty member to stand watch at the main and only unlocked entrance.

As evening came, crowds of Chelseans drifted toward the school. The Chelsea Red Devil basketball team was playing a visiting squad from Williamstown. By the time the game got under way, an anxious Davenport had notified the janitors, the athletic director, and some teachers to watch out for Robert and Jim. Fans and spectators carried word of the cruiser at the Tulloch house as they entered the gym, and the unusual tableau was heightened by the sight of investigators in plainclothes mingling in the crowd and around the periphery of the game, eyes not focused on the action but scanning all around. They stood out because of their dress—neat and much more formal than the country casual of Chelsea—and also because some wore guns on their hips.

Still, spirits in the gym were high. Chelsea not only won the game, but history was made. Brad Johnson became the first Chelsea player to join the "1,000 Point Club" in his junior year. Pouring out of the gym and into the night were happy teammates like Zack Courts and Coltere Savidge, parents, teachers, and kids. They climbed into pickups and cars and headed down Main Street in the picturesque village blanketed in fresh snow.

But the town's landscape had changed indelibly.

Following the win, Brad Johnson, his family, and a group of people wandered across the street to The Pines to eat, shoot pool, play music, and celebrate the historic scoring achievement. It was at this moment that the mystery of the night deepened.

Just after 10 P.M., Chelseans were brought up short by the sight of a convoy of police vehicles lumbering slowly into town from the south. For a small town that didn't have its own squad car and for the most part didn't lock its doors, it was an alien invasion, a close encounter of an unprecedented kind.

The usual rumble through town was the sound of a tractor pulling a spreader, or one of Jack Johnson's logging trucks. But here came a caravan of five state police cruisers along with a sixth vehicle, an over-sized Vermont State Police forensics truck. Driving the front cruiser and leading the way to the Tulloch house was the detective who'd spoken to Pat Davenport earlier in the day, Ray Keefe. He'd never been part of such a massive convoy, which had actually been twice as big until reaching the town line. That was when half the convoy turned off to head up West Hill to the Parker house.

Chelseans, especially kids, began cruising Main Street, gawking at the convoy and wondering, Why the show of force? "We drove by Robert's house and saw all these police cars, and we're like Ohmygod," said Kip Battey. Speculation quickly heated up—What had Robert and Jim done? "We were figuring," said Battey, "oh man, they broke into someone's house." In another car were Gaelen McKee, Sada Dumont, Casey Purcell, and Katie Allen. "They must have stolen a car!" Sada Dumont said, only half-serious. "Or robbed a store!" someone else chimed in. None of them thought it could really be anything that bad. Tyler Vermette and Matt Butryman had been at The Pines when they decided to jump in Tyler's mom's car. The huge police presence took their breath away. "Holy smokes!" Matt said. The two boys counted the number of police vehicles outside the Tulloch place and figured the trouble was deep. But the worst they could come up with was that Robert and Jim "must have done something on the computer." If that was the case, Tyler thought as he drove home, "No big deal—well, a big deal, but not that bad."

Coltere Savidge and Zack Courts were wondering what was up as they headed north on Main Street. Coltere was driving Zack to his home a few houses down from the Tullochs'. The two seniors slowed and eyeballed the police. "Have you ever cut yourself and looked down and gone, 'Oh, crap,'" he said later. "You know it's gonna hurt, but it hasn't started yet. That's how it was. We knew there was no good reason for a forensics truck to be outside any house."

But, like everyone else, Zack and Coltere had no idea what was really happening. Coltere dropped Zack off and Zack headed into his house. He was home alone; his father was away for the weekend. Coltere headed north on Route 110 to his house, just over the town line in Washington. His parents, David and Mary, were there, as was his younger brother, Cabot, and everyone talked about the basketball win and the strange police invasion. The Savidge boys decided to do what Chelseans often do come the weekend—rent a movie.

Coltere drove back to the center of Chelsea in his mother's Subaru Forester. He was inside Will's Store, holding the Nicolas Cage car-theft movie *Gone in 60 Seconds,* when two men approached him and asked whether he knew Robert Tulloch and Jim Parker. The men were dressed in plainclothes but had ID badges hanging around their necks, showing one was with the Vermont State Police and one was from New Hampshire.

They showed Coltere photographs of the two boys from their licenses.

"Yeah, I know those kids," said Coltere.

The investigators said they'd like to question him.

Brad Johnson's older brother was also in the store, and after he returned to The Pines, word spread quickly that the police wanted to question Coltere Savidge. Nervous about the whole thing, Coltere called home. After a couple of telephone conversations between him and his parents, and then the investigators and his parents, Coltere drove home to pick up his father.

Father and son were ushered into a conference room at the Orange County sheriff's office near the North Common. It was past 11 P.M., and David Savidge sensed urgency among the officers. Still, no one knew why police were after Robert and Jim. "Maybe it was just a breaking and entering thing, one of Robert and Jimmy's things that had gone wrong," Coltere hoped. Or maybe, he thought, they ran away again.

The questions began: Do Robert and Jim have any camps in the area? No, said Coltere. What do you know about the boys' first trip west two weeks ago? Not much, said Coltere; they'd said they wanted to go rock climbing in Colorado. Did Robert and Jim use drugs? No. Have they acted strangely lately? Not really. Did Robert and Jim spend much time on the Internet? Not really, Coltere replied. No more than most kids.

Did Robert and Jim ever show an interest in knives?

Did you ever see them on the Internet shopping for knives?

Coltere answered "No" to both questions, but this was when Coltere and David Savidge finally began to understand why the police had invaded Chelsea.

David Savidge interrupted: "Can you tell us about this?" he asked.

No, the two troopers replied.

"Does this have anything to do with drugs?"

No, the troopers said. This is much worse.

"More serious than drugs?"

Yes, they said. Extremely serious.

The troopers had adopted the same mantra Detective Sergeant Ray Keefe had used with Pat Davenport: "Extremely serious." They told the Savidges that was all they could say.

"You will know tomorrow," one said. "In the morning there will be reporters all over this town."

David Savidge began putting it all together: the presence of a New Hampshire detective in Vermont; a situation described by investigators as more serious than drugs or drug dealing—"extremely serious." The media on its way en masse.

The Savidges silently left the sheriff's office, climbed into their car, and drove home past the Tulloch house. Father and son looked at each other and spoke a shared thought: "This has to do with the Zantop murders."

It was around midnight, and the two now were among the first to know the answer to the mystery of a long, strange day in Chelsea.

Soon other Chelseans began discovering the horrifying news. Town Clerk Diane Mattoon was about to go to bed when her sister-in-law called to share the conclusion sweeping through town. "What are you talking about?" Mattoon said, dismissing the notion.

Robert Tulloch and Jim Parker paddle a homemade raft down the First Branch of
the White River in their hometown of Chelsea, Vermont, in May 2000.
(Photo courtesy of Patricia Davenport)

Sixth grade yearbook photo
of Robert Tulloch.

Sixth grade yearbook photo
of Jim Parker.

ABOVE: Robert Tulloch
pretends to cut his finger
while watched by his friend
and debate partner Kip Battey.
(*Chelsea Public School
yearbook photo*)

RIGHT: Jim Parker dressed as
the Big Bad Wolf for the
Winter Carnival in Chelsea,
Vermont, in early 2000.
(*Chelsea Public School
yearbook photo*)

LEFT: Jim Parker after dyeing his hair blond for his sophomore year class photo. (*Chelsea Public School yearbook photo*)

BELOW: Robert Tulloch (*second from left*) clowns around with (*from left*): Casey Purcell, faculty advisor Alyson Mahoney, Lucy Johnson, and Ellen Knudsen. Purcell would join with Johnson and Knudsen to seek Robert's impeachment as President of the Student Council. (*Chelsea Public School yearbook photo*)

The Tulloch home on Main Street in Chelsea, Vermont, with a sign erected after Robert became a suspect in the murders of Half and Susanne Zantop. The window of Robert's bedroom is on the second floor, far left, facing the street. *(Boston Globe photo/Barry Chin)*

The abandoned farmhouse in Vershire, Vermont, that Robert Tulloch and Jim Parker used in an unsuccessful mail-fraud scheme. Later, they dug makeshift graves in an adjacent field, where they planned to bury their first intended victims. *(Photograph by Mitchell Zuckoff)*

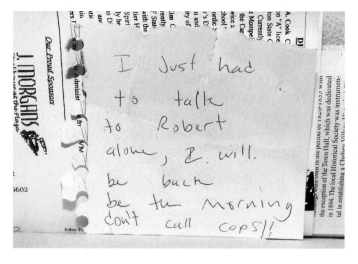

The note Jim Parker left his parents the morning of February 16, 2001, before he and Robert Tulloch began their flight from justice. *(New Hampshire State Police photo)*

The two SOG SEAL 2000 knives used to murder Half and Susanne Zantop, wrapped in makeshift sheaths, in a cardboard citrus box where investigators found them in Robert Tulloch's bedroom. *(New Hampshire State Police photo)*

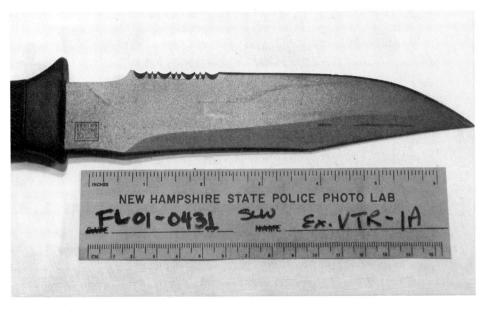

One of the SOG SEAL 2000 knives, labeled as evidence.
(New Hampshire State Police photo)

Robert Tulloch's Vasque workboots, which matched a partial bloody bootprint at the Zantops' home after the murders. *(New Hampshire State Police photo)*

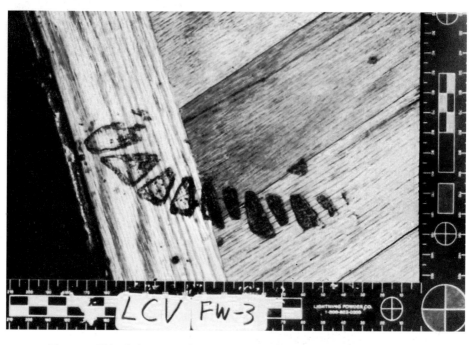

The partial bloody bootprint that linked Robert Tulloch to the Zantop murders.
(New Hampshire State Police photo)

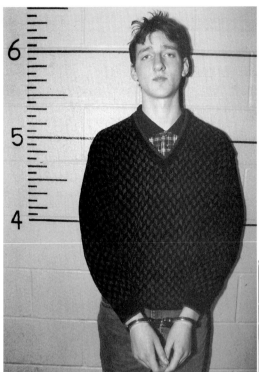

LEFT: Robert Tulloch, in custody of Indiana authorities, before his return to New Hampshire. (*New Hampshire State Police photo*)

BELOW: Sergeant Bill Ward, whose impersonation of a trucker led to the arrests of Robert Tulloch and Jim Parker, outside the Henry County, Indiana, courthouse the day the two fugitives were captured. (*Photo by U. E. Bush*)

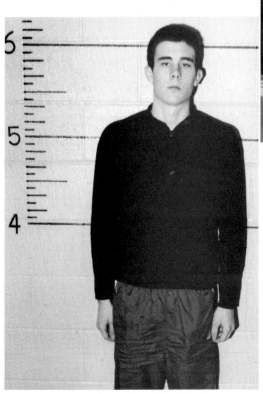

Jim Parker, in custody of Indiana authorities, before his return to New Hampshire. (*New Hampshire State Police photo*)

RIGHT: Robert Tulloch escorted to Lebanon District Court by Hanover, New Hampshire, police officers upon his return from Indiana. (Boston Globe *photo/Barry Chin*)

BELOW: Henry County, Indiana, sheriff's deputies escort Jim Parker to court for an extradition hearing. (Boston Globe *photo*)

Joan and John Parker, April 2002. (Boston Globe *photo*)

Diane Tulloch gets into a car with Mike Tulloch
driving, March 2001. (Boston Globe *photo*)

ABOVE: Becky Tulloch Johnson and Kienan Tulloch in Grafton County Superior Court for their brother Robert's plea and sentencing hearing, April 4, 2002. (Boston Globe *photo by Wendy Maeda*)

RIGHT: Christiana Usenza, Robert Tulloch's girlfriend, April 2001. (Boston Globe *photo*)

Assistant Attorney General Kelly Ayotte and Hanover Police Chief Nick Giaccone at a press conference during the search for the Zantops' murderers. (Boston Globe *photo/John Blanding*)

New Hampshire State Police Trooper Chuck West, who worked with Hanover Police Detective Frank Moran to trace the murder weapons to Robert Tulloch and Jim Parker. (Boston Globe *photo*)

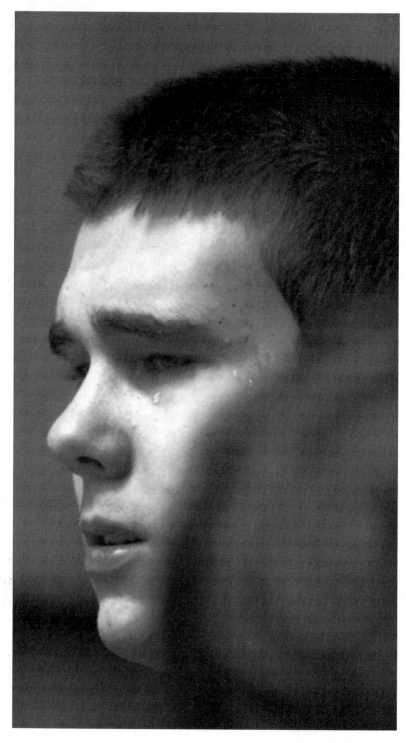

Jim Parker cries at his sentencing hearing, April 4, 2002.
(Pool courtroom photo via AP)

Robert Tulloch smirks as he is brought to court for his plea and
sentencing hearing, April 4, 2002. (Boston Globe *photo*)

Aerial photograph of Half and Susanne's home at 115 Trescott Road
in Etna, New Hampshire. (Boston Globe *photo/David Ryan*)

Half Zantop, at twenty-seven, climbing the South Face of Cathedral Peak in Yosemite National Park in 1965. *(Photo by Alex Bertulis)*

LEFT: An undated photo of Half and Susanne Zantop. (Boston Globe *photo/ Tom Landers*)

BELOW: Veronika *(left)* and Mariana Zantop after Jim Parker's sentencing, April 4, 2002. (*Pool photo via AP*)

Head shots of Half
and Susanne Zantop.
(*Photos provided to the media
by Dartmouth College*)

Mattoon at least got the news from a relative. Others were hit right between the eyes by strangers. Pat Davenport was fast asleep when the phone rang about fifteen minutes after midnight. Pulling herself awake, the principal thought, "Late calls usually mean bad news." It was a reporter from the *Boston Globe,* asking her "opinion of the prime suspect in the Zantop murders, Robert Tulloch." Only then did she understand fully the depth of Ray Keefe's concern that Robert and Jim not be allowed in the school.

Racing through her mind was the same thought that worried Keefe and other police officers all day—the possibility of Columbine redux. But Davenport had little time to process the news. As soon as she hung up—she gave the *Globe* reporter nothing worth printing—the phone rang again, and then again—more than sixty-five calls over the next seventy-two hours.

Home alone in his house, Zack Courts was watching *The Tonight Show with Jay Leno* when he answered his telephone. The caller was a reporter from the *Boston Herald* who wanted to know about the two boys suspected of slaying the Zantops. Questions came nonstop, and Zack, knocked for a loop, found himself answering one after another about Robert, the only one whose name was identified publicly so far. "He's got hobbies, he's got friends," Zack was quoted saying. "He's an extremely intelligent person, very quick-witted." For Zack the news was unfathomable.

"I'd have to say he didn't do it," Zack told the reporter. "He's not like that. I mean, it's always possible, but Robert, no way, man."

Suddenly done, the reporter hung up and moved on. Zack, in shock, held the receiver. He called Coltere and blurted out all he could recall about the interview. Coltere listened and then told Zack that he already knew, that he and his dad had figured it all out during his questioning by police.

"You OK?" Coltere asked.

"Well, I don't know," said Zack.

"My mom says you should come up here right away."

Coltere drove back into town and scooped him up. Zack spent the next several nights sleeping over at Coltere's house. The boys tried watching *Gone in 60 Seconds,* but had trouble paying attention. They had trouble sleeping that night, too—catching only about three hours. Gone in the last six hours was any sense of peace.

"We were kinda scared shitless," said Coltere.

The next morning, Dr. Andy Pomerantz was lying in bed listening to National Public Radio. He was waiting for the popular show *Car Talk,* which was part of his usual Saturday-morning ritual of lingering in bed and gazing lazily out a big window into the woods. He and his wife, Jill, liked to take their morning coffee slowly and then Andy would put on his gear and head out to cross-country ski.

Pomerantz was only half-listening when his wife said, "Did you hear that? They mentioned Chelsea on the radio." Pomerantz turned up the volume. He listened hard, but the news report had moved on to the economy or some other topic. Nothing more about Chelsea. But Jill Pomerantz told her husband she was certain she'd heard Chelsea mentioned on NPR. The couple sat anxiously awaiting the next news cycle.

Then it came: a nationwide search was under way for two teenagers from Chelsea, Vermont, suspected of murdering Dartmouth professors Half and Susanne Zantop in their New Hampshire home.

Pomerantz felt like a tree had fallen on his chest. The small town ran through him; Chelsea was in his soul, defining who he was. These two boys, he was thinking, are our kids, too. He reeled at the news, flashes of Robert and Jim racing through his head. He pictured young Jimmy running up the basketball court. He recalled seeing Robert the previous summer at the wedding of Robert's sister Becky and Charles Johnson, one of Jack and Annette's sons. Robert hadn't been very friendly that day, a mood Pomerantz chalked up to normal teenage angst.

The flashing images kept coming, in no particular order. He pictured Robert and Jim paddling together at the raft race during the Spring Festival, and remembered how tall and strong they looked. Kids grew up so fast, he recalled thinking at the time, a truism that never ceased to amaze him.

The psychiatrist found himself pacing around his house. His wife telephoned a friend, and the friend had already heard the news. It was a scene being repeated time and time again: heads were shaking, hearts were dropping, stomachs were falling, as despair and disbelief swept through town. The news had to be a mistake, thought most. No way two Chelsea boys could have done this. This was wrong. Maybe, some even thought, a police frame-up. It seemed beyond belief. As a psychiatrist, Pomerantz had witnessed despair, and this was what it looked like.

Teacher DeRoss Kellogg was at his home in Bethel when he and his wife, Imogen, heard on the radio that the big break in the Zantop case involved Robert and Jim. Kellogg collapsed into a chair in his living room. "Life has changed forever," he told her. Kellogg felt paralyzed. He sat in the chair for an hour, zoning out. In her Main Street house, poet Cora Brooks, having watched the police take over the Tulloch home across the street, was thinking like a lifelong pacifist: this had to be a horrible police mistake, an abuse of police power. Not for a second that morning did she think Robert and Jim could have killed the Zantops. "Killing like this involves jumping off the edge of existence, with no thought of consequences," she said. "It is incomprehensible." Two boys who had memorized her *Sock Monster* story couldn't have taken such a leap, she thought.

Tyler Vermette, who'd gone to sleep thinking his friends had gotten swept up in some sort of computer crime, awoke and saw a newspaper headline: "WANTED."

"My heart pretty much sank to my feet," he said.

One town over, in Vershire, Andrew Patti dropped by a neighbor's house to say hello. "Did you see the article in the newspaper?" the neighbor asked. Patti looked at the headline, then glanced at the photograph that accompanied it. The caption said it was Robert Tulloch, wanted in connection with the Zantop murders.

"Holy shit!" Patti said. It was the face he had seen through the windowpanes of his front door seven months earlier. Patti thought back to the young man who claimed his car had broken down and who seemed so intent on getting Patti to open the door. Patti thought about how he had flashed his gun to scare the visitor, then launched into a five-minute soliloquy.

"Goddamn it, this is why we have to have the Second Amendment! This is why you've got to be able to have a gun," he yelled. "If it wasn't for that goddamn Glock I'd be dead today and so would my son. That goddamned gun saved our lives!"

The paper didn't print a photograph of Jim Parker—as a sixteen-year-old, he briefly enjoyed some added privileges as a juvenile. But his name and photograph would soon come out as well. Then Patti would be in for another surprise. After the frightening incident at his front door, Patti had scouted around for a builder to install a locking storm door and a secure new sliding door around back, to make it harder for anyone to get in. To safeguard his family, Patti had hired a builder everyone in the village recommended as competent and trustworthy: John Parker.

By late morning, Coltere Savidge and Zack Courts were up and out of Coltere's house and heading back to Zack's house so he could get a change of clothes. The convoy of police vehicles in the village was now outnumbered by television camera trucks, media vans, and reporters racing around in cars. A small-town boy like the rest, Zack had never seen anything like it. Chelsea's quiet Main Street had gone insane, he thought.

The moment Coltere pulled into Zack's driveway, reporters moved toward them in a swarm, shouting questions. You know Tulloch? What about Parker? C'mon, you must know them.

No, no, no, the boys said, shaking their heads as they ducked and ran inside.

The boys headed over to Tyler Vermette's house just south of the village, where a bunch of boys, mostly members of the basketball team, were gathering: Brad Johnson, Kip Battey and his brother Nick, and Coltere's younger brother Cabot. Even surrounded by the warmth of some of his closest friends, Zack felt numb.

They decided to stay away from town and the reporters, but were soon glued to the news on CNN and other television channels that kept replaying the press conferences showcasing police and New Hampshire prosecutors discussing the Zantops and the manhunt for Robert and Jim. "We were torturing ourselves," Zack said, "but we couldn't help it."

Eventually the spell was broken by Tyler's father, Mark, the varsity basketball coach. He wanted his players to talk about the game scheduled for that night in Barre. The players had a choice. In light of the circumstances, the coach was willing to postpone the game. To a boy, they said, Let's play. "If something horrible was happening, I'd rather play a basketball game than sit in a chair and look at the wall," said Zack. It seemed logical. Don't dwell on the news. Stay active and play the game, they figured.

They figured wrong. Coltere Savidge was known around Chelsea as a stoic kid, a school leader, a poised athlete. Tall, light-haired, and handsomely built, he was low-key and showed little emotion. Teachers considered him a role model to younger kids. "If Coltere ever swears, it turns people's heads," said Zack. But during the game Coltere couldn't get into any kind of rhythm. He couldn't find his game head. In the first outing against the Websterville team, the Chelsea Red Devils had won 59–53. This time Chelsea was flat and getting its butt kicked, and Coltere's sloppy, unfocused play was part of the problem. "It was weird, very weird," Coltere said. He was trying not to think about Robert and Jim and the police manhunt, "but it was always in the back of my head." The second half began with his team trailing. "I just wasn't in my right mind."

Losing a battle for an offensive rebound, an opponent elbowed Coltere in the face and Coltere went down. But no foul was called. The Websterville players took off down court on a fast break and scored. Coltere smoldered as he climbed up off the floor. A few plays later, Coltere felt the referee missed another call, and that was it.

Coltere blew up, something his teammates and coach had never witnessed before on the court. The senior began swearing and flailing and then went over and kicked the wall. The referee was not impressed. Coltere was called for a technical foul.

"I've gotten my share of fouls, but never a technical."

The game was a lost cause, a complete bust. The final score was 54–40, and afterward Coltere strode into the locker room and began tearing off his red jersey. He kicked open the door to one of the bathroom stalls. Teammates streaming into the locker room heard the unthinkable sound of Coltere Savidge crying. The locker room fell silent. Zack Courts realized he hadn't seen Coltere cry since they were in kindergarten.

Coltere emerged a few minutes later and went to a bench, avoiding eye contact. He tried to undress, but was suddenly back in the bathroom crying some more.

Coltere was shedding the town's tears. Other teammates began crying, too.

Someone tried to comfort Coltere. Take it easy, man, it's gonna be OK.

Coltere would have none of it. "I'm not gonna take it easy," he said. "My friends are murderers and that's not OK."

Within hours of their arrival in Chelsea on Friday night, investigators found themselves propelled on a fast track. The engine was an evidentiary bonanza, one that would remain a secret from Chelseans and the rest of the world for several weeks.

The police operation had been assembled quickly once the boys' disappearance was reported that morning. Nearly two dozen New Hampshire and Vermont detectives and crime scene specialists mobilized at the state police barracks in Bethel near Interstate 89. They crowded into the small "Troopers' Room" in the center of the low-slung, pre-fab cement building.

Then the wait began for prosecutors to obtain court-approved search warrants.

The two cruisers that Chelsea residents noticed outside the Tulloch and Parker homes were sent there mid-afternoon to secure each home until the warrants were ready, and to keep tabs on the parents. John Parker was followed when he left his house and drove down West Hill to the post office and then to the gym located next to The Pines for a workout. No one was home at the Tullochs' when a trooper first swung by near two in the afternoon, but an hour later Michael Tulloch's red pickup was spotted in the yard. Vermont State Police Trooper Michael O'Neil explained to the elder Tulloch that a search team would arrive at some point later in the day. Mike Tulloch, shaken, telephoned Dan Sedon, the lawyer whose firm had handled the closing on their house. Sedon wasn't available, so Tulloch left a message. Diane Tulloch arrived home from work around four o'clock to find a trooper with her husband.

The Parkers, moving about, kept police wondering—were Joan and John doing anything to impede the investigation? The Tullochs, meanwhile, stayed put. It was a tense holding action all around until the warrants arrived. Moving about town between the two homes were Chuck West and Frank Moran. Then, around five o'clock that evening, Moran happened to telephone the Hanover station to check in, and his chief told him about a preliminary finding: a confirmed match between Jim's fingerprints and one lifted from a sheath found in the Zantops' study. Moran quickly called West with the news, and the murmurings passed from investigator to investigator. Police were getting over their initial hesitation about a murder case that had brought them into Chelsea and to two apparently wholesome families. Although the fingerprint didn't prove Robert and Jim were the killers—it could have been left on the sheath earlier—it confirmed suspicions that the SEAL 2000s Jim bought were the same ones used to kill the professors.

While the wait for the warrants continued, the hunt for Robert and Jim was well under way. With each passing hour, investigators' worries increased. Would the boys elude the dragnet? Were they already dead by their own hands? Would they embark on a violent crime spree? By

6:30 Friday night, a briefing at the barracks was held to finalize team assignments. Shortly after nine o'clock, the warrants finally arrived, and within the hour the convoy was en route to Chelsea, led by Ray Keefe. The thirty-four-year-old Vermont detective had been assigned to oversee the search of the Tulloch house, while another group of investigators would comb through the Parker house.

Dan Sedon hadn't been able to return the call from Mike Tulloch until around five o'clock. Sedon, a thirty-five-year-old criminal-defense attorney with a decade of practice under his belt, had spent the day in Burlington working on a run-of-the-mill case. When he called back, Mike and Diane told him about the trooper at their house and the fact that police wanted to conduct a search. Sedon wasn't overly concerned at first. In his criminal-law experience, a warrant is a warrant is a warrant—it could be about almost anything, from drugs to stolen sneakers. Calling from a commuter parking lot off I-89, Sedon said he'd get there as soon as he could. He needed to stop for gas for his Toyota 4-Runner, return other calls, and check in with his wife.

His wife, however, changed his outlook. When he called to say he'd be swinging by the Tullochs and would be home later, she told him: Dan, this has to do with the Zantops. The Zantops? Yes, she said, troopers were seen in the village and the rumor is that it's connected to the murdered professors. Sedon was stunned. Like most everyone, and especially because he was a criminal lawyer, he'd been intrigued by the crime and followed it closely, mostly by reading about it online. "It was a big mystery, and so weird, a murder case with an international flavor and an Ivy League frosting," said Sedon. "With all the hallmarks of a passion killing." Never once did he imagine a link between the deaths and the cozy community of Chelsea.

Sedon hurried to the Tullochs' house and right away sensed the seriousness. Trooper Mike O'Neil, along with a second trooper, told him a search warrant was in the works and that Vermont's state police crime scene search team would arrive once it was issued. Sedon was also given a heads-up about the police operation that was being assembled. It would be an uncommon show of force. Ordinarily one cruiser, maybe two, would be involved in a search, even in most murder cases. This, Sedon realized, was a full-court press, not only involving Vermont State Police, but New Hampshire troopers as well. The officers wouldn't specify the purpose of the search—the name Zantop wouldn't pass their lips—uttering only the police mantra of the day: "This is serious."

But Sedon could read between the lines. The size of the unfolding police operation told him that investigators were after Robert and Jim not just because they might possess relevant information about the unsolved murders, but because they were suspects. Sedon met privately with the Tullochs to explain the pre-search lockdown and how it might take hours before the paperwork was in order and the actual search would begin.

He found the couple initially unable to grasp what he was saying. Mike said little and Diane reacted as a host, making coffee for the two troopers and tea for Sedon. Everyone had to step over the family dog, Ruby, and the two cats that wouldn't budge from the legs of the kitchen's wood-burning stove.

If it was going to be a while, Diane had an idea: "Let's all watch a movie. I'll order some pizzas."

Diane and Mike went to the living room and put in a movie, *Air Force One,* with Harrison Ford playing the president during a terrorist hijacking. The couple sat down and invited the troopers to do the same. The troopers stayed in the kitchen, while Sedon joined them, half-incredulous. "Here she is, inviting two hulking troopers to join them to watch a movie," Sedon said later. It was at once an awkward moment for the troopers and evidence of a huge disconnect for the Tullochs. To Diane, the interest police had in Robert was some huge misunderstanding that simply had to be straightened out. "They just had so much faith in Robert," Sedon said.

The Tullochs were the epicenter of the same disbelief that would soon spread throughout the community. Sedon wasn't even sure how much Mike and Diane knew about the Zantop case. They rarely read newspapers or watched the TV news; in fact, the TV in the living room had no cable connection and was used almost exclusively with a VCR to play movies. Sedon realized they thought there was no way Robert could be involved in a murder.

At first, Sedon didn't have the heart to shake them out of their fantasy. They watched the movie and got to the part where the hijackers seized Air Force One, when, around eight o'clock, the telephone rang. The movie was put on hold, as the troopers and Sedon were told the warrant had been approved and should be in hand at the Bethel barracks any minute. It was a wake-up call for Sedon, who now impressed upon Diane and Mike that they didn't want to be home when the police descended. To the uninitiated, he said, a search of one's home is disturbing. He would handle it. Finally, the weight of the moment began to take hold. "It was like watching a slow-motion train wreck," Sedon said about seeing the Tullochs recognize the stakes.

Diane and Mike never finished watching the thriller. The drama of real life was outpacing fiction. Mike drove Diane to their daughter Becky's house and returned. Sedon and Mike Tulloch hunkered down in the kitchen to await the search team's arrival. Occasionally Sedon stepped out back in the cold for a cigarette. Mike Tulloch, a former smoker, broke his abstinence from tobacco and joined him.

While troopers temporarily blocked what little traffic there was on Main Street to allow the forensics truck to back into the Tullochs' driveway, Ray Keefe went to the back door, the only door the family really used. He was met by Dan Sedon. The two knew one another from "the circuit," the name given to the commute between courthouses that lawyers and police make as part of their work. Both men were about the same age, liked one another, and had always gotten along. Keefe was a solidly built detective, medium height, his light-brown hair cut in a modified flattop. He'd been in the Major Crimes Unit six years and had worked on about fifteen homicides. Known for his easy banter, Keefe was the picture of crisp professionalism: black dress pants, polished black Florsheims, a blue dress shirt, blue tie, and a blazer. Under the blazer he wore a .40-caliber Sig Sauer semiautomatic.

Both men knew the drill. Keefe handed Sedon the warrant and the attorney lodged his objection to the police presence at the house all afternoon, and now the search.

"Duly noted," Keefe said. "Let's go." Keefe entered the kitchen and had Sedon and Mike Tulloch lead him upstairs to Robert's room. Members of the crime scene search team began unloading equipment and hauling it into the kitchen. Keefe noted the boy's room was in the front corner of the house, a location that gave it a separate feeling from other rooms. Parts of the house, the detective observed, were in disrepair, a not uncommon condition for such an old home. Moving about, he detected a homey feel.

Stepping into the room, Keefe was struck by the ordinariness of it: the basic teenager's room—messy and disorganized. The mattress on the floor, a chair, a stand-up closet, a bookshelf, and clothes scattered all about. Keefe thought a climbing device attached on one wall near the ceiling looked unusual for a teenager's room. A workout buff himself, Keefe could tell it was a tool for the serious rock climber who wanted to build finger strength by hanging from different ledges protruding from the molded, three-foot-wide panel. In fact, the Tullochs had just bought the device for Robert in a bid to lift his spirits; the deep cut in his leg had made it impossible to climb at his usual gym, Petra Cliffs in Burlington, and they thought the hanging board would give him something to do.

Keefe then gave way to the five-person search team. From the Vermont State Police there were Lieutenant Tom Hanlon, supervisor of Vermont's crime scene search team, and Garry Lawrence, a civilian technician from the state forensic lab. From the New Hampshire State Police there were Detective Sergeant James White and Troopers Bob Estabrook and Kathy Kimball. They were looking for anything and everything having to do with Robert, a search that included the laundry room off the kitchen but principally focused on his bedroom. Robert's writings, his computer, his e-mail correspondence, his footwear and shoe boxes, especially Vasque hiking boots other than the ones he had already surrendered, his clothing, blood or trace evidence (meaning hair or fingerprints)—this was the evidentiary wish list investigators had in mind when they slipped on rubber gloves and headed upstairs. Of course, in any homicide, investigators always had the murder weapon in mind, but searches rarely yielded the actual weapons; it was more often about combing meticulously for trace evidence.

Keefe, Sedon, and Mike Tulloch stayed downstairs. Taking a cigarette break outside, Sedon saw flashes of white light exploding from Robert's room. This was the search's first phase, as Trooper Kathy Kimball took well over a hundred photographs to document Robert's room. She moved through the room producing a photo gallery that included shots of the secondhand bureau, bookcase, and chairs; the *Roget's Thesaurus* and the *National Debate Handbook* resting next to a clock radio on the bureau behind the door; the strange indentations and long lines, almost like a cat's scratches, that marred one of the door jams; Robert's name written on the wood in black marker; the climbing ropes and rock-climbing magazine tossed on the rolled-up extra mattress; the blemished wall where plaster was missing; the socks and underwear hanging from a metal drying rack; the bookcase where stacks of books occupied several shelves, and fourteen video and computer games, such as *Rally, Soldier of Fortune,* and *Tomb Raider II,* were stored on the bottom shelf. Kimball photographed everything.

Meanwhile, more and more reporters were assembling around the property line, and television trucks had arrived with their own lights and camera feeds. The Tulloch telephone kept ringing, and it was always another reporter, but Sedon kept answering anyway in case the caller turned out to be Robert. If Robert called, Sedon wanted the first voice the boy heard to be the family's attorney, not that of a state police detective.

The search team had entered the house at 10:45 P.M. The setup and photography took about an hour. During this time, two new troopers arrived for the night shift of "securing" the house and the grounds, taking over from the troopers who'd been there since mid-afternoon. One was Jocelyn Stohl, the trooper who'd run into Robert and Jim on Bethel Mountain Road in the snowstorm a month earlier, on January 19. Inevitably she asked herself a question—what if? What if she hadn't been en route to an emergency? What if other troopers hadn't been tied up with accidents and she'd been able to call for backup? What if she'd searched the car and learned what the boys were up to? Would murder have been averted? No matter how many times she asked herself those questions, she knew she'd never have the answers. Stohl made her way past the crowd of media and some Chelseans who'd gathered outside. She walked into the kitchen, where Keefe, Sedon, and Mike Tulloch sat. Outwardly she displayed her usual military bearing; inwardly, Stohl looked around at the house and town under siege and felt deep sadness.

It was after midnight when the actual search finally got under way, and Keefe left the kitchen and climbed the stairs toward Robert's room. Intending just to check on things, he right away heard the search team talking. He sensed a buzz, an energy in the air. Despite the sexy drama of cop shows like *CSI: Crime Scene Investigation,* a search team usually kept its head down and plodded along. But as he went to look inside, Keefe overheard chatter in Robert's room. Jim White, one of the New Hampshire investigators, saw Keefe coming and greeted him with huge news: "We've got knives!"

Keefe was taken aback. But he wanted to know more, because everyone in Vermont seemed to own knives of one sort or another. What kind of knives? Keefe wanted to know. What kind of knives?

Just moments before, Garry Lawrence, wearing rubber gloves, had been drawn to a cardboard Florida Citrus box on the floor near a wastebasket. It was in one corner of Robert's room, nearly obscured by the bureau with the clock radio that was behind the door. Jim White and Bob Estabrook were inspecting other parts of the room. Tom Hanlon and Kathy Kimball were downstairs, taking photographs of the laundry room. The box was closed, and several writing notebooks and pads rested on top. Lawrence moved the notebooks, putting them atop the wastebasket. He opened the flaps of the box. Inside he saw a deep stack of Marvel comic books. But that's not what caught his eye. Resting on top of the comic books were two bundles made of duct tape wrapped around cloth—a mitten for one, a sock for the other—making them look like foot-long mummies. They were makeshift sheaths, and protruding from each was a black, molded handle of a SOG SEAL 2000 combat knife.

The technician had struck forensics gold. If the sheaths left at the Zantops' house were the glass slippers of the investigation, Lawrence had found the feet on which they fit. Laboratory testing would be necessary, including DNA analysis of what appeared to be bloodstains, but Keefe and the others began to think they'd caught a big break.

"You don't often get the murder weapons," Keefe said in an extreme understatement.

A long day suddenly accelerated into higher gear. Keefe, White, and the others went back downstairs to notify Hanlon of the find, and Kathy Kimball hustled upstairs to photograph the box and its contents.

Sedon noticed the flurry of activity. He saw the investigators had a bounce in their step, a lift to their expressions, an energy that had replaced the flat look and bearing typical of the monotony of a painstaking search. It was the last thing a defense attorney wanted to see. He stopped Keefe.

"Why is everyone so happy?"

Keefe paused. He liked Sedon but wasn't about to reveal the discovery of such pivotal evidence. "Well," Keefe said, "I'll tell you this— I wish this was my case."

Sedon got the point. Right then he knew they'd found something vital in Robert's room. Maybe it was blood. Maybe it was a weapon. Whatever it was, Sedon knew they'd seized evidence that tied Robert Tulloch to the Zantops.

Together, the two knives became ITEM ONE in the search team's inventory of evidence seized. By 1:30 A.M., Hanlon and Lawrence had carefully marked and packaged the knives and brought them outside to the forensics truck. By three o'clock Saturday morning, February 17, the knives were secure in the state police crime lab located in Waterbury, Vermont, where testing could begin.

It was the search team's first and best find. The search was suspended for the night and resumed again by eleven o'clock Saturday morning. During the thirty-three total hours of police occupation, lasting until just before midnight Saturday, searchers methodically examined Robert's room and the laundry room near the kitchen. They made hand-drawn sketches of the house's floor plan, took photographs, and logged every item they seized as possibly having some evidentiary value. It was an excruciatingly slow process. Each item was placed in a bag, and the line of bags in a first-floor room got longer and longer. During all this time, a parallel search was under way of Jim's room at his house on West Hill. In the end, searchers seized more than two hundred items from the boys, including their computers, notebooks, writings, Band-Aids and Ace bandages, a book about Hitler titled *Der Fuehrer,* blue jeans, shirts, and socks. Throughout Saturday, investigators came and went, and Saturday night the two key prosecutors, Kelly Ayotte and Mike Delaney, made a cameo appearance at the Tulloch house.

For all that was ultimately seized, Lawrence's discovery of the two SOG SEAL knives around midnight Friday was a eureka moment. Although it would remain a secret for weeks to come, inside the circle of investigators word spread rapidly from White to Keefe and from the searchers at the Tulloch house to their colleagues at the Parkers, where Chuck West was stationed outside in the drifting snow.

Chuck, you're not going to believe this, Frank Moran said shortly after midnight. It was déjà vu in that Moran was again passing along good news, though this was even better than the fingerprint match he reported earlier in the day.

What's up, Frank?

Moran told him about the knives, and the two investigators stood together outside the Parker house allowing the significance to sink in.

Things were falling into place, West thought. The hard work, all of it, was paying dividends. Even so, it was no time to gloat or celebrate. No time to let up. Time instead to maintain focus, keep pressing, and not get ahead of themselves.

They had the murder weapons, West thought, now let's find those boys. Maybe then we can figure out why these killings happened.

15

On the Run

When Robert and Jim first came begging for a ride at the Sturbridge Isles truck stop, trucker Rowdy Kyle Tucker turned them down flat. But his wife and traveling partner, Nancy Lee Tucker, had other ideas. The thought of the two stranded boys gnawed at her as she picked at her dinner. Nancy told her husband she thought they might be runaways because "they looked pretty fresh, not like they'd been out on the road a long time." The Tuckers, Alabama residents in their thirties with two young daughters, had been married for a decade. That was long enough for Rowdy to know what his wife was thinking.

"You ain't gonna be happy until we give them boys a ride, are you?" he said.

"It's snowing out there. Coming down hard," Nancy answered.

"Do what you want to do."

Nancy jumped up from the table and ran to a television lounge where she had last seen the pair. "Y'all want to go, let's go," she told them. A look of relief washed over the boys.

Robert told the couple his name was Sam. Jim introduced himself as Tyler. Despite Christiana's efforts to help Robert pick a new name, he and Jim fell back on the names of two classmates: Sam Sherman and Tyler Vermette. Jim thought they sounded like "normal names" that wouldn't attract attention.

"Sam" and "Tyler" told the Tuckers they were headed to Southern California in search of jobs on boats. The Tuckers were sympathetic to young men with wanderlust and gave them each $10 so they could buy provisions for the ride before leaving Sturbridge. Once inside the truck, a 1999 Peterbilt with green flames painted on the cab, Rowdy watched the road while Nancy kept an eye on their riders. She had the impression that "Sam"—Robert—was the kind of kid who might have gotten into a fight with his father and had taken off to prove himself. "Tyler"—Jim—gave her the impression of a follower, a nervous young man on the timid side. At one point they were whispering so intimately, their bodies so close together, she thought they might be gay. She gave them the phone number of her lesbian sister in Modesto, California, so they could look her up when they reached the coast.

When Rowdy left the cab to take care of business, Sam/Robert climbed into the driver's seat and played around like a kid.

"How long does it take to learn to drive one of these things?" he asked Nancy.

"You have to go to school—six to eight weeks," she answered.

Then he noticed the thirty-two gauges on the dashboard. "Do you have to watch all these gauges all the time?" he wondered.

"Yep," Nancy said, "all of them all the time." That cooled his ardor for trucking.

As the hours went by, the Tuckers started to think there was something shady about these two. Rowdy told his wife to zip down the dividing curtain between the back of the cab and the seats up front, so if "Sam" and "Tyler" tried to jump them, at least they'd have some warning. But nothing untoward happened, and soon they were talking again. Nancy urged them to turn on the TV or the radio, but they repeatedly declined.

The Tuckers drove the two to the TA truck stop in Columbia, New Jersey, near the Pennsylvania border, some 220 miles southwest of Sturbridge. They arrived around mid-afternoon Saturday, February 17—the ride took so long because Rowdy had to make nearly a half-dozen stops on the way from Sturbridge. Before they parted ways, the Tuckers let "Sam" and "Tyler" use their CB radio to seek out truckers going farther westward. The couple got on the air, too, to vouch for the pair.

After trying for about fifteen minutes, one trucker on the CB said he wasn't sure he'd be able to drive the boys, but he agreed to let them hang out and sleep in his cab until they found a ride. Robert and Jim said their good-byes to the Tuckers and holed up with the other trucker for the rest of that day and overnight until Sunday morning.

The trucker had a satellite television hookup in the cab, and at one point a news show began reporting about two young men from Chelsea, Vermont, who had fled after being questioned in the murder of two Dartmouth professors. As soon as the report began, "Sam" and "Tyler" asked the trucker to switch to the Weather Channel, and he did. He showed no sign of connecting his bunkmates to the wanted teens.

The trucker's name was James Hicks and he was hauling a load of M&Ms from New Jersey to Chicago. He was forty-five, a barrel-chested man with a handlebar moustache. Sitting alone in his Freightliner cab at the TA truck stop, Hicks was tired and feeling unsure about making the trip. He had never before driven with hitch-hikers, but when he heard Robert and Jim calling out on the CB, he decided that having company might help. Hicks was thinking about his own sons, one seventeen and the other thirteen, back home in Sumter, South Carolina. A third son, fourteen years old, had died four months earlier in a motorcycle accident. "I got three boys," Hicks explained later. "One's in heaven and two are still here, and I just felt sorry for them."

When Robert and Jim climbed into his truck, Hicks thought they looked bone-tired. He tried to strike up conversation but didn't get very far. He asked if they missed their parents. "No, not really," they answered. He could tell they didn't want to talk, and he never got their names, fake or otherwise.

Hicks gave the pair a sheet and let them crawl into the top bunk of his cab. Soon they were fast asleep.

Meanwhile, with help from John Moran's tip about the brief stop at the Sturbridge Service Center, authorities picked up Robert and Jim's trail.

Although they had dodged the media dragnet by asking Hicks to switch to the Weather Channel, Robert and Jim began to realize they had miscalculated the response to their flight. As Jim put it, "We didn't expect any type of big media thing." In fact, it was national news—the Big Story—from the moment late Friday night when authorities announced that arrest warrants had been issued, the suspects were running, and the public should consider them armed and dangerous. The story only grew larger as the weekend continued without arrests, competing for attention with the death of race-car driver Dale Earnhardt at the Daytona 500.

After John Moran's tip, authorities focused their search around Sturbridge, in case Robert and Jim had holed up there. Proof that they had been and gone came more than a day later. Massachusetts State Trooper Walter Combs had been told to keep an eye out for the missing teens as part of his regular tour of duty. Combs, at forty-six a veteran trooper, checked out motel parking lots, looking for Parker's car. Then he had a better idea. Combs thought two teenagers with little cash wouldn't spend it on lodging, so he focused on area truck stops.

The trooper's first stop turned up nothing, so he went to the Sturbridge Isles. Driving around back, Combs noticed that only one car was covered with a frosting of snow—which meant it must've been there a couple of days. When he got closer, he noticed a sliver of green on the license plate—Vermont's color. Concerned that Robert and Jim might be hiding inside, Combs pulled his cruiser around to block the car into its spot. He walked carefully toward the car and peered through the windshield to see empty seats littered with knapsacks and crackers. Then he confirmed the car was in fact a 1987 silver Audi 5000. He looked more closely at the license plate: Vermont CDG690. The fugitives had abandoned their car.

As he stood by the car waiting for backup, Combs's biggest worry was that Robert and Jim had hitchhiked a ride with a trucker, and the trucker might be their next victim.

Robert and Jim awoke in Hicks's truck at about two in the morning on Monday, February 19. Their exhaustion had eased, but now they were hungry. Millions of M&Ms were rattling around in the semi-trailer behind the cab, but Hicks handed them chips and soda. An hour or so later, Hicks was driving west through Indiana, some six hundred miles from Sturbridge. Despite all their hours together, they exchanged little conversation or information about one another, and now it was time to part ways. Hicks was heading north to Chicago while they wanted to continue west. He reached for his CB handset: "Can anybody give a ride to two boys who want to go to California?" He mentioned that they were hitchhiking from New Jersey.

By then, based on Combs's discovery of the Audi, police had viewed security videotapes taken at the Sturbridge Isles. One showed the boys getting into a white 1999 Peterbilt with green flames painted on the hood. Authorities quickly traced its owner, and from there began tracking the Tuckers' progress using a sophisticated Global Positioning System device that homed in on a truck-mounted beacon. They got the Tuckers' cell phone number from Rowdy's boss, but police didn't dare call it. They feared a call might spook two armed and dangerous fugitives who might be holding the Tuckers hostage. As it turned out, by the time authorities began tracking the Tuckers, the couple had already handed off the boys to Hicks. Afterward, the Tuckers went out "trashing around"—killing time between required stops—and had gotten lost on an abandoned logging road, making it difficult for FBI agents and local authorities to find them.

When the Tuckers finally made their way back to a main road, they drove to a truck stop in Brookville, Pennsylvania, to get some sleep. A few hours later, late on the morning of Sunday, February 18, their truck was surrounded by gun-pointing FBI agents and an entire SWAT team. The Tuckers told the agents how they had dropped off the boys at the TA truck stop and how "Sam" and "Tyler" had gotten a ride from a trucker heading west.

Early the next morning, while the manhunt was sweeping westward, Hicks was on the CB, describing two boys hitchhiking from New Jersey looking for a ride to California. Puzzle pieces were falling into place.

Hicks waited a moment then heard a man's voice come back: "Sure, I can."

As they spoke, Hicks was approaching the Flying J Travel Plaza in Spiceland, Indiana. That would be a fine spot to meet, said the voice on the other end of the CB. "Why don't you just drop them off at the fuel desk?" he said.

"OK," Hicks answered.

Hicks pulled into the Flying J at about 3:45 in the morning and began saying his good-byes. As a parting gift, he reached into his wallet and gave his young riders $10 for breakfast. That increased their combined stake to $146.04.

As Hicks's time with Robert and Jim was nearing an end, *The Dartmouth* newspaper was preparing to print a letter from a man named Jim Moody of Ithaca, New York. "I'm so afraid these boys might kill themselves, being so cornered, so afraid, so guilty," he wrote. "Whatever their involvement with the Zantop murder is, let's face it, the Zantops are dead. Can't we have compassion for these two boys on the run? Can't you appeal to the Attorney General to make some kind of national media statement that . . . they should not now act rashly, and that all efforts will be made to treat them fairly? . . . Seize the moment. Save these two kids' lives. Now."

A day later, *The Dartmouth* would print two letters slamming Moody. "I can't believe that anyone would be afraid of these two boys committing suicide rather than take responsibility for their alleged involvement in this horrendous crime," wrote a Susan Waterman. "If someone wants to save the boys, look into what can enable two young people to carry out such a horrific act. Focus on saving other boys from becoming the kind of person who could do this."

Unknown to Hicks or his passengers, the man on the other end of the CB conversation was Sergeant Bill Ward, a twenty-two-year veteran of the Henry County, Indiana, sheriff's department.

Ward was working the overnight shift, and earlier that evening he'd been at the Flying J with three fellow officers, enjoying a post-midnight meal he called lunch. The restaurant had opened just two weeks earlier, so it was a nice break in their year-in, year-out routine. While they ate, Ward told the other officers about a report he had heard on CNN *Headline News* about two teenage males wanted for murder in New Hampshire who were believed to be hitchhiking across the country. By virtue of geography, Indiana might be a stop along their route. And if it were, they'd probably pass through Henry County, which was bisected by Interstate 70, one of the nation's busiest east-west highways. Keep an eye out, Ward said.

The officers left the Flying J to begin their patrols, but later in the shift Ward circled back to the truck stop. He was patrolling the semi-trailer parking area when he heard Hicks's CB call for a hitchhiker handoff. After pretending to be a trucker and responding with his casual, "Sure, I can," Ward called two of the officers he had met with earlier, deputies Landon Dean and Chris Newkirk. It was Newkirk's night off, but he couldn't sleep, so he came to work. When Newkirk arrived on duty, he hadn't even heard about the Dartmouth murders.

Ward told the deputies to join him back at the Flying J. Ward doubted his planned rendezvous would involve the two teens who were the focus of an all-points "wanted" bulletin. That would be too easy, he thought. Still, here were two male teenage hitchhikers heading toward California. It was worth checking out, and he wanted backup just in case.

Ward picked up his cell phone and called a dispatcher to get descriptions of the Vermont teens sent out by the Justice Department's

National Crime Information Center. The dispatcher had earlier received a call from a trucker who heard Hicks's CB message and alerted authorities to the possibility that the hitchhikers were the boys on the news. The dispatcher connected Ward and the tipster trucker, who said he thought he saw the two teens at the truck stop's west fuel pump island, trying to hitch another ride.

Head over there, Ward told Dean and Newkirk. Dean drove his cruiser to the fuel pumps and hit the brakes in front of a parked semi. Newkirk pulled in from behind, blocking it in. Standing near the gas pumps in the early morning darkness were two tired-looking young men with backpacks on the ground at their feet. When Ward drove up, he immediately saw a strong resemblance to the photos he had seen on CNN and the descriptions he'd gotten from the dispatcher. He approached cautiously.

The officers separated the pair. Ward asked the one with dark spiky hair for identification. The teen said he didn't have any. Ward asked his name, and Jim answered, "Tyler J. Jones." Ward asked what the "J" stood for. The young man paused. "Jeffrey," he said after a beat. Asked his date of birth, the young man paused a second time. Then he said April 3, 1982, pausing between month, date, and year. In response to more questions, the young man told Ward he had been born in Encino, but he didn't know how to spell that city's name. He said he had set out from California and had hitchhiked to Salem, Massachusetts, in search of a job. That hadn't worked out, so now he was heading back west. He said his traveling companion was named Tom, but he didn't know a last name.

The other hitchhiker, Robert, swaddled in several layers of clothing, was doing an even worse job of lying, despite years of practice. He couldn't remember his Social Security number, so Dean asked his date of birth. The young man said he was born on "March 40, 1982" then corrected himself to March 30, 1982. His lousy act fell apart completely when he heard the name Robert W. Tulloch over the dispatch radio. "It's me you are looking for," he told Dean calmly. "You've got us."

It was 4:07 in the morning on February 19, twenty-four days after the murders, three days after Robert and Jim took flight, two days since the commando knives were discovered in Robert's room, a thousand miles from their homes. After all the talk about killing cops to avoid capture, neither Robert nor Jim resisted arrest. It was their last moment as a team, and their symbiotic bravado deserted them both.

Hicks was still at the Flying J when the deputies arrived, and he stood nearby as his former riders were questioned. Just before they were taken away, one of the two, he wasn't sure which, looked at him and said: "I'm sorry." One of the deputies retrieved Hicks's $10. They wouldn't need it for breakfast. "There is free food in jail," Hicks said.

Hicks had his money back, but he was soon out of a job. When his bosses at Martin Transport of Mondovi, Wisconsin, found out what happened, Hicks was fired for violating the company's strict no-riders policy.

"I have no regrets," Hicks said that day. "Everything seemed so set up for them to be captured here. Maybe it was supposed to happen. I actually feel lucky."

The same fate awaited Rowdy Kyle Tucker: he, too, was fired for breaking company policy on hitchhikers. He and Nancy shrugged it off.

Back in New Hampshire, Attorney General Philip McLaughlin called Mariana Zantop to inform her of the arrests. "For the daughters of Mr. and Mrs. Zantop, time stopped on January 27," McLaughlin told reporters afterward. "I think that they approve of what happened today, but I am sure it's cold comfort."

By the morning of Robert and Jim's arrests, modern crisis management had arrived in Chelsea.

In 1963, when President John F. Kennedy was assassinated, the response was to get schoolchildren out of school and home to their families. But the playbook had long since changed; it now called for elders to ground and reassure kids by maintaining their everyday routines, which meant getting them back into school for collective coping and counseling and the comfort that can come from the repetition of the mundane.

Ever since she'd been awakened by a reporter's telephone call, principal Pat Davenport had been working nonstop to come up with a plan for Monday's return to school. "Mrs. D.," as she was often called, was a veteran educator, a soft-spoken, fiftyish woman with reddish-brown hair who projected a firm but gentle image. She became principal in Chelsea in 1993 after working for eight years at a New Hampshire school and, before that, for fourteen years as an English teacher and administrator at Hanover's Richmond Middle School. Near the end of her tenure there, one of the young students at Richmond was a bright girl named Veronika Zantop.

Davenport huddled with teachers, school board members, and parents, and decided to open the day with an assembly, a gathering in the gym of grades seven through twelve. She talked to Andy Pomerantz and asked for his help. Pomerantz told her his expertise was in geriatrics, not pediatrics. But Davenport said that didn't matter. He was a Chelsean, a parent, and a psychiatrist. He understood the murder case had changed Chelsea forever, making the world seem a dangerous place. His help was vital. Pomerantz agreed to participate.

During the weekend planning, Davenport ignored the telephone messages piling up from reporters. But she did meet with investigators, who were trying quickly to learn as much as possible about the fugitive boys. Davenport told them Robert was "bright and inquisitive." She said Jim was also a good student, though not on Robert's level. Jim was the artistic one, a gifted actor and musician. Davenport went over the boys' recent school history, the fact that Jim had tried Spaulding High School in Barre in the fall and Robert had not been in school at all. She mentioned that Jim seemed "subdued" in school the previous week or so. She also mentioned that Robert, in addition to being bright, could come off as "arrogant." Davenport told investigators he'd acted up with a couple of teachers and generally thought "he was too smart for Chelsea."

But even with that, the first impression given of the boys was largely positive. Davenport's words were repeated, in essence, by other teachers who sat down with investigators. Time and again, teachers talked about the boys' talents and sociability and intelligence, qualities tempered, perhaps, by their acting full of themselves, a touch of grandiosity. But all in all, they were two well-liked Chelsea boys. Only math teacher Paul Callens seemed to offer a glimpse of another side. Callens liked the boys, but he gave investigators a coarser view. He recalled the trouble they'd gotten into the previous spring for going into the Purcells' house when no one was home; he was struck by how unaffected and "carefree" their response was. Jim Parker, he said, returned in January from Spaulding saying, "Spaulding sucked." That's how he'd put it to Callens, and Jim seemed upset he'd even gone there at all. Callens said anger seemed brewing in Robert the past year, and that he would display resentment toward people with money. Recently, Robert had seemed down, he said.

The darker notes, however, were not the prevailing ones filling the notebooks of investigators. Nor were those the qualities that came up during the school assembly that began first thing Monday morning. Right after attendance, kids filed out of the school's side doorway and walked across a parking area to the gym. Standing at center court at a microphone were Pomerantz and Davenport. They were set up right next to the school insignia, the face of a fiery-red devil, painted on the floor.

The principal began the assembly with a declaration: "We love them." She then explained that Robert and Jim had been accused of a horrific crime. She discussed generally how the judicial system works. She mentioned Half and Susanne, and the suffering of the Zantop family and Dartmouth community. Mainly Davenport wanted every-one to know that teachers and parents were available to help Chelsea's kids cope and continue with their schoolwork and activities. She encouraged the students to talk about their feelings, but she also stressed that saying nothing—silence—was all right, too.

Pomerantz was glad she'd made the point about silence—there was plenty of it during the gathering that lasted nearly ninety minutes. Pomerantz understood that after trauma people first needed reassurance about essentials—safety, food, housing—and he tried to maintain focus on these fundamentals. Only occasionally did a question come up. Would Chelsea's kids be ostracized or worse when they traveled to Hanover? What about safety in the Chelsea school? The most provocative comment centered on the boys' flight. Why'd they run? "Because they're guilty!" someone yelled, and others testily rose to Robert and Jim's defense.

The most poignant moment came when basketball coach Mark Vermette, Tyler's father, stood at the microphone and talked about the Saturday night game. He described the locker room scene and how affected his players had been by the murder case and the manhunt for Robert and Jim. Seeing strong boys cry made him realize the depth of the hurt.

In the back, unable to sit in the bleachers, stood Zack Courts. His heart was pounding harder than it had ever before. Waves of heat rushed through his body, and his chest felt as though it would explode. Seated in another part of the gym was Coltere Savidge. He listened to his coach talking about players who meant a lot to him and who were having a hard time, and Coltere knew the coach was talking about him. Then, as he was finishing up, the coach's voice cracked and his shoulders shook as he asked for the town to turn out for the next game, to support the boys. He began to cry quietly.

Coltere began crying, too. The senior stood up and met Mark Vermette as the coach walked away from the microphone, and the two stood side by side at the door. Needing to get out, Coltere then left hurriedly. Zack soon followed. He could take no more.

When the assembly ended, many students filed back into the main building. It was close to eleven, and an effort was made to resume classes, but little work got done. Coltere, his brother Cabot, Zack, Tyler, and other boys left school grounds and gathered at Matt Butryman's house to hang out, shoot pool, and watch CNN's nonstop coverage of their friends' arrests in Indiana.

To get to Matt's house, the boys had to make their way through the phalanx of news reporters lined up just off school property on South Common. This was the media's main staging area, and reporters chased after just about any Chelsea teenager they spotted, trying to get an interview about Robert and Jim. The media circus alarmed everyone in town; Chelseans always viewed the nation's Big Story on television, not live and in person.

Kids traded stories about dodging reporters or granting brief interviews. In one newscast, Brad Johnson spotted his red GMC pickup in the background of a panning shot of the pocket-sized village. Tyler Vermette gave a comment to NBC News and then saw it broadcast. It all seemed so unreal, he thought. "It's like you look on TV at one of these shootings in some high school and you're like, 'Oh my god, that's *huge* national news.' But now you look at the news and all my friends are on TV." Christiana Usenza, pursued more than most as Robert's girlfriend, went so far as to issue a press release the day before the school assembly. "I strongly believe that they are innocent and incapable of committing such a horrible crime," she said. "It is unbearable to hear their names mixed up in this mess! I have no idea where they are or why they took off. I'm sure they are scared and just want to come home and be safe with their family and friends."

Reporters weren't the only ones pursuing Robert and Jim's friends; investigators were, too. Coltere Savidge was apparently the first who was buttonholed and interviewed, but in the weeks to come Zack Courts, Casey Purcell, Sada Dumont, Clyde Haggerty, Julia Purcell, Anna Mulligan, Ivy Mix, Tess Mix, and others sat down for police interviews.

Gaelen McKee told investigators: "These are two kids who really like attention. . . . When they find an opportunity, they take it." He said he doubted they were guilty, but added: "This is either a bad coincidence or they actually did it." Asked about Robert and Jim's connections to Dartmouth, Gaelen said: "They hated Hanover. . . . They were just not into the whole college-prep atmosphere."

Some kids were evasive with investigators, and one girl made a wild accusation that a third Chelsea teen should be considered a possible suspect: Zack Courts. The girl said Zack, Robert, and Jim were like "the three musketeers," but under questioning, her story fell apart. She admitted she didn't like going to school in Chelsea and thought she might be able to transfer by suggesting that a third killer was still on the loose, attending classes at the Chelsea Public School. But most of the kids were helpful, providing details about the boys' lives, while most still conveyed disbelief Robert and Jim could ever be involved in a murder.

It didn't take long for townsfolk to get fed up with the media onslaught. Editorial cartoonist Jeff Danziger captured Chelsea's disdain. He drew a cartoon showing a car with two reporters stuck in the snow on the side of the road. Five Chelseans, armed with shovels, throw more snow on the car rather than digging it out. The caption read: "Freedom of the Press. Newspaper reporters covering the murder case slide off the road in Chelsea. Local residents grab shovels and come running." The cartoon was clipped, copied, and pinned to bulletin boards all around town.

How do you feel about Robert and Jim? That was the question hurled at Chelseans over and over again: Your friends are murder suspects—so how do you feel? The question made kids like Tyler Vermette sick. How do you feel? He wanted to snap right back: "How would you feel if your heart just got ripped out?"

Shorn of their aliases, searched and handcuffed, Robert and Jim were taken to the Henry County Jail, in New Castle, Indiana, some fifty miles east of Indianapolis. As day broke, they were fingerprinted and photographed wearing zebra-striped jail uniforms. During his face-forward shot, Jim—inmate 97797—stared straight at the camera, his usual smile replaced by a tight line; Robert—inmate 97795—gazed off somewhere to his left. Both looked deflated.

The jail rarely held teenage prisoners, and Sheriff Kim Cronk was concerned about placing them with the general population of mostly small-time adult offenders. Robert was taken to a weight room, where he sat on a mattress on the floor crying, a pile of crumpled tissues at his side. When jail officer Adam Bowman came to check on him, Robert said through his tears, "I can't believe what I have done." Bowman, at twenty-one a virtual peer, tried to get Robert to talk instead about what it was like in Vermont. But soon Robert's attention turned back to his predicament: "Am I going to spend the rest of my life in jail?" Bowman said he had no idea and again changed the subject.

Jim was held in an interview room, where he buried his head under a blanket. He cried even harder than Robert, going through several boxes of tissues. Both were placed on suicide watches from the moment they entered the jail. Surveillance cameras tracked their every move.

When Cronk talked with Robert, the teen mentioned several times that he was involved in student council, as if that might somehow impress his jailer and demonstrate that he wasn't a criminal. Tired and hungry, what Robert wanted most was a bowl of cereal and a bed roll. When Cronk checked on Jim, the young inmate asked what New Castle was like outside the jail. Cronk described the quiet little town that is home to the Indiana Basketball Hall of Fame. It was the kind of place that under different circumstances Jim might well have visited with his basketball-loving father. The local motto: "We have what you're looking for!"

When they heard about the arrests, John and Joan Parker made flight arrangements and called San Diego lawyer Doug Brown, John Parker's close friend and college roommate at Ohio Wesleyan. Brown dropped everything and said he'd meet them in Indiana.

When the Parkers arrived later that day, they spent an emotional half-hour with their son. "Jimmy, we love you," they told him. Then, on lawyers' orders, they told him: "Before we get into anything, Jim . . . we don't want you to talk about anything about the case." Then they all cried and hugged.

"I want to go home," Jim told them. "I don't want to be, don't want to be in jail."

One thing they didn't talk about was Robert. Jim never asked about him.

Major Jay Davis, commander of the Henry County Jail, said the Parkers were allowed what is known in the corrections trade as a "contact visit"—they could touch and hold Jim, rather than speak through glass—because of his tender age. As a result, Jim was in no rush to waive extradition, knowing such privileges wouldn't be offered as readily in New Hampshire.

After one visit with their son, John and Joan emerged looking spent and holding hands. "We'd just like to say that we love Jimmy very much," John Parker said outside the jail. He said he and his wife also wanted "to thank the Henry County Sheriff's Department for how they've handled this whole situation. Thank you."

In the end, Jim waived extradition on Friday, February 23, four days after the arrests, at a hearing attended by his father, Brown, and Kevin Ellis, a family friend and public relations executive from Chelsea whose home John Parker had built. Joan Parker was nowhere in sight.

At first, John Parker sat in the walnut courtroom pews behind his son, but then he and Ellis moved across the courtroom so they could make eye contact with the young murder suspect. Jim was spared having to wear jail garb, choosing instead navy exercise pants with yellow stripes down the legs, a black turtleneck, and new Spalding basketball shoes.

Outside the Henry County courthouse, John Parker had only one comment: "I cannot believe that Jimmy was capable of committing this crime."

The next day, Jim flew back east aboard a small FBI plane. "It was a good trip," said Hanover Police Chief Nick Giaccone, who accompanied Jim on the flight. "He's in good shape. Very cooperative and very quiet."

Because Jim was sixteen, still a juvenile under New Hampshire law, he would spend the next three months at a juvenile detention center in Concord. When he turned seventeen in May, he'd be transferred to a county jail.

Jim followed his parents' and lawyers' advice and kept his mouth shut, but Robert slipped. Six hours after his arrest, dressed in a jail-issue blue barn-jacket for warmth, Robert was led to an interview room at the Henry County Jail. Tears streamed down his face as he sat at a wood-veneer table before Indiana-based FBI agent William Donaldson.

"It's gonna be all right," Donaldson said to the crying boy.

Robert pitched forward, putting his head down on the table and covering his face with his cuffed hands.

"I don't think it's going to be all right," he sobbed.

"We're gonna talk about it, OK?" the FBI agent said.

"How's Jim doing?" Robert asked.

"We'll talk about that, OK?" Donaldson said.

As his cuffs were removed by a Henry County sheriff's sergeant, Robert asked: "Can I get some Kleenex?" The sergeant, Elmer New, handed him a half roll of toilet paper and Robert ripped off one piece after another to wipe his tears, then squeezed the used papers into ragged balls.

"Take a deep breath for me," Donaldson said, trying to get Robert to stop crying.

"I don't have to worry about a lawyer or anything, do I?" Robert asked.

"We're gonna talk about that," the FBI agent answered. Donaldson told Robert that authorities in New Hampshire had spoken to his mother and father, and at the mention of his parents Robert again brought his hands to his face to hide his tears.

Donaldson went over a juvenile rights form that was a beginner's version of the Miranda warning adult suspects receive. Then Donaldson asked Robert if he had any questions.

"How is Jim doing?" Robert asked a second time.

"We can talk about that. We can talk about that. He's like you," Donaldson said in reference to Robert's emotional state.

"Do you think I'll be tried as an adult?"

"You know," the FBI agent said, "I can't answer that, I really can't."

Robert began weeping again. Donaldson told him: "OK, I know it's hard."

As Donaldson waited for Robert to compose himself, the teen made the first of a series of statements that were vague yet incriminating, statements that would be his only recorded words of remorse—though that remorse was reserved entirely for himself and Jim.

Choking with tears, Robert said: "It was pretty easy to throw my life away. It should have been a little harder, you know? Or maybe if I should be, have been, less, 'Oh, I know everything.' But, you know, like a house of cards, you know, it takes, what, seventeen years to build it, and then you just blow it away. And you can never put it back up."

Soon after, Donaldson told Robert that he would shut off the audio and video recorders to allow Robert to speak with his parents privately by phone, to discuss whether he wanted to answer questions about the case. In the meantime, Donaldson left the room and Robert got the mistaken impression that the video recorder had already been turned off. Alone in the room, thinking no one could see or hear him, Robert clasped his hands together and stared upward, like a penitent seeking absolution for mortal sins.

"Jim, I'm so sorry," Robert wept to the ceiling. "Jim, I'm so sorry. Maybe if I'd used my brain a little more. So sorry for everything. I'm so sorry." His throat filled with phlegm from crying and the remnants of the flu, and Robert leaned down and spit into a garbage basket. Then he slurped water from a mug on the table. "I'm so sorry, Jim," he repeated, rocking back in his chair as Donaldson returned to the room.

Out of camera range, Sergeant Elmer New heard even more. "Robert stated he wished he had not involved John Parker's son. Robert stated God does not like quitters," New wrote in a detailed report. "Robert stated he could not understand how a person could get manslaughter for hitting a person with a car and it lasted only two seconds, yet it only took ten seconds to change my [Robert's] life. Robert stated he wished he could sit down with his mother and have dinner and do as she said. . . . Robert stated that he had screwed up and it would take twenty to thirty years for he and his family to get over it."

On the advice of his parents and lawyers, Robert declined to answer questions from the FBI agent or other investigators. But by then it was too late; he had already said plenty.

The next day, Robert appeared in Henry County Superior Court, handcuffed, shackled, and wearing a brown-and-black V-neck sweater, Levi's jeans, and Reebok running shoes. His old self returned, as he joked with jail officer Adam Bowman that he never wore those kinds of sneakers or sweater. Bowman shook his hand and wished Robert good luck.

Michael Tulloch sat stoically in the courtroom, his hat literally in his hand, as his son waived extradition and agreed to return to New Hampshire. Diane stayed home—they could only afford one round-trip airfare. Reached by telephone, she told reporters: "We love our son very much and want the press to know that he's innocent until proven guilty." Outside their house they posted a sign: NO MEDIA ALLOWED.

Robert and Jim's paths diverged almost from the moment they were placed in separate cells in Henry County. Except for a brief view of each other through a window, there was no contact or communication, a forced separation that would remain in effect far longer than either could imagine.

16

A Chelsea Embrace

Few were sleeping soundly in Chelsea, and that included Dr. Andy Pomerantz. He'd stood by Pat Davenport's side at the principal's school assembly just hours after the arrests, and now it was his turn: He was in charge of a community meeting scheduled for three days later at the United Church of Chelsea. Welcome were townsfolk who wanted to talk about the murders, the boys' capture in Indiana, and their community under siege. Prominent Chelseans—the educators, parents, and selectmen—all knew they were winging it, trying to confront and manage a crisis none of them had ever known before. Pomerantz was actually one who had a foot in each of the colliding worlds—Chelsea and Dartmouth.

The "hippie doctor," the sobriquet he'd acquired soon after moving to Chelsea in 1972 with his long hair and medical degree from the University of Chicago, had for years been a general practitioner with an office in the village. More recently, after becoming a psychiatrist, he'd taken a position with the VA Medical Center in White River Junction, as chief of mental health and behavioral sciences. In that role, he also held an appointment as assistant professor of psychiatry at Dartmouth Medical School.

The switch—from country doctor to a hospital-affiliated psychiatrist—symbolized more than a career change. It captured as well a broader change in the Chelsea mindset. Not so long ago, Chelseans, including flatlanders like Pomerantz, made only occasional journeys south to places like Hanover or West Lebanon, where in the early 1970s the region's first shopping center was built. Trips back then were a big event. "People would pack up the family and make the adventure trip down to West Lebanon," Pomerantz said, "and if I was going to drive down from Chelsea to Hanover I would check my oil, make sure my car was properly tuned up."

But no matter how routine the daily commute had long since become, Pomerantz's heart and soul remained firmly planted in his town. Indeed, tacked on the wall of his hospital office was a map Pomerantz used to show visitors why he and his family lived there: the isolation that had mostly withstood time. "I have a thirty-three mile commute every morning and twenty miles of it is a twisty, two-lane road before I reach the interstate," he said. "Chelsea's still pretty much out of the way."

But the anonymity was gone. Chelsea was in the grip of a media hurricane, the focus of a nation fascinated by the killing of the Zantops. Following the school assembly on Monday, an almost immediate urgency had arisen for another meeting—this time for parents in town. The assembly seemed to help ground the kids, and afterward Pomerantz and educators realized: What about the mothers and fathers? Pomerantz, who specialized in trauma, knew that the town's kids would be turning to parents and teachers for support and security. The ever-cool teen might be the last to acknowledge this, but Pomerantz understood: kids really do need to know that parents have their world under control. It was how kids maintained their bearings. By Tuesday, then, word went out about a meeting to be held at the church Thursday night, with Pomerantz hoping parents would find strength in numbers.

But Pomerantz, like other Chelseans, was himself turned inside out, and there was no sign of any letup in the aftershocks following the original news about Robert and Jim. The disclosure that the boys were wanted for murder was a roundhouse punch to the face, and the fast-paced developments that followed were slaps back and forth across the cheeks that left Pomerantz and most all Chelseans staggered and woozy. While Pomerantz and the Friends of Chelsea School on Wednesday were putting in play plans for the meeting, Robert was brought back to New Hampshire for his arraignment in Grafton County Superior Court and the start of his incarceration in the county jail. News about the case gushed nonstop in local and national papers and on television and radio. There was no escaping the gale-force coverage—reports that continued to deepen the wound, from the disclosure about a bootprint in blood investigators found inside the Zantop home to the partial fingerprints on a knife sheath that linked the boys to the killings. There also were the quick media snapshots of Chelsea that residents considered tabloid assaults on town life, as if beneath the postcard veneer roiled a weird, real-life *Blue Velvet* of depravity and deceit. Pomerantz was having nightmares about the case, and he wasn't the only one. Treating trauma might be one of his specialties, but what about when he was one of the traumatized?

The morning of the meeting Pomerantz also awoke to the realization that what began as a comfort session for parents had ballooned into something bigger. The hunger for connection ran beyond parents. Even on such short notice, Pomerantz and other organizers now knew to expect several hundred people to show up at the church. News of the meeting, spread mostly by word of mouth, had also been picked up by the media. Pomerantz left his home to the ringing of the telephone in his ears and arrived at his hospital office to a pile of phone messages and a secretary at wit's end. From the start he'd made a decision not to talk to reporters—too much was happening too fast. But he and other town leaders were realizing their ad hoc policy of no comment was wrongheaded and would have to end. The early media reports streaming out of Chelsea were quoting anyone in town whom scrambling reporters could get to talk. In some instances reporters managed to lasso a town leader or longtime resident, but too often they grabbed the nearest warm body, which meant kids and young drifters—the corner-hangers stationed on Main Street outside the pizza shop and the South Common for hours on end. The early outside view of Chelsea was coming from them—many of whom didn't live in town and many of whom didn't know Robert and Jim, although their comments gave the impression they were experts on both. "Most responsible people were refusing to talk to media," Pomerantz said later, "which left a whole other group of people who were getting quoted, and the world was getting a skewed view of Chelsea." It was a lesson in Mass Media 101. Pomerantz and other town leaders began to discuss opening up and talking to reporters. But Pomerantz first wanted to get the community together, where this very point would be made. The calls and messages went unreturned.

Pomerantz couldn't get any real work done. He was anxious, full of doubts, even panic. "In a daze pretty much all day," he wrote in a journal. For five days Pomerantz had been fielding questions from neighbors and friends that ran the gamut—some afraid and fearful for their safety, others angry at the school, the media, the police, or all three—while at the same time shifting roles "between shrink and community person." Pomerantz wanted to bear down and focus the meeting on how adults could best support the town's children. He hoped that parents would have some of their trust in each other and their kids restored, but he wasn't sure he'd be able to harness the passion and panic he'd detected even as he reached a clear idea about his role.

To escape the telephone calls at the hospital, Pomerantz left work early. To escape the telephone calls at home, Pomerantz headed into the woods to seek the solitude of cross-country skiing. More than ever he was looking for the angle of repose he usually found by skiing across the snowy hills of Chelsea. But not this time. "Tried skiing in the woods, but noisy clatter and ice stopped this," he wrote in his journal. Pomerantz fretted. "Pacing, wondering if this could work. Risk or no risk? Called on for something I have never done before and didn't consider my strong suit. But this is my town."

Thirty minutes before the meeting was scheduled to begin, he drove into town from his home up a dirt road off Route 110. The snow-covered North Common was surrounded by reporters. The nearly two hundred-year-old church was all lit up, awash in the klieg lights of television satellite trucks. An orange glow filled the church's stained-glass windows. It was eerie, as bright as midday. A light snow began to fall.

"There's Dr. P. now," one reporter said, and suddenly reporters moved en masse. The common seemed to tilt in Pomerantz's direction. He gave them little, reiterating organizers' position that no media would be allowed inside, and that the meeting was to support families, not to find blame or to explore the boys' possible role in the slayings. To enforce the no-media rule, a uniformed deputy sheriff stood guard at the entrance to the white-steepled church. Seeing all the people work their way inside in twos and threes, past the hordes of reporters, Pomerantz thought, "They're more scared, confused than me." He recognized many faces, but not all. It was clear the meeting had attracted newcomers and old-timers alike, people who got along well and some who didn't, but neighbors all. As he was climbing the steps, part of a headline flashed through his mind. It had said, "Chelsea Psychiatrist." He couldn't recall the rest of the headline, which was atop a news story about the meeting just minutes from starting. But Pomerantz had enjoyed fleeting comic relief at a word combination that could be read to mean a psychiatrist whose patient was a town, just as "child psychiatrist" signaled a therapist who treated children. Thinking about the phrase, he smiled—the idea of it, that he was a community's shrink. Yeah, right.

Dan Sedon arrived in time to take one of the few remaining seats in a rear pew. The young lawyer had come with his wife and a friend, succumbing like so many had on short notice to a pull as relentless as gravity. He felt a need to be there, not just as a member of the community but also in his capacity as counsel to the Tullochs, to see what people were saying about the case. He didn't intend to speak. Sedon thought barring the media was constitutionally suspect, but he wasn't about to complain, not on a night like this, not during a time in town like this. Sedon planned to be a fly on the wall.

The temperature outside was well below freezing, but inside it was steamy from shared body heat. The church was packed with nearly three hundred people, a number that approached a quarter of Chelsea's population. People were seated in pews and standing along the two side walls and in back. The low buzz of chatter ended when Pomerantz, up front, said they should start. He began by referring to the newspaper headline, and then he shrugged and remarked that "Chelsea Psychiatrist" must mean he was the town's therapist. The joke seemed to break the tension; some smiled, some laughed, and some rolled their eyes. The body language in the room relaxed momentarily, as if in a collective sigh.

Pomerantz said his main concern was Chelsea's children. "The kids need us right now. The kids are confused. The adults are confused. I'm confused." Pomerantz was emphasizing that he was one of them—a Chelsea parent and family man—not an objective therapist conducting an intervention. He wanted to use his understanding of the people and their town to guide the meeting, "rather than trying to work the thing intellectually." That meant allowing people to vent and express whatever crossed their minds and then trying to guide the discussion back to the kids. At first, ideas bounced off the walls, at times like non sequiturs. Several residents dwelled on the brutality of the killings, but most spoke about a kind of paralysis—the inability to wrap their heads around the idea that Robert and Jim had killed the Zantops. It had to be a giant misunderstanding. Someone mentioned Robert's fleeting effort at the start of his junior year to open a teen center. If that effort had succeeded, asked the woman who brought it up, would the boys be in jail now? Someone else complained about the "media assault" on Chelsea and its citizens, as if the town was to blame for the murders. "The media says we are heathens," the offended resident said. Another said maybe the negativity wasn't so bad: "We don't want them to like us and move here," he said, openly sarcastic. Comments about the media segued into a point Pomerantz wanted to make. He urged residents to talk to reporters and share Chelsea's strengths. Their silence so far had ceded the floor to the sometimes careless-talking corner-hangers. The discussion shifted again when a woman told the story of a classmate in grade school who had committed a murder, a tragedy that still haunted her. The woman's point was that they all needed to take care of their kids, and it was an anecdote that brought the room back to where Pomerantz wanted to be: "Kids need their parents in times like this."

More than anything else, residents voiced concern for the two teens accused of murder—distress that often came out emotionally, sometimes with tears. There was even some talk about baking the boys cookies. "People worried about two innocent boys in jail," Pomerantz would write in his journal. From the back, Cora Brooks shot up her hand and took the floor. She wanted to ease peoples' minds. The white-haired poet and teacher knew firsthand what she was talking about. One day in the early 1970s she was in Lebanon, New Hampshire, to demonstrate against the Vietnam War. To make her point, Brooks had plopped down in front of a bus loaded with military draftees en route to their medical examinations. Soon joined by other protesters, Brooks and the others were arrested by police and carted off to the Grafton County Jail, where Robert was now incarcerated. "I mopped floors in that jail and, as far as jails go, it wasn't that bad," Cora Brooks told the others.

Near the front of the church stood a large flip chart on an easel, placed there by one of the meeting's organizers, Phil Mulligan, Anna's father and a member of Friends of Chelsea School. The poster-sized chart was there to allow Pomerantz and anyone else to scribble down topics or ideas that arose. But after someone wondered how the community might convey support for Robert and Jim, another mentioned maybe they should send a card. Pointing to the unused flip chart, Pomerantz said people could come up later to write messages and greetings to the boys.

In his seat near Cora Brooks, Dan Sedon was more skeptical than most. The idea of writing a note to the boys on the flip chart took him aback. He hadn't expected the atmosphere to be "so pro–Robert and Jimmy." But Sedon was in a different place from everyone else, both professionally and psychologically. Not only was he a criminal defense attorney, he knew facts that no one else in the church did. He'd seen thirty or so bags of evidence taken from the Tullochs' house. Most notably, he'd figured out since the Friday-night search that investigators had found the knives. So it took him a moment, but once he recognized his unique status, the general mood made sense. It was an instinctive response—a community rallying around two of its kids in trouble. Feelings for the boys were rooted in the loyalty that was part of the gospel of a family-oriented town. In the absence of knowledge about what investigators had found, people around Sedon spoke passionately about "our kids," meaning not just Robert and Jim but all children growing up in Chelsea. Sedon found himself thinking "it was like open group therapy."

The line of commentary turned legal—several people worried that the boys would be railroaded at trial in New Hampshire, and another wondered whether a defense fund for the boys was in order. Pomerantz spotted Sedon and asked the attorney for help in fielding the legal questions. Sedon stood, reluctantly, and began to identify himself when Pomerantz urged him to come up front. Sedon ended up taking questions for nearly fifteen minutes about trials and criminal procedure, a discussion that included his explanation that a trial in a high-profile case like this would be at least a year away. Sedon told the audience the Tullochs were grateful to those who had dropped off groceries, and said the couple had stayed away from the meeting because they wanted others to feel they could speak freely. Regarding Robert's defense, Sedon said the boy had a pair of top-shelf defense attorneys in New Hampshire public defenders Richard Guerriero and Barbara Keshen. "Even if the family had the money, I'm not sure they could do any better," Sedon said. Someone asked about Jim, and Sedon said he couldn't speak for the Parkers, and when someone asked if the families might need financial help to cover expenses, Sedon replied that might be an idea to explore.

But he reiterated he didn't see a need for a defense fund. Guerriero and Keshen, he repeated, are as good as it gets.

When a couple of psychology-related questions came up, Pomerantz happily called on two counselors in attendance from a community mental-health agency. This way Pomerantz could stay with the crowd— one of the townsfolk. Scanning the standing-room-only sanctuary, he sensed the meeting was just what these people needed—each other.

Pomerantz could see that both new and old Chelsea were well represented. Cora Brooks, like himself, was part of the 1970s hippie influx. Not far from Cora stood Doug Lyford, Cora's polar opposite. He was old Chelsea—the Lyford family went back five generations in town. Lyford was fifty-four, a Vietnam War veteran who grew up dirt poor and was one of those no-nonsense Vermonters. "There was no money, but there was always work to do—we always had a farm," Lyford once said about his boyhood. "In the early sixties, we almost starved to death on the farm. There was just no money." To help out, a teenaged Doug drove a milk truck after school and worked on the town's road crew. "I never had to worry about free time—my father made sure we didn't have much." He graduated from high school in 1965 with fourteen others, and five days into his freshman year at Vermont Tech his draft notice arrived in the mail. Lyford didn't try to get a college deferral; he obeyed orders and reported for service. Returning home after combat duty, Lyford earned a degree from the University of Vermont. For thirty years he taught math and industrial arts to high school students in Chelsea—a popular math teacher, in part because he'd put lessons in real-life terms. "It was stuff you needed," said a teenager named Rob Olsen who'd had Lyford for math in eighth grade. "He would write problems like: how much fence do you need to buy to fence a field that is X big. Or you have a field that's a certain size, and how many cows can you put on the field if each cow eats X amount of grass." Lyford retired after the 2000 school year, but retired was in quotes. He was busy most days from before sunrise until after sunset, either logging, caring for eleven farms with a partner ("We hay and plow, that's what we do"), or trying to keep up with the maintenance on a collection of old John Deere tractors he either used in his farm work or stored in other people's barns around town. The tractors were a hobby—at least that's how he justified it to his wife, Karen, who worked as a secretary in the school office. "I guess my status around here is I got a bunch of old John Deere tractors," Lyford said. "I had seventeen but I sold some of them. The reason is I can't keep up with the flat tires, the dead batteries, and gummed-up carburetors. With that many, I can't even keep track of 'em." The cap-wearing Lyford had a barrel chest and a habit of removing his cap as he talked so he could run his thick fingers back and forth across the top of his crew cut. The retired teacher no longer had to work, of course, but he couldn't help himself. "It's an itch that gets under your hide, and you just have to be doing this farm work all the time."

Lyford was also a town selectman, one of a number of town leaders who had been huddling with Pomerantz and other local experts to fashion a way to cope with the murders. The case had generated a notoriety that was unwanted and, to their eyes, unwarranted. And like nearly everyone, Lyford took it personally. "I don't like to have these big, black headlines in the paper," he said, "because Chelsea is not a big, black-headline-producing town."

Now in church was a juxtaposition for all to see: Doug Lyford and Cora Brooks—the proud Vietnam War veteran and the outspoken anti-war protester. The community meeting, Pomerantz realized, could have gone much differently, dividing people further and leaving the town even more adrift. Pomerantz knew this, because he could sense that some in the crowd, particularly older Chelseans, were not comfortable with the generally positive talk about the Tullochs and Parkers. Lyford, for one, saw the world more black and white than did many of the newcomers, and at times he'd spoken frankly about changes in Chelsea that troubled him: "The town of Chelsea hasn't changed a bit. It's just the people in it who have changed." Or he would say, "We're seein' a lot more people movin' here that are comin' from money, and they don't have the same family values that a lot of the old families used to have." He did not single out the Tullochs or Parkers by name, but, said Lyford, "Parents used to have a lot more control, and now it seems a lot of parents are letting somebody else raise their children." The kids of Chelsea, he'd say, "have a lot more free time than they ever had before, and I think a lot of them, instead of having to work for money, their parents just give it to them." Lyford was all common sense: "If you go looking for trouble you're usually going to find it."

Pomerantz didn't know if Lyford on this night was holding his tongue, but he certainly knew Lyford well enough to suspect what he was thinking. Pomerantz did, however, sense an undercurrent of dissent to the support for Robert and Jim. Not everyone was happy, for example, about making a "community greeting card" out of the flip chart. Having invited people to jot down messages toward the end of the meeting, Pomerantz watched as a handful in the audience got up and headed right out the door. Those departing included Pomerantz's longtime neighbor Carol Olsen, the elected town constable. "I did not think it was appropriate to be sending them a card," Olsen said two days later. "If anything, we should be sending the Zantops a card." But at the meeting Olsen had kept quiet. "I knew that some were furious but kept their mouths shut," Pomerantz said. "I attributed their silence to their own awareness at some gut level that it was not the time."

Pomerantz was right—it wasn't a time for rancor. Most in the room had been swept up as one. Near the three-hour mark, the number of questions had finally begun to wind down, and Pomerantz could sense the gathering had succeeded in providing a stabilizing effect. He wasn't alone. In back, Cora Brooks was experiencing a unity she'd never before seen in town. Beforehand, Brooks wouldn't have been surprised if the discussion had grown testy, with the principal dividing line drawn between old timers and the relative newcomers. Both the Parker and Tulloch families were lumped into the latter group, a category in which the grown-ups were often called "granola parents" and the children were "crunchy kids." The old-time Chelseans were a conservative and proud lot. "There's a dignity here to your longevity," Brooks said. "Chelsea is like a deck of cards with suits and kings, queens, and jacks, and if you're born into one of those suits you're going to end up as the town clerk or some other town position, or run some local business, and have a really significant position in the community, a position you are not likely to get if you move to Scarsdale or North Carolina or even Burlington. So you stay. Or if you leave, you come back." But this night those divisions were tucked away.

The exclamation point on Brooks's sense of harmony came when she found herself standing next to Doug Lyford as they were filing out of the church at the meeting's end. The two Chelseans had quarreled in the past, mostly over issues related to Lyford's role as a town selectman. A recent dust-up had erupted over the town's "ditch project" to alleviate minor seasonal flooding in a brook that ran behind town hall and property along the east side of Main Street. Lyford called Brooks to notify her that engineers would be walking in her backyard on Main Street as part of a survey of land affected by the project. Lyford considered it a courtesy call, but the selectman ran headlong into the "question authority" ethos of a veteran protester. Brooks told Lyford in no uncertain terms the surveyors weren't allowed on her land. The conversation soured quickly and Brooks ended the matter by hanging up the phone.

In church, Brooks became conscious of Lyford's presence by her side, and then she felt Lyford's hand touch her arm. Their eyes met. "We may not agree about much," he told her. "Maybe not about anything. But I do know if I was in trouble, you'd be there." It was, to Brooks, a communal moment that defined Chelsea.

"There was this shared grief," she said. "People are really individuals here and don't expect to agree about a lot of things, and it wasn't so much that people agreed at the meeting as they allowed themselves to feel together the devastating news—that these boys were in police custody and if they did it or were innocent, no way it wasn't a tragedy, no matter what you thought."

Said Lyford, "Two people can be madder 'n hell at each other today, and an issue comes up and they can be side by side working on it. That's always been true about Chelsea. It's everybody's family in this town."

Exiting into the cold and the bright lights cast by the big-city television trucks, most people put their heads down and waved off the reporters and television crews that emerged from the shadows. Sedon and his wife hurried off to their car, the packed snow squeaking underfoot. Yet a few locals made themselves available to the media. "My heart goes out to the two Zantop children," said Doug Lyford, whose remarks appeared in a *New York Times* story about the meeting. "These are our children. . . . I think a lot of us feel maybe we have failed a little bit. Maybe we weren't keeping enough control."

Cars pulled out into the snow-covered streets and into the night. Most people headed home, but some pulled into The Pines' parking lot alongside a row of snowmobiles. Inside the town's only bar the kitchen was humming. A TV was tuned to the hit show *Survivor.*

"It's possible that two of Chelsea's children have done something terrible," Pomerantz said. "Sometimes people do very bad things. It doesn't mean that there's something wrong with our community." For weeks to come, Pomerantz would remain mystified at the nation's interest in his tiny town in the midst of news about a Japanese trawler accidentally sunk by an American submarine, President Clinton's travails, and the capture of an FBI counterintelligence expert who became a double agent. He told his journal: "Submarine, Clinton, spy scandal, and still we are the news."

Two bulletin boards—one outside Chelsea Town Hall and a larger "Town Talk" board outside Will's Store—were centrally located for notices that might interest residents. Posters might announce an upcoming performance at the school, a request for information about some unsolved act of vandalism, such as a small fire set on the handicap ramp leading into Town Hall, or such seasonal activities as the annual Cabin Fever Dance, the spring road rally, or the summertime farmers' market held weekly on the North Common. By early March a new flyer appeared outside Town Hall headlined "Chelsea Community Cares." Below the headline was a photograph of the quintessential New England village.

The text read: "We are community members interested in offering support to the families of James Parker and Robert Tulloch during this difficult time. Please help us by contributing funds to offset the financial burdens related to food, lodging, and travel expenses, telephone bills, and lost wages. (This is not intended as a defense fund)." Donations could be made to either or both families, and a post office box was listed.

The issue of a legal defense had been put to rest at the community meeting, but the idea of a family expense fund took hold almost immediately. Key organizers included schoolteacher DeRoss Kellogg, who'd expressed his devotion to Robert and had begun visiting him in jail, and dairy farmer Ron Allen, who was a close friend of John and Joan Parker.

Generally, Allen retrieved the money sent to the post office box and deposited it in a joint bank account in the families' names, from which the Tullochs and Parkers could withdraw funds as needed. Kellogg and his wife would then write thank-you notes after getting a list of donors' names from Allen. Most donations, said Kellogg, "included very nice notes saying how they had compassion for the families." By late April—about two months after the fund was set up—Kellogg said donations exceeded $10,000. He said nearly half of the roughly 120 donors were from Chelsea or surrounding towns and most of the remaining contributions came from around New England. "We had several donors from Hanover, a couple of them even went to the trouble to let us know that they worked for Dartmouth College—yeah, try to figure that one out," Kellogg wrote in an e-mail about the fund. "We've had several donations from the Boston area, a couple of large donations from New York City, a couple of donations from California (Joan Parker's relatives?), and one from a U.S. ambassador who happened to be at a conference in Portsmouth and took the time to drive up to Chelsea to personally give me a check." To reporters, Kellogg mentioned a donation that came from a woman living in Washington, D.C., who had read about the murders. "She had a couple of sons herself who were near that age," he said. The fund's existence brought the veteran teacher a rush of media attention. "I've had offers to appear on *Good Morning America* etc. ad nauseam," he told an acquaintance with barely concealed pride.

Not everyone was supportive. Two men began arguing one day

about the stack of flyers on the counter of the village food store—one favored the fund as the right thing to do, the other complained it was all wrong. Neither man would back down, and the pair nearly came to blows, but the store owner quickly stepped in and insisted they leave. The story of the near-fight spread around town and ended up in local newspapers.

Both Ron Allen and DeRoss Kellogg bumped into a fair share of criticism. "I've heard a few people ask, 'Why are you raising money for murderers?'" said Allen. Put on the defensive, the two men stressed that the fund wasn't for the boys' legal costs but for their families' expenses. "I know people are upset with it," said Kellogg. "But I know they haven't held it against me in any way. We've agreed to disagree."

Pomerantz played the role of facilitator at two more community meetings. Each time fewer people came. There was a meeting in early March at the church, but this time the few dozen who showed up gathered in a room downstairs instead of the main sanctuary. Outside only a single TV truck stood watch. Just two newspaper reporters appeared to see if the meeting would generate news. The main topic, again, was parenting and parental angst. "Wondering how we know if our kids could kill someone," Pomerantz wrote in his journal. Again, there was an outpouring of community guilt, which Pomerantz fielded by employing a line that was becoming a mantra of sorts: "Chelsea didn't kill the Zantops." Some talked about "parenting workshops," but nothing definite was planned. Overall, Pomerantz sensed a town in grief. "Loss of innocence," he noted. Feeling increasingly like he truly was a therapist treating a community, Pomerantz explored the subtext of hard feelings he'd detected at the first meeting. He encouraged people to discuss their feelings and, he said later, "there was an open expression of positives and negatives about the town, the school, and the children."

Pomerantz wondered if the third meeting, in early April, was needed. "Will anyone show up for this one?" Pomerantz asked his journal. He was convinced the first meeting had been a necessity. But he was wary about overdoing it. "In my mind I was mostly wondering if we needed more meetings or if it was time to drop out," he said later. "The worst thing about shrinks is that we often don't know when to stop."

Talking regularly to people around town, Pomerantz found that, "The people closest to the Parkers and Tullochs were, as might be expected, upset, and probably stayed that way." Beyond that circle, however, he found Chelseans who had gotten on with their day-to-day lives. "Confronted by trauma, most people do just fine eventually," Pomerantz wrote. "It seemed that wherever I went people had moved on to other things. More worried about sugaring season and stuff like that." Progress hardly came in a straight line, however. More like stutter steps. The student play scheduled for a March performance at Chelsea Public School was cancelled abruptly in late February. The one-act play, titled *Juvie,* included scenes of teenage violence and murder—the kind of tough and challenging subject matter from which art is drawn. But the drama now seemed too close to Chelsea's reality.

Even so, the decision to deep-six the show didn't come easily—after all this was Chelsea, where dramatic arts were as rooted as the oldest oaks in town. Pat Davenport, the school principal, found herself walking a high-wire act—at once trying to keep kids busy and as close to a regular schedule as possible, but also coping with the extraordinary impact of the two classmates' arrests for murder. Davenport knew a dramatic production would ordinarily provide an antidote of sorts for students, an escape from the pain they felt in their everyday lives. "When they were in character at least they weren't themselves in Chelsea right now," said Davenport, a former English teacher. But this play, she decided, was too much. "It is a good play," she said, but "a raw topic." Some students were upset with her, but the principal held firm: "Now is not the time for this."

Like almost everyone around Chelsea, Davenport was struggling to find her footing. During the school vacation in late February she embraced the chance to flee the area. In a matter of weeks, she'd been worn down by events and, like many, blamed the "invasion of the media" for making the tragedy of the Zantop murders worse. "The press took over the community." Davenport was relieved that she and her husband had a trip planned to visit relatives near Washington, D.C. "Hate is probably too strong a word to describe my feeling toward the media," she said later. "But it had lost its validity with me. I was having this feeling, why can't they go away? Why are they doing this? Why is this so important?" Her first and only concern was "to make sure the children felt safe and supported, and it was hard for kids to get to school without going past the press."

In Washington, D.C., she and her husband filled their days with visits to the Kennedy Center, museums, and historic sites, but when someone suggested the Freedom Forum, the school principal hesitated. The center, devoted to the nation's press, was not on her list of things to do. "The last thing I wanted to do was see anything to do with the media." She ended up going anyway, and was immediately glad she did. "They have a sense there—the staff—that this is not just a museum but a statement of values and of the importance of a free press." She was mesmerized by an exhibit of Pulitzer Prize–winning photographs, particularly a portrait of a black family, sharecroppers who had been ousted from their homestead after the father tried to register to vote. Only a free press, thought Davenport, could capture so dramatically the penalty a race of people paid for trying to vote. "I realized once again how hard people fight for rights, and a free press is part of that effort. I saw the importance of the press bearing witness." The getaway gave her a chance to take a deep breath, and the Freedom Forum visit, she said later, "became a turning point for me to getting back and having a better balance in my view of the press." Not that she became a fan. Returning home, she despaired at finding thirty-six messages from reporters on her answering machine. But she'd gained insight into the "struggle trying to balance the rest of the world needing to know and the people here going through shock and grieving and needing to be left alone."

It seemed any Chelsean who went away on vacation had a story to tell. People everywhere seemed to know about the case and wanted to talk about it. "You say 'Chelsea' and people go, 'Oh, that's where those kids are from,'" said high school sophomore Rob Olsen. Returning from their annual trip to Florida, Jack and Annette Johnson and their son Brad said talk about the murder was constant, to the point where they considered hiding the fact they were Vermonters. While on vacation the year before, the Johnsons had confronted teasing patter about Vermont's new civil-union law permitting same-sex marriages. The bad jokes about homosexual couples migrating to Vermont were reason enough at the time to avoid mentioning where they were from, but the noisy talk about the murders was even worse.

"It's part of the town now," Annette Johnson said repeatedly.

During late winter and spring, the case had to be acknowledged at public meetings as an unscripted item on the agenda. The murders came up right away at the annual town meeting in early March, before the wrangling over property taxes and a new school budget could begin in earnest as it did every year. Before the two hundred or so people assembled, Stephen Gould, the school board chairman, offered the board's support to the Tullochs, the Parkers, and to the Zantops' daughters. "It's still going to be a rough road ahead," Gould said about life in their hometown. "We don't know what news we're going to hear in the future." But whatever may come, he said, "We have our strength to see our way through this."

Others found a sense of purpose in applying for an education grant from the 21st Century Fund to build the long talked-about teen center.

Still, Pomerantz seemed correct about the tug of daily life beginning to reassert itself by the time the third meeting was scheduled for April 12. "Slow arrivals," he noted in his journal about a gathering the media didn't even know about. "Don't need the gym, music room will be OK. Good acoustics anyway." Present at the meeting was an attorney who answered questions for an hour about criminal procedure in New Hampshire. "Glad we had him," noted Pomerantz. "At least we all know what happens next." The next hour was spent discussing whether to meet again. "Do we need another meeting?" Pomerantz wrote afterward. "Guess not."

Come spring, visitors passing through Chelsea on their way to Vermont tourist sites wouldn't detect anything amiss—outwardly. The big-city television satellite trucks, a mainstay in town for weeks, were long gone. Instead, tourists might see Doug Lyford chugging along Main Street aboard one of his John Deere tractors en route to yet another field that he and his partner were tending. Over at the school, the varsity baseball team's afternoon games were drawing as many as eighty parents and kids. The crowd sat on blankets and folding beach chairs on the steep, grassy hill that overlooked the playing field. The team featured a lineup that included many of Robert and Jim's friends: Kip Battey in left field, Zack Courts in center field, Brad Johnson in right, and Tyler Vermette at second base. The boys had had a rough start, winning just two games against six losses by early May. But in a May 22 game against a visiting team from Bethel, the Chelsea Red Devils exploded for seven runs in the first inning on its way to a 13–4 win. Brad Johnson pounded a single to center field to drive in one of the runs during the big inning. Elsewhere in town the talk was about maple sugaring—a season that for many hadn't gone as well as past ones. The weather conditions hadn't been consistently favorable to get the clear, sweet sap running freely from tree trunks into the taps. Ideal sugar weather meant freezing-cold temperatures at night followed by sunny, warm days. The sixteen inches of snow that fell on April Fool's Day was no laughing matter to the many who then had to shovel out their taps and sugarhouses. Sugaring was a hobby for some, while loggers like Jack Johnson and his family did it because hauling logs was impossible during the March mud season. "Sugaring keeps us busy," Jack said. The family's sugarhouse, where sap was slowly boiled into maple syrup, was operated around the clock, mainly by his two eldest sons. Conditions notwithstanding, Chelseans such as Town Clerk Diane Mattoon and her husband had a pretty good year with their 511 taps, and roadside signs appeared at farms and homes announcing the sale of this year's yield.

With the Chelsea Town Hall closed on Fridays, Diane Mattoon began spending part of her day off in the woods near her land, picking fiddleheads in the damp beds along brooks and streams. Growing wild, the bright-green fern has a tightly coiled tip that resembles the top of a violin. Chefs and restaurateurs around New England covet them for their earthy flavor and as an exotic addition to spring-season menus. But Mattoon, who was fifty-nine, had her own family recipes and traditions: "You pick 'em and pickle 'em." She seasoned them in vinegar, dill, red pepper flakes, and garlic. "You can serve them with Saltines or eat them just like a pickle. Or you can sauté them in butter and garlic." She and a friend filled a five-gallon pail one outing. To Chelseans like Mattoon, if it wasn't fiddleheads, it was always something. By early June, Mattoon was out in the woods again, this time gathering mushrooms. Mattoon liked to freeze morel mushrooms and then, come winter, create a rich sauce using brandy and heavy cream that she'd pour over homemade bread fried on both sides. "It's very rich— and it's out of this world," she'd say. Then there was the weekend in mid-May when the civic club from Tunbridge, the next town south of Chelsea, took over the auditorium in Chelsea's Town Hall to stage its 49th Annual Minstrel Show. Inside the songs rang out—selections included "Happy Days Are Here Again" and "Grand Old Flag"—and Mattoon helped out at the door selling tickets.

But it was a surface calm, fragile at best. Worry quickly spread, for example, on the heels of a mysterious incident in the village early one evening in May. Few knew exactly what happened, but the talk was about a car pulling into town carrying a couple of out-of-towners. The two strangers were looking for someone, and a foot chase and a minor altercation ensued. The county sheriff's office got involved and questioned a few teens, but nothing came of it. Even so, eleven parents and teachers showed up at the regular June 5 selectmen's meeting. Principal Pat Davenport attended, as did Diane Mattoon. "People were jumpy, especially since what we've been through," Mattoon said later. "The feeling was to not brush stuff off, as we maybe had done in the past, but to look harder at the seemingly little things to make sure it's not a sign of something worse." They discussed paying for more patrols in town by the county sheriff's department. The selectmen's report for a meeting usually devoted to such mundane matters as road repairs noted, "Because there is a sense of panic in town now, more presence at this time might help with citizens' peace of mind."

Gone was the stillness of Chelsea's slow time. It wasn't as if there was no other news to concern Vermonters. Federal agents descended on a farm in East Warren in March to seize 234 sheep believed to be infected with a variant of mad cow disease. But no matter what else briefly claimed the spotlight, the Zantop case wouldn't go away.

There was the news that a grand jury was meeting in New Hampshire, and that subpoenas had gone to Chelsea kids including Zack Courts and Gaelen McKee. The boys were questioned under oath about the times they'd entered the two houses with Robert and Jim when no one was home, the so-called B&Es. Bigger still was word that investigators and prosecutors were going to question John and Joan Parker and Mike, Diane, and Kienan Tulloch on March 16.

The Tullochs were interviewed at the Hanover Police Department, the Parkers in the more comfortable confines of a private attorney's office in White River Junction. Both families had attorneys present, as they faced a lineup of interrogators that included prosecutors Kelly Ayotte and Mike Delaney and the key New Hampshire State Police investigators: Chuck West, Frank Moran, Robert Bruno, and Russ Hubbard.

The separate questioning of each member of the Parker and Tulloch families followed a similar format: What was the family's connection to Hanover? What was their knowledge of the Zantops? What about Robert and Jim's connection to Hanover? To the Zantops? There were other questions about the boys, their friendship, and their actions from the date of the murder on January 27 and after, but the principal questions were aimed at trying to make headway on the matter that bedeviled investigators and the public: motive. Why had Robert and Jim gone to 115 Trescott Road, and exactly what happened inside the house?

Eight hours later investigators had little to show for the effort. None of the family members provided anything tangible to explain how or why Robert and Jim ended up in Hanover. John Parker told West and Moran that except for a new foundation he'd just poured he'd never built homes in the Hanover area. Parker said he had "no feeling, I mean no information" about Jim's views on Dartmouth College. Joan Parker said she'd never worked as a racquetball instructor in Hanover. West asked her, "What connection did Jimmy have with Hanover?" Joan replied, "Nothing that I know of." Covering all possible angles, investigators asked each parent about the rumors of an affair involving one of the parents and either Half or Susanne Zantop. "I think it's crazy," John Parker said. He'd never met either Zantop. Joan Parker said the same.

"Were you involved in any kind of relationship with Half Zantop?" Frank Moran asked Joan Parker.

"No," she said.

"Or his wife?"

"No."

"Do you know of anyone who had been involved in a relationship with Half or Susanne Zantop?"

"No. I've never heard of them before."

Seeming frustrated, Chuck West at one point tangled with John Parker, pushing the father on whether he would lie to protect Jim. "Are you more comfortable protecting your son than answering our questions truthfully?" the detective asked.

"That's a tough question," Parker replied. "They're both important to me." Seconds later, he insisted, "I won't say things that will protect my son by not telling the truth."

The sessions with the Tullochs were similarly frustrating for authorities. Diane Tulloch said she knew of no possible connection between Robert and either Hanover or the Zantops. "I was not even aware that Robert was into this area. This is not an area we usually go to." Mike Tulloch echoed his wife. "Our family, generally speaking, is not oriented toward Hanover," he said. "Robert's involvement in

Hanover with the Zantops, I, I, have no knowledge of it." Questioned about extramarital affairs with the victims, Tulloch dismissed the rumors. "When we first heard about it, [Diane] laughed, um, so it's kind of a laughable situation from our point of view."

Of the four parents, the reclusive Mike Tulloch was clearly the most uncomfortable. His voice was frequently inaudible and his responses were often tortured in their syntax and littered with "ums" and "uhs." His interview was also remarkable for its detachment. There was a distance in the way he talked about Robert, as though he had only secondhand knowledge of his son's life. He couldn't say whether Robert and Christiana had a close relationship. "Um, if they were, I, I, I, I didn't see it. Uh, it, it seemed more casual to me." Mike was only vaguely aware of Robert's wanderlust in the past year. "I think it was France at one time, and then it was Australia. Um, France was with Jimmy. Australia, as I remember, was just Robert. I could be wrong about that, though." Mike said he thought Robert at one point had sought a grant through his school to help pay for travel, but the father didn't know for sure if Robert ever applied.

"He didn't get the grant apparently," was all he could say about the outcome.

Then came a moment when Mike didn't recognize the inside of his own house in a photograph taken during the police search in February. The photograph showed an interior wall and a doorjamb on which markings had been carved. Investigators, stymied in their quest to understand the killings, wondered if there might be some sort of clue or hidden meaning to the delta-shaped pattern. Neither Diane Tulloch nor her son Kienan thought so. Mike Tulloch said he'd never seen the markings before.

"Where, where in the house is it, do you know?" he asked.

When Bruno told him, Mike remained unenlightened. He'd never seen the markings, didn't have a clue. "I never really went into his room and looked around," admitted the father.

Father and son got no closer after Robert and Jim's incarceration. Mike Tulloch was only a sporadic visitor to the Grafton County Jail; by contrast, Diane was a regular during twice-weekly visiting hours.

Teacher DeRoss Kellogg also routinely made the hour-long drive to see his prized pupil. Meanwhile, John and Joan Parker were seeing Jim as much as they could. The Parkers also hired a therapist to see Jim weekly and made arrangements with the Chelsea Public School so Jim could resume his studies and earn his high school diploma. Similar arrangements were set up for Robert, but he ended up rejecting the schoolwork and the chance to get his diploma from Chelsea.

By the end of the daylong police interviews, the families were spent. But they were also unwavering in their support of Robert and Jim. During each interview investigators reviewed the incriminating physical evidence against the boys, including the discovery of the two SOG SEAL knives in Robert's room, the dramatic breakthrough that still hadn't been made public. But each family member expressed incredulity that Robert and Jim could kill.

"There's got to be some other explanation," said John Parker.

Diane Tulloch explained how she and Mike gave Robert a lot of space because he was trustworthy. Then she blurted out, "This is, I just trusted him. Um, this is, this is not really a, a Robert I really know, this kind of stuff." And she knew her son well. "He was, um, very close. I mean, is. I treat him like he, he doesn't exist anymore. We're very close."

Kienan Tulloch, before breaking down in tears, began by offering a philosophical defense of his brother. "Everybody's capable of murder, but no, I don't think he did it."

The families were sticking by the boys despite learning about the mounting physical evidence, but the public forum was a different matter altogether. Townspeople learned two weeks after the families were interviewed that two combat knives were found in Robert's room, and that blood detected on the foot-long knives matched Susanne's DNA. What's more, documents made public in court in New Hampshire revealed that Jim's fingerprints were on the knife sheaths found by investigators in Half's study, and a bloody footprint in the Zantop home matched Robert's left boot.

For weeks after Robert and Jim were arrested, Chelseans had steadfastly rejected the notion that two Chelsea boys could be involved in murder. They might not be Eagle Scouts, but cold-blooded killers—no way. It had to be a horrible mistake, a case of police incompetence or, worse, two country boys being framed.

But disclosures about the knives in Robert's room had the force of a tidal wave. It was cold, hard evidence that left many feeling ill. Kip Battey began saying about his two pals: "It looks like it happened, you know, and that they are involved." Even DeRoss Kellogg acknowledged in May, "The physical evidence is really tough." The teacher was nonetheless determined to stick by Robert, the former student he regarded as family. "Do you have a son?" Kellogg would ask. "If your son was accused of committing a serious crime, would you stop loving him?" During Robert's arraignment on murder charges May 1, a brief hearing that lasted less than five minutes, Kellogg called out to Robert in court to let the boy know he was there. "The media went zonkers when I called out to him," Kellogg later wrote in an e-mail. "It was all I could do to get my wife and myself back to our car." Before driving off, though, Kellogg tarried long enough to give reporters a view of Robert to compete with the portrait of a killer. "I enjoyed his quick wit and his desire to learn," the teacher said about the Robert he knew in sixth grade. "He was one of those kids—every teacher gets one or two a year, that you say, 'Boy, I wouldn't mind if my classroom was full of kids like this.'"

The steady run of incriminating details began to wear down the people of Chelsea. "If this turns out to be true, these boys who came by on Halloween as kids, it's a sorrow for all of us, and it's a worse sorrow, to me, than losing two boys to suicide," said Cora Brooks. Comments began increasingly to take the boys' guilt for granted. "How stupid is that?" Diane Mattoon said about the fact the boys hid the murder weapons in Robert's bedroom—a stupidity that seemed ironic in that Robert always acted like he was so smart. Hardest hit were the grown-ups—Chelsea parents.

"People want to know if they are responsible in some way," said Andy Pomerantz. The conversation at dinner tables and at The Pines or at Dixie II's had moved beyond the initial blow to the cosmic: the mysterious *how* and *why*. People in Chelsea began speculating about possible motives, ranging from a thrill kill to a burglary gone bad to a crime of passion.

"I refer to it mentally every day," said David Savidge. His daily drive to work in Chelsea village took him past the Tullochs' home on Main Street, and he often looked up at Robert's bedroom window. "Everyone is thinking, 'What went wrong?'" Savidge said. Why would two Chelsea boys do this?

The youth reaction, it turned out, was different. While their parents went on guilt trips, most teens shrugged off the hunt for explanations, at least outwardly. In late May, around the time of Jim's birthday, Tyler Vermette decided to write about his classmate in a journal for psychology class. He shared old memories, like the big birthday parties Jim had when they were in grade school. "I wrote about how I missed him," Tyler said.

Sophomore Sada Dumont said kids at school would sometimes just start talking about the two boys "as though they are not even in jail." She said, "Somebody I know is in love with Jim still and was just saying how hot he was, and she went off about that. You wouldn't even think he was not around." The occasional dinnertime talk at the Dumont house revealed a generational divide: "She wants to know why they did it," Sada said about her mom, "and I want to know why they are being framed."

Mostly Chelsea's teens would say they weren't trying to figure out what happened in the Zantops' house. Why waste the time, they'd say, obsessing about the unknowable. Coltere Savidge, as straight and steady as they come, had little interest in his parents' anxious excavation to find meaning. "My parents stay up and wonder how, and why, and what could we have done?" Coltere said. "I think that is completely ridiculous, because you are just speculating on something you have no information about whatsoever. So you're going to drive yourself crazy thinking about it."

17

Two Graduations

On Sunday, June 10, Hanover's College on a Hill celebrated its 231st graduation ceremony. Lexuses, BMWs, and Mercedeses moved in a procession along Wheelock and Main Streets. Green-and-white tents sprung up like giant mushrooms, some held in place with scaffolding disguised as Ionic pillars. Parking was impossible, except for fiftieth reunion celebrants from the class of '51, who had special privileges. Cell phones were everywhere, as were women in strappy sundresses and floppy hats, men in blazers and rep or bow ties, and well-groomed purebred dogs, with a glut of golden retrievers. State and local police kept traffic moving and an already civilized crowd civil. Music from a brass ensemble in the Baker Library Tower provided the feel of a medieval festival.

The elegant Daniel Webster Room at the Hanover Inn, across from the Green, was serving a lunch menu with appetizers of iced Spinney

Creek oysters with cucumber and Roma tomato relish for $7.95, escargot with soft polenta and beurre rouge for $7.75, and entrées of crispy grilled sweetbreads for $22 and grilled mahimahi for $26. The Gap store opened early to catch the cotton-loving Sunday morning graduation crowds. Outside Lou's Bakery, card tables brimmed with huge muffins, fresh bagels, orange juice, and gourmet coffee. In front of College Supplies, an old woman and a young girl sold disposable cameras and blank tapes for camcorders. They were competing with the official 2001 Dartmouth Commencement Video, a $45 tape spliced together from film shot by a team of green-shirted cameramen.

One hundred eighty-eight flagpoles, each ten feet tall, ringed the Green. From them flew a United Nations' worth of flags. Thousands of folding chairs were arranged in impossibly straight lines, and young attendants wandered through the crowd offering free bottles of Vermont Pure Natural Spring Water. With temperatures hovering around eighty degrees, the sixty-four-page commencement program was widely recognized for its effectiveness as a fan.

The college's official Heirlooms and Artifacts were taken from their sacred resting places like crown jewels brought to a coronation. Among them were the 1769 parchment charter that established the school with the permission of England's King George III; the ornate, gold-and-silver, 1785 Flude Medal worn by the college president; and the 1848 Lord Dartmouth's Cup, borne exclusively by the College Usher when escorting the venerated members of the Dartmouth Board of Trustees to the viewing stand.

At ten in the morning, the 1,050 undergraduates and 515 graduates lined up behind the flags of Dartmouth and the United States to march down the center of the Green. Proud mothers and fathers crowded the four-abreast graduates, snapping pictures and offering flowers, kisses, and handshakes. One mother slathered sunscreen on the neck and ears of her gowned son while he stood obediently still. A lone bagpiper began to play and the rows of new graduates broke cleanly in half, to allow their professors to walk through an aisle they created. "C'mon guys, smile," one professor in a scarlet red gown exhorted. "It's a great day. Exams are over."

Many of the graduates wore sunglasses and a few wore Hawaiian leis. But the most common accessory was a ribbon bearing the inscription "Half & Susanne." The ribbons, in Susanne's favorite color, purple, were the idea of two graduate students in the earth sciences department, Todd Myse and Margaret Quinn. It was the most noticeable reference to the murders, but not the only one.

"We know all too well that no community is apart from the intrusion of tragedy," college President James Wright said in his speech to the departing seniors. "No peaceable kingdom is immune from violence. But the test of a community is not whether it is protected from bad and evil, but rather how it responds to these things when they come upon us without warning or reason. By this test, we can, in the midst of our pain, take pride."

He never mentioned the Zantops by name, but his reference was universally understood. It was hard to find physical remnants of Half around the campus, but a few remained of Susanne: A pink lipstick kiss graced her photo on a faculty roster, and one of her winter-term course offerings—"Topics in Literary Theory: Postcolonialism"—was still listed on a bulletin board in Dartmouth Hall.

The student speakers said nothing about the Zantops. The valedictorian, Brian Stults, who had a perfect 4.0 average in his double major of mathematical social sciences and quantitative political science, talked about the "adversity" Dartmouth graduates faced. He didn't mean murdered professors. He meant competing with Harvard in sports, taking organic chemistry classes, and choosing among the different dining halls for dinner.

The commencement speaker, former secretary of state Madeleine Albright, urged the graduates to be "doers," not "drifters." Then she offered job counseling: "I hope people really do look at international careers, because national boundaries are very much out of date." It was a sentiment Half and Susanne might have spoken themselves.

After the traditional hymns were sung and the diplomas were handed out, the crowd rose to join in the singing of the Dartmouth Alma Mater, ending with the lines:

For the sons of Dartmouth,
For the daughters of Dartmouth,
Around the world they keep for her,
Their old undying faith;
They have the still North in their soul,
The hill-winds in their breath;
And the granite of New Hampshire
Is made part of them till death.

Then the brass ensemble began playing again, accompanied by the bells of the Baker Library, and the graduates marched out. Lunch reservations would soon be kept, graduation presents opened, and good-byes said.

As Dartmouth enjoyed its most festive day, the Zantop home on Trescott Road was deserted. None of Half and Susanne's protégés would be dropping by after the ceremony to show off their caps and gowns. None would quietly take Half aside to thank him for his patient teaching, or Susanne for her inspiration and energy.

There would be no big meal for friends and colleagues, no talk of the summer-vacation weeks to come at the Hiram Blake Camp. No wine glasses held high, no new recipes to try, no updates on Veronika and Mariana's progress in the world. No Susanne and Half stepping outside to stand together, Half's arm around Susanne's shoulder, Susanne's arm around Half's waist, to watch the sunset in the mountains of Vermont.

In two weeks, New Hampshire authorities would return to the house for yet another search. A dozen state troopers and Hanover police detectives, including Chuck West and Frank Moran, would walk shoulder to shoulder, scouring the grounds for more than four hours. The sight of them would renew unpleasant memories for neighbors of the night five months earlier when Roxana Verona found the bodies. Lead prosecutor Kelly Ayotte would explain only that the ground had been covered with snow the last time investigators visited, and it was possible the spring thaw exposed more evidence. Nothing was found.

A more complete explanation for the timing of the final search of the Zantops' property would follow two weeks later. A new real estate listing would appear on Page C7 of *The Valley News*: "115 Trescott Road, Etna. Lovely, private 3+ acre setting, 3 BR, 2.5 BA, First Floor Master Suite. Offered at $475,000." The home would soon have new owners, and Ayotte and her team wanted to be sure only memories were left behind.

One thing Ayotte didn't need to worry about was having enough resources to press her case. The week before the Dartmouth graduation, New Hampshire's governor and executive council set aside an extra $100,000 to help prosecute Robert and Jim. Attorney General Philip McLaughlin said the money would be spent on experts in crime-scene reconstruction, DNA evidence, computer forensics, and psychiatry. Left unstated was the common understanding that this case was so high-profile that New Hampshire didn't dare screw it up.

Only one member of the executive council, Ruth Griffin, voted against the appropriation. She was annoyed that similar attention hadn't been devoted to an unsolved, ten-year-old double murder of a poor, black couple in Portsmouth. "If the case in Hanover is so very important," Griffin wanted to know, "why isn't the case in Portsmouth just as important?"

As Dartmouth's graduation day ebbed, an unnatural quiet enveloped the Zantop house. The bird feeders were uncharacteristically empty, hosta and ferns grew lush and untamed around the front yard, and the lawn would soon need a trim. Susanne's old-fashioned drying rack was empty and forlorn. Half's boat was gone.

As New Hampshire's attorney general was fond of saying, time had stopped on January 27. Long past their useful season, two sets of cross-country skis, one long and one short, remained propped against the house, like loyal pets standing guard at their masters' grave, waiting endlessly for their return.

Two days before the Dartmouth graduation, the Chelsea Public School staged a downscale version of the same rite of passage. On a perfect spring evening, the town turned out in force to wish its daughters and sons Godspeed as they ventured out into the world. Robert Tulloch's class was moving ahead without him, though he and Jim Parker remained very much in the public eye and private thoughts.

Three weeks earlier, Colorado Governor Bill Owens had released a two-hundred-page report on the 1999 massacre at Columbine High School. Its bottom line was that if local and school officials and the killers' parents had acted on clear signals from the troubled triggermen, the tragedy might have been averted. The report concluded that everyone around the murderers had ignored a series of blatant red flags showing "suicidal and violent tendencies" during the year before they went on a shooting spree at their school. The signals mentioned were quite public at the time, including the boys' arrest for breaking into an electrician's van; their suspension from school for hacking into the school computer system; the discovery by the police of a pipe bomb behind one boy's house; an essay written by one that described a school siege; and a homemade videotape showing the boys brandishing their weapons and describing their plans for a massacre.

The report's finding made national news. Chelseans were as startled as the rest of the country by all the missed danger signs. Comparing notes, though, they were left wondering about their situation. The creepy, public buildup to murder by Columbine students Dylan Klebold and Eric Harris didn't sound at all like Chelsea's own Robert Tulloch and Jim Parker. The disconnect only made all the more vexing the conduct of their own boys. Where were the red flags, the in-your-face, murderous clues that the Colorado town had overlooked?

It was seventy degrees as dusk approached on the evening of the Chelsea graduation. The sky was a cloudless blue, the air carried a hint of fresh flowers, and the tree-covered mountains that ringed the valley town wore a coat of leaves that looked dense enough to walk across. Jersey cows chewed cud in pungent fields, and stacks of fresh cordwood patiently waited for the following winter. Signs advertising maple syrup competed with those urging Vermonters to "Impeach Jeffords," as punishment for Senator Jim Jeffords's decision two weeks earlier to quit the Republican Party and become an Independent.

Mud-caked Subarus and rust-eaten pickup trucks moved slowly up and down Main Street. A family of six tumbled out of an old minivan held together with duct tape to grab a pizza dinner. American flags dangled from poles on farmhouses, S&L Video Plus did a steady trade, while Dixie II restaurant sat empty. On Dixie's menu were pancakes with Vermont maple syrup for $2.75; a Dixie burger with onions, mushrooms, and cheddar, for $3.75; and Dixie's chicken fillet for the same price. For atmosphere, there was floral wallpaper, plastic table-cloths, a wood-burning stove, and a television atop a stainless-steel milk dispenser.

As the start of the festivities approached, four boys gathered at the basketball court in the center of town, taking faraway shots that rarely came close to the backboard. Instead of moving closer, they tested their range by edging even farther away, with predictable results. Ten minutes of perfect shooting—all misses—was enough to bore them, so they walked across the street to the misspelled Chelsea Laundramat to sit on the front steps and share a cigarette.

By 5:30 P.M. the graduates started to arrive at the South Common, where seven hundred folding chairs were arranged in rows in the shadow a fifty-foot maple tree. Sunlight bounced off the snow-white Orange County Courthouse at the far end of the common. Six ushers, including Tyler Vermette and Matt Butryman, handed out eight-page programs listing the graduates and detailing all Commencement Week events.

By 6 P.M. the crowd overflowed the folding chairs by some two hundred people, meaning the equivalent of nearly the entire population of Chelsea was on hand to witness the passage of thirty-nine newly minted graduates. John Parker was among them, hanging toward the back of the crowd and exchanging quiet hellos with friends and acquaintances. Joan Parker didn't come, and neither did Mike or Diane Tulloch. The Tullochs' house, a short walk down Main Street from the ceremonies, was dark.

When the crowd was seated, friends and neighbors chatted and laughed, leaning over from one row to the next to offer greetings. Some stood on chairs, calling out to latecomers. The dress was Chelsea

Casual—tie-dyed shirts outnumbered ties, and shorts outnumbered khakis. Footwear ran to Birkenstocks, running shoes, work boots, and clogs for men as well as women. Children passed time with games of duck, duck, goose. No one talked on cell phones; as always, they didn't work in the valley. A black-and-tan Labrador-collie mix wandered through the crowd, collecting pats.

At 6:30 P.M., the graduates walked out of the school building and onto the adjacent common to "Pomp and Circumstance," played by a school band with adults filling in on tuba and trombone. The girls wore silver gowns, the boys black—together, the class colors—and each carried a single red rose. They walked two-by-two. Had Robert been among them, there would have been twenty pairs. In his absence, the thirty-ninth graduate was left to walk alone, giving the procession the look of military jets flying a missing-man formation. A dozen of the seniors had been with Robert in DeRoss Kellogg's sixth grade class.

The graduates found their places in front of a banner with the class motto printed in silver letters on a black background: "The future belongs to those who see possibilities before they become obvious." The class chose two decades-old songs to be remembered by: "School's Out for Summer" by Alice Cooper and "Staying Alive" by the Bee Gees.

Principal Pat Davenport took the microphone and praised a class she called "supportive, stimulating, cooperative, and caring." Without mentioning the missing class member or his best friend, Davenport congratulated the town for coming together to support the new graduates. "As a community we have much to be proud of," she said, her voice cracking.

The valedictorian was Anna Mulligan, who had succeeded Robert as student council president. She had spent a semester at the Mountain School and would be attending Brown University. In florid prose, Mulligan talked about a trip she had taken to Ghana and described how guilty she felt being a tourist in a Third World country. Salutatorian William Funk IV, en route to Norwich University, happily remembered second grade with Kip Battey and Zack Courts, and reminisced about later school years with other friends. He didn't mention

Robert or Jim, but like Davenport, tried to reassure the crowd: "It does take a whole village to raise a child, and looking at my peers, it looks like you did a good job."

Before collecting their diplomas, nearly all the graduates received some kind of award, scholarship, or both. Anna Mulligan collected an armful. Coltere Savidge won the coveted Balfour Award, for his combination of all-around "scholarship, loyalty, and achievement." Kip Battey, Robert's erstwhile debate partner, received a speaking award.

The closest anyone came to a direct reference to the killings was guest speaker Willem Lange, a New England essayist who, it happened, lived in the Zantops' town. "It would be foolish of me to try to pretend there isn't a very sad connection between your town and my village of Etna," he said. "Personally, I feel that the connection is largely the creation of various media, to whom getting a story is sometimes more important than the privacy or feelings of the people involved. We may regret that, but wishing it weren't so won't change it. . . . Our job here this evening is to put that behind us, at least temporarily, and focus on the work that's ahead of us."

Lange then decried "the disintegration of common civility" and urged the graduates to tear down walls that divide people and build bridges to join them. "If ever there was a group of people uniquely qualified to help heal the wounds in the body of our culture, it's you."

Lange's sentiments were well received, but the townspeople knew that before healing could begin they still needed to know why two of their boys were in jail awaiting trial for murder. As more physical evidence was revealed, most Chelseans had come to accept that Robert and Jim had killed the Zantops. But with no known links to the professors and no word of motive from police or prosecutors, the struggle for understanding continued.

To the people of Chelsea, Jim was still the musically gifted class clown, the smiling child of well-respected parents, the native son who didn't like to hunt and was afraid of the dark. Robert was still the whip-smart student council president, the talented debater, the arrogant but harmless son of introverted parents. Together they were the clean-cut, drug-free, fort-building, Frisbee-playing, rock-climbing, fast-driving buddies who might win a raft race one day and entertain the town in a talent show the next.

What the people of Chelsea didn't know was those images were long out of date. The Robert and Jim they thought they knew had disappeared long before they bought knives, put them to use, then took flight from the police.

Part III

18

Jailhouse Snitch

A week after the Dartmouth and Chelsea graduation ceremonies, two men chatted in a brown Ford Crown Victoria driving south along New Hampshire's Route 25. The driver was a young sheriff's deputy with a .40-caliber Glock on his hip. His back-seat passenger was a handcuffed inmate from the Grafton County Jail. They were headed to another New Hampshire county, where the inmate faced charges of forgery and passing bad checks.

As they drove along the two-lane blacktop, the inmate whiled away the time by talking about how he ended up in jail—it was an intricate tale, complete with a motorcycle crash, a coma, and some romantic entanglements along the way. The story ended with him spending his days in maximum security, confined to a cell near one of the teenagers charged with killing the Dartmouth professors.

"That case is a shame," Deputy Chad Morris told his passenger.

The evidence against them looks solid, Morris said, but everyone's still trying to figure out why they did it.

The inmate, a man known to some as "Ranger," thought about that for a minute. It was an opening he'd been waiting for.

Four months earlier, upon his return from Indiana, Robert was driven through the winding roads of Grafton County in northwest New Hampshire to the county seat of North Haverhill. The Zantops' town of Etna was at the southern tip of the county, an hour away and a world removed.

While Etna basks in the intellectual light of Dartmouth, remote North Haverhill does the county's dirty work. Its dominant institution is the fourteen-hundred-acre county complex, which includes the courthouse, a nursing home, the jail, a dairy farm where minimum-security inmates provide the labor, and hundreds of acres of meadows and timber land. The only link between the communities is the main road through North Haverhill: Dartmouth College Highway.

Robert entered the jail through a side entrance, via a steel door that clanked noisily shut behind him. He was led to a closet-sized booking room to be photographed and fingerprinted, after which he sat in a hard chair as a corrections officer raced through a series of questions designed to assess the security risk of each new inmate. In Robert's case, the outcome was a foregone conclusion: Anyone awaiting trial for murder would automatically be held in maximum security, the "Max Unit."

Just a short walk from the booking area, the Max Unit looked like the set of an old prison film. It was a nineteenth-century maze of steel and stone that had absorbed the sour odors and stale breath of untold misfits and miscreants. The unit—home on any given day to about one-third of the jail's ninety inmates—was divided into four rectangular boxes called tiers. Each of the four tiers had the feel of a bus station's overcrowded men's room, a jam of sweaty flesh under dim artificial lights, a place with a numbing gravitational pull to the lowest common denominator. The rules of survival were simple and essential: keep your head down, don't make enemies, and don't stand out. Smarter and more experienced inmates knew a fourth rule: trust no one.

Two sides of each tier were enclosed by steel bars layered with endless coats of industrial gray paint, and the other two sides were solid stone. Each tier had four closely packed cells, with one or two inmates in each. Each cell was no more than six feet wide and eight feet deep. Inside were bunk beds and a toilet at the far end—in full view of any corrections officer or inmate walking past. Outside the cells was a hallway called a catwalk. At three feet wide and thirty feet long, the catwalk was the tier's only common area, a narrow passage where inmates could congregate, though never comfortably.

Just outside the bars at one end of the catwalk was a shelf with a small television set, its controls reachable if one snaked an arm through the bars. MTV and Jerry Springer were the usual fare. The TV was shared by all the men on a tier, but the catwalk was only wide enough for a single plastic chair, so inmates crowded around, body to body in orange Max Unit uniforms, or sat lined up behind one another like riders on a bicycle built for eight. Even that pleasure was limited: an infraction by any one inmate on the tier—drawing a caricature of a corrections officer on the wall, for instance—might result in the shared punishment of a week without television. At the other end of the catwalk was a phone inmates used to make collect calls to anyone who'd accept them at a dollar a minute, or to receive incoming calls from their lawyers. Next to the phone was a small shower with a flimsy plastic curtain.

Before Robert's arrival, prosecutors and jail officials worked out a plan. They planted an undercover officer in his cell, hoping that a teenage inmate new to life behind bars might slip and say something incriminating. The officer—who had spent time with Robert earlier in the day in a holding cell at the Grafton County Sheriff's Office—was equipped with a hidden tape recorder, but he couldn't get it to work. It didn't matter; Robert revealed nothing. They talked about who would get the top bunk and what kind of pizza they liked. Robert's most telling comment was that "nobody should have to live in a place like this." When the undercover officer said his name was Jim, Robert looked away and said only, "I have a friend named Jim."

Some inmates in the Max Unit taped pictures to their cell walls, and Robert and some others kept GE radios purchased for $45 each from the jail commissary. Luckier ones had radios "willed" to them by former cellmates who had been freed or sent on to the state prison in Concord. The commissary also offered a range of junk food, necessities, and semi-luxuries, including $15.99 box fans for the jail's unbearable summer heat, shower shoes for $2, Pert shampoo for $3.25, and greeting cards—"Thinking of You" was a popular choice—for $1.50. There was an inevitable breakdown of haves and have-nots in the jail—the haves had someone on the outside to replenish their commissary accounts.

Robert found one such person in an unlikely place: the Glencliff Home for the Elderly, a state-funded retirement home a few miles from the jail that cared for old people with mental illnesses or developmental disabilities. To the surprise of her friends and colleagues, the home's superintendent, Sandra Knapp, began writing to Robert and then visiting him. Soon the middle-aged woman who looked like a schoolmarm became his most frequent visitor, regularly standing by on visiting days in case none of his family or friends showed up. She sent him books by the dozen and regularly deposited $10 or $20 in his commissary account. One time, Mike Tulloch was about to leave some money for his son, but when he saw Knapp he pocketed his wallet, knowing she would give Robert all he needed. Knapp refused to discuss what drew her to Robert, but once told reporters she considered him "a wonderful young man." Knapp's employees were so disturbed by that comment they bought an ad in a local newspaper. "Our hearts go out to the true victims of this tragedy and we find such statements deeply offensive," they wrote. To Glenn Libby, the jail's superintendent, Knapp was a compassionate woman being used by a manipulative killer. "Robert at times made it clear he's got her on a string," said Libby, whose wife worked for Knapp at the nursing home.

Personal visits for maximum-security inmates at Grafton were allowed just one hour a week, on Saturday mornings, with no physical contact permitted. At most, two adults and two children could visit at one time. In addition to Sandra Knapp, Robert's sixth grade teacher DeRoss Kellogg came regularly. On different visits he brought a friend; Robert's brother, Kienan; his debate partner, Kip Battey; the Chelsea school librarian; and a member of The Crew. Once Kellogg arrived with Mike Tulloch, and Robert's face fell.

The jail visits took a toll on Kellogg, leaving him worn out and wasted. His blood pressure rose. He compared his heartache to "losing a loved one, day after day, with no end in sight." Late in the spring, when Kellogg said he wouldn't be able to visit as often, Robert urged him to at least keep writing. "You said you would send letters now and then," Robert wrote. "Tell you what. I'll mail you like one letter, or maybe two every week, if you keep sending letters all the time. . . . You know my life isn't very good."

As months passed, Kellogg saw changes in his former star pupil. Robert's letters grew shorter and the writing became more jagged, the ideas disjointed. He began calling Kellogg and talking for hours on end. The bills mounted for the Chelsea schoolteacher, but he knew there were few other people who would accept the collect calls.

Kellogg tried to hold on to his carefully constructed image of Robert as a decent, thoughtful young man, fixating on a story Robert told him about asking the corrections officers to place an inmate with a mental disability in his cell to prevent other inmates from abusing him. But Libby told a different version of the story. Robert was the primary abuser, Libby said, at one point crushing the cellmate's glasses and flushing them down the toilet for the sport of it. Libby thought Robert fit the profile of a serial killer, and that only his capture prevented more deaths.

Though Kellogg considered himself crucial to Robert and seemed to bask in the attention he received as Robert's media-friendly defender, Kellogg soon became an irritation to Robert's lawyers. The low point came when Kellogg tried to recruit celebrity lawyer Gerry Spence to the legal team, an unsuccessful attempt that alienated Robert's public defenders, Richard Guerriero and Barbara Keshen.

A friend of Kellogg's sent Robert books on t'ai chi and Zen philosophy. The young inmate also grew enchanted with Ayn Rand, whose philosophy was built on "the concept of man as a heroic being, with his own happiness as the moral purpose of his life, with productive achievement as his noblest activity, and reason as his only absolute." Robert read *The Essential Writings of Ralph Waldo Emerson,* a history of Scotland, Thor Heyerdahl's adventure classic *Kon-Tiki,* and the novel *Cold Mountain,* about a Confederate army deserter's journey home. He didn't like the ending, because the hero died after his long trek.

At Robert's request, Kellogg sent him *Something Wicked This Way Comes* by Ray Bradbury. Investigators had found cassettes for an audio version of the same book when they searched Joan Parker's green Subaru—the car Robert and Jim drove to the Zantops' house. One lyrical passage that Robert would have read describes the characters' symbiotic relationship: "There they go, Jim running slower to stay with Will, Will running faster to stay with Jim. Jim breaking two windows in a haunted house because Will's along, Will breaking one window instead of none, because Jim's watching. God, how we get our fingers in each other's clay. That's friendship, each playing the potter to see what shapes we can make of the other."

A typical day in the Max Unit started with lights on at five in the morning. A corrections officer would yell, "Chow's on the way" and the caged men would grunt in recognition or stay silent in their bunks. Breakfast was optional, so only a few inmates would rouse themselves from the thin, lumpy pads that passed for mattresses. Breakfast arrived by six o'clock, most often eggs, bacon, and soggy toast, prepared at the county nursing home next door to the jail and wheeled on carts through an underground tunnel. There was a time when inmates left their cells and marched through the tunnel to a secure dining room at the nursing home, but that ended with a hostage-taking incident in 1995 led by a former New York City policeman awaiting trial on charges of dismembering his wife.

Robert and the other Max Unit inmates filled the rest of their mornings by hanging out on their bunks, playing cards, making phone calls, reading, and maybe taking a trip to the small collection of books that passed for the jail library. Inmates awaiting trial might have calls or visits from their lawyers, but many slept through the morning altogether, awakening for lunch at eleven, only to go back to sleep and snooze through the afternoon.

The big event of the day came in the afternoon, when all Max Unit inmates were allowed one hour outside their tiers. They decided collectively, with majority rule, whether to spend the hour in an inside recreation room or an outdoor yard. Indoors featured a foosball table, a Ping-Pong table, two treadmills, and a Stairmaster. But the group usually elected to go outside, to a small yard shaped like a lopsided pentagon. Three of the sides were the walls of the jail and the other two were tall fences topped with barbed wire. There was a basketball hoop with a shredded net, but most of the inmates spent the hour lined up along the fence, their fingers entwined in the chain links.

They had a sweeping view down a rolling hill to a meadow, where foxes, deer, and wild turkeys were joined by the occasional coyote or moose. Beyond the meadow was a meandering oxbow of the Connecticut River, then a line of trees that followed a bend in the river. Beyond that was another meadow, just over the state line in Vermont. The vista was a landscape painter's New England ideal.

Despite the view and the chance to breathe fresh air, some inmates chose to stay locked inside rather than stand at the fence. After nearly two decades in the corrections business, Glenn Libby understood why. The view was torture to inmates with wanderlust, who had grown up amid forests and mountains—a shot glass of beer to a hardcore alcoholic. The effect tended to be exaggerated among inmates facing long stretches of prison time. Not long after Robert arrived at the jail, Libby noticed that he was just such an inmate. At first, Robert would spend his hour outside, pining for the woods just out of reach. But then he'd be out of sorts afterward. Soon he began holing up in his cell during recreation hours. A couple of months later, however, Robert surprised Libby by emerging again from his shell and returning for his daily hour at the edge of the great outdoors.

As Grafton County's chief jailer, Libby made a point of noticing things like that. When men were confined in such tight quarters, it paid to watch them closely, to know when things were even slightly out of kilter. Libby kept an especially close eye on Robert, in part because of his celebrity inmate status but also because the superintendent realized that even a small change in his routine, surroundings, or relations with fellow inmates could send him spiraling downward.

Over time, Libby formed a detailed impression of Robert: arrogant, self-centered, a manipulator who prodded and poked to test the limits of his jailers and fellow inmates. Libby saw a young man who tried to "mold people around him to suit his purposes," someone who would coldly calculate every action to benefit himself—even more than typically scheming inmates. "He'd take in everything you said, and like a cash register he'd total it up and then formulate a question or a comeback request," Libby said. Robert got into several full-blown fistfights, usually when he decided to pick on "some inmate who was scrawny." That way, Libby said, he could "flex his muscle in a predatory style."

Late afternoon in the Max Unit was spent watching television, making phone calls, reading, and playing endless games of crazy eights, hearts, and spades. Dinner arrived by 5 P.M., served, like the other meals, on plastic plates filled by a corrections officer then passed through an opening in the bars. Then there were more card games, television, and letter-writing.

Robert wasn't supposed to write to his sometime girlfriend, Christiana Usenza, because she was a potential witness at his trial, just as she had been before the grand jury that in April indicted him for murder. But he devised a plan to skirt that prohibition, enlisting the help of DeRoss Kellogg. If Kellogg received a letter with his first name spelled incorrectly on the envelope—with a lowercase r, "Deross"—it was intended for Christiana, and Kellogg was supposed to pass those letters, unopened, to her. The scheme worked twice.

"God I miss Jim," Robert wrote Christiana. Then, referring to Jim's sister and mother: "Tell Di to tell Jim to remember all those talks we had. I know she probably won't. Joan is really controlling the hell out of that situation." In the other letter, he wrote: "Jim is like my brother. I respect and love him more than anything."

"So many ways to commit suicide," Robert continued. "But I can't do that, not if Jim doesn't want me to. He could be mad at me. I doubt it. He's my hero, you know, him and you. Him because I have seen him. I know how he dealt with this. As smooth as obsidian." It was a reference Half Zantop might have appreciated—comparing Jim to a dense, dark volcanic glass. But there was an apparently unintended meaning in Robert's simile. Obsidian is indeed smooth, but when it cracks, its edges form a sharp curve that can make it a deadly weapon.

"He's amazing," Robert wrote. "I know nothing can break him. It's amazing. He never broke throughout this whole deal."

Robert himself wasn't nearly as tight-lipped. Despite repeated warnings from his lawyers not to talk to anyone about the case, Robert thought he knew best. Ignoring his lawyers' pleas, he befriended two older inmates, who, he seemed to think, could help and protect him if he were convicted and sent to the state prison in Concord. He seemed to enjoy bragging to them about his criminal exploits, as though he could impress them with his capacity for killing and his self-described sangfroid while carrying out a double murder. One was an inmate of American Indian heritage, whom Robert called Chief.

When Chief was sentenced to three-and-half to seven years in another prison instead of Concord, Robert was incensed. He imagined he possessed the means and the power to control the New Hampshire corrections system while making his family rich in the process, and he expressed that grandiosity in a letter to someone close to Chief.

"Chief and I were going to write a book, and make millions," Robert wrote. "Since two Dartmouth professors died, everyone who knew them or lived in New Hampshire or who likes this kind of thing will buy it. And Chief is just the man to write it. I believe you would end up with some 30 million (dollars)." That idea was foiled, Robert explained, when Chief wasn't sent to Concord. But Robert had a plan to fix that.

"I would plead guilty in exchange for Chief getting out in like 4-6 months. Or earlier. That way, we can immediately write the book in those months. He could set me up in Concord. And get out, find a publisher, work out the legal stuff, and make the money. This $3\frac{1}{2}$ to 7 really fucked our plans, but I am not going to let that stop us. I know pleading guilty for a life sentence sounds crazy. But I think I am fucked anyway. And if they will make a deal Chief gets out. I get to spend a few months with him. And then our families get rich. Also, if I plead guilty it might help my friend's case. . . . Burn this letter after you read it. Don't communicate with my mother, all this is too sensitive."

Despite Robert's warnings, authorities got hold of the self-incriminating letter, and his farfetched plan fizzled.

In addition to Chief, Robert also befriended a biker with a history of passing bad checks, who went by the handle "Ranger"—the same man who would later find himself in the back seat of Chad Morris's cruiser.

Lights out at the Grafton County Jail came at eleven o'clock. Some nights, the quiet was broken by the flapping wings of bats followed by yells from inmates.

Sixty miles south, at the modern Belknap County Jail in Laconia, Jim lay on his back on a bench in a living room–sized common area outside his private cell. His long legs hung over the end of the bench, so Jim positioned a chair to support the overflow of his sock-clad feet. He chose his position carefully: rays of natural light filtered down on him through a milky-glass skylight directly overhead. It looked as though he was modeling a passage in the paperback book he was reading, *The Snow Leopard,* Peter Matthiessen's 1978 story of an arduous search for the elusive big cat. "All other creatures look down toward the earth," Matthiessen wrote, "but man was given a face so that he might turn his eyes toward the stars and gaze upon the sky."

Now and then, the former class clown looked up from his prone position to see who was walking past the shatterproof glass that enclosed the common room. If the visitors lingered awhile, watching him, he might raise his arm and offer a cocky wave. Then he'd get up, casually toss a black sweatshirt over his shoulder, and walk into his cell, for privacy.

Taking a break from the book, Jim might fill out a commissary form. The jail supplied Ivory soap for free, but Jim preferred Dial, so he'd pay seventy-five cents for a bar. He didn't like the unlined paper given to inmates, so he paid a dollar for a stack of lined paper. He and Robert shared a distaste for junk food, so for a snack he'd order pretzels for twenty-five cents and a PowerAde drink, Jagged Ice flavor, for seventy-five cents. The cost would be deducted from the commissary account regularly replenished by his parents.

For three months after he was brought back from Indiana, Jim was confined to New Hampshire's juvenile detention center in Concord, a facility with the feel of a strict boarding school. Teens held there ate their meals in a cafeteria setting, and their days were filled with classes and homework. Visiting hours were held three afternoons a week, and when those visits began or ended with hugs, the officers paid no mind. "If there's some demonstration of affection, we're not going to say 'Knock it off,'" said Philip Nadeau, who supervised the detention center. "We realize these are youngsters we're dealing with. They've made some bad decisions, but they still need some support. And the best people to give it to them is their parents."

When Jim turned seventeen in May, he was brought to the Belknap County Jail, in the Lakes Region of central New Hampshire. There was never any consideration of bringing him to Grafton County Jail, where he and Robert would have a chance to work on a new alibi. Jim's move from a juvenile center to an adult jail forced him to adapt to greater confinement, but Belknap wasn't nearly as tough as Grafton.

The Belknap jail was a two-story, almost windowless building made from red cinder-block with a blue-tile stripe, something an unimaginative child might design from Lego blocks. A small portion of the jail dated to the 1800s, but a renovation and addition that opened in June 1989 made Belknap one of the state's most modern correctional facilities. Most strikingly, there were few bars. Cells were enclosed by cinder block and picture window–sized panes of unbreakable glass, through which corrections officers watched inmates as though they were exhibits in a museum.

Like Robert, Jim was automatically classified a maximum-security inmate and issued an orange uniform. That made him a rarity at

Belknap, where Superintendent Joseph Panarello could usually count his high-risk inmates on one hand with a couple fingers left over. Most of the sixty or so inmates at the Belknap jail on any given day were there for petty crimes or domestic offenses, and about half were kept in a minimum-security dorm, where they could pay off their debts to society by working on the county farm, shoveling snow in winter, raking leaves in fall, and sweeping mud off sidewalks the rest of the year.

After his booking and intake interviews, Jim was brought to the "B Unit," just a few steps from the jail's high-tech central station with banks of surveillance monitors. Jim was assigned to B2, an eight-by-ten cell with a single bed, a stainless-steel sink-and-toilet unit, and an unbreakable mirror. It was one of four single-inmate cells in the pod that opened onto the triangular-shaped, four-hundred-square-foot common area called a "day room." The room had a blue pay phone, a television, and a metal picnic table bolted to a gray-painted concrete slab floor. There also were two plastic chairs—one of which Jim used as his footrest—which technically didn't belong in the maximum-security pod. "We let them have the chairs to be nice," said corrections officer Jan Hale, a fifteen-year veteran. That sentiment was foreign to the officers guarding Robert in the Max Unit in Grafton.

The walls of the day room were bare, except for a hand-lettered sign that B Unit inmates would tape to the front window when they wanted to sleep. It read: "Could you please dim the lights."

Maximum-security inmates at Belknap were allowed visitors twice a week, an hour each on Tuesdays and Saturdays—twice the time allowed at Grafton. In addition, Joan and John Parker paid for a therapist to visit Jim weekly to help him adjust to life in jail. Besides the counselor, Jim's parents were his most frequent guests. Joan sometimes brought books about yoga, and Jim soon became devoted to it, spending three or more hours a day in various meditative poses.

One visiting day, Jim's good friend Coltere Savidge came with the Parker family's friend Kevin Ellis. Jim quizzed Coltere on town gossip—mostly who was dating whom—and caught up on news about friends at college. Afterward, Jim told his father he liked having Coltere there; some of his other friends were awkward, but Coltere was at ease, able to keep the conversation alive. Yet Coltere felt strange afterward. There he was with his old friend, talking about what they always talked about, but they were separated by bulletproof glass. Coltere noticed something else, too: Jim seemed older, more sober, less the prankster.

The only break in the Belknap visiting routine came at Christmas time, when Panarello set aside December 20 for maximum-security inmates to have up to five visitors at a time over a three-hour period. Jim drew a Chelsea crowd including his father, Coltere, and Susan Dollenmaier and her twin daughters, Ivy and Tess Mix. Dollenmaier's home had been the target of one of The Crew's breaking-and-eating exploits, but all had been forgiven. Jim hadn't spoken face-to-face with a girl his age in months, and suddenly two were in close proximity. He ignored the rest of the group and focused on Ivy and Tess.

There was no special Christmas visit for Robert at Grafton. There, the only holiday treat was a pizza dinner.

Though the conditions were softer than at Grafton, Jim's daily schedule wasn't much different. At five-thirty every morning, corrections officer Jan Hale radioed the jail's main control room and asked that B Unit cells—she called them "rooms"—be unlocked. Hale flipped on the light and called out, "Get up for breakfast!" Sometimes there'd be only one other inmate in the unit, and sometimes Jim was alone, though at times there were as many as four, one per "room." Those were the times a rousing Monopoly tournament would get under way.

One of Jim's frequent unit mates was a fight-prone young man awaiting sentencing on an assault charge. He was an inmate who, in the words of one corrections officer, had "taken on some of the toughest we've had." But to the surprise of their jailers, he and Jim got along well. Jan Hale said Jim—she always called him James—was a model inmate, quiet and cooperative. Unlike most inmates, he never seemed to harden. The closest he came were a couple times when his usual "schoolboy look" would suddenly be replaced by an "angry flash." Yet that would leave as quickly as it came.

After breakfast, most inmates would go back to sleep, waking again at seven-thirty, when Hale rolled around the "wish cart," containing free supplies for inmates, including pencils, paper, soap, and shampoo. Pencil sharpeners were prohibited in maximum, so the cart carried one for on-the-spot use. Any inmate who wanted to shave would get a razor and shaving cream, both of which had to be returned to an officer within fifteen minutes.

Every morning featured one hour of exercise. Some inmates in the maximum unit adopted Robert's approach of skipping recreation time and staying in their cells, but Jim would never miss his hour outdoors or in the jail gym. Sometimes he would do yoga. More often he would shoot baskets, extending his long arms in a graceful shot that impressed even the jaded jail officers. One time the ball got caught between the hoop and the backboard, and Jim, strong and wiry as ever, grabbed the pole and in a single fluid motion kicked his feet up to the ten-foot-high rim to knock it free. Contact basketball games were prohibited, so Jim and an inmate named Jason sometimes played the shooting contest called HORSE. Each time a player missed, he added a letter of the word, and the first one to get all five letters lost. Jim would take an early lead, but his concentration or confidence would fade, and inevitably Jason would win.

After lunch, Jim worked on his high school diploma. While Robert rejected the offer to receive schoolwork from Chelsea, Jim embraced it. He was the only inmate at Belknap working on a custom-crafted school program, engineered with heavy involvement from Joan Parker. She made sure he received his assignments, and brought his finished work to school so teachers could grade it. Jim did geometry, English, and art, using a small wooden figure as a model for drawing and water-colors.

He filled his days with reading and cards, and sometimes the shared television would be tuned to MTV, a movie, or the news. When reports about the Zantop killings came on, other inmates would get excited, but not Jim. He never spoke about the case. Hale and Panarello described his general demeanor as flat. "He's not emotion-less, but he's not emotional either," Hale said. If she joked with him he might chuckle, but he would never initiate the laugh track. Hale and Panarello were surprised to hear of his Chelsea reputation for clowning. "Not here," Panarello said. Some jail officers considered Jim's demeanor evidence of a cold-blooded streak, but Hale liked him.

Most nights, before being locked in his cell, Jim would wander to the corner of the day room, pick up the pay phone, and call home, collect, to say good-night to his parents.

Sitting in the back seat of Deputy Chad Morris's cruiser driving down Route 25, Ranger saw his opportunity to engage in the time-honored jailhouse tradition of trading information for leniency. When Morris mentioned the mystery of the Zantop case, Ranger pounced. He told Morris that his cellmate Robert Tulloch had confided in him about the crimes. Ranger then gave Morris three pieces of information specific enough to suggest he knew more.

First, Ranger said, Robert said the crimes were random and that he and his friend Jim Parker were originally going to "do" the Zantops' neighbors but they weren't home. Second, Robert said this was his first killing, and "he was a bit nervous and wanted to get a few under his belt." Third, Ranger told the deputy something solid and verifiable that had yet to be made public: The only item taken from the house was Half Zantop's wallet.

Keep this between us—I'm no rat, Ranger added, almost certainly knowing his request would be ignored.

Yet as days passed, it must have seemed to Ranger that Deputy Morris was inexplicably respecting his wishes. In fact, although Morris had followed the Zantop case with professional interest, he overlooked the significance of his passenger's comments. Morris didn't immediately realize that, in his car that day, from behind the Plexiglas-and-steel cage separating the front and back seats of the Crown Vic, Ranger had become the first person to credibly claim that Robert Tulloch had admitted to the killings and had provided an explanation of sorts as well.

On June 26, fully a week after Ranger's revelations, Morris happened to run into Sergeant Bob Bruno of the New Hampshire State Police, a key member of the Zantop task force. Morris and Bruno were standing in a coffee-break room at the Plymouth Police Department when the conversation with Ranger popped into Morris's mind.

"I transported an individual who told me a few things," he told Bruno. "For what it's worth, you might want to check it out."

"What types of things?" Bruno asked.

When Morris told him, Bruno instantly grasped the significance. At that point, neither Robert nor Jim had shown any willingness to cut a deal, and investigators were stumped and frustrated after four fruitless months of searching for a motive or a link between the Zantops and their killers. Bruno told Morris to write up a report as quickly as possible, and Bruno wrote his own report as well, documenting Morris's comments.

Three days later, Ranger was ushered from jail to the nearby Grafton County Sheriff's Office for a meeting with two New Hampshire state troopers: Mark Mudgett, the sergeant supervising the day-to-day investigation, and Trooper First Class Todd Landry.

"OK, listen," Mudgett told Ranger. "You've obviously had desire to talk to the police about the conversation you had with Mr. Tulloch, and that's why we've asked to meet you here today. . . . Do you remember what he told you?"

"He told me that him and James Parker had murdered the Zantops," Ranger said. "He told me that it was just random. There was no connection between himself and the Zantops. That he went to other houses prior to theirs and when he got there he gained entry to the house by giving the pretense of an environmental survey thing."

"Can I interject?" Mudgett said.

"Yeah," Ranger said.

"This environmental study that you speak about, was this done in preparation for a, some sort of course, or school course, or anything like that?"

"Yeah," Ranger said. "That's just what he used, cause he figured he looked like a college kid and around the town of Hanover, or whatever, people wouldn't suspect that as being odd. That it would be a story that he could use to get in."

"Had he been to any other residences, did he tell you?"

"He had been to, he had tried to gain entry into two different residences, one in Rochester, Vermont, and one, the Zantops' neighbors was the other one," Ranger answered. Without knowing it, Ranger was referring to the homes of Franklin Sanders in Rochester and Bob and Audrey McCollum in Etna. Sanders had told Robert and Jim he was too busy tarring his pool to do a survey, and the McCollums were skiing with their daughter and son-in-law when the killers had come knocking.

"OK. Did he want to go into a home that was, someone was home at?" Mudgett asked.

"Yes," Ranger said.

"And why was that?"

"Because," Ranger answered, "he wanted to kill somebody while he was there."

"OK," Mudgett said. "Any other reason why he wanted to go into a house?"

"He wanted a robbery, he wanted to get money or whatever he could get, but he said that after they had killed the Zantops that he kind of panicked and that he didn't search through the house or anything like that."

Ranger then gave an account of what happened inside the Zantop house on January 27, providing details that hadn't been made public. Ranger's information fit the crime scene with such precision it was impossible to imagine it had come from anyone other than one of the killers.

"OK," Mudgett said afterward. "Let me ask you this . . . and you've been very, very cooperative, and I appreciate that. Did he indicate to you whether they had been saving money or trying to get money for any particular reason, or anything like that?"

"He didn't say anything as to why they were trying to get money or anything like that. He said that, ah, he had wished that he had more money to take off with when they took off, but he didn't tell me the reason," Ranger said. "Because I asked him, I says, ah, 'So, what was this, just another random act of violence in America?' or something like that. And he goes, 'Basically.'"

"Did he ever indicate to you that he had ever met the Zantops before?" Mudgett asked.

"He said he never laid eyes on them before, that he knew of, you know."

"Did he ever tell you as to why he was in that particular area? He and James Parker?"

"He figured that the Dartmouth College area would be well-to-do folks and that he wouldn't have any trouble gaining entry into a house," Ranger said.

"OK. And again, it was because he was going to do this environmental study and that's . . . "

"That," Ranger interrupted, "was his cover story to get into the house."

After providing more background information, Ranger described how Robert explained his relationship with Jim.

"I asked him, I says, 'Is this your idea or was this his?' And he says, 'Nah, it was kind of a mutual decision, but I kind of said the way things went and kind of run the show.'"

Mudgett went back over some details, but by then he had everything he needed—a bounty of information that would focus the investigation, potentially squeeze a confession from one or both killers, or be used to devastating effect at their trials. One hundred fifty-three days after Half and Susanne Zantop were killed, police and prosecutors for the first time knew that they were chosen for death randomly, how their killers tricked their way into the house on Trescott Road, and how the murders took place. On the surface, they also had a motive—robbery—but the way it added up, that was window dressing. The real motive seemed to be murder for its own sake. As Ranger put it, "He wanted to kill somebody while he was there."

Yet, as much as Ranger added to detectives' understanding of the crime, he couldn't explain why Robert was so intent on committing a random murder in the guise of a robbery, or how he had convinced Jim that this was the best way to fulfill their dreams of escaping Chelsea forever. Those answers would have to wait.

After sharing all he knew about the murders, Ranger added a bonus: Robert was plotting to escape from the Grafton County Jail.

Ranger described a plot Robert hatched in which someone would leave a handgun buried just outside the recreation yard fence. He would snake his arm through, dig it out, threaten, kill, or overpower a corrections officer, and force his way to freedom. That plan was flawed by the fact that Robert didn't know anyone who was willing to be a gun-burying accomplice. Anyone but Jim, that is, and he was in no position to help at the moment. As an alternative, Robert thought he would somehow make a wrench to loosen the bolts attaching the fence to its posts, then pull the fence back and run for the tree line in the meadow below. Either of those plans would explain why Robert had suddenly resumed spending his recreation hours outside—he was searching for weak spots in recreation yard security.

"Or, he's going to try to do it from court," Ranger told Mudgett. "I know one time when he went to court he took a piece of paper and stuck it in the waistband of his pants, and he was thinking that he was going to pick his way out of the handcuffs." But Ranger scoffed at that idea, saying he doubted Robert could pull it off.

Some of Robert's extravagantly imagined plans seemed cut from the pages of a comic book and bordered on laugh-out-loud funny. That is, if he wasn't so serious about carrying them out. "I gotta get out of here," he told Ranger, "because when they're transporting Jim to court I want to be able to get him somewhere along the route. . . . I'll kill the two officers that are transporting him."

Then he and Jim could disappear into Canada and live as outlaws, robbing banks and changing their appearances to avoid detection. Robert said his first change would be a nose job.

When Glenn Libby got wind of the breakout fantasies, Robert's life at the Grafton County Jail became even grimmer. He wore shackles whenever he was taken outside the Max Unit for recreation or other activities. His incoming and outgoing mail was logged and screened. His visiting hours were moved into a more secure part of the jail. No longer could he sit in the same room with his visitors; now they spoke through a small window of unbreakable glass. Libby also took general precautions, including reinforcing the recreation yard fence and adding more razor wire at the top.

Security around Robert got even tighter after his mother asked one of the officers how far it was from the jail to the Connecticut River. Libby didn't know if it was idle conversation, and he never had any evidence that Diane Tulloch knew of Robert's escape plans. But Libby knew that Diane rarely spoke with the officers, and for her to suddenly ask that question "raised our antennae all the more." After that, two officers were assigned to all Robert's family visits.

Just before the interview with Ranger ended, Mudgett placed on the record a series of statements to clarify the terms under which Ranger had provided the information. The sergeant knew that lawyers for Robert and Jim might say Ranger had made up the entire story under pressure from authorities or in exchange for a deal to reduce or drop the charges against him. Mudgett said the only thing he would do for Ranger was tell the attorney general's office about his cooperation.

"So when you leave here, you understand that I . . . made no promises to you, no offers of reward, nor was I ever trying to employ you into acting as an agent on behalf of the police," Mudgett said.

"Right."

"You understand that? . . . So by speaking here today, are you speaking on your own free will?"

"Yeah."

"You're not expecting any rewards out of this?"

"Nothing," Ranger said.

"You're doing it for what specific reason?" Mudgett asked.

"I don't think it's right what he did," Ranger answered. "I . . . I . . . I think that what he did was pretty sick, actually. . . . If it was somebody in my family [he killed], I would probably be the one facing the murder trial, you know?"

19

Something Wicked This Way Comes

Nearly six months would pass before the public was told the Zantops were marked for death arbitrarily. But from the moment Ranger became a confidential informant, prosecutors stopped looking for more complicated motives and ended their search for links among the two boys from Chelsea and the two professors from Etna. After all the investigative trails and endless speculation about revenge, rock climbing, sex, scandal, and academic politics, by the summer of 2001 prosecutors were certain the Zantops were murdered for the banal reason that Robert and Jim had come to 115 Trescott Road planning to rob and kill whomever they found there.

For Attorney General Phil McLaughlin and his assistants, Kelly Ayotte and Mike Delaney, the case was falling neatly into place. Physical evidence tying Robert and Jim to the murders was overwhelming—the bloody commando knives found hidden in Robert's bedroom would surely impress a jury, as would Jim's fingerprints, the Zantops' blood on the floor mat of Jim's mother's Subaru, the bloody footprint that matched Robert's Vasque boot, and so on. Robert and Jim's porous alibi about selling the knives at the Army-Navy store wouldn't be much help to the defense. And Ranger's account of Robert's jailhouse musings would add immeasurably to the prosecution's case by reducing or removing questions about provocation.

The case for first-degree murder wasn't a slam dunk—the defendants were teenagers with no known history of violence, represented by highly capable lawyers. Also, as an inmate facing fraud charges, Ranger wasn't an ideal witness, though his cooperation wasn't tainted by any special consideration. He had received nothing—no dropped charges or reduced prison time—for telling his story. Still, investigators and the prosecution team felt confident they had solved the case and assembled all the tools needed to win convictions and long—possibly lifelong—prison terms for Robert and Jim. The only uncertainty that remained for authorities was whether one of the two best friends might turn on the other and offer a firsthand account of the murder, as well as its planning and aftermath, in exchange for a lesser sentence.

However, there was another court entirely separate from the one in which prosecutors were operating—the court of public curiosity. Satisfying the legal standard of guilt or innocence wouldn't fully explain what Robert Tulloch and Jim Parker had done to Half and Susanne Zantop, or why they had done it. Missing was a deeper explanation of what still seemed a senseless butchery.

When reporters invaded Chelsea in February 2001, they heard then retold stories of two bright, clean-cut, well-liked boys from stable homes, one a student council president and talented debater, the other a musically gifted, dramatically inclined class clown. They heard that both shunned alcohol and drugs, had a taste for health food, and devoted themselves to Frisbee playing and rock climbing. By all outward appearances, Robert and Jim seemed like normal, high-spirited teenagers. Neither had a history of mental illness, a criminal record, or even a reputation for delinquency. To some, they were mischievous and a bit arrogant, with a craving for attention and a tendency toward heavy-footed driving. But that hardly qualified them for the stereotype of young killers.

Nothing the prosecution or police had uncovered could explain why these two particular boys would purchase commando knives in a long-planned plot to steal money, kill strangers, and disappear into lives of crime. Investigators were happy to end the inquiry into why Robert and Jim killed Half and Susanne with a straightforward, jury-friendly answer—money. But that wouldn't be enough to make sense of the murders in two New England communities—one missing two elders, one missing two children, and both missing their sense of sheltered innocence. It also wouldn't satisfy a wider world at once repulsed and fascinated by the crime. Even after the official investigation was complete, the answers to the deeper questions surrounding the Zantops' deaths lay hidden in Chelsea.

In early 2000, a year before the killings, other members of The Crew were focusing on school, sports, hobbies, jobs, girlfriends, and plans for college. Robert and Jim's parents and siblings were involved in their own lives of work and school, leaving them little time or inclination to worry about the intensifying friendship. Christiana Usenza had transferred to a high school in Montpelier, and she and Robert rarely saw each other. By choice and by default, Robert and Jim were left largely to their own devices, alone except for each other. With only occasional work with Jim's father, little direction from their parents, and paltry school demands because they were far ahead on graduation credits, Robert and Jim had more freedom than ever and huge swaths of free time on their hands.

Then, by early spring, came Robert's near-impeachment and the debacle at the state debate tournament—two dizzying, self-imposed falls for which he blamed others. Both left him angry and confused— he hadn't done anything wrong, he was certain, so how dare they do this to him? In the bitter wake of those public humiliations, Robert filled his free time by allowing his fertile, febrile imagination to focus on fleeing Chelsea forever, Jim by his side, both of them unfettered by rules of society.

"So now, after defying school for the last five years," he wrote in a school paper at the time, "having regular conflicts with the teachers, enjoying myself by doing exactly what I want, I am ready to depart. School is not for me, and now I can leave. I do not think I was old enough or knowledgeable enough to leave before, but now that I know what I want, I can begin the rest of my life."

He didn't want to go alone—"I have always and will probably always have a real live audience," he wrote in the same paper—and so he began methodically drawing Jim into his web. In their private moments together, in the car, rock climbing, communicating over the Internet, Robert spun fantasies of life on the road that he knew would appeal to the actor in Jim. Robert stoked his immature friend's rebellious streak and preyed on Jim's childish self-image as a bold adventurer-in-waiting. "Ever since we started becoming best friends," Jim would say, "we were doing all this adventurous stuff and, you know, considered ourselves better than everybody else."

They began talking about destinations, focusing first on distant parts of the United States, then looking across one ocean to Italy or France, or another to New Zealand. They looked a little more and settled on Australia, for no better reasons than it was far away, seemed exotic, had a variety of climates, and used English as its primary language.

Under Robert's leadership, they began trying to turn that fantasy into reality by crudely calculating how much it might cost to live down under. Earlier they had blown off a school project to research foreign cultures, but they threw themselves into their secret version of the same assignment, scouring the Internet and the Chelsea Public School library for information. Soon they developed a budget for their travels, estimating their cost of food at between $8 and $18 a day. They figured that would eventually drop to zero, because they would learn how to live off the land or buy what they needed with the spoils of their crimes.

To get started, they decided, they needed an initial stake of about

$10,000, for airfare and enough money to last a year. Robert couldn't be bothered raising that much legally—that would take patience, responsibility, courtesy, hard work, preparation, and genuine planning, none of which he had much use or aptitude for. He became fixated on plotting criminal ways to raise the money.

Most of the initial ideas were Robert's, and then together he and Jim would polish off the rough edges. At times Jim would tire of the scheming and urge that they give it a rest—he wanted to go outside, see movies, play ball tag, and hang around the way they used to—but Robert wouldn't hear of it. He was determined to set in motion their two-man traveling crime team, modern pirates on land and sea.

To other friends, his parents, and his teachers, Robert would casually mention his global travel plans and his disdain for college. He told Christiana Usenza that higher education was a waste of time, which ruined good minds and homogenized society. But privately, with only Jim as audience, assistant, and foil, Robert was allowing his resentments to simmer and his imagination to run free.

At first, Robert and Jim let their minds wander over all manner of potential schemes and scams. They talked about holding up a bank or stealing an ATM machine, and several times walked into banks to scope things out, once driving around back to see what they'd find. But robbing a bank was complicated, and that idea didn't last long.

Some of their scheming in the spring of 2000 took shape during drives to a quarry in Barre, some twenty miles north of Chelsea. During quarry visits a year earlier, Robert had fantasized with Jim about stealing cars and joyriding, but nothing had come of it. Jim didn't like that idea at first, but the more Robert talked about it the better it sounded. Robert used adolescent logic to convince Jim there was no risk, because they would abandon the cars afterward, and then no one would bother looking for them, because the cars would end up returned to their owners. That made sense to Jim and appealed to his sense of fun: "I like driving cars around really fast, and shit like that," he'd say.

An opportunity presented itself on one of their visits to the Barre quarry. A truck was sitting there, unattended, its key in the ignition. So they took turns driving it around. They stole a gas can from the pickup's bed, then headed home. Another day, they drove back to the quarry in a beat-up Mazda pickup that belonged to Robert's family. They figured they'd find the quarry truck and go joyriding again, but with a modified *Thelma and Louise* twist. "We were thinking about driving it off a ledge," Jim said. "You know, jumping out first."

They never got the chance—soon after they began joyriding in the quarry truck, a worker arrived at the rock pit. He placed himself between the truck and the exit, so there was no way out. Robert made a quick decision. His family's Mazda was also in the quarry, so he couldn't avoid capture. But Jim could. Robert told Jim to jump out of the quarry truck before the worker realized there were two of them— Robert would take the heat for them both. Jim obeyed Robert's command, sneaking out of the truck without being seen. He ducked behind some rocks and made his way out of the quarry, then hid alongside a nearby road to wait for Robert.

Jim escaped, but things looked bad for Robert. When the quarry worker saw the stolen gas can in the Mazda, he had Robert red-handed. He also accused Robert of stealing some expensive drill bits that were missing previously. Robert hadn't stolen them, but with the gas can sitting there in plain view, he was in no position to argue his innocence. The quarry worker called the Barre police, and when Chief Michael Stevens questioned Robert, he was struck by the teen's amoral, argumentative insistence that he had done nothing wrong. "Robert stated the pit was not locked, nor [were there] any signs to say he wasn't supposed to be there," Stevens wrote in his report. "Robert Tulloch stated that he . . . felt there was nothing wrong with driving the truck, since the keys were in the truck and he never left the pit area. I informed Robert that it was not his property to use."

Afterward, Robert told Jim that the penalty for their misadventure had been steep—community service and a $1,200 fine. Jim knew that was enough to put a huge dent in the Tulloch family's precarious finances. He couldn't help but feel indebted for the cost he thought Robert had borne for them both.

In fact, Robert had lied to his best friend. There was no community service, no fine—Chief Stevens simply issued a verbal notice of trespass and seized the gas can. At Stevens's insistence, Diane and Michael Tulloch accompanied Robert to the station and gave a statement about what little they knew. Diane later said they expected the authorities to order Robert to attend a juvenile corrections program known as a diversion. "They said they would call back and they never called us back," Diane said. She called to check on the status of the case and was told to keep waiting, but still no one called. "I thought it would have been a good lesson to go through diversion. Maybe, maybe somebody should have called us back on that."

Implied in Diane's wish for official action were two unmistakable points about the Tulloch style of parenting. First, Diane was looking to pass the buck, blaming Barre authorities for failing to take action against her son. Second, it was an acknowledgment that Robert would have ignored any punishment she and Mike tried to hand down. As Jim put it, Robert "didn't listen to them."

Joyriding was fun, but it wouldn't get them out of Chelsea. Unknown to the friends who would later describe them to reporters as law-abiding kids, by the late spring of 2000 Robert and Jim had become single-minded about remaking themselves as criminals.

"We started thinking about illegal activities and we couldn't really share that with other people, because we didn't want to have, like, too many people in our circle of crime," Jim would say. "Eventually we decided to do illegal stuff and so we always felt like we should be working on that and not fooling around and playing and stuff. So we didn't do a lot with our other friends." On two occasions when Robert and Jim did reunite with The Crew in the spring of 2000, they had their breaking-and-eating episodes at the homes of their friends Casey Purcell and Ivy and Tess Mix.

Around that same time, Jim began expressing his solidarity with Robert in his schoolwork. In an autobiographical essay, Jim mentioned how he partnered with Robert in sledding, building forts, playing on the river, "and many, many other activities I can not begin to talk about." The essay continued in the third person: "They were both extreme people. Both fed off each other. Robert was very knowledge-able but lacked a distinct view of everything, his life seemed dull. Jim's intellect greatly increased and continues to. Robert has found himself and is very pleased. Robert is a wonderful surprise to the project. And I am pleased to announce that Robert Tolluch [sic] will be added to the assignment. The two will complete the mission together." He didn't elaborate for the teacher on the nature of that mission.

In a similar school assignment, Robert described himself with his usual self-impressed grandeur as an "incredibly smart, witty, and scheming individual." He credited some of his development to DeRoss Kellogg, his sixth grade teacher. "After DeRoss's class, I would com-pletely ignore the need to perform well in school, and dedicate my life to making myself happy." It was as close to a guiding philosophy as he would ever express, having already decided that society and school had no answers for someone of his great intellect, that self-centered manipulativeness was a trait to be admired, and that God was "a pompous, self-centered jerk."

One of their early get-out-of-Chelsea schemes involved stealing mail from rural mailboxes in the hope they'd find credit card numbers. Fifteen or so attempts, mostly around Vershire, yielded little. Sometimes they'd take a quick look at the letters and stuff them back into their boxes. Other times they'd grab the mail from two or three houses, toss their bounty in the back seat of Jim's Audi, and drive to Robert's house to see what they had reeled in. Once they got a credit card number, but that didn't prove useful. Eventually they burned all the mail they had stolen in the wood stove in Robert's house.

In a variation on their mail-theft scheme, Robert and Jim tried to establish a false address at the abandoned home on Vershire Riding School Road they had once considered a potential clubhouse or ball-tag venue. They cut the grass and put up a new mailbox. Then, as a test, they mailed a box filled with old T-shirts to the house. But it was returned as undeliverable—postal carriers were all locals, and everyone in the area knew the falling-down farmhouse had long been abandoned. It would have been big news around town if someone had bought it. When the T-shirts failed to arrive, Robert and Jim crossed that plan off their list.

Around the same time, they tried a few petty crimes that were more about mischief than money, self-styled tests of their criminal wills. They stole poles from a permanent tent, took a small boat down the First Branch of the White River and left it on the river bank, went joyriding in bulldozers they found at work sites in Tunbridge and South Royalton, and stole grappling hooks and pulleys from a house that had been owned by Kip Battey's father, Ned.

A new money-raising scheme came to life one night in late May 2000, just days after they had partnered to win the raft race in the town's spring festival. Robert and Jim were driving to the movies when they saw a four-wheel-drive, all-terrain vehicle on a trailer next to a home in Barre. A few days after Jim's sixteenth birthday, around two in the morning, they drove Robert's Mazda within a mile of the house and made their way through the dark. They unhinged the rear of the trailer, put the red Honda Foreman ATV into neutral and rolled it off the trailer and through an unplowed cornfield toward the Mazda. Robert had forgotten to bring ramps to make the job easier—he always seemed to forget or overlook at least one key element of the plan—so they wrestled the little vehicle through the field, off a ledge, and into the rear of Robert's pickup.

Once back in Chelsea, they scraped off the serial numbers and touched up the paint to hide their work, then stashed the ATV under a tarp in the woods near Jim's house. They removed the ignition and brought it to a dealer in Essex and told him they'd lost the key. When the dealer made them a new one, they replaced the ignition, shined the ATV, and placed classified ads on eBay and other Internet auction sites. One caught the eye of a man from Massachusetts who was willing to pay up to $3,500—one-third of Robert and Jim's travel budget.

Excited by the prospect, they arranged to meet him in a church parking lot. Robert handled the negotiations while Jim stayed in Robert's pickup, slouching out of sight. The would-be buyer test-drove the knobby-tired vehicle and seemed ready to deal. Then he asked Robert about the title and registration. When Robert said he didn't have them, the man grew angry. He couldn't hand over that much money without a title to prove ownership. How could he know it wasn't stolen? The man and his money went back to Massachusetts.

They brought the ATV back to Jim's house, but couldn't figure out what to do next. They drove it around the woods a few times and talked about chopping it into parts and selling them piecemeal, but eventually abandoned that idea as too risky and unworkable. The ATV sat untended in the woods until December 2000, when a call came in to the Orange County Sheriff's Office about a "suspicious vehicle" on West Hill in Chelsea. The owner got his ATV back, and no arrests were made.

A few weeks after they stole the ATV, Jim's thirst for speed led to the wreck of Robert's little Mazda. Again, Robert took the blame, just as he had done when they were trespassing at the quarry. Robert told his parents that he was at the wheel when the car went too fast around a curb. Diane Tulloch strongly suspected that Jim had been driving and that Robert was lying to protect him. But Robert stuck with his lie and Diane and Mike didn't challenge him on it. Robert's deception paid off: Jim avoided penalties or restitution, and Robert's only punishment was being a teenager in a rural town without wheels of his own. Jim's silver Audi would have to serve them both.

A side from the ever-present goal of raising money, Robert and Jim's early criminal efforts shared one quality that was particularly important to Jim: no physical contact. Jim wasn't burdened by moral or religious teachings that discouraged him from breaking the Golden Rule. He just didn't want to get hurt or get caught: "If we were trying to jump them and they, like, turned around and knocked us out, or um . . . they recognized us, they would go to the police and, you know, give our descriptions and they would find us," he'd say.

But as months passed and one plan failed after another, Robert grew impatient. He began using a twisted logic to persuade his malleable friend that they needed to take the next step. He had already spent months talking to Jim about how they were better and smarter than other people, and how they couldn't be expected to conform to rules and expectations that burdened their inferiors. That groundwork laid, on June 24, 2000, Robert decided it was time to lead Jim down the path to murder.

That morning, Robert, Jim, Christiana Usenza, and some other friends headed northwest from Chelsea to the Sugarbush ski area in Warren, Vermont. Barren of snow, the resort's Mount Ellen was transformed into the raucous Tenth Annual Ben & Jerry's One World–One Heart Festival, a mini-Woodstock where everything was toned down from the original except the tie-dyed shirts. The hippie ice cream impresarios, arguably Vermont's two most famous residents, organized the festival as an opportunity to "celebrate, learn more, listen to great music, get involved, and . . . try some new Ben & Jerry's flavors."

But scoops of coffee almond fudge and bands like Hootie and the Blowfish couldn't hold Robert and Jim's interest, so they left their companions midway through the festival. Jim drove aimlessly around back roads while Robert rode shotgun and riffed on what they should do next. An idea took shape: "Let's break into a house and, you know, steal something." They killed some time casing empty condos—both knew that wealthy flatlanders only used them in winter—but they didn't break in.

As they were driving around, they noticed an elderly couple along the side of the road. Robert turned to Jim with a suggestion: We should park the car, get out, and jump them. We could use rocks to bash their heads, and then we'd take their money and run. It was the first time Robert had spoken of murder for money. Previously he had played with the idea of carjacking, but in those scenarios Robert described leaving the victims alive on the side of the road. Now he was going in for the kill.

Jim briefly considered Robert's suggestion, but then flatly rejected it. But not because it was wrong. Rather, Jim thought it was a classic example of Robert failing to think ahead. That's a terrible idea, Jim told Robert. "People will just catch up with us down the road, and you know, there's a lot of people that knew we were driving back" from the Ben & Jerry's festival. If Robert was wondering how Jim would react to the idea of murder, he had his answer. Jim was ready, as long as the crime was better planned.

Jim kept driving, heading toward home, but Robert wasn't quite finished. They drifted around awhile and returned to their earlier talk of breaking into houses. As they wandered around, they came across Bethel Mountain Road in Rochester and noticed all the fine, secluded homes there. They found one isolated enough to catch their interest, then went around back, broke through a storm door, then knocked in a panel on the security door to unlock it from the inside. They scoured the place but the only thing worth taking was a gray Rubbermaid toolbox, so they grabbed that and put it in the Audi. They drove to another house not far away, where they pried open a window. Jim climbed in and let Robert through the door, but nothing inside caught their interest, so they left.

From that moment on, Robert reinterpreted the events of that day—stressing how easy it would have been to rob and kill the elderly couple, versus how fruitless it had been to break into empty homes—into a case for robbery-murder. They could get whatever cash their targets had, as well as ATM card numbers that would allow them to get even more, and then kill to protect themselves from witnesses. He also told Jim it would be important for them to establish themselves as killers before they headed out on the road, Jim said, "because we were gonna be sort of 'badasses,' you know, when we left." During their endless conversations, Robert had spoken of admiring Hitler for his intelligence, cunning, and mastery of tactics, particularly his ability to manipulate people, while glossing over the morality of murder. Now, in his own small, self-absorbed, narcissistic way, Robert was manipulating Jim.

Jim was skeptical about the "badasses" part of the plan, though he did consider it a valid point at the time. Mostly, he focused on the fantasy aspect, "getting the money and going to a different country, you know. Kind of having fun."

"We could steal things from people and it turned into, you know, killing people," Jim would say. "And as long as we were able to kill people and we . . . got good at stealing things, stealing cars, you know, we could hijack people's boats and we wouldn't really have to, you know, be digging for money everywhere and we could just go wherever we want and then, you know, become these really cool people. And one of our main goals was to find some way to live forever, like just check out all the myths in Egypt or something, we weren't really sure. . . . We wanted to just, like, go to an island with spears and, you know, live there and we would be able to, you know, learn how to hunt really well."

Once Robert had Jim hooked, all that remained was a plot to carry it out.

The first idea was jumping someone on the street. They tried to think of a place where they could find a potential victim alone, out of view of anyone else, so no one could come running to aid the target. That concern led them to settle on a crucial element of their plan: What better place to find people alone than at their homes? All they needed to do was find a secluded house, then figure out a way to ambush the owners, take their money, and kill them.

Three and a half weeks later, in July 2000, Robert and Jim drove the Audi to the abandoned house on Vershire Riding School Road they had used for their failed mail-fraud scheme. Using two of John Parker's shovels, they dug a grave for the bodies they expected to dispose of later that night. They suited up in the commando clothes they had bought from Army-Navy stores and grabbed a backpack Jim had borrowed from his mother and filled with duct tape and rope. They slid old hunting knives into their black military boots and hiked through the woods to Goose Green Road.

They had driven by Andrew and Diane Patti's cedar-shingled house countless times—it was just a few miles from Chelsea. They had cased the house on earlier visits, once breaking a window in a shed out back to see what was inside. This time they had come to do more than look. Robert would use a car-broke-down-can-I-use-your-phone plan, and once inside, they'd tie up whomever they found there, demand their credit and ATM cards, and then kill them. They'd wrap the bodies in plastic bags and then haul them up the road to the grave they had dug.

Shortly after ten that night, Robert used a wire cutter to snip the phone lines to the house, then Jim pulled a knit ski mask over his face. He crouched in the bushes while Robert went to the door. But the plan went awry when Andrew Patti didn't buy Robert's story and flashed his gun. The boys scurried home, defeated, but only for the moment.

In the warm summer weeks that followed, Robert resumed plotting while Jim wallowed in discouragement and fear. He was anxious, troubled that the man in the house had seen Robert's face, and worried that he might have been seen, too.

While they regrouped, they threw themselves into their deepening passion for rock climbing—testing themselves against harder routes, encouraging and trusting one another—and kept busy with routine events and family celebrations. For Jim, there was an eightieth birthday party for his maternal grandmother, Hannah Essery, at her home in San Diego. "They put on a play for me and he acted in it," Essery said later. "It was *Cinderella*. He was the prince. He was a marvelous prince and I can't believe that prince would do anything wrong." A few days later, Robert attended the wedding of his sister Becky and Charles Johnson, one of Jack and Annette Johnsons' boys, at the home of the groom.

But beneath the happy surface of birthday parties and weddings, Robert kept pressing for their big score. First, he supplemented their criminal toolkit. He lied to his mother about needing rock-climbing shoes and used her credit card to order two Stun Master stun guns on the Internet. Jim liked the idea of stun guns, because it would lower the risk that their victims might fight back. Second, Robert abandoned the broken-down-car ruse and adopted a stun-gun-surprise plan.

Diane Tulloch's discovery and confiscation of the stun guns was a setback, but her see-no-evil acceptance of Robert's quick lie—that he and Jim had bought them for the harmless fun of popping street signs off poles—spared them from punishment or discovery. Without Diane Tulloch's knowledge or credit card, they bought two more stun guns.

Although they went high-tech with their weaponry and revised their plan in the weeks after being rebuffed at the Pattis' house, months went by with little forward motion on their criminal enterprise. Jim remained skittish after the Patti debacle. Also, Jim was broadening his horizons and spending less time in Chelsea.

In September 2000, at the start of his junior year, Jim transferred to Spaulding High School, twenty miles north in Barre. He was well ahead on graduation credits in Chelsea, so he could afford a change of scenery, and his parents thought Spaulding would provide more opportunities for his musical talents. Jim had maxed out on Chelsea's music program, and Spaulding had a strong reputation for musical offerings. Maybe he'd also make some new friends there. Jim wanted to try Spaulding for the most basic teenage reason of all: He thought he'd meet new girls. And it worked, if only briefly.

During his second week at Spaulding, he met a pretty girl named Sara Aja in music class—she played trombone and sang vocals in the jazz band. Jim developed a crush on her, and his affection was returned. Sara thought he was sweet and upbeat, funny and thoughtful, with a positive aura and a good heart. She considered him the kind of boy who would break up fights rather than start them, a well-raised young man who was polite and well-mannered. A self-described nerd, Sara liked the gentleness she saw in Jim.

Their friendship grew during the first two months of school. They went for a walk in the woods because he loved the outdoors and wanted to share it with her. They spent time together at a friend's house. Soon Jim began opening up to her. He complained that his parents treated him like a child. He thought he could never please them. Jim told her that he dreamed of running away to Colorado to rock climb, and how he wanted to go out alone to the middle of nowhere to rough it.

Jim confided in Sara that his best friend, Robert, had forced him to jump off a cliff into water when he didn't want to, and that he and Robert got their kicks from driving cars backwards into trees. Jim told Sara that he and Robert had robbed a house "a few years ago." He apparently thought that telling her the break-in occurred just a few months earlier, after the Ben & Jerry's festival, might scare her off. He also told her he regretted having done it.

Over time, Sara got the sense that Jim loved and respected Robert but was captive to him. That didn't surprise her. It seemed consistent with something she had noticed about Jim. Sara thought Jim was hungry for attention and would cling to anyone who showed him some. Robert lavished attention on Jim, and Sara thought Jim would do anything for Robert in return.

Jim wanted Sara to be his girlfriend, but she had recently broken up with another boy and didn't want to get involved so soon. By November it was clear to Jim that Sara only wanted to be friends, and they drifted apart.

If Jim thought he would be recognized for his musical genius at Spaulding, he was in for another disappointment. The music teachers considered him a modest talent who could have been quite good if he wasn't so lazy. He could play bass guitar by ear, but he wasn't as motivated as two other bass players at Spaulding that year. His other teachers were similarly unimpressed.

Jim's English teacher, Martha Morris, called him an imaginative young man with a flair for acting, but someone who seemed turned off to school. He wrote his term paper on *The Hitchhiker's Guide to the Galaxy,* Douglas Adams's comic work of science fiction. Jim liked it so much he checked out a sequel from the school library, *Life, the Universe, and Everything.* Another book he checked out was *On the Road,* Jack Kerouac's classic Beat novel of two disillusioned friends who travel cross-country in search of freedom and meaning, committing petty crimes along the way.

Jim's friends and teachers at Spaulding noticed a sudden change that came over him one day in November when Robert tagged along to school. It was "Shadow Day," when Spaulding students were allowed to bring friends from other schools to their classes. Sara Aja didn't recognize the sweet and funny Jim she knew and liked. He acted different around Robert, trying to emulate his arrogant, witty friend.

Another of Jim's friends at Spaulding, senior Michael Wheeler, also noticed that, normally talkative, Jim grew quiet and subservient around Robert. Wheeler sensed that Robert "ran the show" and looked down on Spaulding and its students. Wheeler liked Jim but considered Robert a jerk.

Throughout the semester, Jim learned it was harder to succeed outside the protective cocoon of Chelsea. The As and Bs he was used to receiving became Bs and Cs at Spaulding. Despite his belief that he possessed a superior intellect, those grades were consistent with the mediocre 1,000 Jim scored on the SAT.

As the months wore on, Jim grew less enamored of Spaulding and began making plans to return to school in Chelsea. Later, Jim would echo Robert's attitude toward the Barre school, even denying the friendships he'd made there. "I didn't really like . . . most of the people," Jim said. "I thought everybody was stupid and I was getting real annoyed with that. I didn't really like the teachers, and Chelsea is a lot nicer."

While Jim was at Spaulding, Robert spent the autumn of 2000 doing next to nothing. Only a few credits shy of graduation, he refused to go to school and showed no inclination toward getting a job. His mother asked him about it, but he ignored her and spent his days reading and doing occasional chores at home.

During the first weeks of the fall, when the tree-studded hills around Chelsea were turning gold, red, and orange, Robert drew closer to Christiana Usenza, talking with her nightly on the phone. They talked about his dreams of spending his days rock climbing and living untouched by society's rules, and then, conversely, of his fantasy of becoming president. Yet as much as they talked, she never felt he completely opened up to her. Something was missing in her quasi-boyfriend, though she could never quite put her finger on it.

As winter approached, Christiana enjoyed their talks less and less. She tried to focus on the Robert she considered wise and compassionate, charming and charismatic, but that Robert was little in evidence. He loved to argue and believed he could outsmart anyone, she thought, and she grew tired of the pleasure he took in testing his skills on her. Once, out of nowhere, Robert told her he was psychotic. Christiana disagreed and told him so. But she noticed that he seemed to like being in a bad mood, and those moods occurred with increasing frequency. Privately, she concluded that he had a superiority complex and maybe a touch of depression. Other times, she thought he was troubled, disturbed even, and that he needed help.

Most of their relationship was over the phone—they saw each other about once every two weeks, and Robert wouldn't hang around when she was with other friends. With their limited contact and increasingly contentious phone talks, Christiana thought about breaking off completely from Robert, but she never went through with it.

When Jim came home from Spaulding after school, he and Robert would immediately hook up. Frequently, Cora Brooks—Robert's neighbor and Jim's former substitute teacher—noticed them walking by her house, alone together, lost in conversation. Once she put them to work, hiring them to move some furniture. As often as possible they'd go rock climbing, usually at their regular club, Petra Cliffs in Burlington, but once, in early October, they climbed at the River Valley Club in Hanover.

On several of their trips out of Chelsea in the fall of 2000 they flirted with resuming their lives of crime. Armed with their stun guns, they spent several afternoons lying in the woods with binoculars, scouting out houses along Bethel Mountain Road and waiting for the owners to come home. "It was ideally supposed to be dark, and then we would run around, like, the back of the car or the side of the car and . . . we would like, either stun them or, like, knock them out with something and then we would tie them up and probably drag them into the house," Jim said. "We'd get their credit card and their ATM number and you know, tie them up and ask them for their information and then we would kill them." Their chosen method was strangulation because it would be a bloodless murder. Then they would bury or otherwise hide the bodies to make it appear their targets were missing persons rather than homicide victims.

One time they spent a half hour outside a house waiting for someone to come home, but the fall air chilled their bones. They began making excuses to each other about why it wouldn't be a good day to carry out their plans. Soon the two would-be "badasses" packed it in.

As it turned out, the only person who ever felt the stun guns' sting was Robert. The experiment began when he suggested that they test their weapons. Jim didn't want to be the guinea pig, so Robert volunteered. Jim gripped the six-inch tall, battery-powered device, flipped the "on" switch, and touched the two metal prongs at the top to Robert's stomach. He held it there long enough for tens of thousands of volts of electricity to course through Robert's body, scrambling his nervous system. Aficionados of nonlethal weapons talk about stun guns' "bite," and Robert gained an immediate appreciation of the term. The burst of energy made his muscles fire rapidly, but randomly, depleting the sugar in his blood and converting it to lactic acid. Robert became disoriented, lost his balance, and slumped to the ground. One selling point for stun guns is that they leave no permanent damage. Soon he was himself again, so he and Jim talked about the experience and assessed whether and for how long the Stun Masters would incapacitate their victims.

On a deeper level, Robert had engineered another exercise in bonding and personal debt. After the quarry incident and the Mazda misadventure, Robert had taken the hits personally and financially, or so he had claimed. By testing the stun guns on himself, he took the hit physically, and he must have known Jim wouldn't forget it.

Another time, Robert suggested they test their appetites for violence by taking a life. Robert argued that it would be good practice, so they wouldn't hesitate when the real time came. He had a candidate all picked out: his dog, Ruby. Jim had seen Robert hit Ruby "just because it was a stupid dog." He thought that was a terrible thing to do, though Jim hadn't protected Robert's dog from the beatings. But this was where Jim drew the line. Jim could accept the idea of needing to kill people to rid themselves of witnesses, but he saw no point to killing a dog. "The thing with killing for me is that I was doing it for the money," Jim said. "I thought, you know, maybe we do need to get used to this, but we're not going to practice on animals or anything like that." Robert recognized that carrying out his plan might seriously alienate Jim, so the dog lived. Again, Robert had tested his accomplice for weaknesses and gained more insight into what he could expect from Jim.

To the surprise of Chelsea debate coach John O'Brien, Robert and Jim appeared at an organizational meeting in the late fall of 2000. Although the boys were no longer in school together, O'Brien thought they seemed closer than ever. They had perfected their comedy routine by then, and were finishing each other's sentences. O'Brien thought their persistent bonding wasn't necessarily good for Robert, Jim, or anyone else. He concluded that they were more disruptive together than on their own.

During the introductory debate meeting, however, they threw themselves into the task. Kip Battey was there, too, and O'Brien listened as the three teens sized up possible recruits in the freshman and sophomore classes. "They were like, 'Nooo, not her, she's terrible. Not him, he's an asshole.' Or, 'He's a really cool guy.' They were very opinionated."

Seeing Robert made O'Brien realize that not only wasn't he attending classes, he had failed in his plan to travel the world. "Oh yeah," Robert told O'Brien. "I'm still trying to get it together." Later, when O'Brien bumped into Robert in town, the debate coach tried to press him on the specifics and even the inspiration for wanting to explore abroad. Robert mentioned *On the Road*, but O'Brien thought he seemed only vaguely familiar with the book or wasn't inspired by it. Rather than describe his own passion for travel, Robert preferred to knock his college-bound classmates.

O'Brien realized that beyond vague talk about Europe, beyond his bravado and brashness, Robert had no concrete plan. It disappointed him: "Chelsea has so few sort of bright, go-getter types, so that the ones who actually could go to college or do something, like Robert, you want to see them do it." One difference O'Brien noticed was in Robert's appearance. He often wore a black sweater and black pants that, in O'Brien's eyes, made him look "somewhat European or bohemian."

O'Brien knew that if Robert had bothered to plan ahead, he not only could have devised a trip, he probably could have gotten money to help pay for it. Anna Mulligan, Robert's teammate in debate, had used Chelsea's new Marilyn and James Haskett Senior Project Fund to help finance a monthlong trip to Ghana. The Hasketts, who had homes in Chelsea and Cambridge, Massachusetts, where James Haskett was an emeritus professor at Harvard, had established the fund with a $10,000 gift dedicated to helping the children who lived in their adopted Vermont community.

After Robert and Jim's cameo appearance at the debate meeting, O'Brien decided to challenge Robert to resume debating, hoping that Robert had outgrown the ugly behavior he displayed at the state debate tournament. At first Robert waved him off, repeating his line about his pending getaway to Europe. But O'Brien kept after him. A regional tournament was scheduled to be held in Chelsea after the holidays, on January 6, 2001, and O'Brien urged Robert to participate. Because of his experience, Robert could be a varsity debater. O'Brien would find someone from another school to team up with him. It would be good experience, the coach told Robert, something to keep him busy.

Intrigued, Robert made a counterproposal. He would participate, but on his terms: he wanted to be a judge. The idea of sitting in judgment, exercising power and control, had special appeal to him. Negotiations ensued and a compromise was reached. Robert would get to decide the fate of others, but only after debating in the first two rounds. O'Brien felt satisfied to have re-enlisted the boy in an organized activity.

With the new year came renewed criminal intent for Robert and Jim. It wasn't triggered by anything in particular—it was simply that enough time had passed since the scare at the Patti house, and Robert was growing restless and vengeful as his fellow seniors were looking ahead to college while he was still stuck in his parents' tumbledown house in Chelsea.

First, though, he and Jim decided to upgrade their weaponry yet again. The stun guns were OK, but they were nonlethal weapons, and Robert wanted something with killing power. One option was the knives they had brought to the Pattis, but those had ordinary blades. If they were going to be traveling killers for hire, they needed specialized weapons. Using money from Christmas, birthdays, and what was left from working for Jim's father, they went on the Internet, searched under "military knives," and settled on the SOG SEAL 2000. Jim thought they seemed the best knives on the market, the most durable, "the right kind of knives to have."

On New Year's Day 2001, Jim and Robert sat together at a computer and typed, "I would like to purchase 2 of your seal 2000 knives." With a click of the computer mouse, the message went to Fox Firearms. That same day, Half and Susanne Zantop stood outside their home and waved good-bye to their daughter Mariana and their two closest friends, Eric Manheimer and Diana Taylor, as they drove out of the driveway onto Trescott Road, heading back to New York after their New Year's celebration.

A day later, Robert and Jim sent their second e-mail to Fox, sealing the deal.

At first, Jim told himself the knives were necessary for their travels. "The main reason why we wanted to get these is because when we were in Australia we wanted to have knives for survival, cutting things, not people," Jim said. "We wanted to get some really good knives that . . . wouldn't break in the middle of the desert."

Eventually, though, he acknowledged the real reason, Robert's reason. The SEAL 2000s "would be better knives for killing people."

On Saturday, January 6, 2001, the long, narrow hallway of the high school wing at Chelsea Public School was crowded with debaters from high schools in Rutland, Brandon, and White River Junction, Vermont, along with a new team from across the river in New Hampshire. It was the first year of debate at Hanover High School, and coach Donna Strange, a debate veteran and wife of the Dartmouth debate coach, had happily accepted John O'Brien's invitation to the Chelsea tournament.

Teens filed past one another in the hall, ducking into and out of the various classrooms being used for the all-day competition. Most of the boys wore jackets and ties, and most of the girls wore dresses, respectful of debate decorum. Some kids recognized one another from other debates and renewed friendships, while others warily eyed each other, sizing up the competition.

Not having participated in any of the Chelsea team meetings, Robert was, as usual, thoroughly unprepared. Yet he was fortunate: He'd been paired with one of the league's smartest and best debaters, Jesse Fjeld of Otter Valley Union High School in Brandon. The topic they had to debate was: "Resolved: That the United States government should significantly increase protection of privacy in one or more of the following areas: employment, medical records, consumer information, search and seizure." It was a complex and challenging subject, exploring the privacy rights of citizens balanced against government interests.

After winning their first round, Robert and Jesse faced a team arguing that electronic surveillance of Internet traffic by government agencies had gotten out of hand and constituted a threat to personal privacy. In presenting their affirmative plan, Robert and Jesse's opponents claimed that the FBI was violating constitutional protections with the aid of an Internet tapping system known as "Carnivore," electronic snoopware capable of scanning millions of e-mails a second.

Regardless of the fact that Robert and Jim had just completed some Internet retail business they surely wanted to keep hidden, Robert and his debate partner were obliged to stake out the position that Carnivore was a necessary tool of law enforcement to prevent wrongdoing. Jesse Fjeld had hard research on Carnivore; not surprising, given that the FBI program was just the sort of topic any well-prepared debate team could expect to confront. Relying on specific points, Jesse attacked the plan. Robert hadn't lifted a research finger, so he had to wing it.

He was all swagger. What's the big deal, he asked his opponents when his turn came. Who cares if the government is looking at a few e-mails? If you're doing something wrong on the Internet, well, you *should* get caught, he said, betraying no trace of the conflict between his words and his behavior. Robert moved around, walking from the front of the classroom over to the other debaters. He moved like a hunter, jutting his chin toward his opponents' faces—So, tell me again, *why* you object to this Carni- Carni-what? Is that what you're saying? Carnivore?

The judge for the round was Hanover High coach Donna Strange. During more than a decade of involvement in debate, she'd never seen anything like this. He was argumentative, dismissive, completely lacking in evidence, rude, insulting, and flamboyant—everything a student debater shouldn't be. An image flashed through her mind: Robert reminded her of Eddie Haskell on steroids. Strange stopped Robert several times in mid-sentence to remind the Chelsea debater to maintain decorum. But Robert only grew more agitated, more provocative.

Strange judged the other team the winner by a large margin. But she wasn't finished. Strange was shaking her head with disappointment, and in a post-debate critique she mostly targeted Robert. It wasn't that Robert had been a bad debater—that would have been OK. Students learn from mistakes. But his complete lack of preparation, combined with his lousy attitude, was an insult. "There's a difference between being a bad debater and making a mockery of it," she told him. The Hanover coach knew she was being harsh, but she cared deeply about the integrity of debate and she could see that under the arrogance and anger, Robert possessed talent. "You're clearly a bright guy who could be very persuasive, with the power to have people follow you," she told him. Don't abuse that power, she warned him.

As Strange spoke, Robert struck a nonchalant pose. Most other debaters would have withered under such a public dressing-down, but Robert wouldn't blink. "He was just laughing about it," she said afterward. The only physical betrayal of his feelings came from his feet.

Robert was pacing. Brimming with pent-up anger, he couldn't wait to get out of there.

Meanwhile, John O'Brien already had his hands full—as coach of the Chelsea debaters, as a judge, and as organizer of the event. As the third round was about to begin, O'Brien noticed Robert duck into the school's science room. Heading in the same direction were two well-dressed girls from Hanover High School. The girls, both juniors, bright and blond, had already made a strong impression. They'd won their first two rounds handily, a start that didn't surprise their coach; Donna Strange had recognized their potential in practice during the fall.

As he watched Robert walk into the science room, O'Brien knew this was what he'd been waiting for—a chance to judge other debaters. Then O'Brien spotted Jim Parker in the hallway, also heading toward the science room, and that gave the coach pause. Jim hadn't been part of the deal. O'Brien calmed himself with the thought that he had already spelled out his expectations for Robert, and Robert had promised he would do a good job.

But now, unknown to O'Brien, Robert had something else in mind entirely. By the luck of the draw, he had a chance for revenge. With Strange's criticisms still ringing in his ears, Robert was judging the Hanover High School novice team.

The girls from Hanover were poised for victory. But when they began their presentation, Robert took over the debate, taunting them, flirting with them, interrupting them with sexual innuendos, all to the howling pleasure and snide reactions of his sidekick, Jim. At one point the Hanover girls protested Robert's bizarre conduct, but Robert and Jim made faces and laughed at them. Robert threatened to reduce their score.

John O'Brien had barely finished judging another debate when the two Hanover girls were at his side, flustered and near tears. O'Brien listened in shock and embarrassment to their story. As he comforted the girls, O'Brien thought of Robert and Jim: "The two of them were like two good dogs put together who became one bad dog. They were mocking the whole thing. They know I'll be upset, they know the people involved in the debate will be upset. But they don't seem to care."

O'Brien felt helpless. The recently revamped Chelsea Public School Student/Parent Handbook addressed harassment explicitly: "Current law makes sexual harassment or any assault a crime. Students have a right to attend Chelsea High School without fear of being bothered by others because of gender, race, ethnicity or disabling condition." The handbook stipulated that "harassment . . . will result in a referral to the principal." But O'Brien didn't know that both Robert and Jim had re-enrolled at the Chelsea school. And Robert's participation in the tournament was a one-time deal. "What am I going to do, kick Robert off the team he's not really on anyway?" O'Brien felt the boys were beyond his reach.

When the Hanover debaters found their coach, they wondered what they had done to deserve such abuse. A thought raced through Donna Strange's mind: payback. "He knew they were my students," the coach said. "It was his way of getting back, a slap in my face. He couldn't respond to me, so he took it out on the girls." Hanover's novice team had won the tournament, but they wouldn't celebrate. "They just talked about how they felt dirty," Strange said, "and how they didn't want to win, and how it didn't matter."

Before she left the Chelsea Public School, Strange searched for Robert, determined to have more words with him, even harsher than her earlier criticism. She looked in the hallway as the tournament wrapped up and she continued to hunt for him at the awards ceremony in the cafeteria. She scanned the room but saw no sign of Robert. He was gone.

The next day, January 7, eager to jumpstart their lives of crime, Robert and Jim sent another e-mail to Fox Firearms: "could you notify me when you receive the money order and when you send out the knives? thank you. Jim."

That same week, Jim again brought Robert to Spaulding for a final Shadow Day before Jim's return to school in Chelsea, and Robert made an even worse impression than on his earlier visit. Music teacher Arthur Zorn saw the pair in the school office and took an immediate dislike to

Robert. The young guest was disparaging the school and exhibiting what Zorn called a domineering personality. Zorn casually called him "Bob," and Robert was quick to correct him; later, other students would tell Zorn that Robert had said he would kill someone for calling him Bob. Zorn noticed that Robert and Jim seemed anxious to leave—as though they had pressing business elsewhere. In passing, Zorn over-heard Robert mention their destination: Hanover, New Hampshire.

On January 11, their impatience growing, Robert and Jim sent their final e-mail to Fox Firearms: "i would like to know if you have received the money order yet, and if you have sent the knives. i sent the money order last week thursday. thanks. Jim."

The next day, the two SOG SEAL 2000 knives arrived at Jim's house—they had Fox send them there because they didn't want Diane Tulloch to intercept another weapons shipment. Together they rushed to Jim's father's wood shop and tore open the white SOG boxes like excited kids at Christmas. From there they went to Robert's house and spent the night testing the knives, throwing them against doors and cutting whatever was at hand to see how sharp they were. Robert carved a design on his sheath—it looked like a stylized dagger blade—so they could tell them apart. When it was time to sleep, they stashed the knives under a pile of socks in Robert's dresser drawer.

Back at school in Chelsea, Robert exhibited signs of a young man who had cast off the bonds of civilized behavior. In an environmental science class he needed to graduate, Robert was rude and disruptive, at first with Jim at his side, and later on his own when Jim was quietly moved to a chemistry class. As Jim put it, "We're pretty, kind of, take the show, like just fooling about and saying the wrong things. Not like swearing or telling the teacher he's an idiot. You know, just kind of making jokes . . . that everyone thinks is funny except for the teacher."

On his own, Robert displayed a mix of profanity and hopelessness that marked a dark departure from the high-spirited, if grandiose, writings during his junior year. The worst of it came in a paper about a famous 1980 wager between ecologist Paul Erlich and economist

Julian Simon. Erlich maintained that the prices of natural resources would rise during the next decade as they became more scarce. Simon had bet Erlich that prices would fall, because resources wouldn't be depleted or alternatives would be found.

"Simon is a fucking idiot," Robert wrote on the assignment. "He believes man is the most important thing on earth, and therefore anything he does is a great achievement. . . . Simon will be dead in 32 years, and his grandchildren will have skin cancer. . . . It is quite obvious we are the only problem the earth has."

Robert's environmental studies teacher was Richard Steckler, one of his favorites in the school. Steckler liked Robert as well, but he had no choice but to respond with force. He returned fire in a note copied to the principal, Pat Davenport.

"Robert," Steckler wrote, "Parking lot language [is] totally uncalled for. Passion OK. So, just why exactly are you taking this class? If you wish to stay, you'll have to turn off the sarcasm and the rude comments directed toward others in the class. (I know you well enough to know that this will be very difficult.)"

In January 2001, Steckler thought he knew Robert. Robert's parents, brother, and sisters thought they knew Robert. Christiana thought she knew Robert. The Crew thought they knew Robert. DeRoss Kellogg and John O'Brien thought they knew Robert. Chelsea, Vermont, thought it knew Robert. But Robert's family, friends, teachers, and small community only imagined they knew him. Each of them saw pieces of the whole, and none took the warning signs he displayed seriously enough to dig deeper or clamp down on him. Even Jim, who knew him best, knew only what Robert wanted him to know, which was only as much as Robert thought Jim could handle.

The real Robert Tulloch emerges only when one carefully sifts through his public and private actions and attitudes—some seemingly inconsequential, some clear danger signals, some unknown to everyone except Jim—during the year leading up to the killings of Half and Susanne Zantop. Individually, the markers are easy to overlook or misread. The complete picture appears only when the elements of Robert's life are placed on top of one another and illuminated, like a picture divided into transparencies then stacked together and projected onto a screen.

First, though, it's necessary to eliminate the false leads and incomplete answers.

Prosecutors and police were eager to streamline the case into a straightforward narrative they knew would appeal to a jury. Seen through that lens, it was nothing more than a house robbery in which young, money-seeking thieves killed two strangers to eliminate witnesses. Certainly that theory was bolstered by Robert and Jim's incessant talk of needing cash to leave town and by the absence of other plausible motives—revenge or murder-for-hire, to name two. But to end the inquiry upon concluding that it was a matter of murder for money is to see only the surface, a view as mistaken as to suggest that because they look the same from the outside, a sleeping volcano is only a mountain.

Trying to raise money through crime to start new lives—grabbing mail, stealing the ATV, dreaming of robbing a bank or carjacking people, and ultimately hunting people—masked a disturbed psychology and murderous nature that had been brewing inside Robert.

Of course, he couldn't simply share with Jim his desire to kill people; that would have made his friend and acolyte run for cover. Rather, Robert understood intuitively that he was the leader of their two-man pack, and that he could bend Jim into whatever shape he wanted as long as he brought him along slowly, playing on Jim's love of adventure and fantasy, fueling his adolescent dreams of escaping protective parents, exploiting his craving for attention, stroking his insecure ego, and overcoming his vague doubts with seemingly watertight logic. It was a seduction of Jim to Robert's worldview. And step by step Jim came along, a vessel waiting to be filled, blinded by what he imagined to be Robert's brilliance reflecting off his own impressive mind.

The real question, then, is what made Robert thirsty for blood. Plenty of young men are frustrated and angry, hungry for money and certain of their own superiority, but few turn toward murder. What was it specifically about Robert that made him want to lash out and launch himself and Jim into new lives as outlaws who would never want, need, or be able to find their way back to "sucky old Chelsea"? A path to the answer can be found in the lines Michael Tulloch wrote about himself just a month before the murders: "It is funny how things, that can deeply affect and even change your life, come to you. Sometimes they are right in front of you, and you do not see them until the time is right." Had they only known what to look for, Robert's parents, friends, teachers, and fellow Chelseans might have recognized that right in front of them was a near-perfect specimen of a true psychopath.

Frequently misused and widely misunderstood, the word "psychopath" requires an explanation. At least some of the confusion comes from its overuse by laymen and the media to describe anyone who commits a horribly violent crime. Another reason is its similarity to the word "psychotic," when in fact the two have almost nothing in common. Psychotics are out of touch with reality, subject to delusions and hallucinations. The speech and motor patterns of a psychotic are often as bizarre and disorderly as his thoughts. A psychotic who commits murder might convincingly maintain that his dog told him to do it. As a result, psychotics can be judged not responsible for the crimes they commit by reason of insanity. Christiana Usenza was correct in telling Robert he wasn't psychotic.

By contrast, psychopaths seem exceedingly normal. They function efficiently in society, often extremely well, and know precisely what they are doing and why. They are often charming, witty, and charismatic. They choose to commit crimes because, in the apt phrase of Dr. Robert D. Hare, one of the foremost researchers on the subject, they are thoroughly "without conscience." In other words, they are sane by legal standards, but lack an essential quality of humanity. As Hare puts it, "Their acts result not from a deranged mind but from a cold, calculating rationality combined with a chilling inability to treat others as thinking, feeling human beings."

No one knows what causes psychopathy, though some studies suggest psychopaths suffer from a neurological defect that prevents them from making emotional connections. There is no evidence it results from social or environmental factors, and nurturing parents seem as likely as abusive or neglectful ones to spawn psychopaths. Put another way, sometimes a child raised with love becomes a cold-blooded killer, and, conversely, most children who suffer horrible upbringings don't become psychopaths. That makes it extremely difficult to predict who might become a psychopath, and equally hard to see one coming before it's too late. Another piece of bad news is that the prognosis for changing psychopaths' thoughts and behaviors through treatment is quite poor.

By Hare's estimation, there are at least two million psychopaths in North America, though only a fraction are potential killers. The others fit Hare's description of psychopaths who are "social predators who charm, manipulate, and ruthlessly plow their way through life, leaving a broad trail of broken hearts, shattered expectations, and empty wallets." Those who do become killers are often the most brutal of all murderers, able, in Hare's words, to "torture and mutilate their victims with about the same sense of concern that we feel when we carve a turkey for Thanksgiving dinner."

A famous literary portrait of psychopathic behaviors appeared twenty-five years before the Zantop murders. *In Cold Blood,* Truman Capote's "nonfiction novel," told the story of two young men, Dick Hickock and Perry Smith, who murdered a successful Kansas farm family, the Clutters. The killers didn't know their victims—they came to the farm in search of money. Smith, who thought himself "special" and felt an affinity with Thoreau, wanted to steal enough cash to travel to Mexico to search for buried treasure. Neither he nor Hickock had anything against the Clutters, who were passive and compliant, but Hickock was intent on "leaving no witnesses." As Smith explained after killing family patriarch Herb Clutter: "I didn't want to harm the man. I thought he was a very nice gentleman. Soft-spoken. I thought so right up to the moment I cut his throat."

To diagnose psychopathy, Hare and others developed a psychological checklist to distinguish it from social deviance or other mental illnesses, such as antisocial personality disorder, which is diagnosed largely on patterns of criminal behaviors. Though Robert exhibited antisocial behavior, the boundaries of that personality disorder aren't broad enough to explain him. Psychopathy includes not just deviant behavior but particular personality traits, many of which by themselves aren't necessarily cause for alarm. Only when a cluster of specific behavior and personality traits appear together can a person be deemed a psychopath.

A psychopath is glib and superficial, grandiose, lacking in emotional depth and empathy, devoid of remorse or guilt, deceitful and manipulative, and unable to make realistic long-term plans. "Psychopaths have a narcissistic and grossly inflated view of their self-worth and importance, a truly astounding egocentricity and sense of entitlement, and see themselves as the center of the universe, as superior beings who are justified in living according to their own rules," Hare wrote in what might well have been a review of one of Robert's school assignments. On the behavior side of the checklist, psychopaths lie with impunity, refuse to accept responsibility for their actions, act impulsively, lack behavior controls, crave excitement, abhor boredom, and commit a variety of antisocial acts.

As a teenager, Robert couldn't satisfy all the criteria for an adult diagnosis of psychopathy, particularly some of the secondary traits and behaviors. For instance, a "parasitic lifestyle" could apply to almost any teen living at home, and "promiscuous sexual behavior" isn't easy in a community as small as Chelsea, particularly for someone without a car of his own. On the other hand, a factor used in assessing young psychopaths is their tendency to lead double lives—as in, plotting murder while outwardly seeming a normal, nonviolent teen in Chelsea, Vermont.

Overall, Robert exhibited an extraordinary number of the traits and behaviors that define the syndrome—more than enough to easily satisfy a diagnosis of psychopathy.

The superficial charm he poured on his fellow students to win election as student council president, followed by his impeachable lack of interest once he got the job. The calculating callousness of suggesting that he and Jim kill his dog. The ease and frequency with which he lied to his mother, his girlfriend, his best friend, the police. The grandiosity, arrogance, and narcissism of his self-description as a "higher being" and an "intellectual giant" who was "born in the same manner as Jesus or Moses." The glibness he showed during school classes and debate competitions despite being wholly unprepared, as well as his inability to recognize his flagrant violation or modulate his anger at the state debate tournament. The crafty manipulation of Jim to ensure he would have the assistance and audience he desired. The risk-taking behavior of his *Thelma and Louise* plan at the quarry. The morally bankrupt way he insisted to the Barre police chief that he had done nothing wrong—the keys were in the truck, so why not drive it? The impulsivity and depravity of his suggestion that they crush the skulls of the old couple near the Ben & Jerry's festival. The escalating pattern of crimes to feed his urges for boredom-breaking thrills. The lack of remorse for the Zantops' deaths, contrasted with the blubbering regret he expressed solely for himself and Jim after their arrests in Indiana.

Psychopaths have what Hare called "an uncanny ability to spot and use 'nurturant' women. . . . Many such women are in the helping professions—nursing, social work, counseling—and tend to look for the goodness of others while overlooking or minimizing their faults." It is difficult to imagine a better definition of Robert's jailhouse friendship with nursing home administrator Sandra Knapp. Moreover, Hare notes, "Psychopaths feel their abilities will enable them to become anything they want to be." Robert's musings about becoming president or ruling the world fit nicely. His criminal seduction of Jim was aided by the tendency of psychopaths to exploit "people's need to find a purpose in their lives." The psychopath's "lack of sustained interest in education" perfectly fit his comments about college.

The contrast between Robert's cool demeanor and Jim's neck-throbbing fear on the night Sergeant Bob Bruno first questioned each of them clearly fit the profile; psychopaths tend to "lack the physiological responses normally associated with fear." Also, the psychopathic "indifference to the welfare of children" came through in

Robert's willingness to kill young Andy Patti or anyone of any age who happened to be in a house they targeted. Even his warped interpretation of Thoreau—they were "two peas in a pod," Robert thought—fit the psychopath's desire to live outside society's rules and expectations, as did his belief that such conventions were unreasonable limits on his exalted self-interest.

His repeated murder attempts even after Andrew Patti waved a gun at him were consistent as well. Jim considered the Patti confrontation a warning that this wasn't such a good idea, but Robert returned almost immediately to criminal fantasies. "The psychopath," Hare says, "carries out his evaluations of a situation—what he will get out of it and at what cost—without the usual anxieties, doubts, and concerns about being humiliated, causing pain, sabotaging future plans, in short, the infinite possibilities that people of conscience consider when deliberating possible actions." Even the purchase of the SOG knives—an apparent act of forward thinking, albeit destructive in nature—can be seen as evidence of a psychopath's poor planning. The unique nature of the knives, and their purchase so close in time and proximity to the murders, sent investigators rushing to Chelsea.

A key expression of his psychopathy was Robert's reliance on crime to raise money to leave Chelsea when working a steady job or tapping into the town's new Haskett fund would have been far more fruitful, not to mention legal. "Just as the great white shark is a natural killing machine, psychopaths naturally slip into the role of criminal," Hare writes. "Their readiness to take advantage of any situation that arises, combined with their lack of the internal controls we know as conscience, creates a potent formula for crime."

On the surface, Robert's affection toward Jim might seem to undermine a claim for psychopathy—human predators are notoriously unfazed by such niceties as loyalty. But Robert's apparent devotion to Jim might be better seen as an extension of his own narcissism. Like the Greek half-god Narcissus for whom narcissism was named, Robert looked into the reflecting pool that was Jim and became enchanted with himself. As one researcher explained, true feelings for another person would prevent someone from twisting his best friend into a killer just so he wouldn't have to go it alone. Indeed, a youth version of the psychopathy checklist modifies the criterion of parasitic lifestyle to take into account cases where someone uses other people to fulfill his needs. The tearful apology he made to Jim at the Indiana sheriff's office might as well be seen as Robert crying for himself.

By mid-January 2001, it was a short psychological trip for Robert to lead Jim back to the impressive houses along the road they had discovered on the day of the Ben & Jerry's festival. Had he not turned the two teens away, too busy to waste time with their bogus survey, Franklin Sanders almost certainly would have died on January 20.

The next week, after a few days of school and more bonding through rock climbing, they carried out their fateful decision: Let's go to Hanover—people there have a lot of money, and since Dartmouth is there maybe they'll be friendlier to student surveyors. There was the added benefit in Robert's mind of furthering his revenge after the Chelsea debate tournament by showing the people of Hanover that they weren't as smart as they thought.

They drove across the river and saw the movie *Snatch*, a furiously violent black comedy in which killing is casual and frequent, and one character flashes a long knife and says calmly: "I'll cut him. I've got a blade." After, they prowled around a house—running up the driveway, ducking behind trees, then running back to the car—like boys playing commando games. They were close to fulfilling their goal, but they still didn't feel quite ready to strike. "Basically," Jim said, "we chickened out and, you know, we needed to get ready to do this, and by this time we had firmly decided what we wanted to do."

They went home, steeled themselves, and settled on a plan. They'd use the environmental survey ruse. Once they got inside a house, Robert would ask for a glass of water. That would be the cue for both of them to jump whoever was in the house and tie them up. They'd unsheathe their SOG SEAL 2000s. They'd threaten their captives to get their ATM codes. Then they'd kill them to eliminate witnesses. Everyone in the house would feel the blade—"if there were any kids we'd have to do the same thing," Jim explained. Simple as that.

Then came January 27, 2001. They drove out of Chelsea, past Judgment Ridge, down the interstate and across the river into Hanover. Cruising in Joan Parker's green Subaru, their knives sharp and ready, Robert and Jim made their way along the winding streets to Trescott Road. First they went to the house where Audrey and Bob McCollum lived. Jim parked the car under the carport. Robert stepped into the cold and snow, swirls of cloudy vapor filling the air with his every breath. This time he felt ready. No turning back, no getting turned away. No more missed opportunities.

Robert knocked on the door. He kept knocking, but no one answered—the McCollums had gone skiing that morning at Suicide Six. Robert got back into the car. They talked it over and agreed: We're not through yet. Let's try next door, the modern house in the woods. Maybe someone's home there.

20

"Slit Her Throat!"

The walkway from the driveway to the front of the blue-gray home was shoveled clear. The shrubs looked like snow cones, and to the left of the front patio a bird feeder dangled from an overhang. The holidays were over, but a decorative wreath still hung to the right of the door, above a stack of firewood. Next to the wood was a flower box, finished for the season. While Robert rang the doorbell, Jim adjusted the blue-and-black Jansport backpack slung over his shoulders. Within seconds the boys could see through the full-length window to the right of the door that someone was coming.

The door swung open and standing in the entry was Half Zantop. He was almost equal in height to the boys—the house was a half-step higher than the patio, enough for Half to look them squarely in the eyes. Standing before them, Robert and Jim saw a trim, warm-looking man with a high forehead and a beard that had gone white with time.

He smiled easily. Half was dressed for the weekend in broken-in blue jeans, a lambswool sweater, and Birkenstock sandals. He'd been up for hours already. Half usually awoke before sunlight and liked to boil water and bring a hot cup of tea to his wife. They'd sit together on the bed, chatting, to start their day. The couple tended to be creatures of routine on weekends, sharing coffee and a biscuit at eleven, a home-made soup for lunch at one, then a short nap. By the time Half answered the door, Susanne Zantop had already called and invited Roxana Verona to come over that night for dinner.

Right away Robert took over. I'm Robert Tulloch, and this is Jim Parker, he told Half. There was no reason not to use their true names; he was confident that if everything went according to plan it wouldn't matter. Half listened intently as Robert launched into his act, telling Half that he and his pal Jim were hoping to take a few minutes to do an interview for a school environmental project. Robert was doing what he thought he did best—talk on the fly, like in debate, certain that his gift with words would persuade the world to see things his way. Robert told Half they were from the Mountain School, a couple of hardworking students trying to complete an assignment on this lovely Saturday morning. He'd made up the part of the Mountain School, but that was an easy bluff since he'd heard so much about it from Kip Battey and Coltere Savidge. Robert spiced up his pitch by mentioning that they wanted to gather opinions on such issues as nuclear power and oil exploration.

Jim, standing by silently, was wearing his carpenter jeans, an L.L. Bean sweater, and his Tecnica boots. Robert was dressed in khaki pants, his hand-me-down Vasque boots, and the black sweater he'd bought at the Army-Navy store in Burlington. It was the same sweater John O'Brien had noticed Robert wearing a lot around Chelsea, a sweater the debate coach thought gave Robert a worldly, European look.

Half was friendly enough—seeming on the one hand keenly inter-ested in the boys and the project Robert was describing but also torn, as if he'd been in the middle of something when they'd knocked.

"Hold on a second. My wife is making lunch. I don't think I can do this."

The boys waited outside on the bluestone patio. The beauty of their decision to target Hanover wasn't just the concentration of wealth, which improved the odds of a big payday, but also that a college town overflowed with students. The unexpected appearance of two teenagers, Robert had told Jim, wouldn't seem odd. No cause for concern or alarm. Not like in Rochester, Vermont, the week before, where that guy in the big new house had slammed the door in their faces.

So far, the way this was going validated Robert's thesis. This guy didn't display an inkling of suspicion, only curiosity. Robert and Jim just had to relax and be themselves.

The door opened again and Half Zantop welcomed the boys into his home.

"You know, I like what the Mountain School does," he said.

Jim followed Robert inside. The boys surely caught their reflection in the large pine mirror that hung in the foyer, both knowing full well they weren't as they appeared. Jim, thinking ahead, realized at this point that they didn't have the tape recorder. It was back in the car, a prop they'd thought would add legitimacy to the fake survey. In their gusto to get to the front door, they'd forgotten it. But if Jim was feeling anxious, Robert showed nothing but cool; he walked confidently behind Half Zantop, like someone coming into his own.

Their host led them from the tiled foyer into the living room with a polished wood floor covered by richly colored Oriental rugs. Robert and Jim could see the house was filled with natural light pouring in through the living room's window-lined south wall. They could see the comfortable furniture, invitingly laid out to encourage guests to sit and stay, and a wooden coffee table covered with books, newspapers, and magazines. Robust potted trees and hanging plants added color and life, and a black, cast-iron wood stove off to the right marked the transition from the living room to a dining room that looked out into the attached greenhouse. The place gave off a cozy, lived-in feeling, a warmth due more to the homeowners than the thermostat set at sixty-eight degrees.

Robert was taking a sculpture class at school, but he and Jim weren't as worldly as they told themselves they were: They lacked the knowledge to appreciate the art that was all around them. Within a few feet of them were a kneeling nude sculpture in bronze by Rodin and a seventeenth-century oil painting by the Dutch master Abraham van Beyern. Together, the sculpture and the still life were worth several times more than the $10,000 the boys budgeted for their mythical exodus to Australia.

As Half led them toward a small study, Robert and Jim couldn't help but notice cooking aromas wafting from the kitchen located to the right of the dining room, where Susanne was preparing lunch. A pot of broth and vegetables simmered on the left front burner of the Whirlpool stove. Susanne was dressed in a black-and-brown sweater and tan corduroy slacks as she chopped herbs, onions, and greens into neat piles on a cutting board. She'd reach for spices from a wall rack mounted near assorted bottles of vitamins and prescription medicine. Two blocks of cheese and three slices of bread occupied another cutting board. An open bottle of Merlot sat in front of the coffee grinder, and a half-full glass was within reach near her chopped greens. Dirty pots and lids filled one of the twin stainless-steel sinks, waiting to be loaded into the KitchenAid dishwasher. A boom box at the corner of the kitchen counter was set to National Public Radio. Robert and Jim couldn't see Susanne, and she didn't look over to see who was with her husband.

The head count was now at two. The boys, of course, hadn't known how many people they'd find home, but had assumed they would find a couple. Once Robert gave the signal of asking their host for a drink—what Jim called "the water thing"—Jim's job was to round up whoever else was in the house and bring them into the room where Robert would be busy overtaking their interviewee. Inside the backpack was most everything they thought they would need—a roll of duct tape and zip ties in the first pouch, two notebooks and, most important, the two SOG SEAL 2000 knives in the main pouch.

Half led the boys past a Yamaha piano with CDs, records, books, and a calendar piled on the wooden bench, and ushered them into the nine-by-sixteen-foot study. The room was made smaller by the floor-to-ceiling bookcases on two walls and an L-shaped desk along the other two. Once he'd decided he could spare the time, Half was giving his visitors his full attention. He moved around the neatly organized room, arranging chairs on the Oriental-style area rug. He turned around an ergonomic stool that normally faced the computer, then took a wooden folding chair and a chair made of metal with a cane seat and back, and turned all three inward, creating an intimate circle. Half settled into the ergonomic chair, which he used to ease his back pains, while Robert took a seat with his back to the desk and Jim sat in the chair next to the study door. They were so close their knees were practically touching, giving it the safe-and-snug feel of a seminar.

Robert could easily see from the scholarly surroundings that he was dealing with a bona fide intellectual, someone who'd succeeded in the world of ideas and higher learning. And not just that. Competing for space with the hundreds of shelved books were memorabilia and photographs illustrating a rich and adventurous life. Color photos of Veronika and Mariana were featured prominently, with several looking over Robert's shoulder at their father.

"Okay, what do you guys want to know?" Half said.

Jim set the backpack on the floor next to his feet. He fumbled with the main pouch and pulled out one of the notebooks. He saw that the tape recorder wasn't the only thing they'd forgotten. Jim couldn't find anything to write with. He asked Half if could borrow a pen, and Half obliged, handing him one from the desk.

Jim scribbled in the notebook as Robert began, but it wasn't as if they'd ever rehearsed the survey or drawn up any questions. Robert just did what he'd always done, whether it was in class at school, running for office, or at a debate; he talked off the cuff, believing he was clever enough to fool even someone as smart as Half. From keeping up with current events, Robert could vaguely talk the talk of such environmental concerns as global warming, the depletion of oil reserves, and the costs and benefits of nuclear power. The ecology class taught by Richard Steckler helped, too. The class had been studying the White River Partnership, a citizens group working to improve the river's watershed. But missing from Robert's rap was any real logic to the line of questioning. No matter how articulate he seemed, Robert was jumping all over the map, and it didn't take Half long to see that Robert was bumbling. Jim could see it, as well, thinking, "We weren't prepared at all."

Patiently, though, Half Zantop accommodated the boys. Wherever he could, he tried to help Robert out, either by guiding the inquiry or coming up with a follow-up or related question that had gone unasked. Half noted to Robert, for example, that different countries dealt with environmental issues differently. When he mentioned that he was originally from Germany, Robert picked up on Half's point and asked Half to compare Germany and the United States' approach to oil as an energy source.

To Robert and Jim's surprise, it came out that Half Zantop was an earth sciences professor at Dartmouth. Jim didn't make much of the coincidence, but Robert got it right away. He understood that this was why he and Jim had gained a foothold in the house. They'd concocted a ruse to do a survey about the environment and were interviewing a professor in the field. How lucky was that? What a contrast to the guy working on his pool who turned out to be a retired utilities executive with no use for environmental surveys. Or, before that, the ill-fated summer night in Vershire when they tried using their broken-down-car story on a gun-toting flatlander. Professor Half Zantop, it turned out, was doing what came naturally to him, which made Robert and Jim the beneficiaries of a devilish brand of serendipity. Robert would laugh afterward about the coincidence, calling it a "funny thing."

Ten minutes or so into the interview, as he scribbled words that were barely legible and completely irrelevant, a thought crossed Jim's mind: Half Zantop was an all right guy. The professor had let them into his home when he was busy. He'd tolerated their clumsy attempt at a survey, and he'd even supplied them with the pen to do the interview. Their host was trying to turn the experience into a teaching moment. When Robert faltered, the professor stepped in and coached him on his interviewing technique. Offering constructive criticism of a student presentation was reflex; Half wanted to help the two high school boys do better.

The professor was smothering the boys with good will, and Jim's thoughts turned mutinous: "We don't need to kill this guy." Under the circumstances, Jim figured, they might as well wrap up the interview and split. Forget the plan this time.

But as Jim was going one way, Robert was going the other. For him, Half's critique, however well-intentioned, was a slap across the face. Though Jim heard Half's comments as innocent suggestions, in Robert's mind they were fighting words. And when Half finished up by telling the already coiled Robert, "You need to be more prepared," Robert had heard more than enough. No matter how gently Half said it, to Robert it was a bitter reprise of the criticism he had silently suffered from the Hanover High School debate coach just three weeks earlier. Then, he couldn't do anything about it but tap his foot and rush out the door when she was done. Now he could answer the insult with an attack of his own.

Half began looking for the telephone number of a friend he thought might help Robert and Jim refine their survey. As Half turned to his desk, Robert leaned forward and reached into the backpack's main pouch.

Eleven months later, seven days before Christmas 2001, two deputies escorted Jim to a small conference room at the Belknap County Sheriff's Department. It was only fifty yards across a snow-covered driveway from the jail where Jim had been held since he turned seventeen in May, but the walk symbolized the huge distance Jim had traveled since being separated from Robert after their arrests. Robert may have told Christiana that Jim was "as smooth as obsidian" and would never break. But Jim had indeed cracked. And just as shattered obsidian produces sharp edges, the new Jim was about to turn dangerous to Robert.

It was a cold, snowy New Hampshire morning under a pewter sky. Jim wore the loose-fitting orange uniform of a maximum-security inmate. He was handcuffed during the walk, but the handcuffs had been removed before he entered the room. Easing himself into a high-

backed black fabric chair, Jim sat quietly at one end of the oblong
table, waiting to begin his confession. Next to him on his side were two
of his attorneys, Cathy Green and Phil Utter. Over Jim's shoulder was
a picture window looking out onto the red-brick façade of the county
jail. The walls in the conference room were painted an industrial
cream color and the carpet was a speckled brown. Jim, feeling a chill,
asked that the window behind him be shut.

Seated in a matching black chair directly across the table was Kelly
Ayotte, the chief prosecutor in the Zantop investigation. She wore her
trademark dark pantsuit. Next to her was her colleague Mike Delaney.
With them was state police Sergeant Mark Mudgett, the hulking, six-
foot-plus investigator who'd interviewed Ranger.

Mudgett sat at the head of the table with Jim on his left and Kelly
Ayotte on his right. In front of him was a tape recorder Mudgett had
brought with him. "Today's date is December 18, 2001," Mudgett
began. "Time according to my watch is twenty-eight minutes past ten
o'clock." He identified the others at the table, then said, "I am going
to turn this conversation over to Attorney Ayotte."

The prosecutor leaned forward, her hands on the table holding the
questions she and Delaney had written beforehand.

"Could you please just tell us what your name is?"

"Jim Parker."

"And, James. Do you mind if I refer to you as James?"

Jim said it was OK.

In a legal sense, Jim's turnaround was the result of a plea bargain
his attorneys and prosecutors had worked out during the previous four
weeks. Before then, Jim's attorneys hadn't much been interested in
plea negotiations. They and Jim's parents had focused their energy
throughout the year on fighting to keep Jim's case in the juvenile system, where even if convicted of murder he'd be released at the age of
twenty-one. Prosecutors had vigorously opposed the move and argued
that Jim should be tried as an adult, side-by-side with Robert, where
they both could face life in prison. Although New Hampshire had a
death penalty, prosecutors decided early on not to seek it, in part
because of the defendants' tender ages. In early November, the prose-

cution's views about trying Jim as an adult prevailed. Within days, Jim's attorneys contacted the prosecutors about cutting a deal.

Legal strategy was one thing, Jim was another. From the start his parents did everything they could to reconnect with their lost boy. They hired a private therapist to see him weekly in the county jail; they made sure he earned his high school diploma from the Chelsea Public School (although Jim's name would go unmentioned at his classmates' graduation in June 2002); they saw to it that he kept up with his music and art; they urged him to focus his mind and spirit through yoga; they accepted his nightly collect calls; and they visited him as often as they could and encouraged friends to do the same. Over time they saw the tether tying him to Robert first loosen and then break; the Parkers began to tell close friends in Chelsea that Jim was becoming his old self again. He was ice melting.

The bargain, finalized in early December, required Jim to plead guilty to being an accomplice to second-degree murder, to cooperate fully with investigators by telling them everything they wanted to know, and to testify against Robert at trial. In return Jim would be sentenced to twenty-five years to life in state prison. Under New Hampshire law, Jim could eventually seek to have his sentence reduced by one-third, a formula which meant that, at a minimum, he would serve sixteen years and eight months.

Publicized in early December, the deal was attacked by many of the Zantops' friends and Dartmouth colleagues, and in newspaper editorials. "He's a demonic murderer," Eric Manheimer, the Zantops' close friend and trustee of their estate, told a reporter. "It's an outrage that the system allows this young man to negotiate his way out of what should be a maximum sentence." Audrey McCollum said, "A crime that was so atrocious and sadistic, it's hard to come to terms with this mild a sentence." The *Union Leader* newspaper went after Ayotte's boss, Phil McLaughlin, condemning the plea bargain and editorializing that the attorney general had been "callously insensitive."

Prosecutors didn't flinch. Their investigation, which included the still-undisclosed account that Ranger had gotten from Robert, showed that Robert was the ringleader. This meant that Jim was the one to negotiate with. The terms of Jim's deal, too, were not unheard of. In a 1997 murder case in which three men killed two teenage girls in Salem, New Hampshire, prosecutors cut a deal with one of the killers, which mirrored Jim's. Like Jim, that killer had to testify against the others, plead guilty to second-degree murder, and spend twenty-five years to life in prison. McLaughlin, facing harsh criticism, understood that friends of the Zantops wouldn't take a macro-judicial view and comprehend the practical reasons for making a deal. "They live in a universe in which they have a gut reaction," he said. "I live in a universe of what's possible and what's impossible." Most important to the authorities, Veronika and Mariana Zantop endorsed the plea bargain.

Jim appeared in court on December 7 to enter his guilty plea. He was reed-thin, his hair was cropped short, and he wore a black pullover jersey, dark blue jeans, and sneakers. Eleven days later he was seated across from Kelly Ayotte in a sheriff's conference room dressed in his orange jailhouse jumpsuit.

Ayotte began by asking Jim general questions about where he was from, about his family and growing up in Chelsea. She asked about his interests and his friends. She asked about Robert, their friendship, and about all the time they spent together in 2000. Jim kept up eye contact as the interview moved along. Like his mother, Jim favored natural foods, which he rarely got to have in jail. Cathy Green had brought him a salad and an organic drink, which Jim ate appreciatively during a break. Occasionally Jim came across as sassy. Ayotte asked him at one point about the different musical bands he played in. "Were you focused on jazz music or a particular type of music?" Jim replied with a hint of sarcasm in his voice, "Well, in the jazz band we do jazz, and in the concert band we did classical music."

Then Ayotte asked Jim to walk her through his and Robert's deepening criminal behavior—stealing mail, the housebreaks, the truck in the quarry, the stolen ATV. Finally, after nearly three hours of questioning, Kelly Ayotte asked Jim Parker about early 2001 and the discovery of the professors' house at 115 Trescott Road.

"What is it that brought you down there that morning on January 27?"

"Well," said Jim, his voice flat and mechanical. "We were going to kill somebody and take their credit cards and get their ATM numbers."

The room's dynamic changed abruptly. Jim stopped making eye contact with his soft-spoken inquisitor. The questions about January 27 kept coming, one after another, and eventually Jim slumped back in the cushioned chair. The two prosecutors could tell they were taking Jim to a place he was loath to revisit.

"Walk me through step by step, walking up to the door," Ayotte said.

"We had a backpack with some paper for writing stuff down," Jim said. "And the knives."

"Let me give you somebody's number near your area that you can talk to," Half told Robert and Jim. He spun in his chair and fussed at his desk looking for the friend's number. He flipped open a regional telephone directory to the "T" section on pages 372–373, scanned the names, but couldn't find it there, either. He turned to his Apple computer and tried an Internet telephone directory, but again no luck.

Meanwhile, behind the professor's back, Robert had quietly removed one of the foot-long combat knives from Jim's backpack. Making no sound, he pulled the knife from its sheath. He folded the fingers of his right hand tightly around the molded black fiberglass grip. The seven-inch stainless-steel blade with serrated teeth was pointed up.

Half remembered that the friend's number might be on a slip of paper in his wallet. He leaned sideways and pulled the wallet from the hip pocket of his jeans. He swiveled back to face the boys as he flipped through the billfold.

Robert sprang from his chair. Lunging forward, he thrust the knife upward, burying the blade deep into the professor's chest. Half let out a terrible scream. Together Robert and Half fell backward over the ergonomic chair and into the floor-to-ceiling bookcase to the left of the computer. A card table toppled to the floor, spilling papers everywhere. Blood poured from Half's chest.

Robert pulled the knife out and thrust it a second time into the teacher's warm flesh. To Robert's mind, each blow with the knife was a deeply satisfying, well-deserved act of revenge. Half's summary of Robert's interviewing shortcomings had, in effect, been the latest in a yearlong string of reality checks exposing the gulf between Robert's self-image as a higher being and the fact that he was plain old Robert of Chelsea. It was one humiliation after another, from the mouths of idiots, as far as Robert was concerned, idiots who didn't appreciate his brilliance and insisted that his chronic slacking undermined his potential. Robert wouldn't acknowledge that it had been lack of preparation that led to his near-impeachment from the student council presidency, and it was the reason his debate season imploded. Lack of preparation had even foiled his and Jim's attempt to get into the Pattis' home in Vershire and then into Franklin Sanders's home in Rochester. The very word itself—"unprepared"—was ricocheting in his head even before Half Zantop spoke it, from the debate tournament fiasco in Chelsea.

Making no sound, Robert plunged the knife into Half's chest again and again. Robert noticed Half's eyes bulge out of their sockets. He slashed his victim's face. Robert said nothing, working in a silent rage. He lorded over the fallen professor, who was dying quickly and unable to offer much of a struggle given the suddenness, the speed, and the intensity of the attack. In his frenzy, Robert missed Half and gouged the bottom shelf of the bookcase near Half's head. Later he missed again and wounded himself above the right knee.

Jim had jumped to his feet seconds after Robert pounced on Half. He reached into the backpack, took out the second knife, and removed the sheath. The room was filled with Half's screams, and Jim watched the blood pool across the front of Half's sweater. Half's legs dangled up over the toppled ergonomic chair. The wicker wastebasket next to the desk was overturned near Half's lower back, blood on it.

Jim was the bystander by the door, but that changed the instant Susanne Zantop ran into the study. Robert wondered later whether Susanne, hearing her husband shrieking, had rushed from the kitchen across the living room thinking Half had suffered a heart attack. But the moment she entered the study and saw the slaughter that was under way she threw herself toward Robert and Half. She screamed in German, grasped at Robert's leg, and reached desperately for her husband. Jim bent down and put his left arm under her shoulder, sweeping Susanne away from Robert and Half.

"Shut up," Jim told Susanne as Robert continued stabbing her husband.

Half was on his back, lifeless; Susanne flailed away in Jim's arms, screaming and trying to break free. The room had erupted into bloody chaos. Robert looked at Jim and locked eyes.

"Slit her throat!" he yelled.

Jim could have pulled Susanne out of the study and saved her life. Or he might have abandoned her and saved himself. But the idea of disobeying Robert never crossed Jim's mind. He and Robert might as well have been clinging to a rock face in the midst of a sudden high-altitude crisis, bonded by their ropes, each boy's safety completely dependent on the other. Robert's months-long seduction had succeeded; now the debts would be repaid, the bond would be cemented. At that moment Jim saw the two of them as one, and he didn't think twice about whether to follow Robert's command. There was no room left in him to hear his own conscience, his mother's voice, his father's, or anyone else's. All he could hear was a cry from his best friend for help.

Pausing only briefly, Jim flexed the muscles of his left arm to steady and subdue Susanne, who though small was kicking and flapping wildly. Jim raised his knife and brought it quickly under her chin. In a single, swift motion, he sliced Susanne Zantop's throat.

Jim let go. Susanne's body dropped, all that fight in her gone the instant the steel blade opened her up. She fell face down across the doorway to the study. Jim could hear gurgling sounds coming from her. "Dying sounds," he realized right away. The blood pooled by Susanne's head and began soaking her pullover sweater.

Half and Susanne were finished, but Robert was not. His most violent psychopathic urgings in full flower, Robert was overdosing on the darkness of the moment. He felt himself "going animal." He took pleasure in the expression on Half's face—a dumb look, Robert decided, which he thought was humorous, such a stupid look as the final expression on such a smart man. Robert leaned down and slit Half's throat. He was puzzled at first when Half didn't bleed much from the fresh cut, then he realized that Half had no blood pressure left from the many other wounds. Robert then stalked over to Susanne. He took his knife and plunged it into her head. It was an experiment, Robert would later tell Jim. He wanted see if the knife would penetrate her skull. He did it again. And again. Each thrust through bone and brain made a horrible sound, Jim thought as he watched, "like jabbing a knife into a pumpkin."

Jim had gone numb, empty of emotion. The moment Robert surprised him by reaching into the backpack for the knife, only one thought crossed his mind: This was business. He would later realize how awful that sounded, but that was how he felt. Like it or not, the time had come to complete the job they'd talked about for so long.

Two extraordinary lives were extinguished in less than ten minutes. Jim felt as if a much longer chunk of time had passed. Robert stood over Susanne once he stopped stabbing her head. Jim moved behind him and grabbed the backpack off the floor. Robert took Half's wallet. Each clutching a knife, they ran from the study. On his way out Robert stepped in a puddle of blood, and a partial bloodstained footprint in the living room marked their departure.

The exit route from the study took them within a few steps of the Rodin sculpture, the oil painting, and other valuable art pieces. The boys, had they been more prepared, would have realized they could have gotten thousands of dollars by fencing the Zantops' art objects. Instead they had the $340 in cash from Half's wallet. By jumping the professor when he did, Robert had discarded their robbery plan. He'd skipped the part about subduing the victims to obtain the bank information that would get them the larger sums they were after. Jim later thought that Robert had lost it—or "clicked," as he called it—once he saw the cash in Half's wallet. But that couldn't be quite right. There was more to Robert's propulsion than the flash of cold cash; Robert had moved to get the knife before Half had even begun reaching into his back pocket for the wallet.

Afterward, Robert lied to Jim, saying he wasn't sure why he went off on Half when he did and ignored their planned cue about the glass of water and all the rest. The truth was that the mission he'd enlisted Jim for was never really about ATM cards, PIN numbers, and money. Robert wanted to kill somebody, and he later told Ranger so, saying he saw the slayings as a "chance to get a few under my belt." Innocently, Half Zantop had given a psychopath a reason to commence the blood-letting, simply by doing to Robert what so many others in his life already had done: question his greatness.

Jim's confession lasted nearly five hours and left everyone in the conference room drained. Signing off, Mudgett even got the date wrong. "OK, we're going to conclude at, ah, 2:30 P.M. on the eighteenth of January." It must have felt as if a month had passed; they'd covered so much ground, concluding with the murders. "I'm back on tape with a clarification," said Mudgett seconds later. "It's *December* 18, 2001."

Once outside the room, Jim was handcuffed and walked back to the jail.

Inside, the two prosecutors conferred briefly with Jim's attorneys about the session and plans for future ones—a second interview would be held January 4, 2002, a third two weeks later, and finally, a brief session on March 7.

The prosecutors packed up their things and headed back to their offices in Concord. Only after they were in their car did they let down their guard. Jim Parker's confession had taken their breath away. In all their experiences with homicide cases, Kelly Ayotte and Mike Delaney had mostly dealt with an older, more seasoned brand of defendant, career-criminal types who rarely gave straight answers, who tended to spin and tailor their responses in self-serving ways. Those interviews required careful, hard questioning from prosecutors. In contrast, Jim had been easy—guileless, frank, and straightforward, almost like a child whose parents had instructed him to tell the school principal the truth. He would make a great witness in court.

The prosecutors talked nonstop, trading highlights from the confession, discussing Jim's demeanor, and brainstorming about the topics they wanted to follow up on. Indeed, at the next interview Ayotte had Jim open with a second run-through of the murders. And it was during a follow-up session that she posed a question she hadn't asked the first time. It was a question she, Delaney, and police investigators had wondered about ever since the day of the murders. It was a question that got to the very heart of how the case was ultimately solved—a break without which Robert and Jim might never have been apprehended, a break that had come from a mistake Robert and Jim made that seemed so careless that investigators and psychiatrists would later wonder whether it meant that the boys, for all their talk about being badasses, had wanted to get caught. Or, if not Robert, perhaps it was Jim who had left the sheaths, consciously or subconsciously hoping that whoever found them would do what he was powerless to do on his own: break free from Robert's grasp before the time came to kill again.

"During the last interview," Ayotte said, "you said that after you let Susanne down, you started packing up the stuff into the backpack. Do you remember talking about that?"

"Yeah," Jim said. "What's the question?"

"When you were packing up the stuff, how come you didn't take the knife sheaths?"

The question hung in the air. During hour after hour of interviews, Jim usually answered questions right away. He usually spoke in a clear voice. But this time Jim paused. This time his voice dropped. Jim knew what Kelly Ayotte was after; the sheaths were what had led Chuck West and his colleagues to Chelsea and to him and Robert.

And that had ultimately led them here.

Jim's voice was barely audible when he finally spoke: "Forgot about them."

21

Hope and
Hopelessness

"Can you read?" Superior Court Judge Peter W. Smith asked.

"Yes, I can."

The judge was looking down from his bench at Robert Tulloch inside Courtroom 3 of the Grafton County Superior Court, and Robert was staring right back. Robert made a face that suggested he considered the judge's literacy question odd and insulting. Traces of a smirk creased his mouth: Of course he could read.

"Is this your signature?" Judge Smith continued. The judge held in his hands the legal paperwork notifying the court that Robert was changing his plea to guilty. The black-robed, gray-haired jurist sat comfortably behind the bench while Robert, shackled, stood stiffly at the defense table, flanked by his two public defenders, Richard Guerriero and Barbara Keshen.

"Yes, it is," Robert said. His voice was firm and self-assured. He wore gray slacks and a white, collared shirt that he'd buttoned to the top. He sported a new, short, choppy haircut—a prison buzz-cut. Robert had asked his jailers for scissors the day before—he knew they were forbidden, but wasn't he always pushing the envelope?—and he was given electric clippers. One of his cellmates, clearly inexperienced in hair care, had done a rough and uneven job.

It was April 4, 2002, in North Haverhill, New Hampshire, and the Zantop murder case was unexpectedly reaching a legal climax. For months the public had eagerly followed news accounts of Robert's upcoming first-degree murder trial, scheduled for late April and featuring Jim Parker as the government's star witness. Prosecutors and defense attorneys had been working frantically to get ready for a trial expected to last at least a month.

Suddenly, Robert folded, deciding early in March to plead guilty to killing the Zantops. The news, when it broke later that month, shocked and surprised; it was the courtroom equivalent of boxer Roberto Duran's famous "No Mas!" fight, when out of the blue, during the eighth round of a title bout, the Panamanian champion threw up his hands and quit. Robert's decision meant there would be no trial, but he still needed to make his admission in open court. For the sake of convenience and legal symmetry, court officials scheduled Jim's sentencing hearing for the same date.

And so, the stage was set for a remarkable day—a final congregation of nearly everyone connected to a case that had been followed from coast to coast. It would be a finale divided into two acts, Robert in the morning and Jim in the afternoon. The once-inseparable friends would be closer to each other than they had been since their separation in Indiana fourteen months earlier, and at different times they would occupy the same holding cell and the same chair in the same courtroom. In keeping with their usual pattern, Jim would be following in Robert's footsteps. But on this day they wouldn't get even the briefest glimpse of each other.

The media began pulling into tiny North Haverhill and filling up the few area motels the night before the hearing. As dawn broke, seven satellite television trucks were lined up like tanks in formation in the courthouse parking lot. Spring was officially two weeks old, but it hadn't arrived in northern New Hampshire. The morning opened to a mix of sun and occasional flurries. Reporters' words formed clouds as they sipped coffee in the thirty-degree chill. They mingled and gossiped at the top of the driveway that sloped down to the courthouse's back entrance, where officials would bring Robert and later Jim. To capture their arrivals, fifteen TV cameras on tripods lined the grassy embankment bordering the driveway. Still photographers were moving around, bobbing and feinting with competitors to position themselves for just the right shot.

More newspaper and radio reporters milled around inside, filling the lobby adjacent to Judge Smith's courtroom. A majority came from newspapers in New Hampshire and Vermont, Boston and other New England cities, but there also were reporters from *Associated Press,* the *New York Times,* the *Washington Post,* the *Los Angeles Times, People* magazine, and, of course, *The Dartmouth.* In all, about three dozen news organizations were on hand. Moving about, too, were "bookers" from network newsmagazine shows who'd been lobbying anyone and everyone close to the Parker and Tulloch families to get the parents to sit for an exclusive interview with one of their celebrity correspondents. Their efforts weren't paying off.

Inside Courtroom 3, even with extra folding chairs, the supply of seats couldn't meet demand. At Robert's hearing, seats were reserved for the Zantop and the Tulloch families and their supporters, as well as key investigators. After that, twenty-three seats remained for the news media, and eleven were left for the general public. Clerks held a lottery to see which reporters got inside. The losing journalists hustled out to monitor the proceedings from the TV trucks that were getting a live feed from the single television camera Judge Smith had reluctantly allowed inside the courtroom.

No one around the courthouse, or North Haverhill for that matter, had ever seen a media invasion like this. To prepare for the day, court administrators had picked the brains of their colleagues in Rockingham County, who had endured the crush of media a dozen years earlier during the sensational case of Pamela Smart, the schoolteacher who convinced her teen lover and his friends to kill her husband. Ordinarily, only a few security guards staffed the Grafton County courthouse; for the big day that was about to unfold, fifteen guards were stationed throughout the building.

Veronika and Mariana Zantop arrived with friends in two cars, driving right past the reporters and down the driveway to the rear entrance. The Tulloch family and Robert's two public defenders arrived a few minutes later, also in two cars, and they used the rear entrance, too. They were all inside by 8:30 A.M.

Soon word spread that Robert was coming. A brown sheriff's cruiser could be seen making its way slowly across the parking lot and toward the back entrance. This time officials allowed photographers and reporters to move in closer—down the driveway and into a long line that formed just outside the drop-off bays. Two deputy sheriffs were in the front seat of the cruiser. Robert sat in the left rear passenger seat. The cruiser began to brake as it curled past the gauntlet of photographers and into the bay. Robert's eyes scanned the row of journalists, absent any expression.

"Robert! Anything to say?" one photographer shouted before Robert had finished climbing out of the back seat, his feet in leg irons and his hands in cuffs. The photographers needed Robert to look their way, but he padded toward the door. "Robert—give us a look!" another shouted desperately. "We want to see your face!"

Robert gave them nothing; he shuffled into the building, his back to the crowd.

Judge Smith opened Robert's hearing with a string of questions he was required by law to ask a defendant who was changing his plea. The sixty-three-year-old judge had a reputation as a no-nonsense arbiter.

He had once worked as an estate tax examiner for the IRS, and in court he projected the image of jurist as judicial accountant. No flights of rhetorical or legal fancy from him. No extended intellectual repartee with counsel over obscure legal hypotheticals.

Except for the voices of the judge and defendant, the capacity-filled courtroom was stone silent. Judge Smith was making sure Robert knew exactly what he was doing—that he was making a competent and informed decision. He told Robert about the legal rights available to all criminal defendants—rights Robert was abandoning by pleading guilty.

"Do you remember what those rights are?"

"Do you want me to list them?" Robert's voice sounded incredulous, as though Judge Smith was making a nuisance of himself. But the judge wouldn't rise to the bait.

"Only if you can."

Robert's brow furrowed. "I have a right to be . . . " He paused. "I have a right to a fair trial, to be represented by counsel. I have a right to a trial by a jury."

The exchange resembled a quick civics lesson on the Bill of Rights. When Robert's voice trailed off because he was unable to recall the other rights he was waiving, the judge filled in the rest. It was like checking off items on a grocery list.

"Do you give up all these rights?" the judge asked.

"Yes, I do."

Perfunctory and brief, the robotic colloquy hardly reflected the dramatic consequences: Robert would live every remaining day of his life and then die in a state prison. That fact wasn't lost on Robert's lawyers. As Judge Smith and Robert finished, Richard Guerriero, who'd been standing next to Robert, turned to the judge. "I have to tell the court that Robert's decision to plead guilty is against our advice," he said.

Until the moment Robert changed his plea, prosecutors, the public, and the press had been gearing up for a murder trial at which

Robert's attorneys were planning to argue he was not guilty by reason of insanity.

That approach had come as an autumn surprise of sorts, filed for the first time the last day of November, or nearly nine months after Robert's arrest. Ordinarily a defendant notifies the court of an insanity claim within ten days or so of arraignment. Explaining Robert's long delay, Guerriero told Judge Smith, "the indications of mental illness were difficult to recognize because of Robert's intelligence and his particular personality." A recent psychiatric evaluation, the public defender said, had discovered that Robert suffered from a "severe mental defect or disease and that his acts were the direct result of the mental defect or disease."

Guerriero did not identify the specific diagnosis or the psychiatrist hired to assess Robert, but the defense team had tapped into the big leagues. Dr. Dorothy Otnow Lewis was a well-known professor of psychiatry at Yale University and New York University School of Medicine who also practiced at New York's Bellevue Hospital (the same hospital, coincidentally, where Dr. Eric Manheimer, the Zantops' close friend, served as medical director).

Lewis, a diminutive, dark-haired woman in her early sixties, had spent years studying the minds of killers—examining up to two hundred murderers by her own count—and she'd testified for the defense as an expert witness in numerous insanity cases. Included on her roster were some of the nation's highest-profile murderers; she examined Mark David Chapman, for example, the man who shot John Lennon. Lewis met for hours with Ted Bundy the day before the charming serial killer's execution; at the end of the long chat Bundy planted a kiss on her cheek. Lewis returned the gesture of affection, giving Bundy a hug and a kiss. She would later enjoy telling others about the moment—she was the last person to kiss Ted Bundy—and eventually recounted it in a 1998 memoir.

To Lewis, most criminals were themselves victims. She was outspoken in her belief that most murderers suffered from some toxic blend of physical and emotional abuse, brain injuries, and mental illness—to such an extent, she usually concluded, that the killers were not criminally responsible for their homicidal conduct. She told writer Malcolm Gladwell in a 1997 interview that when she examined a killer she was on the lookout mainly for signs of childhood abuse and bodily scars.

Lewis and a clinical social worker interviewed Robert on Saturday, November 10, at the Grafton County Jail. She conducted tests and, as she always did, got Robert talking about his childhood, his family, and his feelings. The next day, Lewis was in Chelsea, where she took over Dan Sedon's law office on Main Street to conduct interviews with the Tullochs. She spoke with Mike, Diane, Kienan, and Becky. She learned about Mike's alcoholism, depression, and his long-ago suicide attempt. She learned about Julie's brain condition and possible manic tendencies. Lewis didn't find that Robert had been physically abused as a child. She did, however, report to Guerriero that she found a family predisposition for mental illness and said Robert suffered from a severe psychiatric condition.

Lewis diagnosed Robert as bipolar, a condition that used to be referred to as manic-depression. Full-blown, the illness is not subtle: a person with bipolar disorder swings between extended stretches of mania and major depression. Manic phases feature hyperactivity, sleeplessness, and a feeling of almost unrestrained and inexpressible euphoria, like being high for days on end, fueled by a seemingly endless supply of energy. The bouts of depression are at the other extreme, featuring a deep, inconsolable, crippling anguish that impairs the ability to perform basic tasks of daily life.

Using Lewis as his expert, and the bipolar diagnosis as Robert's mental illness, Guerriero's defense strategy would have revolved around an argument that Robert was hostage to an extreme, manic episode—one that tipped over into psychosis—when he butchered the Zantops.

In Chelsea, the new twist in the case caught people by surprise, and a fair amount of skepticism took hold. It wasn't as if anyone could recall a time when Robert was running around town for days on end, unable to sleep, soaring down Main Street in a high-energy trance. Nor could anyone recall Robert missing school for any stretch of time because he was so depressed he couldn't get out of bed. "He was certainly very bright and mentally complex, but I never saw an insane side to him," said John O'Brien, his debate coach. In his confession, Jim was pointedly asked about Robert's moods and mental state, and each answer he gave revealed that during all their time together Jim had never seen any symptoms of bipolar disorder. Pressed further, Jim said Robert wasn't delusional, wasn't suicidal, and never mentioned hearing voices in his head. He said Robert knew exactly what he was doing. "He knew what his goals were. He knew that he was killing people and afterwards he knew that he had killed somebody."

Most saw the new defense, coming so late, as the legal equivalent of a quarterback throwing a "Hail Mary" pass, lobbing the ball into the end zone and hoping for the best as time runs out. But Guerriero and Keshen understood that New Hampshire's insanity doctrine actually offered Robert some hope—at least in theory. New Hampshire insanity law was unique. The statute said, "A person who is insane at the time he acts is not criminally responsible for his conduct." That's plain enough and not unlike the wording that appeared in other states' laws. What made New Hampshire different was that, unlike in most states, its statute didn't define insanity. It didn't spell out any particular legal test or definition juries must follow. A jury could consider expert and nonexpert testimony and weigh the evidence as it saw fit. "There are all tests because there are no tests," noted one New Hampshire legal expert. In sum, each New Hampshire jury was free to devise its own insanity standard.

Every other state had rules. For example, many had the "right-wrong" test, where the jury's task was to determine whether the defendant could tell right from wrong at the time of the crime—or, to phrase it another way, whether the defendant had the ability to appreciate the wrongfulness of his actions. Another common test is often called the "volitional test" or the "irresistible-impulse test." Juries are instructed to decide whether insanity—voices in the defendant's head, for example—prevented the defendant from controlling himself and conforming to the law.

In the absence of such tests, New Hampshire's law was a blank slate. Expansive rather than restrictive, in theory it could result in a jury's generous interpretation of whether someone's conduct constituted legal insanity. A jury could find that a moody, brooding, arrogant, grandiose, at times exuberant, allegedly bipolar teenager was not criminally responsible when he killed two people with a SOG SEAL 2000 combat knife.

But for all the insanity law's theoretical elasticity, courtroom reality was another matter entirely. To succeed, Robert would have to break a long losing streak. The insanity defense had never been successful at a murder trial in New Hampshire when the case had gone to the jury, according to veteran criminal-law practitioners.

In that sense, New Hampshire was like every other jurisdiction in the United States—insanity defenses were long shots. With his trial a month away, Robert was reminded of that hard fact of legal life. On March 12, 2002, a jury in Houston took fewer than four hours to convict Andrea Yates of murdering her five children. The gruesome trial had been the talk of the nation. Yates, who had a well-documented history of mental illness, said she drowned the kids to save them from Satan. Many pundits commented that if anyone was insane it was a mother who killed her own children. Even prosecutors agreed Yates was psychotic, but they argued she was still criminally responsible, because she was aware that killing was wrong. The jury agreed.

The significance of that case wasn't lost on Robert: If someone as sick as Andrea Yates couldn't succeed with an insanity defense, how could he? The Yates verdict added to the already growing doubts he was having during the winter about going to trial and claiming he was not criminally responsible for the murders because he was bipolar.

First, there were family matters. Initially he and his parents had cooperated with the insanity defense. But that changed quickly. Why are you doing this to us? Diane asked Robert at one point—or words to that effect—during one of their many conversations early in 2002. She and Mike had begun to understand the reality of what an insanity defense would look like at trial. They would most likely have to testify, and their family's troubles would be exposed for all to see. Their beloved privacy, already tattered since Robert's arrest, would be stripped away completely. Diane, especially, was worried a trial would leave her family shattered. She shared her concerns with Robert.

Jim's deal with prosecutors in December had also shaken Robert. "That was a whack," said jail Superintendent Glenn Libby, recalling Robert's reaction to the news. Privately Robert may have felt devastated by Jim's betrayal, but after he got over the initial shock he told his jailers and friends he didn't hold it against Jim. Robert understood, however, that Jim's cooperation was a powerful new element to the prosecution's already strong case.

Indeed, on March 6 Robert was arraigned on a new charge of conspiracy that prosecutors had obtained based on Jim's information. The indictment disclosed the boys' prior attempts against the Pattis in Vershire and Franklin Sanders in Rochester. In their motion to add the conspiracy count to the murder charges, prosecutors argued that the prior acts and the fact that Robert and Jim eventually fled proved they understood their crimes. "All of the acts . . . are properly admissible in the murder trial as evidence of flight, concealment of the crime, consciousness of guilt, requisite mental state at the time of the murders, and premeditation and deliberation." The new conspiracy charge was intended as a legal checkmate to the insanity argument, a countermove to the defense claim that Robert was in a psychotic state and insane when he slashed and killed the Zantops.

More and more Robert saw his case as a loser, so what was the point? He'd thought about pleading guilty as far back as the spring, mentioning that option in the letter he sent to a person close to his jailhouse pal Chief. So it wasn't as if he'd always been gung-ho to have his day in court. Now the state had Jim's testimony to bring life to the mountain of physical evidence.

Early in the new year, then, Robert and his family began talking about Robert simply folding. "There was just too much evidence, too much premeditation, to overcome with an insanity defense," one Tulloch insider explained. "It was like, 'Yeah, like, I can't win, so fuck it.'" Robert's lawyers, Guerriero and Keshen, made clear to the Tullochs they weren't happy with Robert's thinking. Though they often accept settlements in the interest of their clients, criminal lawyers are programmed for battle—go to trial, challenge the state's case, hope for at worst a conviction on a lesser count, appeal a loss. Do all that and more when the client is a seventeen-year-old boy facing life in prison. "Robert stepped off that treadmill, the lawyer mindset," the source said. "He saw there was no way out."

The last thing Robert wanted was to go to trial and be the freak at the center of a three-ring circus. "He saw the trial as a benefit to others, not to him or his family. It would be a dog-and-pony show for the government," the insider said. Robert had grown to despise prosecutor Kelly Ayotte, the source said, and he "didn't want to give her a chance to grandstand." By pleading guilty, he took all that away.

Jail officials were among the first to pick up signs of Robert's new fatalism. In early January, they detected that Robert was again having what Glenn Libby called "jailbreak fantasies." Jailhouse sources told authorities that Robert was seeking to enlist others to create an emergency inside the cellblock. Once the corrections officers responded, Robert and his allies would overwhelm them and take their keys. The intelligence grew sketchy after that. Concern heightened after an actual medical emergency in Robert's cellblock when a new inmate had a breakdown. Libby noticed Robert coolly studying the officers' response, searching for weaknesses.

Libby ordered an immediate crackdown. Robert's cellblock was searched and a "quasi-rope," made from strips of socks and wire from a spiral notebook, was found in the cell next to Robert's. "He was too smart to keep it in his own cell," Libby said. Robert was moved immediately to a different cellblock. He was back to wearing handcuffs and leg irons—just as in the spring—and was put on suicide watch, not because Libby considered him a suicide risk, but rather because he was a security risk. It meant a corrections officer would check on him at least every ten minutes and his cell would be searched every three days. As long as Robert was inside his walls, Libby wouldn't relax those rules.

Robert's restlessness didn't surprise Libby. He took it as part of the teen's growing disenchantment with the idea of an insanity defense. From the very beginning Libby had been puzzled by Robert's willingness to consider insanity at all. To Libby, insanity and Robert Tulloch didn't fit. Robert was calculating, stoic, and more self-possessed than most inmates. He was never on any medication in jail. Most of all, the insanity gambit didn't jibe with the teen's oversized ego. Robert claiming insanity cut against what Libby saw as "his arrogance and his wanting to be perceived as really smart."

In Libby's view, Robert realized "you can't be superior and crazy." Given the choice, Robert would choose superior.

Judge Smith watched Robert sit down after finishing the required Q&A. From the bench, the judge could look out over the prosecutors and see Veronika and Mariana Zantop, seated in the front row of the right side of the gallery. The sisters held hands, surrounded by a cocoon of friends and supporters.

The Tulloch family occupied seats in the front row of the opposite side of the gallery. Mike Tulloch was sitting farthest away, against the wall. He wore darkened glasses that made it impossible to see his eyes. His graying hair was swept back, looking almost unkempt. Diane sat next to him. Her gray-streaked hair hung straight to her shoulders. She wore a red-checkered woolen shirt and black slacks. Their older daughter, Becky Tulloch Johnson, was next, wearing a blue blazer. Kienan was there, too, slouching in his seat. His short brown hair was mussed and peach fuzz covered his chin. He had Robert's nose now and there was no mistaking the two were brothers. The family alternated between staring straight ahead and looking down at the floor. The Tullochs barely said a word to one another during the proceeding, and Robert rarely looked their way.

At 10:05 A.M. Kelly Ayotte made her way to the lectern from the table where she'd been sitting with Mike Delaney. Key state and local investigators were seated in a ring of chairs directly behind them in a show of force and solidarity. The prosecutor was dressed in a periwinkle-colored pantsuit, a black blouse, and black boots. She opened a black notebook, grasped the sides of the lectern, and began reading the state's offer of proof. "If this case had gone to trial," she said, "the state would

have called James Parker to the witness stand. And he would have testified to all the facts and circumstances leading up to and surrounding the
murder of Half and Susanne Zantop."

For the next thirty-seven minutes, Ayotte gave the most detailed
public account of the murders to date. Though her voice cracked at
times, Ayotte's performance was low-key, straightforward, and non-
theatrical. She let the content speak for itself, with Jim Parker as the
government's guide.

"They were bored," Ayotte said to start her story about Robert and
Jim—and that's exactly how Robert looked in court throughout her
narrative. He leaned back into his chair and glared sullenly at the prosecutor as she spoke. He showed little expression, but the smirk
returned when Ayotte told the court how the boys nurtured a fantasy
of running off to Australia to start new lives as "badasses."

The delivery of the facts took a dramatic turn when Ayotte reached
the day of the killings. "On January 27 they were driving to Hanover in
the Parkers' green Subaru," she said. "Jim Parker was driving." Her
voice dropped the better part of an octave and she moved away from
the lectern to mark the transition. She clasped her hands and
described how Robert and Jim first tried the house next door. "They
knocked on the door several times. But no one was home. No one to
let them in. So they left. And they immediately turned their sights to
the house owned by Half and Susanne Zantop." Hearing their parents'
names, Mariana lowered her head and cast her eyes downward, while
Veronika stared straight at Ayotte.

The prosecutor led everyone in the courtroom to the Zantops' front
door, with Half answering it and then making up his mind that he had
time for the two students. Robert and Jim, she said, planned to put
into play the same fake survey they'd tried the week before in
Rochester. "To use an environmental survey to gain access to the residence. To tie up the Zantops. To steal their credit cards, ATM numbers. To threaten the Zantops for their PIN numbers. And then, finally,
to kill them."

The prosecutor described how Robert discarded the plan when he
lunged at Half and started the massacre. "Half was screaming, scream-

ing terribly," Ayotte said. She stressed robbery as the motive for the killings, saying Robert attacked Half after he had pulled out and opened his wallet. She emphasized the cash for legal reasons; one of the charges against Robert was committing a murder "while engaged in the commission of, or while attempting to commit, robbery or burglary while armed with a deadly weapon, the death being caused by the use of such weapon." The government needed to establish robbery as a requisite element of the crime. But that overlooked a key chronological fact—Robert had already moved to take the knife out of Jim's backpack *before* Half reached for his wallet.

Veronika was crying the moment Kelly Ayotte began describing the bloodbath. She raised a tissue to wipe the tears. Mariana kept her head lowered. Robert, meanwhile, was unmoved. Occasionally he leaned over and whispered to Guerriero. He never spoke to Barbara Keshen. Blankly, he listened to the prosecutor finish telling about how investigators broke open the case, and how he and Jim fled and were captured.

Finally came the moment he was waiting for.

"Guilty," Robert said, his voice firm, when court clerk Robert Muh asked how he pleaded to the charge of first-degree murder in the death of Half Zantop.

"Guilty," he repeated when Muh asked about the first-degree murder of Susanne Zantop.

"Guilty," he said to the charge of conspiracy to commit murder.

Before the sentence could be pronounced, Robert had to hear the pain of two of the Zantops' close friends, Dartmouth professor Irene Kacandes and their summer getaway pal Jim Zien. He also had to hear their orphaned daughters.

Veronika and Mariana stood up at 10:48 A.M. and walked together to the lectern. Veronika, thirty, wore a blue blazer, dark skirt, and a white blouse open at the collar. She tucked her shoulder-length blond hair behind her ears. Veronika had her father's height and bearing.

Mariana, twenty-eight, stood by her side. She wore a dark pantsuit, a light-colored blouse, and had a short, simple haircut that resembled her mother's.

Mariana put her right arm around her sister's waist. Veronika held onto the lectern and began by turning to face the prosecutors and investigators. She thanked them for their "absolutely tireless and tenacious work." Her voice sounded fragile. "I can't tell you how important that was for both of us."

Then, for the first time, the sisters stood facing one of their parents' killers, separated by twenty feet and too many qualities to count. Veronika looked across at Robert and then down to read her remarks. "There is no statement in the entire world that can capture the absolute horror, disbelief, pain, sadness, and anger that my sister, my family, and friends have experienced since my parents were murdered."

Mariana lifted her right hand and began rubbing Veronika's back.

"My father's name was Half, which in German means 'to help.' According to family legend, at the time of my father's birth my grandfather, a religious man, closed his eyes, opened the Bible and let fate guide his index finger. From the page on which his finger landed came my father's name."

Veronika began to cry, but she kept going. "My father lived up to his name. . . . That their desire to help, to teach, and to open their home to perfect strangers was abused in such a horrific way makes their deaths seem like the greatest violation.

"Rather than focus on the inhumanity and monstrosity and the sheer stupidity of their brutal and senseless deaths, I've tried to console myself by trying to perpetuate the essence of my parents—two people with true open-heartedness and generosity, who fought for positive change. And my sister and I will continue that fight."

Veronika folded the piece of paper. "Thank you."

"Thank you," Judge Smith said, his voice barely audible.

The sisters returned to their seats where friends reached to touch and embrace them. Mariana wiped her eyes with a tissue. More than a few observers in the gallery, including some hard-bitten reporters, also dabbed tears from their eyes. The courtroom was silent except for the sound of deep sighs.

The only person who appeared unmoved and unimpressed was Robert. During the remarks, he looked straight at Veronika. Robert had looked sad-eyed in many of the photographs taken of him immediately after his arrest; now in court his eyes alternated between cold and empty.

At Judge Smith's command, Robert stood between his lawyers. Judge Smith asked him if he had anything to say, but Robert declined. He didn't dispute any of the facts outlined by prosecutors. He didn't address Veronika and Mariana. He didn't take one final look at his family or at anyone else. He looked straight ahead, waiting for the hearing to end. Court clerk Robert Muh obliged him by pronouncing the sentence Robert knew he'd receive: life in prison without the possibility of parole.

Flanked by two deputy sheriffs, he turned and shuffled out of the courtroom. Just like that, Robert Tulloch was gone.

Kelly Ayotte said afterward that throughout her presentation she was fully aware of Robert's eyes upon her. It didn't unnerve her, because she was so focused on the task at hand. Besides, she said, "I've prosecuted some really awful killers." But, she said, she would always remember the contempt she saw in Robert's eyes.

The morning hearing over, the courtroom emptied in silence. Outside, the Tullochs piled into the two cars parked in a rear lot and drove off. Like Robert, they made no comment. DeRoss Kellogg hung back at the courthouse's front entrance. The teacher had become the self-appointed standard bearer of what he termed Robert's "soft side." "Robert wants it to be known that it is untrue that he had no remorse," he said. Reporters, hungry for quotes and comments, surrounded him, some thrusting microphones at him and the rest jotting notes. Kellogg wanted to dispute what the reporters had just witnessed. The longtime teacher insisted that Robert had "a moral center." Robert, he said, accepted his guilt and was truly sorry for what happened inside the Zantops' study.

Few believed him. Robert's final act to plead guilty, one close Tulloch supporter said later, didn't involve a moral epiphany. "Robert still doesn't get it," the insider said. "He will say 'Killing is wrong,' but mainly he'll say it's wrong because everyone else says it's wrong." It was Robert the psychopath. The most Robert would acknowledge, the insider said, was that he "messed up—his family, and Jim." But over-all, Robert acted as if he'd been caught for marijuana possession, not cold-blooded murder.

"He's scary. Fascinating the way a car accident is fascinating."

While Robert was in court, Jim was waiting his turn in, of all places, Robert's old haunt, the Grafton County Jail. He'd been driven up first thing in the morning from the Belknap County Jail. His last day in Belknap County began like any other. He woke up around six o'clock to a breakfast of hard-boiled eggs, juice, toast, and Cheerios. The differ-ence on this day was that his cell was already cleaned out; his parents had taken his personal belongings during a visit a few days earlier.

The Belknap corrections officer who had seen Jim most mornings for almost a year found him quieter than usual. Jan Hale was used to inmates saying "bye," or "see you around" when they were led away. But Jim left without any parting words for his jailers. He was escorted to the booking area where he peeled out of his orange jumpsuit and put on the blue jeans, white T-shirt, and dark polo shirt his parents had left for him. His hair was freshly cut, but unlike Robert's rough cell-block look, Jim's had been trimmed neatly by a barber who came monthly to the Belknap jail. Two deputy sheriffs were there to take him away. Jim recognized them. They were the same two deputies who in December and January had escorted him from the jail to the con-fessional sessions with prosecutors.

Once inside the Grafton County Jail, Jim waited out the morning in the same cell that Robert had occupied before being transported to the courthouse. Jim would have had no way of knowing this, unless he possessed a sixth sense for Robert's presence. But Jim couldn't help but notice that the overall conditions at the jail where Robert had been held were far more severe than he had endured.

Though Jim's afternoon hearing took place in the same courtroom, before the same judge, with the same prosecutors, and many of the same gallery members, that was where the similarities ended. So much had changed between Robert and Jim. Jim was no longer within the black hole of Robert's gravitational pull. Finally, too late for the Zantops, Jim had let go of the psychic rope that had bonded him to Robert.

Jim was brought into the courtroom at 2:08 P.M., long after Robert had been taken away. His hands and feet were shackled. The tail of his polo shirt was untucked in back. His face was pallid. The courtroom was filled to capacity, just as in the morning. Veronika and Mariana sat with their friends in the same seats as before. The seats that had held the Tulloch family were now filled by John and Joan Parker, along with their friends Kevin Ellis and Bob Sherman. Joan was dressed for mourning, wearing a long, black skirt and a black sweater. At the sight of their son entering the courtroom, John snaked his arm through Joan's and grasped her hand.

Jim, shuffling toward the defense table, scanned the room until he found his parents. They made eye contact, and Jim bit his lip. Cathy Green, one of Jim's attorneys, helped Jim get settled into the same chair at the defense table where Robert had sat.

Prosecutor Kelly Ayotte stood to address the court. Because Jim had pleaded guilty in December, she didn't have to go through the offer of proof she'd delivered in the morning. Instead Ayotte summarized for the judge the plea bargain. John Parker kept his eyes on Ayotte while she spoke. Joan Parker's eyes were fixed on her son. Ayotte told Judge Smith that Jim fully honored his part of the agreement, giving "great information in this case."

Jim flinched when Ayotte mentioned the agreed-upon prison

sentence—twenty-five years to life—but other than that, he listened without expression as the prosecutor spoke. That changed when Veronika and Mariana approached the lectern and Veronika began to read to Jim the same statement, word for word, she'd delivered to Robert.

At that moment, the courtroom saw what a difference a boy makes. As the words reached him, Jim began rocking in his chair. He bit his lip. The first tear rolled down his cheek as Veronika explained the meaning of her father's name in German. Cathy Green noticed Jim's tears and handed him a tissue. Jim couldn't raise his shackled hands, so he lowered his face to wipe his cheeks. He sat up and began taking gulps of air, trying to fight back more tears. He raised his left shoulder and wiped his eyes on his shirt.

When Veronika finished, Jim bent forward again to use the tissue. His mother's head was bowed.

Then it was Jim Zien's turn. "This terrible wrong that you have done can in no way be redeemed by the right you also have done in making this plea. But I want you to know you have done a right, which is to save the Zantop family and friends a great deal more pain." Jim leaned way back in his chair, his Adam's apple bobbing.

"Our hearts are broken," Zien said.

Irene Kacandes strode to the lectern, looking right at Jim. "This is about two beautiful human beings who showered love and affection on each other, their families, and on the people they came into contact with. This is about two people who loved to take walks, teach their classes, write books, go to the movies, have barbecues with their friends, talk to their daughters on the telephone, and help everyone they met—including you! This is about Half and Susanne Zantop, who loved life."

Her voice shattered. "They loved life."

Jim let out a quick burst of air, as though he'd been punched in the gut.

She continued. Half and Susanne's family and friends "think about them, miss them, and cry for them every single day."

Jim once again leaned to wipe tears on his shirt. When Kacandes was finished, Cathy Green stood. "Your Honor, with the court's permission, Jim Parker would like to make a statement."

Jim rocked forward and tried to stand up. But he couldn't. He needed to compose himself. He closed his eyes and took a deep breath. He leaned forward again and this time managed to stand. In front of him on the table was a piece of paper with a statement he'd written out beforehand. Jim ignored it. He rocked on his feet. He took another deep breath.

Forty-seven seconds passed before he could get any words out, a pause that was filled with rocking and deep breathing. It felt more like forty-seven minutes. Jim looked across the courtroom at Veronika and Mariana. "I'm sorry," he said finally. He took another deep breath. "There's not much more I can say than that."

Jim's mouth contorted into the shape made by a baby who is about to cry. Joan raised a hand ever so slightly, as if to reach for him, and then she began to weep. John Parker reached over and held her. Robert Muh, the clerk, talking over the sobs, announced the prison term. He asked Jim, "Do you understand your sentence?"

"Yes," Jim said.

Jim was led away. Before he was gone, he stopped in the doorway and turned his body fully to face his parents. He took one long, last look.

The Parker family and friends left the courtroom first. Veronika and Mariana hung back and were greeted warmly by Ayotte, Mike Delaney, Phil McLaughlin, and other investigators. "Thank you very much," Veronika told Ayotte. Mariana hugged the prosecutor.

Outside, television and radio reporters scrambled to go live with reports about the day's events. Print reporters used pay phones or, if they could catch a signal, cell phones to call their editors. Then they rushed around trying to mop up posthearing comments.

Everyone was talking about the sharply contrasting portraits of Robert and Jim on display. News accounts all stressed the difference.

"Tulloch, reversing his initial plea of insanity, was steely," wrote the *Los Angeles Times*. "Parker shuddered with sobs."

"Parker wept during his hearing," wrote the *Boston Globe*. "Tulloch, presenting the image of an iron-clad killer, locked eyes with the sisters." The newspaper juxtaposed photos of the boys on its front page, having captured Robert smirking and Jim looking forlorn.

"Tulloch appeared stone-faced and unremorseful," wrote *The Dartmouth*. "Parker, by contrast, was barely able to hold back his tears." Dartmouth's student newspaper had no fewer than six reporters working the conclusion of the murder case that had terrorized the college community for months. Yet around Hanover, it seemed almost anticlimactic.

"I don't take any comfort or relief from this. I'm just glad it's behind us," said Dartmouth President James Wright. "I want to think about their lives, what they did, what they meant to this community. That is the more positive, inspiring thing to do."

Chelseans by and large were also trying to move on, even if many remained haunted that two of their own turned out to be killers. "They in no way projected as monstrous children," Principal Pat Davenport said. But it wasn't as if the town had found peace of mind. Davenport felt a chill when she walked into the school library the day after the hearings and saw the *Burlington Free Press*. Someone had drawn targets on the foreheads of Robert and Jim in the front-page photographs of the boys.

Following Jim's sentencing, the various players in the fifteen-month-long drama began peeling off. The Tullochs were the first to leave. Public defenders Richard Guerriero and Barbara Keshen didn't stick around, either. Their expert psychiatrist never got to take the stand for Robert, but in a matter of weeks Dorothy Otnow Lewis would be testifying in a murder case in Chicago for a serial killer named Andrew Urdiales. She found him to be a paranoid schizophrenic and legally insane when he killed two young women. He was convicted anyway and sentenced to death.

Before Veronika and Mariana drove away with their friends,

Veronika gave investigators a half-smile. Several waved back.

Soon the prosecutors and investigators lined up for a press confer-ence staged on the embankment along the courthouse's rear entrance. "Justice has been served in this case," Ayotte said, standing before a dozen or so microphones as the television cameras rolled. Behind her stood nearly twenty officials who'd worked on the case, including her boss, Phil McLaughlin, and her co-prosecutor, Mike Delaney, as well as investigators Chuck West, Frank Moran, and Bob Bruno. Hanover Police Chief Nick Giaccone was there, as was Major Barry Hunter of the New Hampshire State Police along with Sergeant Jim White and troopers Russ Hubbard and Kathy Kimball. Vermont State Police Detective Sergeant Ray Keefe had come, too. "These are the true heroes," Ayotte said.

The Tullochs were gone, but John and Joan Parker made their way to the microphones. They held hands. Their faces were clenched. John spoke first. "Joan and I, we'd like to say to Half and Susanne Zantop's family and friends, Veronika and Mariana and everybody, we're very, very sorry." His voice was plaintive, the words spoken to a chorus of clicking sounds made by the motor drives on news photographers' cameras.

Then it was Joan's turn. She was tearful, her voice shaky. "We hope that in time those hurt by these acts will be able to find peace in their hearts, and forgiveness."

The couple wouldn't take any questions. They turned and walked down to the driveway to their car. Minutes later they cruised past the gaggle of reporters, headed home to Chelsea. The Parkers were in the family's green Subaru. The same green Subaru Jim and Robert had driven the day they killed the Zantops. The car with bloodstains on the floor mat in front. The car was cleaned and the case was officially over, but the bloodstains would never go away. They would haunt the Parkers, the Tullochs, the Zantops, and two small New England com-munities to the end of their days.

Epilogue

In September 2002, more than two years after Robert Tulloch and Jim Parker came to Andrew and Diane Patti's vacation home bent on murder, another unexpected visitor arrived at the house on Goose Green Road. This time the Pattis let him in.

John Parker made the five-mile drive from his Chelsea home in his wife's green Subaru. He parked the car in the driveway, unfurled his long frame, and made his way toward the front porch. He strode silently past the bush where his son had hidden while Robert tried to worm his way into the house with his story about a broken-down car.

The Pattis first met John Parker when he installed a storm door and did other work on their house in the weeks after that strange incident in July 2000. After Jim's arrest, Diane wrote John a letter to say her thoughts and prayers were with him and his wife. John had stopped by not long after that, in the summer of 2001, to thank her.

"How's your son doing?" Diane asked then.

"As good as a child could in that situation," he told her.

But that was before the Pattis learned how close Andrew and Andy had come to being killed. Although Andrew Patti recognized Robert's photograph in the paper as the face he saw through the window, only much later did the Pattis learn the full details—the graves dug nearby, the hunting knife in Robert's boot, Jim waiting to pounce.

The Pattis had never met Joan Parker, and they wouldn't have known what to say to her if they were introduced. But they knew and liked John Parker—they considered him a friendly neighbor and their local contractor, and it bothered them that he hadn't sought them out since the complete facts about that night became public.

Now, five months after his son was sentenced to twenty-five years in prison, John was standing at their front door. Diane greeted him warmly and invited him inside. She saw the pain etched on his face. Andrew came down from upstairs and sent Andy outside. John Parker settled into a wing chair in the living room, Andrew took a chair opposite him, and Diane sat on the couch, the same couch where Andrew and Andy had been reading a story the night Robert came knocking.

John explained that he had driven past the Pattis' house several times, intending to stop, but only now had he worked up the nerve.

"I'm here today asking you to accept my apology for what happened to you that night," John said.

"Absolutely," Andrew Patti said. "Accepted."

"We don't hold you responsible for that," Diane said.

"I hope someday my son might be able to come here and do what I'm doing," John added.

The Pattis said nothing. It was too far in the future to think about.

In Hanover, classes continued, snow turned to mud, and Dartmouth kept churning out Ivy League graduates. The murders were no longer daily news in *The Dartmouth*, but the paper maintained a "Zantop Tragedy Archive." Half and Susanne's lives remained woven into the fabric of the College on a Hill.

Their unfinished works were completed by friends and colleagues, scholarship funds were raised in their names, gifts were donated in their memories, journals were dedicated to them, and academic conferences were held in their honor. More than two years after her death, Susanne's name remained on the computerized German department faculty list, though clicking on the link led not to a list of classes she'd be teaching but to information about the murders.

Perhaps most appropriate of all, a yellowwood tree was planted as a memorial to the Zantops behind Dartmouth Hall. The tree was placed close to a cluster of residence halls, so there would always be students around, just as Susanne and Half would have wanted.

"I think something like this is not put behind easily or ever. It will endure," said Dartmouth President James Wright. "We've all come to recognize there are some pretty awful things that can happen in places where one least expects it. It demonstrates that no place is as isolated from evil as it thinks it is."

For a while, the Zantops' daughters considered razing the house on Trescott Road. But they abandoned that plan and instead sold it to a young family. Not long after, a swing set appeared in the yard and the house came back to life.

In the wider world, the Zantops' deaths became enmeshed in debates about "youth violence." That use-worn phrase was often enhanced by the word "epidemic" to suggest that a virulent form of mayhem was being passed hand to hand or mouth to mouth by previously docile American teens. Some commentators cited the Zantop killings and the Columbine High School massacre in the same breath to suggest that murderous impulses were spreading unchecked from inner cities to restful suburbs and rural retreats. One writer, citing the Zantop murders as Exhibit A, sounded the warning that "an apocalyptic nihilism is taking root in this nation's children."

To be sure, American youths commit a disturbing number of violent crimes compared to their peers in other industrialized countries—there were 1,400 arrests of people under age eighteen for homicide in

1999, the year of Columbine. However, frequently overlooked was the fact that homicides and other violent crimes by teenagers fell sharply for nearly a decade before the Zantop murders; FBI statistics show a 74 percent drop in homicides by youths between 1993 and 2000. Citing those statistics, Jason Ziedenberg of the Justice Policy Institute in Washington sought to muffle the alarm: "In Vermont, New Hampshire, and Maine, an average of six juveniles were arrested every year for murder in the 1970s, five in the 1980s, four in the 1990s, and two in 2000. In 2000, Vermont's 37,000 youths aged fourteen to seventeen accounted for just one homicide and thirty-three violent crimes in the entire state. The inference that random crimes, occurring over half a decade, are somehow evidence of an apocalypse is about as valid as the claim that Timothy McVeigh and Charles Manson are indicative of their adult generations' predisposition to murder."

Meanwhile, in June 2002, the chief justice of the U.S. Supreme Court cited the Zantop murders in an opinion about unchecked freedoms for door-to-door canvassers. Justice William H. Rehnquist used Robert and Jim's environmental survey ruse as an example of the grave dangers he envisioned from allowing everyone from Fuller Brush salesmen to Jehovah's Witnesses to continue pounding the sidewalks without government oversight. The Zantop case, he wrote, "is but one tragic example of the crime threat posed by door-to-door canvassing. . . . If Hanover had a permit requirement, the teens may have been stopped before they achieved their objective." Rehnquist was outvoted 8–1, and doorbell-ringers carried the day.

Beyond the disputes about legal issues and teen crime trends, there was near-unanimous agreement that violence by teenagers remained poorly understood and demanded serious attention. Police, school officials, parent groups, criminologists, psychiatrists, and psychologists raced to develop methods to change behavior patterns, reduce impulsivity and aggression, and teach young predators strategies to slake their thirsts in less destructive ways.

The search for answers also involved brain scientists. The week after Robert pleaded guilty to murder, neuropsychiatrist Bruce Price was advocating the need for brain research to help solve the mysteries of teen violence. "Whether it's Robert Tulloch or other killers, they don't wear a 'C' on their forehead announcing they are criminals; instead, for the most part, they walk around looking like you or I," he warned at a seminar at the Boston University School of Medicine.

Price, chief of neurology at Harvard-affiliated McLean Hospital in Belmont, Massachusetts, admits to a fascination with crime and violence stemming from personal experience. He grew up in Kansas; his family was acquainted with the Clutters, the family whose murders were recounted in *In Cold Blood*. "What trips the switch in someone like Robert Tulloch?" Price wondered. "Between being a seventeen-year-old kid acting out and a kid who goes out and kills? . . . His brain is not processing like most people's. Where is the empathy? The remorse? Something is drastically wrong."

Price dreams of studying Robert in life and then dissecting his brain after death to explore the "neuroanatomic, neurochemical, and genetic determinants" of Robert's violent behavior. The study would include MRI scans of Robert's brain and tests to measure empathy, such as showing Robert beautiful images alternated with horrible ones, perhaps even photos of the Zantop murder scene, and gauging his emotional responses, if any, a technique reminiscent of a scene in the movie *A Clockwork Orange*.

In Price's view, the potential payoff is huge—nothing short of preventing future murders. "If we can identify potential markers for violence when kids are still young, we may be able to guide them down a different path," he said. Robert, then, represents a research prize in brain science. To Price, "it's an absolutely wasted opportunity if we can't study this boy."

When the Zantop case ended with guilty pleas, the prosecutors and investigators moved on to other cases and, in some cases, other jobs.

In January 2003, Attorney General Phil McLaughlin left his post after more than five years as New Hampshire's top prosecutor. A new Republican governor took office and McLaughlin, a Democrat, wasn't his choice for the appointed position. McLaughlin returned to private practice, joining a law firm run by his wife.

The new governor did, however, dip into McLaughlin's office to choose his chief legal counsel: Kelly Ayotte. She left her job as New Hampshire's chief homicide prosecutor undefeated. The third member of the AG's Zantop team, Michael Delaney, remained in the trenches, taking over from Ayotte as chief of the homicide unit.

In October 2002, Chuck West was promoted from trooper first class to sergeant. With the promotion came a reassignment to the Major Crime Unit, the elite investigative team that handles all New Hampshire homicides. He liked the work, but he wasn't thrilled about the commute to the unit's Concord office from his home in the North Country. While waiting for the inevitable call about the next killing, West spent his days pursuing cold cases of unsolved murders. Also promoted was West's knife-hunting partner, Frank Moran of the Hanover Police Department, who rose from detective lieutenant to captain, which made him the second-ranking member of the force, after Chief Nick Giaccone.

"Every time I get stressed out on my job now, I reflect back on the Zantop thing," Moran said two years after the murders. "I have not felt the level of importance or obligation anywhere near that. That case is a source of strength when I start to get frazzled about paperwork or the lack of leads in a case. It's a reality check."

Moran, West, and three other members of the Zantop investigative team—New Hampshire State Police Sergeants Bob Bruno and Mark Mudgett, and Trooper First Class Russ Hubbard—were honored for their work with the Congressional Law Enforcement Award for Dedication and Professionalism.

Special honors also went to the Massachusetts state trooper who spotted Jim Parker's abandoned Audi in the parking lot of the Sturbridge Isles truck stop. Two weeks after Robert pleaded guilty, Trooper Walter Combs received the Meritorious Achievement Award from the International Association of Chiefs of Police Highway Safety

Committee. Meanwhile, Sergeant Bill Ward of Indiana, whose CB radio imitation of a trucker led to the capture of Robert and Jim, received the "Radio Hero Award" from a group called REACT International, a CB radio safety organization. Ward still eats regularly at the Flying J truck stop.

In Chelsea, the day-to-day obsession about the case evolved into something more subtle—the occasional, unpredictable pain of two missing limbs. "It's no longer right there on the edge, where we think about it all the time," David Savidge said. Time does that. Even so, no one expected to forget that two of their boys were brutal killers. "The shock, that will always be there. It's still something so hard for us to believe."

School principal Pat Davenport left Chelsea at the end of the 2002 academic year and became principal of the Woodstock Elementary School. The new Chelsea principal and a revamped school board confronted a budget deficit that was bigger than most Chelseans had realized.

But there was some good new in the fall of 2002. The town won a $90,000 federal grant to develop after-school programs. School officials also raised the number of graduation requirements. Both moves addressed the growing recognition that Chelsea teenagers had too much free time. Block scheduling remained in place.

Dr. Andy Pomerantz, overwhelmed by his on-the-fly attempts to help his traumatized community, ended up putting his experience to a new professional use: He became a consultant to the Vermont Agency of Human Services' trauma policy group. Whenever Pomerantz was able—weather permitting—he found solace and serenity by biking or cross-country skiing in the woods and hills around Chelsea.

Diane Tulloch continued to work as a visiting nurse. A new sign appeared on the front porch of the Tulloch home on Main Street. It read: MICHAEL TULLOCH. MASTER CRAFTSMAN. Yet Mike Tulloch remained as reclusive as ever. Chelseans saw him driving about in his red pickup, and from inside the cab he'd give what one Chelsean called the "finger wave," but that was about it. No stopping or idle chatter for him.

John Parker remained Mike Tulloch's opposite. He didn't skip a beat in his involvement in town affairs—on the recreation committee, playing basketball, and regularly attending the school's athletic events. The same wasn't true for Joan, who became as withdrawn as the Tullochs. On Christmas Eve 2002, a group of friends gathered for a low-key party. John Parker came, but Joan did not. No one asked why; no one needed to.

Christiana Usenza continued working at the health food co-op, while Zack Courts and Casey Purcell headed south to colleges in Boston. Coltere Savidge, after spending his first year after high school working, in the fall of 2002 went off to the College of the Atlantic in Maine. Kip Battey headed west to attend Ohio Wesleyan, but then took off in the spring of 2002 to do some travel. His itinerary included a trip to Australia, of all places. By the fall of 2002 he was back in school.

After Robert's sentencing, members of The Crew had little, if any, contact with him. But Coltere and Zack stayed in touch with Jim, exchanging letters and visiting him in prison. During one visit, Jim asked Coltere what he thought about him being in prison and about what he'd done. Coltere told his longtime friend: If I didn't know you, I'd feel you should spend the rest of your life in prison. But because I do know you I'm glad you'll have the opportunity to get out someday.

They agreed to stay in touch.

Jim quickly acclimated to the New Hampshire State Prison in Concord, home to some 1,350 inmates. In a cold drizzle one late-fall day, Jim could be seen outdoors in a horseshoe pit, working methodically through a series of yoga poses. Alone, dressed in sneakers, green pants, a light hooded sweatshirt, and a blue woolen cap, he slowly extended his arms and legs to move into the Warrior Two position.

"His Jane Fonda workout," said one inmate, watching from across the yard.

Prison officials considered Jim well-behaved and even-keeled. Upon his arrival, he was listed as C-3, a medium-security classification that placed him in the general population. With that came freedom to move about the facility, mingle with other inmates, and attend regular classes and activities.

Jim was assigned to a unit called Medium Custody South. Other than the high walls and concertina wire that surrounded it, the concrete prison block resembled a three-story motel with rows of doors that opened onto balconies. The balconies overlooked a grassy courtyard, picnic tables, a basketball court, two handball courts, and a small flower garden tended by inmates.

Each outside door opened into a twenty-by-twenty-foot day room, or common room, off of which there were ten cells—home to up to twenty inmates. Jim lived on the second level, in a group of cells known as 2C, where the day room was decorated with posters made from completed puzzles of kittens and dolphins.

Taped to Jim's cell door—cell number 3222—was a color picture of the U.S. flag above the words "God Bless America." His guitar hung just inside the cell door. Jim slept on the top bunk, and on a shelf within arm's reach were books on art and music, including *Jazz and Popular Guitar* and *Gray's Anatomy*, which he used for drawing human figures. Other books in his cell were *Power Yoga* and college-level texts, including *Understanding Nutrition* and *The Western Humanities*. Also on Jim's reading list was *Man's Eternal Quest*, a book about meditation, healing, and life after death.

A calendar Jim taped to the cinder-block wall noted his regular activities—guitar lessons on Monday; drama on Tuesday; piano on Thursday; t'ai chi every Friday. Attached to the calendar was his "list of things to remember." It included: "Letters . . . Mom; art paper; Zack; 10:30 see Lt. Hogan . . . Put Di on visit list asap."

Jim wasn't unfriendly behind bars, but neither was he eager to form close bonds. He drew, completed homework for his classes, watched some TV, occasionally played cards, and did his yoga. Other inmates called him quiet, even shy. "He's doing his own time," said Joel Ranstrom, an inmate on Jim's pod. The phrase was admiring prison slang for someone who didn't cause problems for himself or others.

W hile Jim seemed intent on calmly marking the nine thousand or so days of his sentence, Robert went looking for trouble almost from the start.

After a brief period of processing at the Concord prison, he was transferred to New Hampshire's other prison, a smaller facility in Berlin. The idea was to keep Robert and Jim apart—prison officials said they would never spend time together no matter how many years they remained behind bars.

At Berlin, Robert quickly developed a reputation that one corrections official described as "uncooperative"—a euphemism for a potentially dangerous inmate. Robert was often in trouble with corrections officers and alienated fellow inmates by displaying "an attitude that he's better than everyone," the official said. Less than two months after he arrived in Berlin, Robert was attacked by another inmate.

"It's letting him know he's just a punk, a coward," his assailant, Thomas E. Dougherty, told a reporter. Dougherty started the fight in the recreation yard by pushing Robert and ordering him to leave the workout area. Robert walked across the basketball court and glared back at him, Dougherty said, so he ran up to Robert and punched him in the face. The two fell to the ground and began swinging at one another.

"I'm from the old school," said Dougherty, a convicted drug dealer. "Rapists, child molesters, people who kill women, rats, would not be allowed to live and walk freely about the general population [before]." Both he and Robert were treated for cuts and bruises, although Robert came out worse—two black eyes.

Robert's stay in Berlin ended soon after. Prison officials caught wind he was thinking about an escape—they intercepted a letter he'd written to a friend asking for help. Berlin is purely a medium-security facility, and the letter meant Robert was destined for maximum security. By September 2002 Robert was returned to Concord and assigned to New Hampshire's most tightly controlled prison setting.

Grim isolation defined inmate life in the so-called Secured Housing Unit. Even the corrections officers seemed tougher than those assigned to other areas of the prison, partly because they dressed in militaristic uniforms and were never more than a few feet from a wall lined with black riot helmets and Kevlar vests.

Robert spent at least twenty-two hours a day locked inside his eight-by-ten-foot cell, an enclosed box with a concrete floor, a single metal-framed bed, fluorescent lights, and an open stainless-steel toilet. During the brief periods outside his cell, Robert faced limited choices of activities and no contact with fellow inmates. He could take a shower. He could sit alone in one of the indoor day rooms on the cellblock. He could go outside for some fresh air in one of several narrow, high-walled courtyards the officers called "dog runs."

Robert was scheduled to remain in the Secured Housing Unit until he was deemed duly punished and fit to return to medium security. Because he was serving life without parole, and had already gotten into a fight and plotted an escape, corrections officials seemed in no rush to make that ruling.

While Jim could look out of his day room and see over the top of the prison walls to the tree-covered mountain range beyond, Robert's narrow window offered a view of only another wall.

The day Jim was striking the Warrior Two pose in the horseshoe pit, the two Zantop killers were as close as they had been in almost two years, since their capture in Indiana. Robert was less than a hundred yards away from Jim, inside his cell on the H tier of the max unit. But Robert and Jim were separated, as they would be forever, by several high walls and coils of barbed wire. Neither knew how close he was to the other.

One of them might as well have made it to Australia.

Notes on Sources

Chapter 1

Multiple interviews with Andrew, Diane, and Andy Patti.

Transcript of James Parker interrogation; December 18, 2001; January 4 and 14, 2002; March 7, 2002; pp. 14764–14768.

Transcripts of interviews with Andrew Patti and Andrew Patti Jr. by Sergeant Ray Keefe, Lieutenant Frank Moran, and Trooper Russell Lamson, on February 16, 2002.

Chapter 2

Interviews in Chelsea, Vermont, with Jack Johnson, Annette Johnson, Doug Lyford, Andrew Pomerantz, Cora Brooks, David Savidge, and Diane Mattoon.

Transcript of James Parker interrogations, p. 14880.

"Chelsea Municipal Plan: December 1996." Chelsea Planning Board.

A History of Chelsea, Vermont 1784–1984, by W. Sydney Gilman and a committee from the Chelsea Historical Society, pp. 126–127; 152–153; 198–203; 225–270; 277–278; 306–307.

Bertsche, Robert A. "Our Town," *New England Monthly,* April 1985, pp. 41–49.

Lehr, Dick, "It Shouldn't Happen Here," *The Boston Globe Magazine,* July 29, 2001, pp. 10–13; 20–26.

Miller, Peter. "Chelsea, Vermont," *Vermont Life,* Autumn 1972, pp. 14–22.

Chapter 3

Interviews with Jim Reynolds, Haidee Wilson, Alex Bertulis, Wolf Zantop, Marianne Korsukewitz, Thomas Korsukewitz, Jeannine Blackwell, Patricia Herminghouse, Helen Mango, Werner Gocht, Bruce Duncan, Fred Berthold, Irene Kacandes, Richard Birnie, Ned Whittington, Debbie Ludlow, Catie Huisman, Kristina Kleutghen, Julia Henneberry, Erik Wright, Saleeda Salahuddin, James Wright, Margaret Robinson, Susannah Heschel, Fred Berthold, Audrey McCollum.

Remembrances of Sujee Fonseka, Joan Blumberg, Roxana Verona, Eric Manheimer, at the Service of Remembrance and Thanksgiving Celebrating the Lives of Half Zantop and Susanne Zantop, February 3, 2001, Rollins Chapel, Dartmouth College. (Recorded on video.)

Estate documents of Susanne Zantop, Docket no. 2001–0066, Grafton County Probate Court, filed April 19, 2001.

Obituaries of Half and Susanne Zantop, from Dartmouth College, provided by Rand-Wilson Funeral Home.

Curriculum vitae of Susanne and Half Zantop.

Blackwell, Jeannine, and Susanne Zantop, eds. *Bitter Healing: German Women Writers, from 1700 to 1830, An Anthology* (Lincoln, Nebraska: University of Nebraska Press, 1990).

Zantop, Susanne, *Colonial Fantasies: Conquest, Family, and Nation in Precolonial Germany, 1770–1870* (Durham and London: Duke University Press, 1997).

Hanover, New Hampshire, property records of 115 Trescott Road.

Online Berlin apartment rental information.

Copies of notes taken from Half Zantop's last class.

The American Alpine Journal, Volume XIV, Issues No. 38 and 39, p. 174.

The American Alpine Journal, Volume XV, Issues No. 40 and 41, pp. 126–127.

Sambasivan, Aarathi, "Susanne, My Mentor," guest column in *The Dartmouth,* February 1, 2001.

Reynolds, Jim, "The First Day in Hanover," guest column in *The Dartmouth,* January 30, 2001.

Fair, Alan, "Susanne and Half," guest column in *The Dartmouth,* February 6, 2001.

Kay, Melanie, "Remembering Half," guest column in *The Dartmouth,* February 22, 2001.

McCollum, Audrey, "Uncommon Neighbors," guest column in *The Dartmouth.* July 31, 2001.

Zien, Jim, "Uncommonly Human," guest column in *The Dartmouth,* February 2, 2001.

Hirsch, Marianne, and Leo Spitzer, "Remembering Our Friends," guest column in *The Dartmouth,* January 31, 2001.

Chapter 4

Transcript of James Parker interrogation, pp. 14763, 14767, 14769, 14771, 14774–14777, 14856–14859, 14994.

Selected school and other writings by Robert Tulloch and Jim Parker: 1999, 2000, and 2001.

Hanover, New Hampshire, and Vermont State Police report of police interview on February 6, 2002, with Franklin D. Sanders of North Hollow Road, Rochester, Vermont.

Brief telephone interview on July 8, 2002, with Franklin D. Sanders.

Brief telephone interview with Rochester, Vermont, town clerk's office on July 9, 2002.

New Hampshire State Police report of a police interview with Gaelen McKee and Mark McKee on February 18, 2001, in Chelsea, Vermont.

Transcript of June 29, 2001, interview of confidential informant "Ranger" by Sergeant Mark Mudgett and Trooper Todd Landry.

New Hampshire State Police report, dated February 14, 2002, of crime scene tour conducted on February 5, 2002, during which Jim Parker showed investigators sites in Vermont and New Hampshire for various crimes Parker and Robert Tulloch committed.

Vermont State Police Sergeant Jocelyn Stohl's incident report of an encounter with James Parker and Robert Tulloch in Rochester, Vermont, on January 19, 2001. Also, interview with Jocelyn Stohl on July 12, 2002.

Interview with Vermont State Police Detective Sergeant Ray Keefe, July 12, 2002.

Chapter 5

Interviews with Audrey McCollum, Margaret Robinson, Susannah Heschel, Fred Berthold, Jeannine Blackwell, Patricia Herminghouse, Bruce Duncan, Irene Kacandes, Richard Birnie, Ned Whittington, Debbie Ludlow, Catie Huisman, Julia Henneberry, Erik Wright, Saleeda Salahuddin, James Wright.

Remembrances of Sujee Fonseka, Joan Blumberg, Roxana Verona, Eric Manheimer, at the Service of Remembrance and Thanksgiving Celebrating the Lives of Half Zantop and Susanne Zantop, February 3, 2001, Rollins Chapel, Dartmouth College. (Recorded on video.)

Estate documents of Susanne Zantop, Docket no. 2001–0066, Grafton County Probate Court, filed April 19, 2001.

Obituaries of Half and Susanne Zantop, from Dartmouth College, provided by Rand-Wilson Funeral Home.

Hanover property records of 115 Trescott Road

Copies of notes taken from Half's last class.

Hanover Police Department dispatch log from January 27, 2001.

Transcript of James Parker interrogation, pp. 14786–14787.

Transcript of police interview with Eric Manheimer, February 1, 2001.

Sambasivan, Aarathi, "Susanne, My Mentor," guest column in *The Dartmouth*, February 1, 2001.

Fair, Alan, "Susanne and Half," guest column in *The Dartmouth*, February 6, 2001.

McCollum, Audrey, "Uncommon Neighbors," guest column in *The Dartmouth*. July 31, 2001.

Zien, Jim, "Uncommonly Human," guest column in *The Dartmouth*, February 2, 2001.

Hirsch, Marianne, and Leo Spitzer, "Remembering Our Friends," guest column in *The Dartmouth*, January 31, 2001.

Chapter 6

New Hampshire State Police interview with Roxana Verona, January 27, 2001, with follow-up interview January 30, 2001.

Detailed narrative description and sketches of crime scene prepared by Trooper First Class Kathleen M. Kimball and Trooper Michael T. Kegelman, dated April 10–11, 2001.

Police interview with Dr. Robert McCollum, Audrey McCollum, Cynthia McCollum, and John Spellman, January 27, 2001. Also with Audrey McCollum on January 30, 2001, and Robert McCollum on February 5, 2001.

McCollum, Audrey, "A Neighbor Wonders About Her Role as a Media Source: 'Had My Attempt to Honor Dear Friends Actually Caused Harm?'" *Nieman Reports*, September 22, 2001.

Martinez, Jose, "Mystery Leaves Locals Frustrated," *Boston Herald*, February 4, 2001, p. 1.

Interview with Omer Ismail, May 16, 2002.

Multiple interviews with Philip McLaughlin, Kelly Ayotte, and Michael Delaney.

Bubriski, Mark, "Two Profs Dead; Police Investigating Possible Double Murder." Story posted on *The Dartmouth* Web site, 11:15 P.M., January 27, 2001.

Scholer, J. Lawrence, "Dartmouth Mourns Professors," *The Dartmouth Review*, January 29, 2001.

Nitka, Abigail, "Dartmouth Reporters Lead the Way," *Rutland Herald,* February 1, 2001.

Quint, Wilder D., *The Story of Dartmouth* (Boston: Little Brown and Co., 1914).

Nelson, Daniel M., "Knowing Our Place," essay contained in *Miraculously Builded in Our Hearts: A Dartmouth Reader,* Edward Connery Lathem and David M. Shribman, eds. (Hanover, New Hampshire: University Press of New England, 1999), pp. 399–403.

Kreiger, Barbara L., "The Alma Mater," essay contained in *Miraculously Builded in Our Hearts,* pp. 355–362.

Cameron, Kelly, and Tara Kyle, "Students Horrified by Weekend's Events," *The Dartmouth,* January 29, 2001.

Ford, Royal, "New Hampshire Man Charged in Ax Murders of 2 Women," *Boston Globe,* June 18, 1991.

Ford, Royal, "Slain Dartmouth Grad Students Thought They'd Fled Violence." *Boston Globe,* June 19, 1991.

Klein, David, "Past Murders Were Few and Far Between," *The Dartmouth,* January 30, 2001.

Gorsche, Ryan, "Dartmouth's Last Murder," *The Dartmouth Review,* January 29, 2001.

Belkin, Douglas, and Marcella Bombardieri, "Faculty Couple at Dartmouth Slain," *Boston Globe,* January 29, 2001, p. A1.

"A Service of Remembrance and Thanksgiving Celebrating the Lives of Half Zantop and Susanne Liselotte Marianne Zantop," videotape made February 3, 2001, The Media Production Group, Trustees of Dartmouth College.

Police report of Trooper Christopher J. Scott on memorial service surveillance, dated February 7, 2001.

McCollum, Audrey, "Mediaitis," guest column in *The Dartmouth,* February 22, 2001.

Shea, Lois, "Rattled by Deaths, Neighbors Start Locking Doors," *Boston Globe,* January 30, 2001, p. A8.

Belkin, Douglas, "Public Asked to Help Police Solve Dartmouth Case; Keen Awareness Crucial," *Boston Globe,* February 10, 2001, p. B3.

Kenyon, Jim, "Area Has History of Unsolved Killings," *Valley News,* February 11, 2001.

Zuckoff, Mitchell, and Shelley Murphy, "Love Affair Eyed in New Hampshire Killings; Husband Involved with Unidentified Woman, Officials Say," *Boston Globe,* February 16, 2001, p. A1.

Zien, Jim, "Maligning the Zantops," *The Dartmouth,* letters to the editor, February 20, 2001.

Chapter 7

Transcript of James Parker interrogation, pp. 14745, 14747–14748, 14790, 14799, 14803–14811, 14813–14814, 14871–14872.

Selected school and journal writings of Robert Tulloch and James Parker, 1999, 2000, and 2001.

Grossman, Dave, Lieutenant Colonel, *On Killing: The Psychological Cost of Learning to Kill in War and Society* (Little Brown and Co.: 1995).

Chapter 8

Interviews with Andrew Pomerantz, Jack Johnson, Annette Johnson, Brad Johnson, Zack Courts, Kip Battey, Tyler Vermette, John O'Brien, Dan Sedon, Maggie O'Neale, Will Gilman, Doug Brown, Kevin Ellis, DeRoss Kellogg.

Transcript of James Parker interrogation, pp. 14739, 14741, 14742, 14750, 14751, 14755, 14864, 14869, 14871, 14873, 14876, 14877, 14883, 14884.

Transcript of police interviews on March 16, 2001, with Kienan Tulloch (pp. 4798–4841), Diane Tulloch (pp. 4842–4871), Michael Tulloch (pp. 4871–4894), John Parker (pp. 4895–4962), Joan Parker (pp. 4967–5021).

"Life of Robert," a three-page school essay written by Robert Tulloch in 1999–2000.

"Jim: Male Subject 769 10010," an eight-page school essay written by Jim Parker in May 2000.

Search warrant return, dated February 16, 2001, and February 17, 2001, by Vermont State Police, following search of the Tulloch house, 313 Main Street, Chelsea, Vermont.

Hanover Police Department report of March 1, 2001, interview with Hanover Police Officer John Kapusta and his wife, Michelle Kapusta.

New Hampshire State Police report of February 21, 2001, interviews with Chelsea Public School teacher Anne E. Pietryka and with Chelsea Public School guidance counselor Steve Kamen.

Florida interviews with Bart Fletcher, Ginny Luther, Jack Luther, John Donovan, Wilbert and Lucille Varley.

Martin County, Florida, property records.

Mashberg, Tom, and Jack Sullivan, "Tullochs, Parkers: When Evil Happens to 'Good People,'" *Boston Herald,* March 3, 2001, p. 1.

Duggan, Christine, "A Devotion to Craft, and Windsor Chairs," *Valley News,* December 9, 2000.

Tulloch, Michael, "Chairmaking Demo Overcomes Handicaps," *Windsor Chronicles,* Winter 2000, pp. 6, 18.

Chapter 9

Detailed narrative description and sketches of crime scene prepared by Trooper First Class Kathleen M. Kimball and Trooper Michael T. Kegelman, dated April 10–11, 2001.

Interviews with Trooper First Class Charles M. West, March 31, 2001, and July 15, 2002.

International Association of Chiefs of Police 1998 Police Officer of the Year news release, from *www.theiacp.org.*

Twohig Ed, Vermont State Trooper, "Terror in the North Country," in *The Vermont Trooper* (Vermont Troopers Foundation Inc.: 1998).

Sullivan, Robert, "The Echo of Gunfire Lingers in the Mountains of New Hampshire," *Life,* August 1, 1998.

Ziner, Karen Lee, "He Was Hunting People: One Man's Rage Rips Apart a New Hampshire Town," *Providence Journal-Bulletin,* August 24, 1997, p. 1.

Glenn, Amanda (staff sergeant), "MACV-SOG Unit Gets Presidential Award," *Army News Service*, April 10, 2001.

Numerous investigative reports by Detective Charles West and Lieutenant Frank Moran detailing the pursuit of the SOG SEAL 2000 knives. A key document was dated March 15, 2001, written by West, titled "Research of the SOG SEAL 2000 Knives."

Numerous investigative reports focused on Stanley Williams, including January 31, 2001, interview with State Police Detective David McCormack, and transcript of February 4, 2001, interview of Williams at the Phoenix Police Department.

Meek, James, "It Was Dangerous. That Was the Point," *The Guardian*, June 4, 2001.

Williams, Lynda B., "Treatment by the Press," *The Dartmouth*, letters to the editor, February 23, 2001.

Hundreds of reports about the early weeks of the investigation, including tips, police interviews, potential suspects, and forensic reports, were included among more than six thousand pages of police and prosecution files released in June 2002 under the New Hampshire Right to Know Law.

Chapter 10

Interviews with Zack Courts, Coltere Savidge, Sada Dumont, Kip Battey, Tyler Vermette, Matt Butryman, Brad Johnson, Cora Brooks, Pat Davenport, John O'Brien, Dan Sedon.

Transcript of James Parker interrogation, pp. 14740, 14743, 14744, 14745, 14746, 14747, 14843, 14844, 14845, 14854, 14876, 14880, 14882, 14883, 14884, 14886.

Transcripts of police interviews on March 16, 2001, with John Parker, Joan Parker, Michael Tulloch, Diane Tulloch, and Kienan Tulloch.

"Jim: Male Subject 769 10010," an eight-page school essay written by Jim Parker in May 2000.

Police report of interview with Ivy Mix and Susan Dollenmaier at the Orange County Sheriff's Office in Chelsea, Vermont, on March 26, 2001.

Police report of interview with Julia and Francis Purcell at the Orange County Sheriff's Office in Chelsea, Vermont, on March 26, 2001.

Police report of interview with Sada Dumont at the Orange County Sheriff's Office in Chelsea, Vermont, on March 21, 2001.

Police report of interview with Gaelen McKee in Chelsea, Vermont, on February 18, 2001.

Zuckoff, Mitchell, and Douglas Belkin, "Blood on Knife Linked to 2 Victims," *Boston Globe,* March 28, 2001, p. 1.

Hattaway, John, "Finding Focus," *The Boston Globe Magazine,* May 20, 2001.

Valley News newspaper article about Susan Dollenmaier's house, 3/24/01.

Chapter 11

Interviews with Trooper First Class Charles M. West, including March 31, 2001, and July 15, 2002.

Numerous investigative reports by Detective Charles West and Lieutenant Frank Moran detailing the pursuit of the SOG SEAL 2000 knives. A key document was dated March 15, 2001, written by West, titled "Research of the SOG SEAL 2000 Knives."

Hundreds of reports about the early weeks of the investigation, including tips, police interviews, potential suspects, and forensic reports, were included among more than six thousand pages of police and prosecution files released in June 2002 under the New Hampshire Right to Know Law.

Chapter 12

Interviews in 2001 and 2002 with DeRoss Kellogg, Pat Davenport, Zack Courts, Matt Butryman, Cora Brooks, John O'Brien, Paula Routly, Maria Lisa Calta, Johannes Gamba, David F. Kelley, Luke White, William Haines, Gayle Wetzler, William Dritschilo.

Transcript of Jim Parker interrogation, pp. 14880–14882.

New Hampshire State Police interview with Chelsea Public School principal Pat Davenport on February 18, 2001, February 19, 2001, and February 21, 2001.

New Hampshire State Police interview with Kienan Tulloch on March 16, 2001.

Chelsea High School debate team's scoring sheets for the 2000 season. The Chelsea debate team's 2000 affirmative plan, "Let There Be Light."

The Fall 2000 issue of the *Chelsea School News.*

Fine, Gary Alan, *Gifted Tongues: High School Debate and Adolescent Culture* (Princeton, New Jersey: Princeton University Press, 2001).

Duane, Daniel, *El Capitan* (San Francisco: Chronicle Books, 2002).

Tillman, Jodie, and Jeffrey Good, interview with Marilyn Childs, Chelsea High School forensics coach, in *Valley News,* February 18, 2001.

Bombardieri, Marcella, and Tom Farragher, "1 New Hampshire Suspect to be Arraigned Today," *Boston Globe,* February 21, 2001, p. 1.

Chapter 13

Transcript of James Parker interrogation, pp. 14807, 14811–14821, 14839–14840.

Interviews with Detective Chuck West, Kip Battey, Zack Courts, John O'Brien.

Transcripts of police and prosecution interviews with John Parker, Joan Parker, Michael Tulloch, Diane Tulloch, all on March 16, 2001, and Christiana Usenza on February 20, 2001.

Transcript of public defenders' deposition of Sergeant Robert Bruno on November 8, 2001.

Transcript of public defenders' deposition of Trooper First Class Russell Hubbard on December 7, 2001.

Transcript of Detective Chuck West's interview with Jim and John Parker at the Orange County Sheriff's Office in Chelsea, Vermont, on February 15, 2001.

Copy of Jim Parker's handwritten account of his sale of the SOG SEAL 2000 knives, given to police February 15, 2001.

Report written by Detective Chuck West on interview at Jim Parker's home on February 15, 2001.

Report written by Trooper First Class Russell Hubbard on interview at Jim Parker's home on February 15, 2001.

Report written by Trooper First Class Russell Hubbard on interview at Robert Tulloch's home on February 15, 2001.

Report written by Sergeant Robert Bruno on private discussion with Mike and Diane Tulloch at their home on February 15, 2001.

New Hampshire State Police, Vermont State Police, and Hanover Police Department reports on interviews with Charlotte Faccio, Tyler Vermette, Sada Dumont, Rebecca Mulligan, Clyde Haggerty, Joan Feierabend, Richard Steckler, Paul Callens, Bob Sherman, Richard Goldsborough.

Records of e-mails from Jim Parker, Joan Parker, and Diana Parker, collected by police and prosecutors.

Material from Jim Parker's computer hard drive collected by police and prosecutors.

Chapter 14

Interviews in 2001 with Pat Davenport, Kip Battey, Zack Courts, Coltere Savidge, David Savidge, Sada Dumont, Brad Johnson, Jack Johnson, Annette Johnson, Andrew Pomerantz, DeRoss Kellogg, Cora Brooks, Dan Sedon.

Police reports of interviews in early 2001 with Chelsea School administrators and teachers Pat Davenport, Paul Callens, Roger Grow, Steve Kamen, Richard Steckler, and Joyce Feierabend.

Police reports of interviews in early 2001 with Sada Dumont, Susan Kay, Gaelen McKee, Casey Purcell, Grace Lovejoy-Bowmer, Rebecca Mulligan, Clyde Haggerty, Julia and Francis Purcell, Tyler Vermette, Ivy Mix, and Susan Dollenmaier.

Interview with Detective Sergeant Ray Keefe and Trooper Jocelyn Stohl of the Vermont State Police, Bethel Barracks, July 2002.

Interviews with Detective Chuck West.

Interview with Detective Lieutenant Frank Moran of the Hanover, New Hampshire, Police Department.

Police reports by Vermont State Police Detective Sergeant Ray Keefe and other investigators describing the events in Chelsea on February 16–17, 2001.

Zuckoff, Mitchell, and Shelley Murphy, "Vermont Youth Sought in N.H. Killings," *Boston Globe,* February 17, 2001, p. 1.

Richardson, Franci, and Jose Martinez, "Closing In: N.H. Police Hunt Vermont Teen in Prof Killings," *Boston Herald,* February 17, 2001, p. 1.

Various police reports on the crime scene searches of the Tulloch and Parker houses on February 16 and 17, 2001, by the following: Detective Sergeant Ray Keefe of the Vermont State Police; Lieutenant Thomas M. Hanlon, crime scene supervisor of the Vermont State Police; Trooper Michael O'Neil; Trooper Michael Kegelman; Detective Sergeant Jeff Cable of the Vermont State Police; February 16, 2001, affidavit by Sergeant Robert Bruno of the New Hampshire State Police.

Chapter 15

Interviews with Chuck West, John Moran, Kip Battey, Julia Purcell, Zack Courts, Kevin Ellis, Doug Brown, Rowdy Kyle Tucker, and Nancy Lee Tucker.

Transcript of James Parker interrogation, pp. 14825–14837.

Transcripts of police and prosecution interviews with John Parker, Joan Parker, Michael Tulloch, Diane Tulloch, all on March 16, 2001, and Christiana Usenza on February 20, 2001.

Videotaped interview with Robert Tulloch by FBI Special Agent William Donaldson in Henry County (Indiana) Sheriff's Office, February 19, 2001. Official transcript of same interview, filed by New Hampshire State Police Sergeant Mark Mudgett.

Affidavit of Jon E. Provost, Massachusetts State Police trooper, filed February 18, 2001.

Affidavit of Robert Bruno, New Hampshire State Police sergeant, filed February 16, 2001.

Second affidavit of Robert Bruno, New Hampshire State Police sergeant, filed February 23, 2001.

Affidavit of Kathleen Kimball, New Hampshire State Police trooper first class, undated.

Affidavit of Bill Ward, Henry County (Indiana) Sheriff's Department sergeant, filed February 19, 2001.

Search warrant return from Henry County, Indiana, filed February 19, 2001.

Sworn statement of Jail Officer Adam Bowman of Henry County Sheriff's Department, February 27, 2001.

Affidavit of Susan Forey, New Hampshire State Police sergeant, filed February 27, 2001.

Unpublished notes of *Globe* correspondent Kathleen Schuckel at Henry County (Indiana) Courthouse.

Lewis, Rafael, and Patrick J. Calnan, "Suspects May Be Heading West; Two Leave Car, Seek Lift in Mass., N.J.," *Boston Globe,* February 19, 2001, p. A1.

Schuckel, Kathleen, "Sergeant's Motto: Be Prepared," *Boston Globe,* February 20, 2001, p. A10.

Daley, Beth, and Jonathan Wiggs, "Thinking of His Own Sons, Trucker Took a Chance," *Boston Globe,* February 20, 2001, p. A1.

Heslam, Jessica, and Jose Martinez, "Teens Kept Apart for Hearings," *Boston Herald,* February 21, 2001, p. 4.

"Sheriff Blasts Handling of Dartmouth Murder Case," Associated Press story reprinted in the *Rutland Herald,* April 23, 2001.

Lucarelli, Jennifer, "Trooper's Work Honored," *Telegram & Gazette* (Worcester, MA), April 23, 2002, p. A2.

Chapter 16

Interviews with Andrew Pomerantz, along with selections from his journal, DeRoss Kellogg, along with Kellogg's e-mails, Pat Davenport, Dan Sedon, Cora Brooks, Doug Lyford, Diane Mattoon, Jack Johnson, Annette Johnson, David Savidge, Coltere Savidge, Sada Dumont, Tyler Vermette.

New Hampshire State Police interviews with Michael, Diane, and Kienan Tulloch, and John and Joan Parker, Hanover, New Hampshire, March 16, 2001.

Lyford, Ashley, and Marcella Bombardieri, "250 Gather in Pair's Hometown," *Boston Globe,* February 23, 2001, p. 1.

Bombardieri, Marcella, "Vt. Town Tries to Cope with N.H. Slayings," *Boston Globe,* March 7, 2001, p. B1.

Belkin, Douglas, and Stephen Kurkjian, "Friends in N.H. Probe Subpoenaed to Testify," *Boston Globe,* March 12, 2001, p. B1.

Bombardieri, Marcella, "As Vt. Suspects Sit in Jail, Donations Flow to Their Kin," *Boston Globe,* April 22, 2001, p. B3.

Jimenez, Ralph, "In N.H. Slay Case A Not Guilty Plea Trial Date Hearing for Tulloch," *Boston Globe,* May 2, 2001, p. B3.

Marchocki, Kathryn, "$2,000 Raised to Help Families of Accused Vermont Teens," *Union Leader,* April 19, 2001, p. 1.

Rimer, Sara, "Arrests of Youths in Dartmouth Case Leave a Town Searching for Answers," *New York Times,* February 25, 2001.

Tillman, Jody, "Town Tries to Cope," *Valley News,* February 23, 2001.

Hanchett, Doug, and Franci Richardson, "Teens' Community Gathers to Reflect and Ponder," *Boston Herald,* February 23, 2001, p. 1.

Ismail, Omer, "Friends and Relatives of Tulloch and Parker Likely to Receive Subpoenas," *The Dartmouth,* March 11, 2001, p. 1.

Bubriski, Mark, "Chelsea Close to Blows as Case Drags On," *The Dartmouth,* March 24, 2001, p. 1.

Staff reports, "Home Searched for Hate Literature," *Rutland Herald,* February 23, 2001, p. 1.

Delcore, David, "Chelsea High Cancels Play, Debate Match," *Times Argus,* February 23, 2001.

Ring, Wilson, "Vt. Discusses Professor Slayings," Associated Press, February 23, 2001.

Staff report, "Selectmen Reports," *Behind the Times* (Bradford, Vt.), July 2001, p. 19.

Chapter 17

Authors' notes on Chelsea, Vermont, and Dartmouth College commencement exercises, June 8 and 10, 2001, respectively.

Behind the Times, July 2001, p. 19 (for selectmen's meeting on police presence).

Ayotte, Lori, "Zantop Case Proves Costly as AG Seeks $100K More," Associated Press story published in the *Manchester Union Leader,* June 7, 2001.

Hookway, Bob, "New Zantop Search Startles Residents," *Valley News,* June 29, 2001.

Weber, Harry, "Police Search Anew Outside Zantop Home," Associated Press story published in the *Manchester Union Leader,* June 29, 2001.

Coleman, Toby, "Zantops' Etna Home on the Market," *Valley News,* July 23, 2001.

Chapter 18

Interview with Deputy Chad Morris, September 18, 2002. Also, narrative reports filed by Morris and Sergeant Robert Bruno on June 26, 2001.

Transcript of June 29, 2001, interview of confidential informant "Ranger" by Sergeant Mark Mudgett and Trooper Todd Landry.

Statement of Glenn Libby to Trooper Todd Landry dated July 18, 2001, regarding informant's claims about escape plans and the Zantop murders.

Copy of Robert Tulloch's letter detailing his plans to plead guilty and write a book about the case.

Multiple interviews with Glenn Libby, Joseph Panarello, Jan Hale, and several guards who requested anonymity at Belknap County and Grafton County jails.

Interviews with DeRoss Kellogg, David Savidge, Coltere Savidge, and Kevin Ellis.

Investigation report of undercover officer placed in Robert Tulloch's cell, dated February 22, 2001.

Non-redacted excerpts of letters Robert Tulloch wrote to Christiana Usenza, released by prosecutors.

Bombardieri, Marcella, "Age Matters, Dartmouth Suspects Find," *Boston Globe,* March 18, 2001, p. B1.

Chapter 19

Multiple interviews with Phil McLaughlin, Kelly Ayotte, Michael Delaney.

Christiana Usenza subpoena service interview with Detective Lieutenant Frank Moran, January 9, 2002.

"Life of Robert," autobiographical school paper written by Robert Tulloch, "Jim: Male Subject 769 10010," autobiographical school paper written by James Parker, along with other assorted school and journal writings of both.

Transcript of James Parker interrogation, pp. 14733–14739, 14743–14737, 14750, 14752–14758, 14760–14769, 14770–14781, 14784–14785, 14841–14842, 14845–14851, 14854, 14858–14863, 14866–14867, 14871–14872, 14887–14889.

Barre, Vermont, police department, trespassing and theft incident report 00BT00315, including interview with Robert Tulloch and his parents.

Hanover, New Hampshire, and Vermont State Police report of police interview on February 6, 2002, with Franklin D. Sanders of North Hollow Road, Rochester, Vermont.

Transcripts of police interviews on March 16, 2001, with Michael Tulloch, Diane Tulloch, Kienan Tulloch, John Parker, Joan Parker.

Report on theft of ATV from Barre Town Police, May 18, 2000.

Police interviews with Spaulding High School staff and students Dennis Hill, Arthur Zorn, Martha Morris, Sara Aja, Michael Wheeler, Jennifer Lucey, Daniel Bruce.

Interviews with John O'Brien and Donna Strange.

Police interview with Richard Steckler, February 21, 2001.

Interviews with forensic psychiatrist Alison Fife, M.D.

Hare, Robert D., Ph.D., *Without Conscience: The Disturbing World of the Psychopaths Among Us* (New York: The Guilford Press, 1993).

Hare, Robert D., Ph.D., *The Hare Psychopathy Checklist, Revised Manual* (Toronto: Multi-Health Systems, 1993).

Hare, Robert D., Ph.D., "Psychopathy: A Clinical Construct Whose Time Has Come," *Criminal Justice and Behavior*, 23 (1), pp. 25–54.

Hare, Robert D., Ph.D., "Psychopathy and Antisocial Personality Disorder: A Case of Diagnostic Confusion," *Psychiatric Times*, February 1996, Vol. XIII, Issue 2.

Pitchford, Ian, Ph.D., "The Origins of Violence: Is Psychopathy an Adaptation?" *Human Nature Review*, 2001, Vol. 1, pp. 28–36.

Forth, A.E., S.D Hart, and R.D. Hare, "Assessment of Psychopathy in Male Young Offenders," *Psychological Assessment,* 1990, 2, 342–344.

Forth, A.E., and H.C. Burke, "Psychopathy in Adolescence: Assessment, Violence, and Developmental Precursors," in *Psychopathy: Theory, Research and Implications for Society* (Boston: Kluwer Academic Publishers, 1998), pp. 205–229.

Salekin, Randall, Randall Rogers, and Dayli Machin, "Psychopathy in Youth: Pursuing Diagnostic Clarity," *Journal of Youth and Adolescence,* April 1, 2001, pp. 173–195.

American Psychiatric Association, *Diagnostic and Statistical Manual of Mental Disorders* (Washington, D.C.: APA, 4th Edition, 1994).

Chapter 20

Audiotapes of New Hampshire State Police and prosecutor interviews with James Parker, at the Belknap County Sheriff's Department.

Police reports and diagrams of Zantop home, January 27, 2001.

Transcript of New Hampshire State Police interview with "Ranger," June 29, 2001.

Interviews in September 2002 with Kelly Ayotte and Michael Delaney.

Kurkjian, Stephen, "Plea Deal Seen Set in N.H. Killings," *Boston Globe,* December 3, 2001, p. 13.

Bombardieri, Marcella, "Plea Deal Irks Zantop Friends," *Boston Globe,* December 6, 2001, p. B16.

Richardson, Franci, "He's 'Demonic'; Dartmouth Profs' Friend Rips Plea Deal for Teen Killer," *Boston Herald,* December 5, 2001, p. A1.

Zuckoff, Mitchell, and Marcella Bombardieri, "Youth Admits Role in Slayings," *Boston Globe,* December 8, 2001, p. B1.

Editorials on the Zantop case in the *Union Leader,* December 9 and December 17, 2001.

Chapter 21

Videotaped court proceedings and authors' notes of proceedings at the sentencing hearing for James Parker and the plea hearing for Robert Tulloch on April 4, 2002.

Interviews with Glenn Libby, superintendent, Grafton County Jail; Joseph Panarello, superintendent, Belknap County Jail; Jan Hale, corrections officer, Belknap County Jail.

Interviews with Kelly Ayotte, New Hampshire senior assistant attorney general; Michael Delaney, New Hampshire assistant attorney general; Philip McLaughlin, New Hampshire attorney general; Richard Guerriero, New Hampshire public defender; DeRoss Kellogg; attorney Daniel Sedon; Robert Muh, clerk of Haverhill Superior Court; Pat Davenport.

Audiotapes and transcripts of the confessions of Jim Parker to New Hampshire prosecutors and investigators, December 18, 2001, et al.

Scherr, Sonia, "A Chaotic Scene, Unusual for Haverhill Court," *Valley News,* April 5, 2002.

Hookway, Bob, "Tulloch: Life Without Parole," *Valley News,* April 5, 2002.

Kurkjian, Stephen, and Doug Belkin, "Zantop Case Defendant to Cite Insanity," *Boston Globe,* December 1, 2001, p. 1.

Bombardieri, Marcella, and Doug Belkin, "A Silent Tulloch Gets Life in Prison, Parker 25 Years," *Boston Globe,* April 5, 2002, p. 1.

Richardson, Franci, "Teens Defense Eyes Family Mental Woes," *Boston Herald,* March 7, 2002.

Sullivan, Jack, and Franci Richardson, "Pair Show Different Faces in Court," *Boston Herald,* April 5, 2002, p. 1.

Osterman, Rachel, "Tulloch Pleads Guilty to Zantop Murders," *The Dartmouth,* April 5, 2002, p. 1.

Mehren, Elizabeth, "Teen Killers Sentenced," *Los Angeles Times,* April 5, 2002, p. A26.

McGrane, Victoria, "Attorney General Talks About Zantop Case," *The Dartmouth,* May 1, 2002.

Coen, Jeff, "Defendant in Murder Trial Insane, Doctor Says," *Chicago Tribune,* May 4, 2002, Southwest Final, p. 16.

New Hampshire Criminal Statutes, Chapter 628: Responsibility.

Reid, John Phillip, *Chief Justice: The Judicial World of Charles Doe* (Cambridge, Massachusetts: Harvard University Press, 1967).

McNamara, Richard B., *New Hampshire Criminal Practice and Procedure,* chapter 34, sections 1091, 1092, 1093; chapter 29, sections 834, 835, Lexis Law Publishing, 3rd Edition, 1997.

Caplan, Lincoln, "Annals of Law: The Insanity Defense," *The New Yorker,* July 2, 1984, p. 45.

Gladwell, Malcolm, "Crime and Science: Damaged," *The New Yorker,* February 24, 1997.

Epilogue

Interviews with Andrew and Diane Patti, Dr. Bruce H. Price, Kelly Ayotte, Chuck West, Frank Moran, Andy Pomerantz, David Savidge.

November 13, 2002, tour and interviews at the New Hampshire State Prison in Concord.

Powers, Ron, "The Apocalypse of Adolescence," *The Atlantic Monthly,* March 2002, Vol. 289, No. 3, pp. 58–74.

Ziedenberg, Jason, *The Atlantic Monthly,* June 2002, letters to the editor, Vol. 289, No. 6, p. 6.

Marchocki, Kathryn, "Tulloch Gets Two Black Eyes in Prison Scrap," *Union Leader,* July 6, 2002.

Selected Bibliography

Books

A History of Chelsea, Vermont: 1784–1984, authorized by the town in March 1980 and compiled by a committee from the Chelsea Historical Society, Inc.

American Psychiatric Association, *Diagnostic and Statistical Manual of Mental Disorders* (APA, Washington, D.C.: 4th Edition, 1994).

Blackwell, Jeannine, and Susanne Zantop, eds. *Bitter Healing: German Women Writers, from 1700 to 1830, An Anthology* (University of Nebraska Press, Lincoln, Nebraska: 1990).

Bohjalian, Chris, *Midwives* (Harmony Books: 1997).

Bradbury, Ray, *Something Wicked This Way Comes* (Simon and Schuster, 1962).

Brown, Rosellen, *Before and After* (Farrar, Straus and Giroux: 1992).

Capote, Truman, *In Cold Blood* (Random House: 1965).

Carrere, Emmanuel, *The Adversary* (Metropolitan Books: 2000).

Duane, Daniel, *El Capitan* (Chronicle Books: 2002).

Fine, Gary Alan, *Gifted Tongues: High School Debate and Adolescent Culture* (Princeton University Press, Princeton, New Jersey: 2001).

Francis, Eric, *The Dartmouth Murders* (St. Martin's Paperbacks: 2001).

Gourevitch, Philip, *A Cold Case* (Farrar, Straus and Giroux: 2001).

Grossman, Dave, Lieutenant Colonel, *On Killing: The Psychological Cost of Learning to Kill in War and Society* (Little Brown and Co.: 1995).

Hare, Robert D., Ph.D., *Without Conscience: The Disturbing World of the Psychopaths Among Us* (The Guilford Press: 1993).

Jamison, Kay Redfield, *An Unquiet Mind* (Knopf: 1995).

Lefkowitz, Bernard, *Our Guys* (Random House: 1997).

Lewis, Dorothy Otnow, *Guilty by Reason of Insanity* (Ballantine Books: 1998).

McNamara, Richard B., *New Hampshire Criminal Practice and Procedure* (Lexis Publishing: 3rd Edition, 1997).

Mondimore, Francis Mark, M.D., *Bipolar Disorder: A Guide for Patients and Families* (Johns Hopkins University Press: 1997).

Papolos, Demitri F., M.D., and Janice Papolos, *The Bipolar Child* (Broadway Books: 1999).

Pollack, William S., Ph.D., with Todd Shuster, *Real Boys' Voices* (Random House: 2000).

Quint, Wilder D., *The Story of Dartmouth* (Little Brown and Co.: 1914).

Reid, John Phillip, *Chief Justice: The Judicial World of Charles Doe* (Harvard University Press, Cambridge, Massachusetts: 1967).

Thompson, Michael, Ph.D., and Catherine O'Neill Grace, with Lawrence J. Cohen, Ph.D., *Best Friends, Worst Enemies* (Ballantine Books: 2001).

Thompson, Michael, Ph.D., with Teresa Barker, *Speaking of Boys* (Ballantine Books: 2000).

Trilling, Calvin, *Killings* (Ticknor & Fields: 1984).

Zantop, Susanne, *Colonial Fantasies: Conquest, Family, and Nation in Precolonial Germany, 1770–1870* (Duke University Press, Durham and London: 1997).

Articles

Barrett, Greg, "Scientists Search for the Seat of Evil," *USA Today*, May 5, 2001.

Bertscher, Robert A., "Our Town," *New England Monthly*, April 1985.

Brower, M.C., and Bruce H. Price, "Neuropsychiatry of Frontal Lobe Dysfunction in Violent and Criminal Behavior: A Critical Review," *Journal of Neurology, Neurosurgery and Psychiatry*, December 2001, Vol. 71, No. 6.

Caplan, Lincoln, "Annals of Law: The Insanity Defense," *The New Yorker*, July 2, 1984.

Edwards, Tamala M., "Lights, Camera . . . Fred!" *Time*, September 28, 1998.

Filley, Christopher M., M.D., Bruce H. Price, M.D., et al., "Toward an Understanding of Violence: Neurobiological Aspects of Unwarranted Physical Aggression: Aspen Neurobehavioral Conference Consensus Statement," *Neuropsychiatry, Neurophsychology, and Behavioral Neurology*, Vol. 14, No. 1.

Filley, Christopher M., James P. Kelly, and Bruce H. Price, "Violence and the Brain: An Urgent Need for Research," *The Scientist*, April 2, 2001.

Forth, A.E., and H.C. Burke, "Psychopathy in Adolescence: Assessment, Violence, and Developmental Precursors," in *Psychopathy: Theory, Research and Implications for Society* (Kluwer Academic Publishers: 1998).

Forth, A.E., S.D. Hart, and R.D. Hare, "Assessment of Psychopathy in Male Young Offenders, *Psychological Assessment,* 1990, Vol. 2.

Gladwell, Malcolm, "Crime and Science: Damaged," *The New Yorker*, February 1997.

Kreiger, Barbara L., "The Alma Mater," in *Miraculously Builded in Our Hearts: A Dartmouth Reader*, Edward Connery Lathem and David M. Shribman, eds. (University Press of New England, Hanover, New Hampshire: 1999).

Miller, Peter, "Chelsea, Vermont," *Vermont Life*, Autumn 1972.

Nelson, Daniel M., "Knowing Our Place," in *Miraculously Builded in Our Hearts*.

Powers, Ron, "The Apocalypse of Adolescence," *Atlantic Monthly*, March 2002.

Price, Bruce H., Kirk R. Daffner, Robert M. Stowe, and M. Marsel Mesulam, "The Comportmental Learning Disabilities of Early Frontal Lobe Damage," *Brain,* 1990.

Tulloch, Michael, "Chairmaking Demo Overcomes Handicaps," *Windsor Chronicles,* Winter 2000.

Court Cases

The State of New Hampshire v. Blair, 143 N.H. 669, 669 A. 2d 448 (1999).

The State of New Hampshire v. Cegelis, 138 N.H. 249, 638 A. 2d 783 (1994).

Acknowledgments

We began covering the tragedy of the Zantops' deaths for the *Boston Globe,* where we've worked a combined thirty years and where we forged a writing partnership and an enduring friendship. Our *Globe* colleagues Steve Kurkjian, Marcella Bombardieri, and Doug Belkin did remarkable work on this story for the paper, and we're grateful for their insights, their support, and their endurance in the thigh-high snow.

Our friend and longtime colleague Gerry O'Neill read and improved the manuscript and, as always, demonstrated why he's the best newsman we know.

Todd Shuster urged us to team up for this book, and then he and his partner Lane Zachary made it possible. Our editor, Dan Conaway, recognized the potential of this story and the potential in us. We're grateful to him and to Gail Winston. We also thank Nikola Scott, Jill

Schwartzman, Olga Gardner Galvin, and the entire HarperCollins team.

An extra large bouquet to Alison Fife, M.D., our forensic-psychiatrist-on-call, who was enormously generous with her time and her expertise in helping us understand the minds of teenage killers, these two in particular. David Meier, chief homicide prosecutor in Suffolk County, Massachusetts, first suggested we talk with Dr. Fife, and we thank him for that.

The people of Chelsea, Vermont, opened their homes and their thoughts to us, offering valuable insights into their lives and the lives of Robert Tulloch and Jim Parker. We especially want to thank Andy Pomerantz, Jack and Annette Johnson, Brad Johnson, Zack Courts, David and Mary Savidge, Coltere Savidge, Cabot Savidge, Kip Battey, Matt Butryman, Sada Dumont, Tyler Vermette, Rob Olsen, DeRoss Kellogg, Cora Brooks, Doug Lyford, Diane Mattoon, Patricia Davenport, John O'Brien, Ned Battey, Will Gilman, Karen and Jay Keller, Steve Kamen, and Maggie Neale. We're also grateful to Kevin Ellis, Bob Sherman, Doug Brown, Dan Sedon, Johannes Gamba, Luke White, Rowdy Kyle Tucker, Nancy Lee Tucker, Omer Ismail, Ginny Luther, and Bart Fletcher. Very special thanks to Andrew, Diane, and Andy Patti.

Getting to know the Zantops posthumously made us wish we had known them in life. Among those who made clear the enormity of the loss were Jim Reynolds, Wolf Zantop, Alex Bertulis, Dr. Thomas Korsukewitz, Werner Gocht, Helen Mango, Audrey McCollum, Irene Kacandes, and James Wright.

Members of the New Hampshire attorney general's office, most notably Phil McLaughlin, Kelly Ayotte, and Michael Delaney, were unfailingly gracious and as cooperative as the law would allow. Special thanks to Major Barry Hunter and Trooper First Class Chuck West of the New Hampshire State Police; Chief Nick Giaccone and Detective Frank Moran of the Hanover Police Department; and Sergeant Jocelyn Stohl and Detective Sergeant Ray Keefe of the Vermont State Police. They are an honor to their badges and were a great help to us.

Indeed, the entire team of investigators did impressive work, as evidenced by the results and the voluminous files they left behind. Deserving special mention are Lieutenants Russell Conte and Wayne Fortier; Sergeants Mark Mudgett, James White, and Robert Bruno, and Troopers Russell Hubbard and Kathleen Kimball, all of the New Hampshire State Police. Also, Tim Pifer, director of the New Hampshire State Police Laboratory; Major Robert White of the Vermont State Police; Detective Eric Bates and Sergeant Brad Sargent of the Hanover Police Department; and Allison Vachon of the New Hampshire Office of Victim/Witness Assistance. We also owe a debt of gratitude to Glenn Libby of the Grafton County Jail and Joe Panarello and Jan Hale of the Belknap County Jail. The county prisoners of New Hampshire are in good, strong hands. Thanks also to Jeff Lyons at the state prison in Concord.

Mike Nikitas and John Herrholz of NECN shared videotapes and hot coffee with us, and we thank them. Richard Abate was always there to offer valuable and critical insight into the book publishing world. Brian McGrory led us to Richard, and for that and so many other things we thank him. Helene Atwan didn't let contract language stand in the way of this book. Richard Brackett runs the best restaurant in Greater Boston, period.

At the *Globe,* we owe debts to many friends, collegues, and ex-colleagues, among them Matt Storin, who gave us leaves of absence to write this book, Helen Donovan, Louisa Williams, Ben Bradlee Jr., Nick King, Lisa Tuite and the entire *Globe* library staff, Fiona Luis, Sally Jacobs, Larry Tye, Wil Haygood, Joe Kahn, Steve Bailey, Marjorie Pritchard, Ande Zellman, Ken Whitney, and publisher Richard Gilman. We were introduced to each other nearly twenty years ago by Christopher Callahan, who remains a true friend.

Jeff and Andrea Feigelson made sure there was always a warm bed in New York. The same holds true for Jon Tisch. Dave Holahan, Kyn Tolson, and Greg and Tierney Fairchild put up with nonstop chatter about the book, even on the beach when the conversation should have been about waves and body-surfing. Harry Goldgar always comes to mind as a great teacher of literature and writing. Thanks to Bobby Gordon for his interest in our work. Mary C. Velasquez's early support of the book included a bike trip up and down the hills of Chelsea. Ellen Jarrett's encouraging reading of the first draft was just what was needed at that moment. Talks about the case with Jennifer Peter, a fellow journalist and friend, were always illuminating. At the end, Karin Koehn provided an inspiration that felt good and right and made crossing the finish line unexpectedly special.

Our families have been endlessly patient with us, and we could never have written this book without their support.

Sid Zuckoff taught by example that any job worth doing was worth doing right. Gerry Zuckoff was a constant source of warmth and compassion. Allan Zuckoff has always been a beacon, searching out a righteous path and illuminating it for others fortunate enough to follow him. Isabel Zuckoff's curiosity about Robert and Jim helped define the questions that needed to be asked and answered. Eve Zuckoff's clear-eyed sense of right and wrong charted a course through the shades of gray. Suzanne Kreiter, to whom this book is co-dedicated, treads softly on dreams spread under her feet.

Special thanks as well to John and Nancy Lehr, and to John, Kellie, and Julia Lehr. Nick and Christian Lehr, who were always asking how the book was coming along and when it would be finished (that is, when they weren't asking, "What's for dinner?") are, quite simply, the greatest pleasure any father could hope for.